ROYAL CLOCKS

(Overleaf)
It would be hard to envisage a clock with a more regal appearance than the massive musical automata clock by John Smith of Pittenweem.
(From The Queen Mother's Private Collection and reproduced by gracious permission of Her Majesty.)

PITTENWEEM NORTH BRITAIN

Cedric Jagger

ROYAL CLOCKS

The British Monarchy and its Timekeepers 1300–1900

ROBERT HALE · LONDON

First published in Great Britain 1983

ISBN 0 7091 9562 1

Robert Hale Limited
Clerkenwell House
Clerkenwell Green
London EC1

Photoset by BAS Printers Ltd.
Printed in Great Britain by Jolly & Barber Ltd., Rugby,
Warwickshire and bound by Hunter & Foulis Ltd.

Dedicated, by gracious permission,
to
Her Majesty Queen Elizabeth
The Queen Mother
whose interest in, and appreciation of,
fine clocks over very many years
extends to the present day.

Contents

For ease of reference, the number of each illustration has been placed in the margin of the text immediately alongside the particular passage to which it relates.

Introduction

Any kind of contact, however impersonal, between monarch and tradesman might seem, to the traditionalist, to be mutually exclusive; they are at near-opposite ends of an extremely long social scale. Yet, in Britain, quite close associations of this kind have been customary for centuries and are well documented and, to this day, carefully nurtured.

The first formal links seem to have come about when trade and craft Guilds emerged in the City of London. Later known as Livery Companies, on account of the distinctive dress once worn by their members, they have been described as a mixture of trade union, employers' association and friendly society. These bodies derived their by-no-means inconsiderable authority for regulating their crafts within the 'square mile' that constituted the City proper, from Royal Charters granted them by the monarch. Later in the present work it will become clear that the Worshipful Company of Clockmakers is quite young, as such bodies go, having received its Royal Charter as recently as 1631; the first known such association between a monarch and his tradesmen, albeit collectively, dates from 1155, when Henry II granted a Charter to the Weavers' Company. The Drapers received theirs in 1364; and the practice gradually increased as reign succeeded reign although it was never exercised indiscriminately, and one Livery Company is on record as having had to wait several centuries for recognition.

At the same time as the Livery Companies started to make their influence felt on behalf of their members, individual craftsmen of skill and enterprise could be encouraged in the exercise of their talents by a grant taking the form of Royal Letters Patent. This procedure reached a peak during the reign of Elizabeth I, when Patent Rights became properly defined and recognized.

The Royal Warrant of Appointment represented a further refinement, by which the monarch could grant to specific tradesmen the right to supply services or goods to the royal household. Any warrant is simply an authority, commonly used throughout officialdom, requiring the person specified therein to perform an act or service, or take up a particular office. Royal Warrants of Appointment are issued on behalf of the sovereign by the Lord Chamberlain and for some years now have nominated individual grantees rather than firms. They are intended as marks of recognition, giving such persons the right to display the Royal Arms and the words 'By Appointment' on their business stationery, outside their premises and so forth. The precise rules applying to Royal Warrant Holders—of whom there are over eight hundred—are confidential, while they themselves are required to exercise total reticence regarding the responsibilities and privileges accruing to them as a result of such patronage. They have the satisfaction of knowing that the quality of the goods or services which they purvey, and indeed their own integrity, have been exposed to possibly the most critical audience conceivable and not found wanting.

The Royal Warrant itself has undergone changes over the centuries, mostly directed towards avoiding excesses of one kind or another. Clock and watchmakers have certainly not been innocent of sharp practice in the past, in their efforts to drum up trade and outwit competitors. It is often postulated, for instance, that some unscrupulous chronometermakers signed their work 'Maker to the Admiralty' or 'Maker to the Royal Navy' on the basis of the sale of a single timekeeper. Indeed, in the course of an action in the High Court in 1891, it was actually proved that John Forrest, a London maker who had died twenty years previously, and who customarily signed his wares 'Maker to the Admiralty', had never made a chronometer in his life. Similarly, it is not too uncommon to find craft signatures on eighteenth- and early-nineteenth-century timekeepers that lay claim to the patronage of as many as three different members of the royal family of the time, presumably on the assumption that quality and value is directly proportional to the volume of royal support that can be arrogated.

Eventually, measures were taken to restrict this kind of abuse. Throughout the present century, for example, the issuing of Royal Warrants of Appointment has been reserved to the monarch, his or her spouse and the immediate heir to the throne; once qualified, however, such authority is never withdrawn from an executant even though subsequently disbarred by, say, the advent of widowhood.

The Royal Warrant Holders, too, have banded together for their own mutual support. The first occasion, in 1840, seems to have been a spin-off from a celebration in honour of Queen Victoria's birthday: those taking part decided to make it an annual event, and formed themselves into The Royal Tradesmen's Association. This title underwent change in 1895, and again in 1902 when it became The Royal Warrant Holders Association Limited. Finally, in 1907, it received a Royal Charter of Incorporation—just like the Livery Companies of the City of London—and became The Royal Warrant Holders Association, by which title it is known today. It is not without significance that the constitution of this body establishes it as 'not for the purpose of gain, but for enforcing the laws of protection of Persons and Firms holding Royal Warrants of Appointment'.

By one of those typically English caprices, the tradesmen supplying Windsor Castle have an independent association, known as The Windsor, Eton and District Royal Warrant Holders Association, which is, in fact, the older of the two bodies by some thirty years, having been formed in 1810. Most of its members, however, also belong to the Royal Warrant Holders Association since it is the latter which is the executive arm in this particular field.

So much for the relevant organizations at the present day. This book attempts to explore the kinds of relationships that existed at various times between successive British monarchs—together with members of their families—and their horological tradesmen, whether officially appointed or not; to examine such circumstances of the personal and working lives of these craftsmen as are at present known; and finally to describe and appraise the objects that they produced for their royal patrons. There will also be cross-fertilization, as when sovereigns of one period have set out to collect clocks of another; any kind of affinity is tenable. It will become clear that individual monarchs, or small groups of them, have exercised, by their interest, a disproportionately strong influence over events affecting the craft, certainly as practised in London. For instance, three seventeenth-century kings—Charles I, Charles II and William III—not only were major factors in the rise to eminence of such superb workmen as Edward East and Thomas Tompion but were also instrumental in establishing two bodies with an intense interest in the future health of a still-young craft, namely the Worshipful Company of Clockmakers and the Royal Observatory. In the eighteenth century George III, a man of great intellectual attainment with an enquiring and scientific turn of mind, attracted some of the finest products of the native clockmaking of his day into the Royal Collection, where they still remain. In the nineteenth century, and by contrast, George IV, both as Prince Regent and King, included within the breadth of his aesthetic appreciation of French works of art some superb examples of that nation's horological output. The London craft probably reached the peak of its technical achievement during the reign of his niece, Queen Victoria, only then to have to fight for survival against the expansionism of mass-production. Yet in our own time love of fine craftsmanship in clocks prevails, in the deep interest shown in them by Her Majesty Queen Elizabeth The Queen Mother, which dates from long before her widowhood and which has had concrete results in the gradual formation of her own private collection in this field.

It is often asserted not only that the clock was the first machine invented by Man but also that it remained his most sophisticated one for several centuries. By comparison with some other parts of Europe, Britain came rather late in the day to convert to mechanical timekeeping, even though, within a relatively short time as such things go, she was to prove her skills in the making of timepieces of quality and reliability. Before the beginning of the seventeenth century, however, virtually all mechanical timekeepers must have been imported and have been so costly as to preclude their possession by other than the monarch, the richest nobles and courtiers and perhaps a few wealthy merchants. Ecclesiastical foundations, even so, managed to raise sufficient funds to bring craftsmen from elsewhere on the Continent to build and install the enormous iron clocks which were the first manifestations of more universal mechanical timekeeping in Britain, as well as the forerunners of today's large public clocks; and Britain's sovereigns in those early times provided much impetus for the development of these new-fangled but useful devices.

One of the residual confusions remaining to cloud our picture of the earliest periods of time-measurement is the use of words which, despite minor linguistic variations, are all based upon the Latin *horologium*. When, towards the end of the Middle Ages, the wholly non-mechanical timekeeper started to give place to primitive clocks, this usage proved a source of ambiguity which partly explains the relative lack of success, up to the present, in establishing beyond doubt the exact date when the change-over commenced. For the purposes of this book, therefore, the word 'clocks' in the title will be accorded an equally wide-ranging interpretation. Every kind of clock, watch and chronometer of mechanical construction, on the one hand, as well as every sundial, sand-glass, water clock and similar devices of a non-mechanical nature, on the other, will be grist to its mill. It will stop short only of such relatively modern inventions as the quartz crystal, and electronics generally.

It would have been satisfying to be able to claim that this work was, in relation to a seemingly narrow subject, exhaustive. There are a variety of reasons why it cannot be so; and it must be doubtful if such could ever be produced. Many of the earliest references are missing, or frustratingly incomplete, or ambiguous; many formerly royal clocks have passed out of the possession of the sovereign, some into private hands, and traces of these may have been lost; again, many timepieces which were commissioned only to be given away as private or official presents, have now also disappeared from view. Many clocks and watches exist with pretensions to an association with royalty, some demonstrably spurious, some suspect, some believable but incapable of proof. Finally, and most importantly, there is the question of sheer scale. At a recent reckoning, it was discovered that there were about three hundred clocks in Buckingham Palace and about the same number in Windsor Castle. An authoritative source, writing at the beginning of the present century, gave the comparable figures as 170 at the first location and 250 at the second. It is clear that a very large—and apparently still increasing—number of timepieces makes up the royal holding in this field, and when the potential of all the other residences is considered, the figure is likely to be so large that no single volume would suffice to cover them all. Even accepting that many of these objects—perhaps the majority—fall into that category so beloved of the trade, known as 'furnishing clocks' it will still be necessary to be highly selective, for even those clocks that might conceivably be placed in that slightly derogatory classification are likely to be minor masterpieces of their kind, in a palace context. Happily, the Royal Collection contains so many remarkable examples of the clockmaker's skill which are of the very highest quality and originality, that there has been no shortage of material from which to choose.

(Overleaf) *Her Majesty The Queen, accompanied by H.R.H. Princess Margaret and Lady Sarah Armstrong-Jones, admiring the four-dialled astronomical clock by Christopher Pinchbeck, when it was publicly exhibited in 1974.* (Thompson Organisation)

1 Marking time: Palace practice prior to 1600

By about the year 1300, mechanical time-measurement had appeared in Britain, albeit on a very small scale. Before that time—and for several centuries after it—non-mechanical methods prevailed, these including not only the common sundial but also various devices which related the passing of time to the flow or consumption of a familiar commodity. Among these were the water clock (clepsydra), the sand-glass, the burning-candle clock and a related contrivance which burned oil from a calibrated glass tank, and a number of others. The earliest mechanical clocks were connected with religious institutions, they having the greatest need for accurate timekeeping in order to regulate their offices properly. It was natural that the monarch also should interest himself in a development of such obvious utility.

The earliest records that are likely, on present evidence, to relate to the existence of mechanical clocks are comparatively few and can be easily summarized. In 1283, in the Annals of Dunstable Priory of the Austin Canons, in Bedfordshire, occurs the entry '*Eodem anno fecimus horologium quod est supra pulpitum collocatum.*' ('That year we made the clock which is set above the rood-screen.') It seems likely that '*pulpitum*' in this context meant rood-screen and loft or gallery, probably of stone and well able to take the weight of a monastic mechanical alarm, so that this was not just the acquisition of another clepsydra. This underlines the fact, perhaps, that at this early period clocks almost certainly had no dials and hands, as we know them, but were simply mechanical alarms to warn of the imminence of a holy office.

After this beginning, references become frequent, although still the crucial word is '*horologium*'. In 1284, one Roger de Ropford, with his wife and family, received a tenement in Paignton at a nominal rent, in return for repairs to the organ and clock in Exeter Cathedral; they also drew rations from the Chapter of Exeter. From then on there are regular references to such matters in this cathedral city.

In London, in the *Compotus Bracini* (brewer's account) of St Paul's Cathedral for the year 1286, a clockmaker—Bartholomew Orologiario—drew rations, including measures of beer. It is probable that he was an outside expert brought in to undertake special work and not on the regular staff.

The first association of royalty with such operations as these is more of a tradition than anything else. It is said that a clock tower was built in Westminster Palace in 1288 and that it was funded from fines imposed by Edward I upon those of his judges found guilty of corruption and other malpractices, and especially naming Chief Justice Hengham. There appears to be no basis whatever for this story, and in fact, as will be seen, this tower was built in Edward III's reign between 1365 and 1367, by two masons, Thomas de Hardegrey and Maurice Yonge, working under the supervision of Henry Yevele.

The list of these earliest clocks, probably mechanical ones, extends then to Merton College, Oxford *c.* 1288, Norwich Cathedral Priory in 1290, Ely Abbey (Benedictine) in 1291, Canterbury Cathedral in 1292, the first clock in Salisbury Cathedral in 1306, Norwich Cathedral Priory again in 1322; and then other cathedrals and churches follow in swift pursuit, Lincoln in 1324, St Albans Abbey (Benedictine) in 1327, Durham in 1360.

Before the last-mentioned had come into being, however, we find the first definite record of royal interest in clocks of this early, monumental type. Between 1351 and 1354 the first clock ordered by Edward III for Windsor Castle was installed in the Great Tower. It took carpenters, working more or less continuously on the project, more than six months to construct a room for the clock, which was itself made in London by three clockmakers from Lombardy. After they had delivered the clock, together with a great profusion of accessories and spares—wire of different kinds, cord and lines of various weights, iron bars and other ironwork, a hammer weighing 160lbs, and much more—it took them $6\frac{1}{2}$ weeks in 1352 to erect the machine and set it going. Associated with it was a large bell, which had been transported from Aldgate to Windsor; and it required 99 lbs of ironwork alone, in order to install it in the Tower. It is further noted that the roof of the clock house was protected with lead, while in 1353 the clock was enclosed in a cupboard. This is not the end of the story, however. Whatever may have been the fate of the Aldgate bell, it became necessary to replace it with a new one twenty years later. There is reference to it in a works account of 1375–7.

The same monarch was also concerned, as we have just seen, with the next large clock in the chronology of such devices. In the Palace of Westminster, in 1365, a start was made on a clock tower, immediately opposite the Great Hall and at the end of the King's Garden. This took two years to complete. A bell for it was made by John Belleyetere in 1366–7; and by May 1370 there is a record of the payment of 6d per day wages to one John Nicole 'keeper of the great clock of the lord king within the palace of Westminster'. It is interesting to note that this bell, one of three ordered by the King, weighed 4 tons; in 1698 it was transferred to St Paul's.

Another one of these bells was destined for the castle of Queenborough, on the Isle of Sheppey, which Edward III was building. No accounts relating to the clock survive, but it was probably installed before 1370. During 1373–4 the belfry was roofed with lead, and a clockmaker called John Lyncolne—probably the same man as the John Nicole who was associated with the Westminster Palace clock—came from London to repair it, taking five days in the process. The clock figures in an inventory of 1393, which also mentions a small hanging clock in the chapel.

Edward III's interest and influence can be traced in two other historic clocks. At Sheen, in Surrey, where he had a favourite residence, there seems to have been a clock in use before 1366, and, ten years later, carpenters constructed a belfry for it. Of more wide-ranging interest, however, is a Patent provided by the King in 1368 ensuring safe conduct for three Flemish clockmakers to come to England for one year, in order to pursue their craft. The date coincides with the transport of the third of Belleyetere's bells, from Westminster to King's Langley Manor, in August of that year. The bell was accompanied by a supply of accessories—iron bolts, staples, nails and chains for the

1. *The Salisbury Cathedral clock: as found in the roof of that building, prior to restoration.* (Alan Lloyd Collection)

clock. The following year, a carpenter made a clock case, while the belfry and clock room were roofed with lead in 1370.

Particular interest in this last clock focuses upon the three Flemish craftsmen, two named Vrieman and one called Suiveyt, all from Delft. It is possible that they were associated not only with the clock at King's Langley but also with those at Queenborough and, conceivably, at Westminster Palace. This must suggest that, as bells had been provided for already, there was no competent English clockmaker available at that period. After 1369, however, John Lyncolne or Nicole was formally appointed Royal Clockmaker.

At this point, it might be desirable to consider what clocks from this era looked like; and, conveniently, one of the next clocks in this chronological sequence still
survives. The basis for attributing to it the date 1386 is 1
an original Deed from that year leasing a shop from the 2
Dean and Chapter, at 16 shillings *per annum* for forty years, to Reginald and Alice Glover on condition that they maintain the clock in the belfry of the Canon's cloister of Salisbury Cathedral. The late R. P. Howgrave-Graham, who was one of the first researchers in this specialized area of horology, showed that the cathedral clock was commissioned by Bishop

2. (Above) *The Salisbury Cathedral clock after restoration in 1956, and now located on the floor of the building.* (Alan Lloyd Collection)

Ralph Erghum, who was at Salisbury from 1375 to 1388; he also considered that Bishop Erghum was responsible for the Wells Cathedral clock, since he was translated to the See of Bath and Wells in 1388, 3
remaining there until 1400. If this is the case, it is not unreasonable to suppose that the same craftsmen made both machines. The Salisbury clock, which remained actually in use until 1884, was renovated in 1956 and is now kept on display, while the Wells clock, much altered, is maintained in running-order in the Science Museum in London. This clock was certainly fully installed by 1392.

Both these machines are of substantial proportions, and made by smithing techniques, since the specialized tools for such operations as cutting the teeth of wheels were still to come. The clock at Wells was more complicated than that at Salisbury, possessing an extra train of wheels to strike quarters in addition to that striking the hours; but even this was not unique. Much earlier in the same century the Abbot of St Albans, one Richard of Wallingford, devised a clock which struck the hours, actuated an astrolabe dial and also represented the motions of the sun, moon and perhaps the planets. Finally, there was a mechanism depicting age and eclipses of the moon. It was not entirely completed

3. (Below) *The Wells Cathedral clock.* (Science Museum: on loan from the Dean & Chapter, Wells Cathedral.)

before his death in 1336 but seems to have been finished by other hands by 1350. Strangely, considering his interest in such matters, Edward III is said to have censured the expenditure of so much money on such a project, to which the Abbot replied that when he died, nobody else was capable of carrying on the work.

4 The horological inclinations of Richard II are
5 reflected in the survival of his horary quadrant. In effect an altitude sundial, this versatile device can be made to show equal or unequal hours, sometimes both; in the present case, the quadrant shows equal hours. Dated 1399 and made of brass which was once gilt, it is described in detail in Dr. Frank Ward's '*A Catalogue of European Scientific Instruments . . .*', published by the British Museum, (where this fine instrument is preserved), in 1981. The evidence of ownership is particularly interesting in that it consists of a rebus.* *Chambers Dictionary* defines this as the 'enigmatical expression of a name by pictures punningly representing parts of the word. . . .' The design, in this case, includes a stag and a crown, together with the inscription 'Pri 3 Di 3 pascha fi'. A very similar dial, but dated a year earlier, is to be found in Dorchester Museum.

While they do not seem to have demonstrated the same pioneering interest in mechanical horology as did Edward III, his successors at least continued to maintain their existing large clocks. Henry IV is said to have appointed a clockmaker, with an appropriate salary, to look after the Westminster machine, while Henry V, in the first year of his reign, 1413, appointed Henry Berton to the same office, at the by now traditional stipend of 6d per day. Henry VI gave the keeping of the clock over to William Warby, Dean of St Stephens, at the same rate of remuneration; but during his reign some extra attention, over and above the normal routine, seems to have been necessary, for in three successive years there is mention of a clockmaker named Thomas receiving what might nowadays be called a retainer, of 13s 4d a year, together with extra sums of money for undertaking repairs, as also for providing two 'great ropes', one weighing 52 lb and the other 49 lb, charged for at three-halfpence per pound.

The circumstances under which clocks were manufactured at this time are also worth brief consideration. In the fourteenth and fifteenth centuries, demand for these new-fangled devices was insufficiently great to allow for the emergence of specialists, so that the earliest clockmakers were mainly blacksmiths, locksmiths or gun-founders, craftsmen accustomed to working in metal who could also, when required, produce or repair clocks. Nowhere other than thin on the ground, the numbers of such skilled men varied substantially from country to country, Germany being particularly well-placed in this regard. It was for this reason that Edward III had found it necessary to import the skills to build his clocks at King's Langley and elsewhere, just as Bishop Erghum was to do at Salisbury. However, the situation started to change during the sixteenth and seventeenth centuries, as domestic clocks and watches became less of a rarity, since the techniques required were different from those of the blacksmiths and locksmiths, and much more closely allied to those of the goldsmiths, the smaller timepieces being more expensive contrivances owned by wealthy people. Thus, a clear-cut distinction

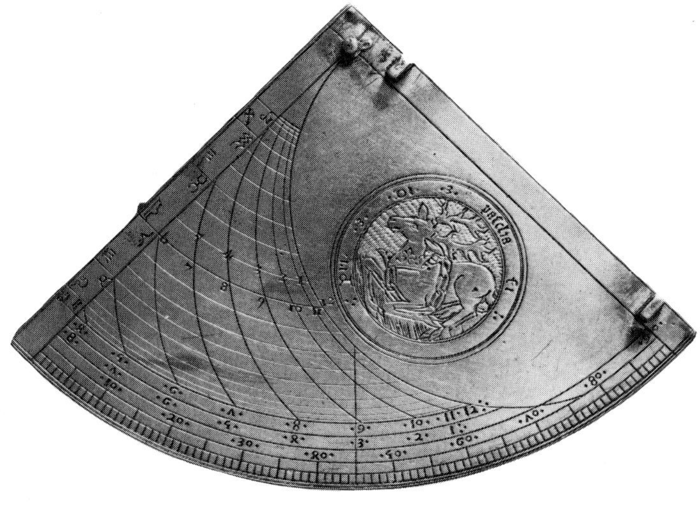

4. (Top) *Quadrant made for Richard II, dated 1399: obverse.* (British Museum)

5. (Above) *Quadrant made for Richard II, dated 1399: reverse.* (British Museum)

*Richard II's badge, 'a white Hart lodged' [lying down], is thought by some authorities to derive from the white hind device favoured by his mother Joan, the Fair Maid of Kent. However, he was not her heir, so that it might seem more likely simply to be punning upon his name, 'Rich-hart'.

developed between makers of the big public clocks—in England, these tended to be known as 'Great Clockmakers'—and those of little clocks, and eventually watches.

It is easy to become so involved with the fascinating story of the emergent years of mechanical timekeeping that the continuation unabated of the common use of non-mechanical devices gets altogether ignored. Yet clocks were still for the use and edification of the privileged few, and even royalty continued, in the main, to resort to sundials and the like.

6. *Portrait of Nicholas Kratzer, after Hans Holbein, 1528.* (National Portrait Gallery, London)

The comprehension, design and manufacture of sun-
6 dials implies a good working knowledge of astronomy. One of the most successful royal dial-makers was one Nicholas Kratzer, or Cratzer, who was so employed by Henry VIII.

Kratzer was a Bavarian, born in Munich in 1487. He studied first at Cologne and Wittenberg and, by 1517, had become Wolsey Lecturer and Fellow of Corpus Christi College, Oxford, his subjects being, in his own words, 'Astronomy, and the supplement to Astronomy, the mundane sphere of John of Holywood, the composition of the Astrolabe and the geography of Ptolemy'. Apparently his appointment was by the King's command; and, in 1519, he became the sixteenth-century equivalent of Astronomer Royal to Henry VIII, at a salary of 100 shillings a quarter. His practical work at Oxford, consisting of two exterior dials, has simply been allowed to disintegrate over the centuries, and only odd sketches of them remain; however, a small portable dial which he made for Cardinal Wolsey survives there, in the Museum of the History of Science.

Several anecdotes concerning Kratzer have also been preserved. It is said that the King asked him, on one occasion, how it was that, after so many years in England, he had still not learned to speak the language, to which he replied, 'Pardon, your Highness, but how can a man learn English in only thirty years?' A letter from Cuthbert Tunstal, Master of the Rolls to Cardinal Wolsey, dated 12th October 1520, states,

> Please it your Grace to understand that here, in these parts [Tunstal was writing from Germany] I met with a servant of the King's called Nicholas Cratzer, a German, devisor of the King's horologes, who showed me how the King had licensed him to be absent for a season, and that he was ready to return to England, whom I desired to tarry, until I might write to the King's Highness, to know his pleasure whether he would suffer him to be in company with me for a season, until the assembling of the electors were past.

On a purely material level there is, in a book of the payments made by the Treasurer of the Household from Candlemas-day, 29 Henry VIII to Midsummer 33 Henry VIII, the entry: 'Nicholas Cratzer, Astronomer, received five pounds, as his quarter's wages.' This was in the year 1538.

Holbein the painter—that is, Hans Holbein the Younger—who seems to have been fascinated with the paraphernalia of horology, was a friend of Kratzer and painted a famous portrait of him in 1528, which is now in the Louvre. He painted another portrait of him—or at least it is said to be from his workshop—which has recently been acquired by the National Portrait Gallery in London. He is also said to have helped him by designing cases and decoration for clocks and sundials; and, in his famous picture of 'The Family of Sir Thomas More', painted between 1526 and 1530, there is a hanging clock having some superficial likeness to the one supposedly given by Henry VIII to Anne Boleyn on their wedding-day (*q.v.*). Kratzer died in 1547; he left behind several manuscript works, notably *Canones Horoptri* (Bodleian Library: MS Bodley No. 504) and *De Compositione Horologiorum*. In his old college at Oxford is preserved his manuscript *De Horologiis* (Corpus Christi College MS No. 152) which contains, *inter alia*, a statement that many of the directions for dialling were taken from a manuscript in the Carthusian Monastery at Auerbach, near Vienna.

Kratzer enjoyed the friendship of the famous men of his day, such as Dürer and Erasmus. It was thought until comparatively recently that Kratzer might have been concerned with the original astronomical clock at Hampton Court Palace, since the wrought-iron frame was marked with the date 1540 and the letters 'N.O.' or possibly 'N.C.'. This, however, is now known to refer to Nicholas Oursian, more usually called Urseau, to whom we shall come in due course; but Kratzer may have been involved with the astronomical work on this masterpiece.

So far our attention has been occupied with large public or semi-public clocks, the first manifestation of the application of machinery to time-measurement. Surviving domestic clocks prior to 1550 are extremely rare, although it seems possible that they may first have come into use up to a century earlier. So long as they continued to be weight-driven, they could hardly be considered portable and were normally supported upon a wall bracket or by spikes. They were really little more than scaled-down versions of the large clocks already mentioned and are generally categorized today as Gothic clocks, presumably from the style of the decoration which is often incorporated into the corner-posts of the frame and the four straps supporting the one or more bells that surmount the movement. The matter of portability was resolved, of course, only when it became possible to make spring-driven clocks, an advance which seems unlikely to have occurred before the last quarter of the fifteenth century, at the earliest.

So much for such records as remain from the earlier centuries of the period at present under review. Turning now to the sixteenth century, mention has already been made of the monumental astronomical clock at Hampton Court Palace, and that will be as good a starting-point as any at which to return to palace practice.

On 8th March 1880, *The Times* devoted an article to the Hampton Court clock, and it will be helpful to quote substantial extracts from this, with annotations in the light of later research. The article starts:

> 7 The antique and curious dial of the clock over the gate-tower in the second quadrangle at Hampton Court Palace, has lately been replaced and, with new works, again shows not only the hours of the day and night, but also, among other things, the days of the month, the motion of the sun and moon, the age of the moon, the phases and quarters of the moon, and the moon's southing. The dial is composed of three separate copper discs of different sizes, with a common centre but revolving at varying rates. The smallest of these is three feet three and a half inches in diameter, and in the middle of this is a slightly projected globe painted to represent the earth. The quarters marked on the centre disc by thick lines are numbered with large figures, and around the edge this disc is divided into twenty-four parts, a red arrow painted on the second disc pointing to these figures and showing at once the quarter in which the moon is, and the time of southing. Next to the figure of the earth in this centre disc a circular hole, ten inches in diameter, allows a smaller disc, travelling behind, to show the phases of the moon. On the second disc, four feet one and a half inches in diameter, but of which only the outer rim is seen, are twenty-nine divisions, and a triangular pointer, projecting from behind the central disc, shows the moon's age in days. The largest of the three discs is seven feet ten inches in diameter. There are many circles painted on so much of the rim of this as is seen; the inner, or—following the order above observed, and proceeding from the centre—the first circle, giving the names of the months, the second the days of the month (only twenty-eight for February), the third the signs of the zodiac, and on the rim, with thirty degrees for each space filled by a sign, a circle divided into three hundred and sixty parts. A long pointer with a gilded figure of the sun attached, projecting from behind the second disc, shows on this third or outermost disc of the dial the day of the month and the position of the sun in the ecliptic. This pointer performs another duty, acting like the hour hand of an ordinary clock, and shows the time of day or night as it passes the twenty-four figures—two sets of twelve—painted on the stonework within which the dial revolves. The diameter of this outer immovable circle on the stone is nine feet eight inches, and the figures of the hours, roman numerals, are nine inches in length.

Complicated though this description may sound, it becomes clear when read in conjunction with an illustration of the dial of this remarkable clock (see figure 7). The dial is important, too, as being the only part of the original machine that remains, albeit still performing the functions it was first intended to do; and finally, of course, it is as good an example as one could wish for of the large, complex public clocks that had sprung up in some numbers all over Europe, mainly on ecclesiastical establishments. The Hampton Court clock purports to show the Ptolemaic system of planetary motions; there are examples in which the purely astronomical information shades off into the realms of astrology, which suggests that there was a strong superstitious element in the make-up of those to whose everyday lives such clocks were of importance.

The only remaining indication of the date and maker of the original mechanism of the Hampton Court clock is to be found incised in part of the wrought-iron framework to which the dial is fixed. This reads 'N.O. 8
1540'. It is now generally considered that this refers to Nicholas Oursian, often called Urseau—there are at least seven different versions of his name to be found in

7. *Dial of astronomical clock, Hampton Court Palace.* (Crown Copyright)

8. *Detail of movement of Hampton Court clock, showing the inscription 'N.O. 1540'* (Crown Copyright)

contemporary records, not to mention 'Nicholas the Astronomer', although the last-named might equally refer to Kratzer. Oursian's life is dealt with in more detail elsewhere in this chapter. It seems likely that he was at Hampton Court constructing and installing the big clock, from about 1538 to 1542; but he was, of course, equally at home with smaller devices, as witness his gift to his monarch—in this case, Mary—on New Year's Day 1556, of 'a fair cloke, in a case, cover with blake vellat'. On this occasion, he is identified as Nicholas Ursin.

Sadly, the original Hampton Court mechanism of 1540 has disappeared long since; and although the vicissitudes through which the machine has passed over the centuries mainly belong later in this work, it will be more convenient to gather them all together here. They make sorry reading.

Many craftsmen seem to have had a hand in maintaining this big clock, over the years. There is, for instance, reference to a painting—or perhaps it should be re-painting—of 'the great dial at Hampton Court' in 1575, by a certain George Gaver, 'serjeante painter'; later, the famous Thomas Tompion is quoted, erroneously, as having been concerned with it, but it would seem that the clock was again altered and repaired between 1760 and 1800. William Derham, Canon of Windsor, but best known perhaps as the author of *The Artificial Clock-maker*, published in 1696 and one of the first printed works in English on the subject, described the condition of the clock in 1711, when it had been recently repaired by Langley Bradley. With premises in Fenchurch Street, it was Bradley who made the clock for St Paul's Cathedral. In the case of the Hampton Court clock, Bradley had found that parts of the movement had been removed 'by some ignorant workman, as he supposed'—thus *The Times* article again—but even after he had finished work on it, Derham concluded that it could not have performed its functions accurately. Indeed it seems probable that the astronomical action had long been useless, for, as early as 1649, another clock dial had been placed on the other side of the gate-tower, over the entrance to the Great Hall, and a striking-part had been added to the clock mechanism. In 1835 the original clock mechanism was finally removed, and nobody knows what happened to it. Another clock mechanism was installed at that time, and it was that machine which was about to be removed when this newspaper article appeared in 1880. That second mechanism bore an inscription as follows: 'This clock, originally made for the Queen's Palace in St. James's, and for many years in use there, was, A.D. 1835, by command of His Majesty King William IV, altered and adapted to suit Hampton Court Palace, by B. L. Vulliamy, clock-maker to the King'.

On another part of the movement was found a further inscription reading 'Vulliamy, London, No. 352, A.D. 1799'. Very much more will be said later in this book, about this family of clockmakers of Swiss extraction who served the Royal Family for so many years. So far as Benjamin Lewis Vulliamy is concerned, however, it must be said that no other nineteenth-century maker did more to destroy, quite needlessly, some of the great examples of Britain's horological heritage; and it is difficult to escape the conclusion that, in most cases, this was done for self-aggrandizement.

The Vulliamy movement in the Hampton Court clock had not had sufficient power to drive the astronomical dial, which was taken down and stored in a workshop at the Palace, the gap left being filled in simply with a painted board. *The Times* takes up the story again:

> When Mr Bland, of the firm of Gillett & Bland, who have been commissioned by the Office of Works to make a new clock, examined the wheels by which the dials were to be moved, he found by the number of teeth in some of the wheels that the astronomical clock could not possibly have served its purpose. New wheels have, therefore, been cut, the work being done by machinery driven by steam at the works of Messrs. Gillett & Bland, at West Croydon. The new clock made by this firm to replace Vulliamy's drives both the astronomical dial and the hands of the ordinary clock-face on the opposite or western side of the tower. In the mechanism many ingenious contrivances, some of them introduced and patented by the firm, have been employed; and while the clock is guaranteed not to vary more than five seconds a week, it is not expected to vary even so much as that.

For those who are interested, there follows a long technical description of the movement with its double three-legged gravity escapement and compensation pendulum, made of zinc and iron tubes—'compensation' means, in this context, a construction designed to counteract the expansion and contraction of the length of the pendulum rod due to changes in temperature, which would naturally affect its timekeeping—and since even *The Times* comments, about part of the machine, that 'it is, however, of too complicated a nature to be intelligibly explained without diagrams', we may perhaps be excused for omitting it. Clearly much ingenuity of design was indeed required; the pendulum, beating $1\frac{1}{4}$ seconds, was shorter than might have been desired, simply since the apartments below the clock chamber were occupied by one of the Palace residents and there was not depth enough to hang a longer one. Then again it is pointed out that the hands do not advance continuously but jump forward every quarter of a minute; this is to counteract the adverse effects of the weight of the hands themselves and the pressure of the wind upon them. This is a very real consideration in large clocks.

By contrast, Henry VIII's liking for small clocks, both for his own use and as gifts to his friends and favourites, is well documented. The word 'watch' was often used at this period for any small timekeeper, and thus, when William Derham mentions being told of an 'eight-day watch' that belonged to that sovereign, the context clearly indicates a weight-driven timepiece.

Many of these doubtless beautiful objects seem to have been made by immigrant French craftsmen, of whom not a great deal is known aside from records of payments made to them. Piers and Nicholas Plantart, for example, were receiving wages at the rate of £4 *per annum* in 1521. Vincent Keney—there are several different spellings of his name—came originally from Normandy, where he is known to have been working in Rouen in 1524. By 1530 he was employed at Hampton Court, but seems only to have stayed about ten years; and by 1540 he had been appointed Keeper of the Rouen Cathedral clock. He died in 1553. Sebastian le Seney also originated in Normandy, coming to this country in 1537. He was soon taken into the King's employment at a salary of 20s 8d a quarter. In 1541 he became a naturalized citizen, went to live in Westminster and, in 1546, took charge of the Westminster Palace clock at a fee of £10 a year. He died about 1549. But perhaps the best-known of these foreign workmen was Nicholas Oursian, mentioned elsewhere in this chapter. First records in which he is named appear in 1532, when he was paid £5 3s 'for stuf made for the King's Grace'. From then on he occurs frequently in the royal accounts, receiving 20s 8d a quarter, apparently the customary salary in those days for this level of employee. Probably his best-known work was the clock at Hampton Court Palace, of which he was appointed Keeper at the princely wage of 4d *per diem*. Like le Seney—and in the same year—he, too, became a naturalized citizen, papers of denization being issued to his home in Westminster on 12th March 1541. He was still living there in 1568, with two Protestant refugee assistants, one French and one Dutch; and by that time he was also responsible for the clocks at Oatlands and Westminster, as well as Hampton Court. He did not die until 1590, having held office in four reigns. Some authorities, in view of his seemingly very long life span, have speculated that there may have been two Nicholas Oursians, perhaps father and son, during the period in question, but there is no evidence to support such a conclusion.

Sebastian le Seney has one special claim to our attention, in the survival of a superb astrolabe made by
him for Henry VIII about 1545. Dr. Frank Ward, 9
author of the recently-published catalogue of European 10
scientific instruments in the British Museum, describes this device as 'a skeletonised celestial globe, pressed flat', going on to show, however, what a remarkably complex instrument it was. Telling the time by it was not usually just a matter of direct observation but, even if this were a minor disadvantage, there was com-

9. (Left) *Henry VIII's astrolabe, ca 1545; obverse, and beside it the second plate.* (British Museum)

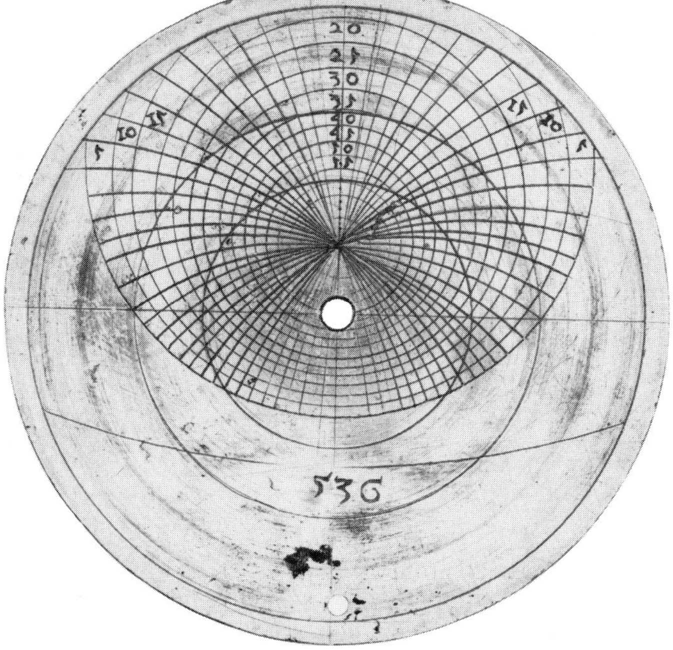

pensation to be found in its use as a kind of astronomical computer. The astrolabe could be made to predict, for example, the times of sunrise and sunset, as well as the altitude and azimuth of the sun at any time and date, together with similar information in respect of those fixed stars for which any particular astrolabe had been programmed. Evidence of the ownership of le Seney's astrolabe is to be found in the shield with its Royal Arms flanked by the letters 'H.R.', while elsewhere appears the inscription 'ROY HENRY PAR LA GRASE DE DEIV'. This instrument, which is housed in the British Museum, bears the maker's signature: 'BASTIEN LE SENEY FACIT'.

The subject of immigrant clockmakers working for the Crown at this period has been explored recently by Clive Ponsford, in an article entitled 'French Clockmakers at Nonsuch', (*Antiquarian Horology*, Vol. XIII, No. 3, March 1982, pp. 294–5). It seems that Henry VIII began to build Nonsuch Palace in 1538, on a site near Cheam, in Surrey, which had formerly accommodated the village and church of Cudlington. The palace, upon which some £23,000 had up-to-then been lavished, was in partial use by 1545 although not wholly completed when the King died two years later. The calendar of *State Letters and Papers* covering this period, which places both monarch and Privy Council

10. (Left) *Henry VIII's astrolabe; reverse.* (British Museum)

at Nonsuch on 5th July 1545, also contains various references to letters of denization—these under the heading 'Aliens'—and also to certain clockmakers, in particular Sebastian Le Sene (or Lesney, etc.) and Nicholas Worston (Oursian, Urseau, etc), although not specifically in connection with Nonsuch. However, further light is shed by a volume entitled *Letters of Denization and Acts of Naturalization for Aliens in England 1509–1603*, which is number eight in the Huguenot Society series and was published in 1893. Edited by William Page, F.S.A., this includes a group of clockmakers who were granted letters of denization—that is to say, they became English citizens—on 1st July 1544. The source of this data is *Westminster Deniz. Roll 36 Henry 8*.

First on the list is John Demolyn, clockmaker, born in Normandy and resident in England 15 years, who is married to an English woman. There then follows a group of six, all French and all working on the Nonsuch clock; their names are Peter Mare, Dedie Colls (or Collo), Charles Durrant, John Brisbrough, Robert Lamberd and Mathewe Bachlatt. In the case of the four last-mentioned, repeat entries on 11th July contain, in three cases, modified name spelling, perhaps in an attempt at anglicization, these now reading Brisborowe, Lambert and Mathew Bachlat. Finally there is John Votier, born in Rone (*sic*) and 12 years in England—he is also listed again on 11th July—and John Riche, of Frampton, smith, aged 50 and with two children, 20 years in England, who 'is allowed for his qualities as a clockmaker'. Although no trace of the Nonsuch clock remains, it is thought to have been comparable with the one at Hampton Court; and Clive Ponsford concludes by speculating whether the clock in Dover Castle, another of Henry VIII's foundations, and which bears the monogram 'RL', could perhaps have been made by Robert Lamberd. The clock itself is in the Science Museum. It is a tantalising puzzle.

Although most of these royal craftsmen seem to have come to England from elsewhere in Europe, there are one or two who may have been native to these shores. Two makers, for instance, share the surname Tracellion or Trasillion, which has a good Cornish ring to it. In 1515, John of this name received a quarter's wages of 30s 5d and an identical payment was made to an Anthony in 1528; all further trace has disappeared by 1530. Whether these were one and the same man—such records were never noted for their detailed accuracy—or, perhaps, father and son, is not known. Another seemingly native English name at this time is that of John Fitzwater. He became a royal clockmaker from 1530, having made the clock for the second gatehouse at Hampton Court; and subsequently Keeper of the Hampton Court clock, with a payment in this regard of 27s 8d being recorded in 1532. It seems likely, however, that he was not a very successful clockmaker, as Nicholas Oursian was frequently called in to overhaul Fitzwater's own clock at Hampton Court; and by 1538 Fitzwater had been transferred from that job to look after the clock at the palace at Newhall Boreham, in Essex. That this was a demotion is amply illustrated by his new salary, 13s 4d per quarter. Nevertheless, he continued in the King's employ, albeit in a much reduced role.

Further concrete examples of Henry VIII's predilections in clocks are to be found in 'Privy Purse Expenses from 1529 to 1532', in the version edited by Sir Harry Nicholas, an early-nineteenth-century antiquary. In July 1530, £15 was paid to the Frenchman who sold the King 'ij clokks at [W]Oking'. In the following month was paid to 'a Frenchman called Drulardy, for iij dyalls and a clokk for the King's Grace the sum of £15'. In December of the same year, £19 6s 8d was 'paid to Vincent Keney clok maker for xj clokks and dyalls'. In this same series are cited payments to Nicholas the Astronomer, for mending a clock, but whether this was Kratzer or Urseau is not clear. By January 1532 the practice was still continuing, a payment being noted 'to the French clokmaker for ij clokks xxx corons [crowns], and a reward of xx corons, in all lv corons'. Presumably they did get their sums right, and the missing five corons were duly accounted for. On 15th March of that same year was 'paid to one Lycile, a widowe, for vij cloke cases, xxx.s a pece'. There is also mention of a clock 'of iron with sondry dores of copper graven showing howe the see doth ebbe and flowe', which is said to have been presented to Henry VIII by John Poynet, Bishop of Winchester. Of even more interest, however, is an Inventory of certain valuable effects in the Palace of Westminster in 1542, among which are described the following clocks:

Item, oone Clocke of iron with a case of glasse, the frame of the same case being iron gilt with iij plumettes of led and two belles whiche stryketh the quarter and half of an hower.

Item, oone Larum or Watch of iron, the case being likewise iron gilt, with two plumettes of led.

Item, oone Clocke of copper and gilt, with a man in the toppe of the same of like copper, holding the King in his armes sett in silver and gilt, standing upon a fote of walnuttre garnishid with xij pillours of like wodde.

Item, oone Clocke of iron with a Larum to the same, with the Kinges armes crownyd upon the same, with iij counterpoyses of copper, two of them wrythen and gilt, and the iij. de playne and nott gilt, with iij. smaller counterpoyses of like copper and gilt.

Item, oone Clocke of iron having dores of copper and not gilt, with iij belles and two men that stryketh the hower, and upon the top of the bell and egle gilt sett upon a case of iron colourid red, with iij great plomettes of copper and iij. smale plomettes to the same, and the same clock having the change of the moone upon it.

Item, oone Clocke of copper and gilt, with a chyme to the same, showing all the daies of the yere and the planettes, with iij moving dialles to the same, oone of them beyng silver ennamuled blewe and the xij. signes gilt, with thre great counterpoyses of copper gilt, and iij. very smale counterpoyses of like copper gilt.

Item, oone Clocke of copper and gilt, with a chyme to the same at the half hower, having the chainge of the moone, the Kinges armes graven upon the ij. dores, with iij. great plumettes of copper gilt, engraven with the Kinges and Quene Annes letters, and two smale plumettes like acorns gilt, and the iij. de wrethen all gilt.

Item, oone rounde Clocke of iron, with sondry dores of copper graven, showing howe the see doth ebbe and flowe, and with a case of glasse sett in iron gilt, standing upon a foote or case of wodde, with iij. great counterpoyses and two smale of copper, and the iij. de smale oone being of led.

Item, oone Clocke of iron, a larum to the same, stryking butt oone stroke at the half hower, with a case of glasse sett in iron gilt and payntid, with iij great and iij. smale plomettes of led.

Item, oone Clocke of iron garnisshid with copper and gilt, with a George upon the top of the same, which Clocke goyth withowte any counterpoyse.

These effects were seemingly entrusted to Sir Anthony Denny, as Keeper of the Palace of Westminster in 1542. This favourite of the King, born in 1501, was a privy councillor who obtained grants of various manors and lands of dissolved monasteries, was knighted in 1544 and appointed by Henry VIII in 1547 to be counsellor to his son and successor, Edward VI. In the same year he also became a Member of Parliament, and died in 1549 only two years after Edward VI ascended the throne. In that year, 1542, however, Denny seems to have given the King a singular New Year's gift, in the form of a clock, said to have been designed by Holbein, which 'had on its summit a clock driven by wheelwork, below which were before and after noon dials, showing time by shadows; and beneath them was a clepsydra, indicating the quarters of an hour by means of a fluid'.

When reviewing inventory material of this period, there must inevitably be speculation as to whether, in some instances, the objects concerned may have been spring-driven and conceivably small enough to be described as watches. For example, another entry from the same source, covering the payment of 10 guineas, a large sum for those days, was paid for a 'clock' in a gold case. Was this perhaps a watch?—yet it is most uncommon, before the second quarter of the seventeenth century, for watches to be cased up in precious metals. It is doubtful if we shall ever know. However, it does seem that the very last item from the Inventory which is listed above, may have been a spring-driven timekeeper.

By this time, appointments of royal clockmakers were becoming more numerous, suggesting that skilled native craftsmen were no longer so scarce. For instance, there is a record of payments made in 1550 on behalf of the King, to 'Allaine Bawdyson, clockemaker, by vertue of the K's warrant under his prevye signet dated at the palaice of Westminster the thurde daye of Aprill A^{o} Regis Edwardi sexti iij ^{cio} the wages or fee of viij by daye which Sebastian Lysney [Le Seney, *q.v.*], clockemaker, late enjoyed &c. xij^{li} iiij^{s}'.

From this point in mid-century there remains intact one fine royal artefact for horological use, in the shape of the horary quadrant of Edward VI. The nature of
such a device has already been described, in relation to 11
a similar survival in respect of Richard II. This present 12
quadrant is dated 'Anno Domini 1551' and there are also the words 'Edwardus Rex' together with several sets of initials. These include 'W.B.', 'J.C.' (or possibly 'T.C.') and 'T.G.' These have been identified by Dr. Frank Ward as relating to William Buckley, Sir John Cheke and Thomas Gemini. Buckley, a Fellow of King's College, Cambridge was Tutor to the Court Pages by 1551. He had also made a ring dial for Princess Elizabeth in 1546, with a tract on its use. Sir John Cheke was the Royal Tutor in 1548, and Provost of King's College until 1557. From 1544 to 1551 he was tutor to Prince Edward, who was, at the age of sixteen in 1547, to become King Edward VI. Finally, Thomas Gemini was engaged as instrument-maker and engraver in London from 1545 to 1562. All three men were also to be associated with an astrolabe made for Edward VI in 1552, which is now preserved in the Royal Belgian Observatory in Brussels.

Peripheral references to horology are also starting to appear. In the Calendar of State Papers under the date 25th December 1551, for example, there is a letter from Sir William Pickering (1516–75), who was a courtier and diplomat and, at that time, ambassador in Paris, to Sir William Cecil (1520–98), who served at least three monarchs in a long life but is best known as the Lord Burghley who was responsible for the execution of Mary, Queen of Scots, in 1587. In this letter are references to a book entitled *L'Horloge de Princes*. Next, Sir John Cheke (1514–57), who was Secretary of State in 1553, but originally a Greek scholar and university professor, and well liked in royal circles, having been granted a pension by Henry VIII and some Church

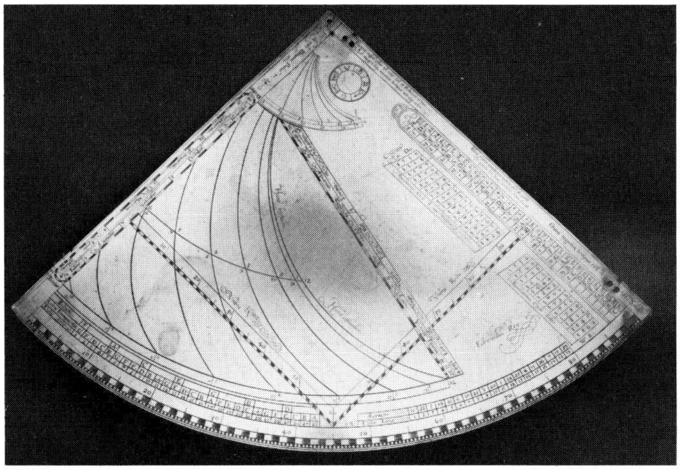

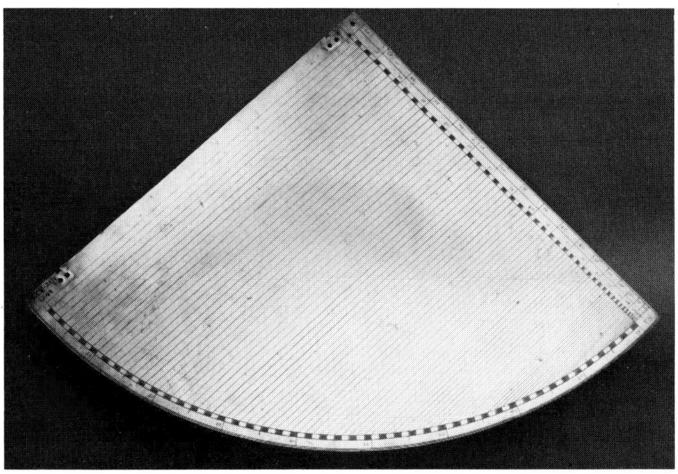

11. (Top) *Quadrant made for Edward VI, dated 1551: obverse.* (British Museum)

12. (Above) *Quadrant made for Edward VI, dated 1551: reverse.* (British Museum)

lands by Edward VI, describes how the latter king gave him a clock 'by which 'tis probable his Majesty with his schoolmaster had studied many an Hour'—thus reports John Strype, the historian and biographer, in 1705. The clock passed from Cheke to Dr Edwin Sandys, Bishop of Winchester, who seems to have given it in turn to Lord Burghley, this in 1563. His covering letter is said to have run:

Suche ys the barreness of this Countrie that yt bringith nothing forth fitt to remember youe withall, and therfor I am bold to present youe with an olde Clock, in the stead of a Newyears gift, which I trust ye will the rather accept because yt was your olde masters of happy memorie King Edward's, and afterwards your lovinge and learned brother's Mr. Cheeke's; and synce, hys who thinkith himself in many respectes most bounden unto youe.

Nicholas Urseau continued to serve as clockmaker to Queen Mary, and there is a reference, from the first year of her reign, in which his name is now spelt 'Ursewe'. Listed in the same *Booke of Fees and Offices* is a certain 'Cloke keper, John de Moylym', who seems likely to be the craftsman sometimes identified as John Demolyn. He is thought to have been of French extraction, but living in England by 1544. There is extant an account of New Year gifts presented to Queen Mary in 1556, one of them from Urseau which was described earlier (see page 7) and also 'a cloke with a lambe on it of copper, guilt' from John Demolyn.

Mary, Queen of Scots, was also said to have possessed a number of watches, such as the one with its movement enclosed in a rock-crystal case shaped like a coffin. Another was a large oval watch, said to have been found immediately after the Queen's escape from imprisonment in Lochleven Castle; this watch bore the maker's name, 'F. Le Grande', but it is unlikely to be the François of that surname who worked in Rouen, for his date is usually listed as 1617. It is also said that, while still in Fotheringay Castle and just before her execution, Mary gave a watch to the castle governor as a token of her gratitude for his civil treatment of her. Reputedly, she also gave a watch to John Knox, the reformer, 'as a pledge of amity', this watch being in an octagonal rock-crystal case, $1\frac{1}{2}$ inches long with a concave silver lid on either side. The maker was 'N. Forsaict a Paris'; it is tempting to identify this maker with a certain Nicholas Forfaict, Forfait or Forfect, but he was seemingly in Paris from 1606 to 1613. Another of the ill-fated Queen's watches is described as small—about an inch in diameter—round, and in a black shagreen case studded with gold stars, and with a central cross formed of fleur-de-lys. Unusually for that period, the dial is said to be of white enamel, 'somewhat larger than a shilling'; and the maker's name, 'Etienne Hubert à Rouen', is shared by several makers, presumably succeeding members of the same family, of whom the earliest cannot be placed before about 1620.

The period which is the subject of this present chapter concludes with Queen Elizabeth I, during whose reign it might appear that watches and domestic clocks, albeit confined to the wealthy, were at last becoming more generally familiar objects in Britain. Even so, these must, at first, have been imported, for most skilled craftsmen working on mechanical time-keepers in this country were foreign. It would also appear that no Wills of clock- and watchmakers are to be found up to this time, and indeed mentions of timepieces in any testaments are exceedingly rare.

There is the Will of Archbishop Parker, dated 5th April 1575, which includes bequests of a '*horologium*' valued at £54 4s to the Bishop of Ely, and to the same beneficiary 'my stick of Indian cane which hath a watch in the top of it'. There was also the case of Anne, Duchess of Somerset, whose Will, dated 14th July 1586, left to her daughter-in-law, Lady Catherine Grey, 'a clock of gold, worth about £30'. But such references are the exception rather than the rule.

The first royal clockmaker whose Will can be traced was Bartholomew Newsam. There is no suggestion that he was other than a native-born Briton, and so can perhaps claim to be the first really important horologist to emerge from these islands. There is some probability that he was born at York, although the year is not known. At some time he moved to London, and seems to have carried on business as a clockmaker from about the year of Queen Elizabeth's accession. On 8th April 1565 he obtained from the Crown a thirty-year Lease of premises in the Strand, close to Somerset House, and he appears to have resided there for the remainder of his life. He was not only skilled in his craft but on friendly terms with men of influence such as Sir Philip Sidney, well known as soldier, statesman, poet and courtier. In 1572, he was granted the office of clockmaker to the Queen in reversion after the death or surrender of N. V. (presumably Nicholas Urseau), while, under date 1590, he finally obtained it, Urseau being now described as 'deceased'. However, he was Clock-keeper to the Queen prior to 1582, for on 4th June 1583, under Privy Seal, he was paid 32s 8d for 'mending of clocks during the past year'. Thus it would seem that Newsam (or Newsham, as it is sometimes spelt) was the first to combine the offices of Clock-keeper and Clockmaker, hitherto kept separate; this is apparent from items in Queen Elizabeth's household accounts, recording payments of £18 annually as a fee for the clockmaker, while the clock-keeper received £12 13s 4d *per annum*.

Several important events seem to have occurred to Newsam in 1583. On 5th August he wrote to Sir Francis Walsingham, statesman and Secretary of State dealing in foreign affairs, desiring him to favour Newsam's petition, apparently for an extension of his Lease. He had already asked Sir Philip Sidney to speak for him in this matter, and this was presumably a subtle reinforcing of his position, since Sidney was Walsingham's son-in-law. Whether he got exactly what he wanted, in the end, is unclear; suffice it to say that, by Letters Patent dated 6th September 1583, he received a Lease for twenty-one years of lands at Fleete in Lincolnshire formerly the property of the Duke of Suffolk, also a water-mill at Wymondham, in Norfolk, together with fishing-rights, as well as various other parcels of land in different parts of the country, and in London.

He died before 18th December 1593, so that his tenure of office in his double capacity had been but a short one. His Will, which is dated in 1586, states that he had married on 10th September 1565, his wife's maiden name being Younge; the ceremony took place at St Mary Le Strand, and this was only a few months, of course, after he had obtained his Lease on premises that must have been very close at hand to the church. He was survived not only by his widow—forename, presumably, stated to be Parnell—but also by four children, William, Edward, Margaret and Rose. The first-named was born, we are told, on 27th December 1570.

Newsam's Will contains some fascinating bequests. His son Edward was to have his father's tools 'on condicion he become a clockmaker as I am'; all except, that is, his 'best Vice save one' and certain other specified implements, which he left to John Newsam, clockmaker of York and clearly a close relative. Indeed, a maker of this name made a clock for Ousebridge chapel in 1593. The other implements, apart from the vice, make unfamiliar reading, viz. 'a beckhorne to stand upon borde, a great forehammer, and to [two] hand hammers, a grete longe beckhorne in my backe shoppe'. Should his son Edward fail to become a clockmaker, then 'I will the foresaid tooles to be sold by my executors.' Incidentally, a beckhorne—or beck-iron—was a small anvil.

However, it is the images conjured up by the timepieces included in Newsam's Will that are of even greater interest, and his friends, to whom he bequeathed them, must have felt most favoured. These range from 'a sonne dyall of copper gylte' and 'a chamber clocke of fyve markes price', to 'one crystall jewell with a watche in it, garnished with goulde'—this one to John Hill—and again, 'one watch gylte to show the hower' to his 'very lovinge friend Mr. Barnarde Dewhurst'. There is also 'a strikinge clocke, in a silken purse, and a sonne dyall to stande upon a post in his garden' to another friend, Albane Stepneth Esquire.

Although relatively little of Newsam's work has survived,* it is possible to obtain a little perception of his skills from the above descriptions. There is, for example, in the Cheapside Hoard in the Museum of London—this enormous recovery of Jacobean and Elizabethan

* In the British Museum there is preserved a quite magnificent set of drawing instruments in a square, tall and beautifully enriched gilt case. On the bottom of this, in a cartouche, appears the name 'Barthelmewe Newsum'. Thought to date *c.* 1570, it is conceivable that the existence of Newsam's name indicates ownership only, but it is perhaps more probable that he was the maker.

13. *Six-sided emerald containing a watch, from the so-called Cheapside Hoard.* (Museum of London)

jewellery, discovered under a house in Cheapside in
13 1912, is thought to have been a jeweller's stock-in-trade—a single six-sided emerald into which is sunk a watch, with gold and enamel embellishments. It is not possible to establish the maker of this supremely beautiful article, since the movement has, over the centuries, become corroded into its precious-stone case and cannot be removed. However, it fits very well Newsam's 'crystall jewel with a watche in it'. Then again, there is in the British Museum a striking clock in
14 a square brass case, gilded and engraved; the base is about $2\frac{1}{2}$ inches square, the height 4 inches, but augmented by an ornamental domed and perforated superstructure which brings the overall height to $6\frac{1}{2}$ inches. The movement is arranged in two stages, one above the other, the framing for it consisting of three plates held in place by four corner-posts. The going-
15 mechanism is between the upper and middle plates, while the striking part of the movement is between the middle and lower plates. Both trains have fusees, which are very long and with little curvature in their profiles. They are connected to their spring-barrels with gut line, rather than the later fusee chains. Wheels are of iron, while the plates, posts and barrels are of brass. The signature inscribed on the movement—which, incidentally, has no screws in its construction—is 'Bartilmewe Newsum'. This clock is particularly important not only because of its fine workmanship but also on account of its originality—it has been preserved from subsequent modification which, in an object of this kind and age, is very rare. Its small size and obvious portability certainly suggest that it might, at one time, have been enclosed 'in a silken purse', probably with draw-strings and carried at the waist.

Like her predecessors, there can be no doubting Queen Elizabeth's predilection for clocks and watches. Of the former, there is one contemporary account describing a piece of clockwork consisting of 'an Aethiop riding upon a rhinoceros, with four attendants, who all make their obeisance when it strikes the hour; these are all put into motion by winding up the machine'. The descriptions of watches presented to the Queen are, however, of singular interest; in the year 1572, for example, she received 'one armlet or shakell of golde, all over fairely garnishedd with rubyes and dyamondes, haveing in the closeing thearof a clocke'. In that same year, too, another gift is said to have been 'a juell, being a chrsolite garnished with golde, flagon facyon, thone side sett with two emeraldes, thother side haveing in it a clocke'.

An inventory of clocks and watches in Queen Elizabeth's possession contains no less than twenty-four separate items, the descriptions of which underline perhaps the most salient features of portable time-keepers at this period, which is that they were far more to be regarded as pieces of jewellery for personal adornment than as serious functional time-measuring instruments. That this must have been so we know, simply from a contemplation of the technical achievement at that time. The mechanism was robust, and it worked—but not for another three-quarters of a century was there to be development of those elements which could materially improve the time-keeping performance of these early clocks and watches. So, we can rejoice with the Queen, without any great concern about their functional accuracy, at such timepieces as

> one clock of gold curiously wrought with flowers and beastes, with a queene on the toppe on the one side; and on the other side a beare and a ragged staffe of sparkes of diamonds, fullie furnished with diamonds and rubies of sundry sortes and bignes; one emerode under it, a faier table diamond with a ragged staffe in the foyle thereof, and a faier rubie under it squared; and a pearle pendaunt on either side of the clocke.

The 'bear and ragged staff' was the heraldic device of

14. *Clock by Bartholomew Newsam: the case.* (British Museum)

15. *Clock by Bartholomew Newsam: the movement.* (British Museum)

the Earl of Leicester, who was Master of the Horse; and another gift in this same vein, although deriving from the Countess of Derby, consisted of 'a white beare of gold and mother of perle, holding a ragged staffe, standing upon a tonne of golde, whearin is a clocke, the same tonne-staffe garnished with dyamondes and rubyes'. Then there is 'one clocke of golde wrought like deyses and paunseyes', garnished with diamonds, rubies, emeralds and pearls, and with 'a pendant acorne'. Another gold clock had, on one side, a horse bearing a globe, with a crown above it; yet another had a mouse on top, and another a 'frogge'. The variety seems to have been endless; and even such an uninteresting device as an hour-glass seems to have been made the object of fabulous decoration, when one reads 'Item, an hower glasse sett in golde with 6 emerods, 3 turquesses, two rubyies, and xv small diamondes with 6 perles'.

It will be abundantly clear from the foregoing that most of our knowledge of royal domestic clocks and watches of the sixteenth century and earlier stems from documentary records. In recent times the Royal Collection has been totally lacking in such objects; those that still exist in inventories must in reality have been disposed of for their intrinsic value during times of financial stringency. It is true that the very occasional early timepiece has graced the private collection of a member of the Royal Family; such a one, for instance, was prominent among the objects of vertu that were sold following the death in 1965 of HRH The Princess Royal. This was a superb South German silver rectangular clock casket raised on four ball feet, and 16
with the sides and slightly domed top most elaborately pierced and engraved with a crowned monogram, coats-of-arms, mythological figures, putti and masks, all in a setting of scrolling flowering foliage. The clock, having a verge movement of watch size, is located in the centre of the lid, with its silver chapter ring upon a platform which surmounts the domed area and which is embellished with winged satyrs and further scrolling foliage. The signature on the movement is 'Seb. Schwarz Nurnberg', presumably the same Sebald

16. (Above) *The casket clock which was once the property of H.R.H. the late Princess Royal.* (Christie's, London)

Schwarz of that city who is listed as active in 1580, although this particular object could well be somewhat later.

In the event, just one timepiece seems to have survived from this early period—the sixteenth century—which can, with the greatest confidence, be identified from inventory descriptions as possessing authentic royal antecedents; and a truly magnificent object it is. Sadly, when this clock appeared on the market some years ago, an unexpected and insurmountable combination of adverse circumstances prevented its being acquired for the nation. In the end, however, it was purchased by the Worshipful Company of Goldsmiths as a remarkable addition to their already supreme collection of historic gold and silver artefacts, so that it is almost certainly as permanently located in Britain as would have been the case had it gone to the British Museum, where it would have been equally as welcome.

It may be interesting, first, to consider the documen-
17 tary references to this object, described by the auc-
18 19 tioneers as 'A Highly Important Royal Tudor Clock-
20 Salt'. It appears first in an inventory entitled 'The Kinges Juelhous in the charge of Sur Anthony Aucher, Knight Master and Tresorer of the same made in 1550'. Two copies of this manuscript exist, one in the British Library (Add. MS 46348) and the other in the library of the Society of Antiquaries. From the latter (fol. 105b) can be found

Item one salte of silver and gilt wt a cover standing uppon vi rounde Balles of Jasper wt vi white Agath heddes standing in collitts of silver within the same a rounde cristall and therein a Clocke wt seames and other joyntes of Latten and Iron apperteyning to the same The Salte garnished wt course stones and certein hanginge perles the cover garnished wt small white heddes of Agath and small counterfeite Emereuds having a man sitting uppon an Eagle uppon the Toppe of the cover weing altogether cviii oz.

There are a number of later references recorded, from which can be derived a glimpse of the subsequent fortunes of this remarkable object. Inventories taken in 1559 and 1574, the first in the National Library of Scotland (MS 2825) and the second in the British Library (Harley MS 1650), virtually copy the foregoing description, save that the word 'seames' of the 1550

17. (Below) *The Royal Tudor clock-salt: its appearance in 1967 and prior to the removal of later additions.* (Christie's, London)

19. (Above) *The Royal Tudor clock-salt: detail of upper gallery.* (Goldsmiths' Company, London)

18. (Left) *The Royal Tudor clock-salt, as seen today.* (Goldsmiths' Company, London)

20. (Below) *The Royal Tudor clock-salt: detail of lower area.* (Goldsmiths' Company, London)

version is replaced by 'a chyme' in both the later editions, while there is an addition, at the end, of the words 'lacking divers stones'. These losses apparently include 'the white heddes of Agath' in the cover, or perhaps the sides of the Salt, which are now set with garnets. Yet a further inventory of 1597 (British Library Stowe MS 555) copies these descriptions.

In the 1574 inventory already mentioned, there were no less than seven Salts containing clocks–for easy reference, see *The Jewels and Plate of Queen Elizabeth I—The Inventory of 1574*, by A. J. Collins, London, 1955. The present example is item number 914, the 'certein hanginge perles' presumably being suspended from small rings which are still present below the lower edge of the sides of the hexagonal Salt in the upper part. For the next chronological reference, it is necessary to turn to 'A true and pfect inventory of all the Plate and Jewells now being in the Upper Jewell House of the Tower in the Charge of Sir Henry Mildmay, together with an appraisement of them made and taken in the 13th, 14th and 15th daies of August 1649' (*Archaeologia* XV from a manuscript in the possession of Reverend John Brand read to the Society of Antiquaries 17th May 1804 and now lost). There is an entry in this which reads: 'Two faire large Saltes of Silver Gilt with a clocke in it, garnished with 6 ivory heads about the bottom and enriched with Stones and little Gold heads Enamelled with a man upon a Faulcon on ye top of it valued at £40'. If there seems to be a confusion of numbers in the foregoing, the most likely explanation is that the enumerator mistook the hexagonal base of the object for another Salt—in addition, that is, to the one at the top—in which case 'two faire large saltes' would have been quite correct albeit in combination with a singular 'Clocke' and also 'ye top of it'. The certificates of the Treasurers of the Sale of the royal property (PRO, SP 29/447) give a list of the buyers and the prices paid, in which this item is annotated 'Sold Mr Smith ye 31 Decr 1649 for £43'.

This fascinating creation was sold at auction by Messrs Christie's in 1967, and the background outlined above is based upon the research published in their catalogue on that occasion. From that same source, the following is the auctioneer's description of the object as it now appears:

A HIGHLY IMPORTANT ROYAL TUDOR CLOCK-SALT, of silver-gilt enriched with cameo busts, semi-precious stones and enamel, with later additions—13¾″(34.0 cm.) high, probably German, circa 1540.

The hexagonal base standing on six mottled grey agate spheres with panels to the sides each set with a shell cameo cut in very high relief with a male or female bust on a blue enamel ground gilt with arabesques, with bands of acanthus foliage above and below, the dome supported by six double scroll mounts with a shell at the base of each and containing a glass cylinder with the later movement within; above this a pierced dome for the bell cast and chased with ribs and urn motifs with gables above heads of fabulous animals with figures of putti between surmounted by an octagonal salt-cellar treated in similar manner to the base but set with garnets and small loops below, with similar gables above and a calix of alternate ribs, as on the dome, and leaf motifs containing a later white enamel sphere on which the hour is indicated by a figure of a Roman soldier which stands at the base of the dome.

Following the 1649 inventory, there does not seem to be any further record of this clock-salt until it turned up at the South Kensington Loan Exhibition of 1862, when it was exhibited by W. B. Stopford Esq., grandfather of Colonel Nigel Stopford Sackville, CBE, the vendor in 1967. In 1862, it was described (exhibit no. 7448) as French, *c.*1520. The cameos are comparable with two in the British Museum and one in the Royal Collection at Windsor Castle. Apart from this object, only two other items from the 1574 inventory have been identified up to the present time, neither of them clocks. Nevertheless, the mere fact that, even in the twentieth century, it is still possible for such treasures to emerge from obscurity and to be recognized for their true worth, does at least leave some hope for other such discoveries in the future.

2 Stuart patrons sponsor a Golden Era

Prior to 1600, native-born clock- and watchmakers in Britain were almost unknown; only Bartholomew Newsam seems to have achieved any eminence in this, at that period, highly specialized field. As the century turned, however, the situation started to improve but—as indeed was the case with any changes in those far-off days—it was a very slow process.

The first maker of substance to emerge was Rainulph (Randulph) Bull; and he is best known on account of work he did on the Westminster Palace clock. There is an oft-quoted entry under date 1st April 1617, which reads:

By Order, dated 29th March 1617. To Ranulph Bull, keeper of his Majesty's clock in his Majesty's palace at Westminster, the sum of £56 13s 4d in full satisfaction and discharge of and for divers sums by him disbursed for mending the said clock, in taking the same and other quarter clocks all in pieces, and repairing the same in wheels, pulleys, hammers, weights, and in all other parts, and in new hanging, wiring and cording of the same clock, and other necessary reparations thereunto belonging, the charge whereof, with his own workmanship and travail therein, doth amount to the sum aforesaid, appearing by a note of the particular demands, delivered upon his oath, taken before one of the Barons of his Majesty's Exchequer, without account or imprest to be made thereof. By writ, dated 27th March 1617, £56 13s 4d.

This extract is from Devon's *Issues of the Exchequer*.

Randulph Bull is generally considered to have flourished during the period *c.*1590 to 1617 or later,
21 bridging the change of century; and several watches by
22 him have been recorded, including one in the British Museum which is dated 1590. As usual, however, there are other hazy details which only tend to cloud the issue yet cannot be ignored. There is a record of a maker called Edmund Bull, who can be placed at work during the period *c.*1610–30—his watches are repre-

21. (Above left) *Watch by Randulph Bull dated 1590: general view.* (British Museum)

22. (Above right) *Watch by Randulph Bull: the movement.* (British Museum)

sented in several of the great public collections—and yet another, Emmanuel Bull, who is generally placed ante-1618 and who was the King's clockmaker. Were these one and the same man, and were they any relation to Rainulph? Sadly, the records have not revealed the answer, up to the present time.

The only other important craftsman during this bridging period in which the indigenous artisan gradually took over from foreign immigrants—until,

23. *Star Watch by David Ramsay, open to reveal dial.* (Clockmakers' Company, London)

24. *Star Watch by David Ramsay, showing the movement.* (Clockmakers' Company, London)

that is, the revocation of the Edict of Nantes brought many more to these shores—is Michael Nouwen. Active from *c.*1580 to 1613, he is likely to have been born of parents who originated in Flanders; his father was certainly Andrewe Noway, who came to London in 1571. He is considered to have been an exceptionally fine maker, which is borne out by the surviving specimens of his work; yet in an age when the greatest craftsmen invariably gravitated to the Court, he does not seem to have had any royal associations whatever.

The next emerging royal clockmaker is David Ramsay, of whom there are more detailed records. The *Dictionary of National Biography* places him as one of the Ramsays of Dalhousie, but this is disputed by other authorities, who place his origins in Dundee; his date of birth is unknown, but his earliest work seems to appear *c.*1600. There was a well-known family of the name of Ramsay in Dundee at this time, who had care of the town's clocks, and David was probably related to them.

There is no record of where he received his training, but it is tempting to think that this was in France, since much of his surviving work shows clear indications of French influence. There is other evidence of this, too. The hinged covers of the front and back of one of his early watches are engraved with scenes of the Annunciation and the Nativity, themes which would have made the watch almost impossible to dispose of in Scotland, where anything savouring of popery would have received a poor reception indeed. There is also the evidence of Ramsay's son William, who is quoted as saying, 'When James I succeeded to the crown of England, he sent into France for my father, who was there, and made him page of the bedchamber and keeper of his Majesty's clocks and watches.' Finally, several watches of what might be called Ramsay's
'French period' are signed 'David Ramsay, Scotus, me 25 26 27
fecit', a form of identification that would have been unnecessary had the watches actually been made in Scotland.

There are many references to Ramsay in royal records of the time. The earliest appears to be an entry in the account of money expended by Sir David Murray, Kt., Keeper of the Privy Purse to Henry, Prince of Wales, who died in 1612. This reads: 'Watches three bought of Mr. Ramsay the Clockmaker lxjli' (£61). In the same account among the 'Guyftes and Rewardes' there is an item 'Mr. Ramsay the clockemaker xjs' (11s).

In 1613, James I gave Ramsay a pension of £200 *per annum*. This was quickly followed by a further, and illuminating, award:

25th November 1613	Grant to David Ramsay, Clockmaker Extraordinary, of a pension of £50 *per annum*.

Three years later saw the start of a steady stream of such grants and payments:

1616	Warrant to pay David Ramsay, Clockmaker, £234 10s due to him for purchase and repair of clocks and watches for the King.
1618	Grant to David Ramsay of the office of Chief Clockmaker to the King, with fees and allowances for workmanship.
27th July 1619	Grant to David Ramsay, the King's Clockmaker, born in Scotland, of denization. [i.e. he became an English citizen].
30th March 1622	Warrant to pay David Ramsay, Clockmaker, £113 for work for the late Prince Henry and for watches and clocks for the King. [Henry Frederick, Prince of Wales, and James I's eldest son, died of typhoid fever in 1612.]
30th September 1622	Warrant to pay £232 15s to David Ramsay, the King's Clockmaker, for repairing clocks at Theobalds, Oatlands and Westminster, and for making a chime of bells adjoining to the clock at Theobalds.
25th January 1626	Warrant to pay to David Ramsay, for coins to be given by the King at the close of his coronation.

By now, of course, he owed fealty to Charles I, who had ascended the throne the previous year. The entries continue:

17th March 1627	Warrant to pay to David Ramsay, Page of the Bedchamber and clockmaker, £441 3s 4d for work done for his late Majesty, and £358 16s 8d in lieu of diet and bouche of court. [This appears to refer to the mode of living and the service, especially from the kitchens, which such an appointment would normally carry with it.]
10th July 1628	Warrant to pay to David Ramsay, £415 for clocks and other necessaries delivered for the King's service.
1632	Warrant to pay David Ramsay, clockmaker, on his bills, for one year £219.

The date of Ramsay's death has not been traced but appears to have been *c.*1654. He left behind a legacy of superbly decorative and well-made watches, now to be found mainly in the great public collections; one or two small clocks of his are also known, including a beautiful square table clock in the Victoria and Albert Museum. There are contemporary references describing some of his work, too, such as that among the *State Papers* of 1653, wherein are two receipts taken from the Jewel House at Whitehall soon after the death of Charles I. These read:

18 die Feb. 1649	Recd. one clocke with divers mocions, two globes, one case for a clocke, and a glasse, one Bullet Clocke, one clocke with five bells, and one other clocke, all which were lying at Whitehall late in the charge of David Ramsay.
On the same date	One other clocke in a Bow received from Ramsay.

Ramsay must be one of the very few notable clockmakers to feature in a work of fiction. Sir Walter Scott introduces him as 'Constructor of Horologes to His most Sacred Majesty James I' in his novel *The Fortunes of Nigel*, which appeared in 1822. He does not come well out of this: 'a tall, thin, lathy skeleton' of an old man, extending his lean jaws into an alarming grin, must suggest considerable licence on the author's part. He is further described as a shopkeeper with premises a few yards to the east of Temple Bar; whereas Ramsay's son William, in a postscript of 1653 to his work *Vox Stellarum*, which he had dedicated to his father the previous year, writes 'From my study in my father's house in Holborn, within two doors of the "Wounded Hart", near the King's Gate'. That, too, is probably where he died.

Ramsay seems to have been a man of many parts. Excellent craftsman he certainly was, and adept at business he must have been, also well thought of in the highest circles in the land, without doubt. He is said to have been a student of the occult sciences, and William Lilley the astrologer (1602–81) relates how he accompanied Ramsay to Westminster at night to make some experiments with the object of locating treasure by use of divining-rods. Ramsay was also an inveterate patentee; Woodcroft's *Alphabetical Index of Patentees of Inventions* lists no fewer than eight in his name, all lodged between 1618 and 1638, none of them being concerned with any aspect of horology.

Ramsay's eminence in his own time may also be inferred from the fact of his being appointed to the office of Master, when the clockmakers of the City of London first received their Royal Charter of Incorporation. Sworn into office on 12th October 1632 by Sir George Whitmore, Lord Mayor, he never seems to have taken any active part in the management of the Company's affairs, and his deputy, Henry Archer, presided at most official occasions held during his term of office. The fact
23 24 that the Company preserves a superb watch, shaped like a six-pointed star, made by him, is entirely fortuitous; it is a relatively recent acquisition. Sadly, in view of his great importance as one of the early pioneers in Britain of mechanical horology, there seems to be no timepiece by him with any proven royal associations; there is a small table clock in the Victoria and Albert Museum, to be described later, which has been accredited to the patronage of James I, but there can be no certainty of it.

References to horology which involve King James I are varied. One account, of a State Progress to Theobald's in 1603, mentions that he stopped at the Bell Inn at Edmonton and, desirous of discovering how many vehicles passed that establishment within a given period, 'called for an houreglasse', which was duly provided. This must be as graphic a reflection upon the state of development of mechanical methods of time-measurement then in vogue as could be imagined. Nevertheless, there are also numerous examples of his interest in those new-fangled devices. Included in the *State Papers* of his reign, for instance, is a letter dated 4th August 1609 from Sir Julius Caesar (1558–1636), who was then Chancellor of the Exchequer, to the Clerks of the Signet, requesting them to prepare a warrant in the sum of £300 in favour of a certain Dutchman called Hans Niloe, 'for a clock with music and motions'. Later that same month, on the 17th, Sir Julius intimated that he was being pressed by Niloe for this payment. It fell to James I also, in 1622, to receive the petition of London clockmakers complaining of the unfair competition of foreigners practising their craft, which, as it turned out, was the initial step that led to the establishment of the Worshipful Company of Clockmakers. Two years before, however, in 1620, a London Pageant given in the King's honour included 'a

25. (Below left) *Gold and rock crystal watch by David Ramsay, dial view.* (Clockmakers' Company, London)

26. (Below right) *Gold and rock crystal watch by David Ramsay, showing movement with signature.* (Clockmakers' Company, London)

27. (Below) *Gold and rock crystal watch by David Ramsay: side view of movement seen through the crystal band of the case.* (Clockmakers' Company, London)

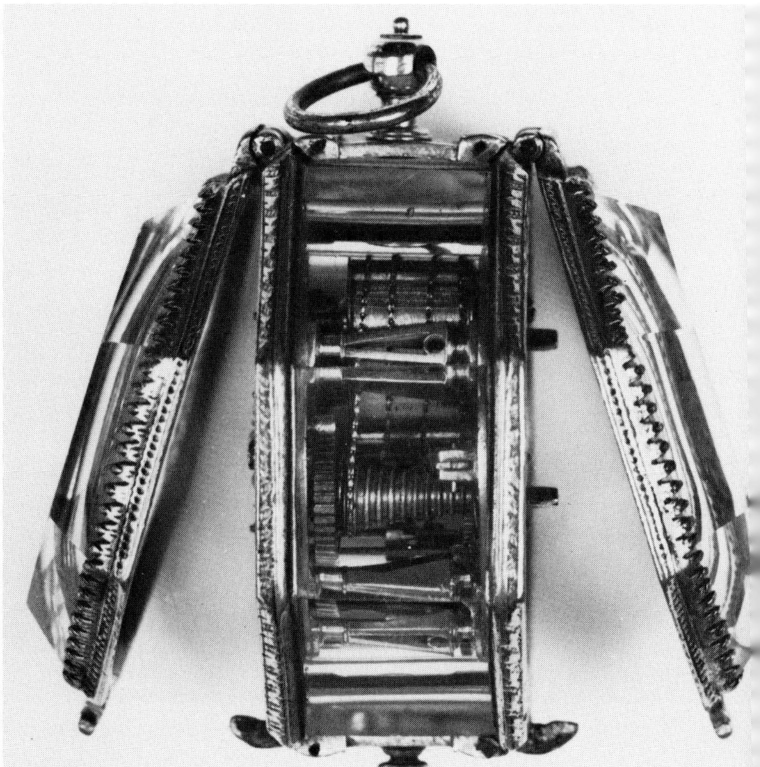

chariot painted fulle with houre-glasses and sundialls; the fore-wheeles were two globes, and the hinder wheeles were like two church-dialls. Within it aged Time was drawne, seated upon an houre-glasse'.

There is some descriptive record of the actual clocks and watches that passed through the royal hands of that period. One particularly evocative reference, quoted verbatim from Wood's *Curiosities of Clocks and Watches*, runs as follows:

On April 18th 1623, James I wrote from Windsor a letter to his 'sweete boyes', who were then in Spain; and therewith sent certain jewels for their companion, the Duke of Buckingham, to give away. One jewel was, according to a contemporary inventory, 'a clocke of goulde, garnisht on the one side with letters of dyamondes: Dieu et mon droyte; and on the other side, a crosse of dyamondes fullie garnisht, with a pendante of dyamondes'. The king in his letter said 'the watche is the richest and fittest for some olde ladie in my opinion'. With this royal opinion before us, we are induced to consider whether his majesty thought that a timekeeper was better suited to an elderly lady because of her nearness to the grave; or that the favour and influence of an aged woman, as against those of a young one, were more worth a costly trinket; or that youthful beauty did not require a blaze of diamonds to enhance its attractions. Later we find a warrant of indemnity to the Lord High Treasurer for having delivered certain jewels to James I, that were sent into Spain as above mentioned, dated July 7th, 1623; in which document the 'clocke of goulde' is mentioned.

Other mouth-watering descriptions of royal clocks and watches come direct from contemporary documents. In October 1605, for instance, it was ordered that £100 be paid to a clockmaker named Uldrich Henche 'for a clock, in manner of a branch, made by him, and set up in his Highness's chamber at Whitehall'. Two years later, in July 1607, 'to Humphrey Flood, goldsmith, or his assigns, the sum of £120, in full satisfaction and payment for a clock covered with gold and set with diamonds and rubies, and by him delivered to his Majesty's use, at the price of £220, whereof received £100'. First Britten, and then Baillie, in their standard reference works, quote Flood's dates as 1607–17, but without revealing any source of this information; and apart from this, no other information appears to have come to light regarding either of these craftsmen.

Many watches have been accredited to James I, either for his own personal use or for gift presentation by him. One which might seem, at least from the nineteenth-century description—for its present whereabout are not known—to warrant such a provenance, was exhibited at the Archaeological Institute on 7th December 1849, by a certain Mr Frederick Ouvry. Shaped like a flattened egg, and in a plain silver outer case, its inner case was engraved on one surface with a representation of Christ healing a cripple, with King James's motto 'Beati pacifici' above the royal arms. On the reverse appears the Good Samaritan, with the inscription 'S. Lucas, c.10'. Inside the lid, according to this same description, was a well-executed engraved portrait of the King, with his style and title. Round the rim were the rose, the harp and the thistle, crowned with the initials 'J.R.'. There was both calendar and lunar work 'and other things'—which are not specified—included in the dial arrangements, and the movement was signed 'David Ramsay, Scotus, me fecit'. The inner case had a rotatable keyhole-cover in the shape of a shield—to prevent dust entering the movement through the winding-hole—and, seemingly, this also concealed the name of the engraver of the elaborate case; this was quoted as 'Gerhardt de Heck, sculps.' but there is no trace of any such craftsman in the standard biographical dictionaries of engravers. The plain outer case of silver is reminiscent, not only in its simplicity but also in its shape, of one form of the excessively plain 'Puritan Watch', which became commonplace during the second quarter of the seventeenth century; it would not appear to accord with the flamboyant style of the rest of the timepiece and may therefore have been an afterthought.

Arguably the greatest horological personality of the seventeenth century—if only because of his enormously long life-span, more especially considering the period when he lived—was Edward East. He lived so long, in fact, that it was thought for years that there were two clockmakers with the same name, perhaps related; and it is only due to the research of the late H. Alan Lloyd, a well-known antiquarian horologist who died in 1969, that this matter was eventually sorted out.

Edward East, then, was born at Southill, in Bedfordshire—which is only a few miles from Northill, where Thomas Tompion, the other possible contender with East for the above-mentioned distinction, was born. East was baptized at Southill on 22nd August 1602, and on 27th March 1618, when he was $15\frac{1}{2}$ years old, he was apprenticed to a goldsmith called Richard Rogers, for a period of eight years. On 8th February 1627, East was made Free by Service—that is to say, he obtained his Freedom to work for himself, under his own name, and to sign his work himself and probably to take apprentices for training.

This was, of course, before the Clockmakers' Company was formed, and East was simply following the course of many another clockmaker in taking up the Freedom of any reasonably relevant Livery Company, just to be allowed to work within the City of London. When the Clockmakers' Company was at length

28. (Above) *Coach watch movement by Edward East: the dial incorporates an alarm setting ring.* (Clockmakers' Company, London)

29. (Below) *The movement back plate of the Edward East coach watch: three winding squares are needed, for going, striking and alarm trains.* (Clockmakers' Company, London)

formed, in 1631, East immediately transferred, becoming the junior member of the original Court of Assistants of that body. He eventually gravitated to the supreme office of Master, serving both in 1645 and 1652.

Lloyd considered that East's early work in watches bore witness to his training as a goldsmith; yet his clocks were remarkable for their extreme simplicity, resulting in an elegance and an architectural form that made them outstanding even in their own day.

In addition to his work, East remained active in the Clockmakers' Company so that, when it applied, in 1671, for a Grant of Arms, it was remarked then that he was the only member of the original Court of Assistants still alive; and when Henry Jones, one of East's apprentices, himself became Master of the Company in 1692, he recorded that Mr East wished to donate £100 during his lifetime for the benefit of the poor, a gift which was in fact registered in the following year.

East apparently moved to Hampton, in Middlesex, towards the end of his life. In his Will, which is dated 21st July 1688, he describes himself as 'Edward East, Watchmaker, Citizen and Goldsmith of London'; the Will was proved on 3rd February 1696/7. He was thus ninety-five years old when he died.

This most eminent of early horologists was Watchmaker to Charles I, his premises being in Pall Mall, near the Tennis Court. The Prince of Wales, subsequently Charles II, frequently played tennis, so that East's proximity was a convenient arrangement,
the stakes for this sport being often set at an 'Edwardus 30
East', as His Royal Highness is reputed to have called it; 31
that is, a watch of East's making. Another of the anecdotes concerning this craftsman is retailed in *Memoirs of the two last years of the reign of King Charles I* by Sir Thomas Herbert, Groom of the Chambers to His Majesty, in the 1815 edition, pages 148 and 173:

> Another night His Majesty (Charles I) appointed Mr. Herbert to come into his Bed Chamber an hour sooner than usual in the morning; but it so happened that he overslept his time, and awaken'd not untill the King's silver bell hasten'd him in. Herbert (said the King), you have not observed the command I gave last night. He acknowledg'd his fault. Well (said the King), I will order you for the future; you shall have a Gold
> Alarm-Watch, which, as there may be cause, shall awake 28
> you; write to the Earl of Pembroke to send me such a one 29
> presently. The Earl immediately sent to Mr. East, his Watchmaker in Fleet Street, about it; of which more will be said at his Majesty's coming to St. James's. . . . The Earl delivered to a Military Officer who was going to St. James's the Gold Watch that had the Alarm desiring him to give it to Mr. Herbert, to present it to the King.

Further light is shed on this matter in a delightful little work entitled *A History of Watches and other Timekeepers*

30. (Above) *A typical 'Puritan' watch by Edward East, so-called on account of its total lack of decoration.* (Clockmakers' Company, London)

31. (Above right) *Movement of an Edward East 'Puritan' watch.* (Clockmakers' Company, London)

by James Francis Kendal, which was published by Crosby, Lockwood & Son, London, in 1892. The author, a principal in the well-known watchmaking firm of Kendal & Dent, of Cheapside, died at the age of sixty-seven in 1911. On page 76 of the book appears the following statement:

In the possession of Mr. Alfred Morrison is a Warrant, dated June 23, 1649, from the Committee of Public Revenue to Thomas Fauconbridge, Esq., Receiver-General, authorising him to pay 'unto Mr Edward East, watchmaker, the some of fortie pounds for a watch and a Larum of gould by him made for the late King Charles by directions of the Earle of Pembrooke by order of the Committee, and delivered for the late King's use the xvii. of January last'. It is worthy of note that the watch was supplied but a fortnight before the execution of Charles I.

It is perhaps also worthy of note that the owner of this deed, despite the fairly commonplace name, was in fact a noted collector of works of art in his day. Alfred Morrison (1821–97) had houses at Fonthill and Carlton House Terrace, which he filled with objects reflecting his special interests, these including autographs and manuscripts such as the papers of Sir Richard Bulstrode. Presumably the means by which he fulfilled his artistic instincts derived from the fortune which his father, James Morrison (1790–1857), had amassed as a draper, who afterwards became an influential politician and Member of Parliament.

Nevertheless, there is a sad ending to this episode concerning the gold alarm watch for Mr Herbert. His memoirs take up the story sometime later when, having occasion to see the Earl of Pembroke—who was his cousin—the latter asked if the watch had been safely delivered and how the King liked it. Mr Herbert had to tell him that it had never been delivered and that he had many times since seen the officer in question, but that nothing whatever had been said about the watch. The Earl was very angry; but 'such was the severity of the Times, that it was then judged dangerous to reflect upon such a Person, being a Favourite of the time, so as no notice was taken of it. Nevertheless, Mr. Herbert (at the Earl's desire) acquainted his Majesty therewith, who gave the Earl his Thanks, and said "Ah! Had he not told the Officer it was for me, it would probably have been delivered; he well knew how short a time I could enjoy it" '.

The precise date of East's removal from Pall Mall to Fleet Street does not seem to have been recorded, but it must have been before 1635, by which time he is listed in a manuscript *Return of Strangers within the Ward of Farringdon Without* as being there, in the parish of St Dunstan's in the West. Furthermore, he employed there a certain Dutchman called Elias Dupree. Lady Anne Fanshaw (1625–80), the talented wife of the diplomat Sir Richard Fanshaw, who shared in all her husband's missions of whatsoever kind, states in her memoir of her husband that when she came from France in the autumn of 1646, she lodged in Fleet Street at Mr East's the watchmaker. Later, East was to move yet again, for the *London Gazette*, 22nd–26th January 1690, refers to Mr East 'at the Sun, outside Temple Bar'—possibly still Fleet Street, but some distance from St Dunstan's.

The fees paid to royal craftsmen must have been quite substantial, according to the money values of the time. In East's case, for instance, there is an entry in the *Calendar of State Papers (Domestic)* of a grant in 1662 to East of the office of 'chief clockmaker and keeper of the Privy clocks, fee 12d. per day and £3 6s. 8d. livery'—indicating that East was expected to wear a uniform when exercising this function. In the self-same year there is also entered a warrant to swear in *James* East, the King's servant, as clockmaker to the Queen; it seems almost certain that this is an error and that the reference is still to Edward East. Sad to record, there does not seem to be any representation of East's work in the Royal Collection at the present time.

Anecdotes regarding Charles I and his watches have already been retailed; and there are records of the latter, some not quite so credible, which feature elsewhere in this book. The King's interest, however, is undisputed. He seems, for example, to have maintained two watches beside his bed, one of gold and the other of silver, which he customarily wound up before retiring; they were then placed on a stool nearby, before a lamp. It is said that his last moments prior to execution were regulated by a clock in Whitehall which, according to the *Gentleman's Magazine* in 1799, eventually passed into the hands of a Mrs Forrester and was installed by her at Great Brickhill, in Buckinghamshire. It is likely that a public clock would have figured in such circumstances, but whether it was the one described will probably never be known, since Mrs Forrester's effects were dispersed by public sale after her demise, and all trace of this clock has been lost.

In the second half of the century, the more eminent London makers included Henry Jones. He came to the metropolis from Bouldre, near Southampton—where his father was vicar—to take up an apprenticeship with Benjamin Hill, to whom he was bound on 22nd August 1654. However, this association was short-lived, certainly to Jones's long-term advantage, for he was 'turned over'—the curious terminology used when transferring an apprentice from one master to another—to the great Edward East. Thus started a friendship which lasted throughout the remainder of their lives, Jones dying only in 1695, two years before East.

Jones became a master clockmaker, being admitted to the Freedom of the Worshipful Company on 6th July 1663, a most significant time in the evolution of the domestic clock since the pendulum development had only arrived in London through the aegis of the Fromanteels some five years before, and the pendulum clock was thus in its infancy. Few of Jones's early clocks survive, however—indeed, he was never what could be called a prolific clockmaker— but those that do, reflect a considerable affinity with East's work.

The Clockmakers' Company occupied much of Jones's time throughout his working life, and references to him on all sorts of counts are legion in the Minute Books of the Company's Court Meetings. He had the occasional quarrel with other craftsmen, such as Robert Seignior and John Nicasius; and he sat on several committees which reviewed the conduct of the Company in relation to its Charter and Ordinances. At the same time he progressed up through the various offices of that body, culminating in his election as Master in 1691.

His working premises seem always to have been in the Inner Temple area, contemporary references varying between 'Inner Temple Gate', 'Inner Temple Lane', or plainly 'of ye Inner Temple'. The Rate Books of the parish of St Dunstan's in the West, the famous Fleet Street church, reveal that Jones shared, with one George Petty, the 'Precinct next Temple Bar, Falcon Court, (Fleet) Street Side' from early 1672 and he was still there in 1680. It was St Dunstan's Church that became Jones's final resting-place, and there is a fine memorial tablet to him there. His widow, Hannah, was also buried there, in 1708, having reached the age of eighty-three.

It is a curious thing that, despite his eminence in the craft and as a craftsman, Jones never received any formal royal appointment. Probably he was overshadowed first by East and subsequently by Tompion. He certainly made at least one clock to the King's commission, and this is described in connection with Robert Seignior, *q.v.* It is clear that Charles II gave that particular clock away, but, nevertheless, the present-day Royal Collection does include a typical example of his work. Located at Sandringham, this is a bracket 32
clock in ebonized case of bell-top form, with gilt mounts 33
and a finely engraved back plate. It is signed only on the back plate 'Henry Jones in the Temple'. The measurements of this fine two-train clock are height 13 inches, width $9\frac{3}{4}$ inches and depth 6 inches; and it appears to be a purchase of this century, since it bears Percy Webster's ivorine plaque on the back. The business of this internationally known dealer finally closed with the sale of his remaining stock by Sotheby's in 1954.

A famous family of four seventeenth-century clockmakers were the Knibbs; and two of them had royal associations in their own time, although again they

32. *Bracket clock by Henry Jones, at Sandringham.* (Royal Collection)

33. *Movement of the Henry Jones bracket clock.* (Royal Collection)

appear to be unrepresented in the present-day Royal Collection.

Samuel Knibb, born in 1625, started his working life in Newport Pagnell but later set up business in London, where he was admitted to the Clockmakers' Company by Redemption—that is to say, he paid for the privilege—in 1663. He seems to have started in Westminster, where he is first listed in 1662, but subsequently moved to Threadneedle Street, and a partnership with another maker, Henry Sutton, in the making of mathematical instruments.

Relatively little is known about Samuel Knibb and his working circumstances, apart from the occasional binding of his apprentices, and indeed the exact date of his death has not so far been discovered, although extrapolation from other known occurrences suggests that this must have taken place *c.*1670.

It is a remarkable supposition that apparently only five clocks by Samuel Knibb have survived, and it is inconceivable that he made so few. Stylistic similarities suggest that he must have worked in very close association with Ahasuerus Fromanteel, one of the family of Dutch clockmakers who pioneered the pendulum clock in Britain, and they both seem to have employed the same casemaker. Each of the clocks signed by Samuel Knibb is a complicated creation, which only further confuses the situation.

Of these five clocks, one was formerly in the Royal
Collection at Windsor Castle. This was the only long- 34
case clock so far attributed to this maker. Furthermore, the movement had three trains, i.e. it was quarter-striking, and it was set in a case veneered with a much-figured wood, thought to be either kingwood or cocuswood. From the only surviving photograph of this clock it appears that the case has at some time been altered, the base having been cut down and a plinth added. It is known that this clock was at Windsor Castle earlier in the present century—it has been hazarded that it was in fact made for Charles II—but it is believed now to be in America, and no trace of it has been seen since 1926.

The other member of the Knibb family of interest in the present context is Joseph, who was born in 1640. He was a cousin of Samuel, to whom he was apprenticed in 1655 or thereabouts; he moved to Oxford about 1662, having served the customary seven years indenture, and this was at about the same time that Samuel moved to London.

Joseph seemingly had difficulty in settling into Oxford, on account of the antagonism of local craftsmen who regarded him as an interloper. When this obstacle had been satisfactorily overcome, he carried out successful experiments with a seconds-beating pendulum which prompted him to move to London in

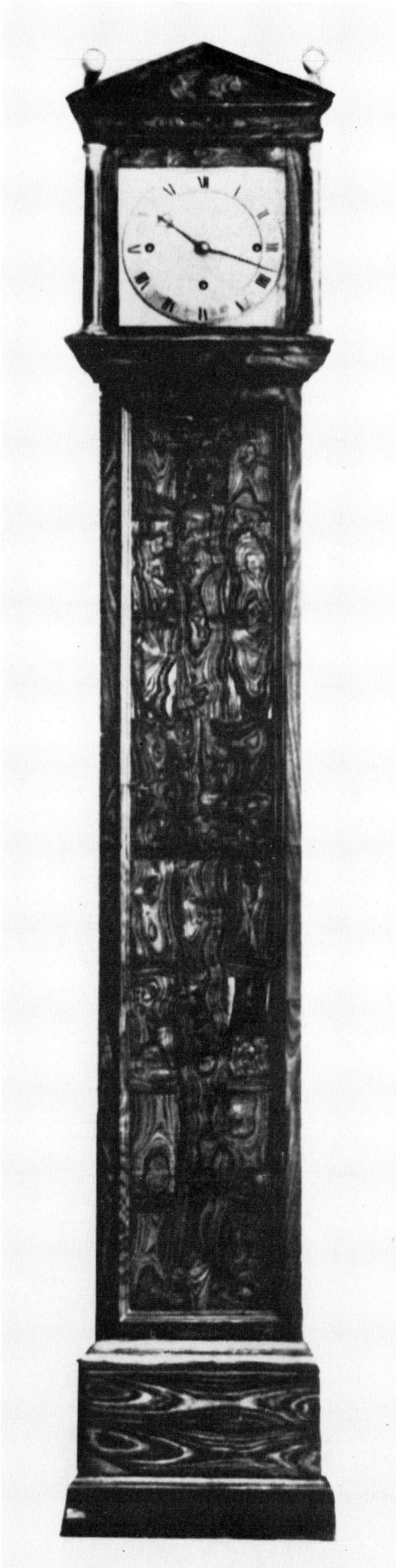

34. (Left) *Three-train longcase clock by Samuel Knibb, formerly at Windsor Castle.* (R. A. Lee)

35. (Right) *Silver-mounted bracket clock by Joseph Knibb, dated 1677.* (Private collection)

36. (Below right) *Movement of the Joseph Knibb bracket clock showing unique signature.* (Private collection)

1670. There, he was quickly absorbed into the Clockmakers' Company, and it seems likely that he took over Samuel Knibb's workshop on the latter's death.

Innovation seems to have been Joseph Knibb's forte, and he is credited with inventing several methods of hour-striking, as well as various escapement improvements. In 1675, when he is listed as a rate-collector for St Dunstan's in the West, his business address was 'The Dyal' near Serjeants Inn in Fleet Street, and later, in 1693, he moved to 'The Clock Dyal' in Suffolk Street, near Charing Cross.

Although undoubtedly qualified, Joseph Knibb never seems to have aspired to high office in the Clockmakers' Company. He was elected a Steward in 1684 and an Assistant in 1689, but that is as far as he went. He must have been in a big way of business, for there are more than two hundred of his clocks still surviving, which suggests that he might have made double that number throughout his working life. It has also been suggested that he had the most prosperous clock business in London when he retired in 1697—the year East died—and moved to Hanslop, in Buckinghamshire. Even then, he did not wholly discard his craft—there are a few of his clocks existing that are signed 'Hanslop'—and he did not die until 1711, by which time he was seventy-one years of age.

Mention has been made elsewhere of the remarkable auction sale which took place in 1843, of clocks belonging to the Duke of Sussex. This included two long-case clocks made by Joseph Knibb which came originally from the Duke of York's collection, and an ebony-cased night clock said to have been designed by Prince Rupert, the son of Elizabeth, daughter of James I. This last clock survives but shows no proof-positive of any royal connection. Yet Joseph Knibb certainly did enjoy royal patronage, as a turret clock by him was formerly installed above the State Entrance to the quadrangle at Windsor Castle. It is recorded that the clock bore the signature 'Joseph Knibb Londini 1677', and it is probably in respect of this clock that there is an entry in the Secret Service payment book in 1682, 'to Mr. Knibb by His Said Majesty's Command upon a bill for clock work £141'. Sadly, the turret clock was taken down in 1829, when alterations were being carried out by Sir Jeffrey Wyatville, and a new one by B. L. Vulliamy was substituted. Of the original clock there now

See 2[illegible] and 2[illegible]

appears to be no trace whatever. It has been suggested that it was the twin of another Joseph Knibb turret clock installed in Burley Church in Leicestershire, which has been recently restored; but no proof of this is known to the author. There has recently come to light, however, a superb silver-mounted bracket clock, its velvet-covered dial having silver chapter ring, winged cherub spandrels and elaborately pierced centre plate all in a somewhat untypical style—as indeed is that of the signature on the back plate, which reads 'Joseph Knibb Londini Invenit et fecit Anno Domini 1677'. There is said to be documented provenance that this clock was given by George III to his surgeon in 1809; sadly, investigation has not borne out this claim, nor that the clock might be one purchased by Charles II, who is rumoured to have purchased two silver-mounted spring clocks by Joseph Knibb. All these claims are unsubstantiated at present; yet this is a fine and interesting clock, which might well have some royal antecedents if they could only be uncovered. 35 36

The tiny representation of Samuel Knibb's output is not unique. Another such eminent craftsman in his own time, but whose surviving clocks probably do not number more than a dozen or so, with perhaps half as many watches, is Robert Seignior; and he did enjoy the privilege and prestige of a royal appointment, albeit under rather curious circumstances.

Seignior was born in 1645, being baptized on 26th May in that year at St Dunstan's in the West—yet another famous clockmaker to be associated with that church. His father was George Seignior, a Fleet Street tailor, a member of the Barber-Surgeons' Company and altogether a man of some standing in the community.

About 1660, Robert Seignior was apprenticed to John Nicasius—the same clockmaker with whom Henry Jones had quarrelled—and he was subsequently admitted to the Freedom of the Clockmakers' Company on 17th April 1667. The next year, on 8th June, he followed the age-old precept for the ambitious young man by marrying his master's daughter, An (*sic*) Nicasius, 'by Banns', in St Dunstan's Church.

Seignior must have been an angry young man, even a rebel, for he constantly chafed under the discipline to which the still-young Company submitted its members. In 1671 he called the Master and Assistants a 'Company of Cheating Knaves' and accused the Master of maligning him in a coffee-house. He was fined 20 shillings for 'this offence and scandall' but must have made other suitable amends, for half the fine was later returned to him. He also got into trouble over apprentices, as the numbers of these allowed to enter the craft were very strictly controlled; and Seignior tried to evade the regulations by persuading a clock-maker with no apprentices, called Samuel Vernon, to bind Francis Draycott apprentice on his behalf. On the other hand, he also suffered the indignity of having one of his apprentices desert him to go and work elsewhere.

Local records seem to suggest that Seignior set up in business at 'The Dyall' in Exchange Alley, a tiny thoroughfare running between Cornhill and Lombard Street, soon after becoming a master clockmaker, and he remained there until his death. His son and heir was baptized George, presumably after his grandfather, on 4th January 1671.

When dealing earlier with Henry Jones, it was mentioned that he had made at least one royal clock; and this emerges from the Clockmakers' Company Court Minutes of a meeting held on 19th January 1674, when Seignior had his most potentially serious brush with the Company. The Minute in question reads:

> Mr Henry Jones Clockmaker acquainted this Court that he, having heretofore made for the King a clock of the value of one hundred and fifty pounds whereon was engraved Henricus Jones Londini with which it stood in his Maj'ties closett about seaven yeares, but being by his Maj'ty given unto a Lady it came to the hands of Robert Seignior Clockmaker to make some addition to the works . . . who hath taken out, or caused Edward Staunton Clockmaker or some other person to take out, the name of the said Henry Jones and caused some other person to engrave thereon Robert Seignior in Exchange Alley London.

37. *A conventional bracket clock by Robert Seignior.* (Private collection)

A full-scale investigation was ordered, but in the end the whole complaint seems to have been discreetly dropped. Seignior remained totally unperturbed throughout; and the most likely explanation is that the Company had very little power to act in this kind of situation. Interestingly the only clock utilizing this long 38
form of signature so far recorded—for the usual form is simply 'Robert Seignior London' (or 'Londini')—is a night clock in the Conservatoire des Arts et Métiers in Paris. There are signs that this clock has been altered in certain respects, the dial not being as originally made; and the case is missing altogether. Carrying the speculation a stage further, there is a tradition that Charles II gave one of Henry Jones's clocks to Mrs Jane Lane after the Battle of Worcester, as a token of appreciation of her services during that arduous operation. It is tempting to think that this might be that very clock; but there is no evidence to support this supposition whatsoever.

Nevertheless, a connection between the monarch and Robert Seignior is indisputable, for he was appointed Chief Clockmaker by Letters Patent under the Great Seal dated 28th August 1674 (PRO reference: C66/3157, No. 23). The corresponding Privy Seal warrant which preceded this grant reads:

> *Robert Seignior—Watchmaker*
>
> These are to require you to sweare and admitt Robert Seignior in the place and quality of Watchmaker and Clockmaker for makeing and mending his Maj'ties watches and clocks in Ordinary without ffee until the Death, Surrender or other Determinacion of Edward East. And then to enjoy the same places with ffee together with all other profitts, allowances and priviledges thereto belonginge in as full and ample manner as the said Edward East or any other person whatsoever. And this shalbe your Warrant. Given under my hand this first day of August 1674 in ye 26 yeare of His Maj. Reine.
>
> To the Gentlemen Ushers, dayly Wayters in Ordinary to His Maj'tie, or one of them.

None of Seignior's work is to be found in the Royal Collection today, and indeed, since East outlived him by nearly a decade, it is doubtful if he ever got much of a look-in where such important patronage was con-

38. *Movement of night clock by Robert Seignior.* (Conservatoire des Arts et Métiers, Paris)

cerned. There is one record only of a royal commission being placed with him, and this occurs in a manuscript copy of a 'Schedule of Receipts and Payments by Henry Guy, Esq., for the Secret Services of His late Majesty King Charles the Second . . .'. Under date 9th December 1682 occurs the following entry:

> To Rbt. Seignior, for a clock bought of him and sett up in the Trea'ry Chambers, for the use of the Commissioners of His said Maj'ties Trea'ry . . . . . £20.

Yet Seignior must have been highly regarded in his day. He was a friend of Tompion and of Robert Hooke—the three used to meet in Garaway's Coffee-house in Exchange Alley, and he figures in Hooke's celebrated
37 diary. Seignior's existing work reflects many of Tompion's special characteristics, such as plates that are latched together rather than pinned. Even so, he remained aloof—so far as he could—from the Clockmakers' Company throughout his life, preferring to pay a large fine in 1678 rather than serve the office of Steward; and in 1682, despite surviving two ballots and being finally chosen for the Court of Assistants, he disregarded two summonses and was never sworn into office. On 19th December 1685, being 'at this time not in perfect health of body but of sound and perfect mind and memory . . .', he signed his Will; he died the following year and was buried on 8th November 1686 'as neare the bodies of my wife and sonne as conveniently may be' in the now-demolished church of St Peter-the-Poor. Even to this day Seignior remains something of an enigma, and his long and complicated Will does nothing to dispel the mystery which surrounds him. One of the beneficiaries, for instance, was one Baptist May, Esq. (1629–98), who was Keeper of the Privy Purse to Charles II and generally regarded as an expert in bribery and corruption. Of him the *Dictionary of National Biography* says, *inter alia*, that he 'developed a taste for fine pictures, possessing, among others, a fine portrait of Moll Davis playing a guitar, by Sir Peter Lely'. Seignior's bequest to him—'my Italian picture of Madonna'—might seem highly appropriate!

The greatest makers of the later seventeenth-century will be dealt with in another chapter since, in the main, they spanned the end of that period—and the change of royal dynasty—surviving well into the eighteenth. There remain several important clocks and watches currently in royal ownership, however, which should be included in this part of the work. The first is a turret clock made—curiously, in view of the preference shown, by most monarchs, for London workmanship—by a country maker, albeit a very competent one.

This is the remarkable clock in the Curfew Tower at 39 40 41
Windsor Castle. The work of John Davis of that town, it is dated 1689. The Curfew Tower itself was built by Henry III in 1227 to defend the north-west approaches, but it has been altered in comparatively recent times, and especially in 1863 when the stone facing on the street side was renewed and the present conical roof added, after the model of Carcassonne in southern France. There are several dormer windows in this, and above the one looking directly towards the town is the clock mechanism. It would seem that the present dial must have been part of the last-century modifications, since, to reach it, the transmission from the clock has to be at least 60 feet long and includes three right-angled bends with all the gearing associated with that kind of problem.

Apart from the escape wheel, it would appear that virtually all the mechanism of this clock is original; and it is remarkable, in particular, for its carillon work. A

39 (Left) *The Curfew Tower clock in Windsor Castle, as seen from the outside.* (The Dean and Canons of Windsor)

40. (Centre left) *Movement of the Curfew Tower clock.* (The Dean and Canons of Windsor)

41. (Bottom left) *Carillon mechanism of the Curfew Tower clock.* (The Dean and Canons of Windsor)

42. (Right) *Octagonal rock crystal watch by Henry Grendon: dial view with outer case.* (Royal Collection)

43. (Below right) *Movement of watch by Henry Grendon, showing the full signature. This watch is kept in Windsor Castle.* (Royal Collection)

large wooden drum, at least 2 feet in diameter, is studded with wooden pegs like the pinned cylinder in an old-fashioned musical box—and works in exactly the same way. A toothed wheel integral with it revolves when this action is unlocked, turning the drum, so that the pegs can operate hammers to sound bells. Unlike many musical movements of this kind, there is no sign that there have ever been any alterations, such as changes of tune, and it is likely that this clock performs in exactly the same manner as when it was first made. Indeed, for years the tune was unintelligible, and it was not until an inspection by Sir George Elvey in 1874 that it was discovered that some of the pegs on the pin-barrel had dropped out. As soon as these were replaced, the music became identifiable as the old Psalm tune *St Davids*, which was immediately followed by a chime known to all campanologists as *The King's Change*. The music is played every three hours.

The Davis family is well known in seventeenth-century local history, John's father, William, was blacksmith both to the King and to the Corporation, and an ardent Royalist who had carried out various works at Windsor Castle during the reign of Charles I. Not unexpectedly in a man of such loyalty, he continued to do work for the castle during Cromwell's period of ascendancy but refused to accept any money for it. John himself seems to have had a small output—a handful of domestic clocks by him are recorded, but only the one large clock. He is dated as active 1678–89, a very small span for somebody obviously so skilled; and his other productions include a fine small lantern clock and a walnut long-case clock with a pendulum beating $1\frac{1}{4}$ seconds. There seems to have been yet another generation of this family, for a second John Davis of Windsor, usually described as John Davis junior, was making turret clocks in the middle of the eighteenth century, and a handful of these have been recorded.

There are two important watches from this period which should not pass unnoticed; their antecedents have something in common, in that neither of them has been in the Royal Collection ever since they were

44. (Left) *Coach watch with striking and alarm actions, by David Bouguet: dial view.* (Royal Collection)

46. (Below) *The movement of the coach watch by David Bouguet. This watch is also kept in Windsor Castle.* (Royal Collection)

45. (Left) *David Bouguet's coach watch: the superb silver case.* (Royal Collection)

manufactured, and both were probably made within a few years of one another.

42 The first watch is in an octagonal rock-crystal case,
43 which is notable for the unusually large facets cut upon its surface; small, it measures only $1\frac{1}{2}$ inches on its longer axis and $1\frac{3}{32}$ inches on the shorter. The movement is conventional of its type and is signed on the back plate 'Henry Grendon in y^{e} Exchange fecit'. Very little seems ever to have come to light about this maker, save that he was admitted to the Freedom of the Clockmakers' Company in 1640. He certainly had a facility with his dials, for the one fitted to this watch, which is of all-over engraved silver and has its centre enriched with a floral motif, is of the highest quality. The leather protective outer case is embellished with silver pinwork in a formal design.

The fascinating aspect of this watch lies in its history. Charles II, fleeing after his defeat at the Battle of Worcester in 1651, put up for some days with a Colonel Lane, at Bentley Hall near Wolverhampton. From there he travelled to Bristol on horseback, disguised as the serving-man of Jane Lane, the colonel's sister, who rode pillion behind him. It was an adventurous, even traumatic, experience for both of them; and on arrival in Bristol, the King is said to have given Jane Lane this watch in recognition of her resource and bravery. Preserved in the Lane family, the watch was finally restored to the Royal Collection in 1928, when Major-General Sir John Lane presented it to King George V. There is no reason to doubt the accuracy of this provenance although it must be remembered that Charles II is also credited with having given Jane Lane a clock by Henry Jones on this self-same occasion, and a second watch, this one gold and bejewelled, after the Restoration. Perhaps the lady shared the King's compulsive fascination with timepieces!

The second watch is large—the extreme outer diameter of the case is no less than $4\frac{3}{4}$ inches—and is
44 called a travelling clock-watch. Signed 'D. Bouguet
45 46 Londini', and dating *c*.1650, it not only strikes the hours like a clock, hence its self-explanatory title, but is also fitted with an alarm, which was considered an essential adjunct for the traveller in those far-off days. This is a superb object in all respects. Its massive case is enriched with a profusion of engraved and pierced decoration—the holes were needed to permit the sound of the bell to be heard—of a most unusual type; the motifs employed include six parrots in varying poses, interspersed with six human figures radiating from a central boss, which takes a spiralling foliate form. The overall effect is almost tropical in its imagery, while the freshness of the workmanship must point to the existence, at some time, of a protective outer case, probably leather-covered over a shaped wooden carcase. As to the fine movement with its large silver cock and count-wheel, decorated hammer-head and substantial blued-steel components, its size alone must make it almost unique; the diameter of the plates is $4\frac{1}{16}$ inches.

This fine watch of David Bouguet's was given to King William IV by Countess Howe; and it became his favourite for use when journeying, even though much more accurate timekeepers would have been easily accessible to him. Its earlier history is, unfortunately, not known.

As his name suggests, David Bouguet was of French extraction and almost certainly a dispossessed Huguenot. He first appears in London in 1628, as a member of the Blacksmiths' Company, which might imply a date of birth *c*.1607. He became one of the first members of the Clockmakers' Company in 1632, only a year after its Charter was granted; and he died in 1665. It is said that he left a widow, Dorcas Bouguet, who continues to appear in the Company's books long after David's death; but since this was clearly a skilled clockmaker, who took two apprentices, Thomas Knight and Thomas Walker, during the closing decades of the century, such an identification can only be tentative.

David Bouguet had two sons, Solomon and David junior, who followed in his footsteps; and yet another generation emerged in the person of Solomon junior, who was still active in Company affairs at the century's end. David Bouguet's work was of a very high order, but surviving examples are by no means common. Advertisements in the *London Gazette* describing watches of his that had gone astray, suggest that his business premises, at least for some of his life, were at 'Black Fryars', although the signature on his wares is not specific in this regard.

Contemporary diarists are not above mentioning royal clocks and watches. John Evelyn, under date 24th February 1655, reports:

> I was shew'd a table clock whose ballance was onely a chrystall ball sliding on parallel wyers without being at all fixed, but rolling from stage to stage till falling on a spring conceal'd from sight, it was throwne up to the upmost channel againe, made with an imperceptible declivity, in this continual vicissitude of motion prettily entertaining the eye every halfe minute, and the next halfe giving progress to the hand that shew'd the houre, and giving notice by a small bell, so as in 120 halfe minutes, or periods of the bullet's falling on the ejaculatorie spring, the clock part struck. This very extraordinarie piece (richly adorn'd) had been presented by some German Prince to our late King, and was now in possession of the Usurper, value 200.l.

Later, on 1st November 1660, Evelyn writes:

> I went with some of my relations to Court, to shew them his Maties cabinet and closset of rarities.... Here I saw ...

among the clocks, one that shew'd the rising and setting of the Sun in ye Zodiaq, the Sunn represented by a face and raies of gold, upon an azure skie, observing ye diurnal and annual motion, rising and setting behind a landscape of hills, the work of our famous Fromantel.

This seems to be the only contemporary reference to a clock by any of the Fromanteel family being in royal possession, although the application of the pendulum for clockwork was conveyed from Holland to Britain by John and first offered for sale by his master, Ahasuerus, by means of an advertisement in *The Commonwealth Mercury* in 1658. As to clocks with 'bullets', Samuel Pepys, in his diary under date 28th July 1660, reports: 'To Westminster, and there met Mr. Henson, who had formerly had the brave clock that went with bullets (which is now taken away from him by the king, it being his goods).'

The interest shown in antique clocks by HM Queen Elizabeth The Queen Mother has been described elsewhere. In that part of Her Majesty's collection at her London home, Clarence House, there is a typical late-seventeenth-century spring clock in ebonized case by Edward Stanton, sometimes spelt Staunton. Of a slightly Puritan appearance, with gilt embellishments confined to the bell top, the dial is unsigned; it does appear likely, however, that the chapter ring has been replaced, and that would have been a probable location for a dial signature at this time. There is a fine signature engraved within a lambrequin on the extensively decorated back plate of the movement. Originally the clock was the conventional two-train mechanism with added pull-repeating, but this latter also has at some time been stripped out. The clock was presented to Her Majesty many years ago now, by the Edinburgh Tradesmen's Association.

Stanton is one of those fine London makers whose work continues to turn up from time to time, and whose life spanned that important period of change when the architectural influence to which clocks and their cases were subjected gradually gave way to less severe treatments. He was apprenticed on 27th December 1655 and appears to have had two masters, Francis Bowen and Nathaniel Allen. He was admitted to the Freedom of the Clockmakers' Company on 19th January 1662 and served the highest offices, starting as Junior Warden in 1693 and finishing as Master in 1696. He is thought to have died *c.*1707. The Wetherfield Collection included a magnificent architecturally-styled three-train clock, giving three-part ting-tang striking on three bells, of about 1665; and Cescinsky and Webster's *English Domestic Clocks* illustrates, at figure 88, a burr walnut long-case clock of eight days duration, with striking-train and bolt-and-shutter maintaining-power. Stanton's only recorded business premises were in Leadenhall Street.

3 George I brings an epoch to an end

Most of those craftsmen whose working lives were wholly encompassed within the seventeenth century have been reviewed in Chapter 2; the exceptions were Joseph Knibb, who barely survived the first decade beyond it, being then a man approaching his seventieth year, and Edward Stanton, who died *c.*1707. However, there did emerge during this same period a small group of pre-eminent clockmakers in London, whose work attracted royal attention and whose lives and influence spilled over more decisively into the eighteenth century, thus embracing a notable change of royal House as well as the substantial differences between, say, the Court of Charles II and that of George II. It seems desirable to treat these makers in isolation not only from those who went before but also from those who succeeded them.

Arguably the least among this important group but, from his surviving work, a maker of great quality nonetheless, was Joseph Windmills. Not very much appears to be known about his earliest antecedents. When he was admitted to the Freedom of the Clockmakers' Company in 1671, he was even then described as a 'great clockmaker', indicating his specialization in large public clocks, and it seems almost certain that he transferred from another Livery Company. William Million, another 'great clockmaker' who was admitted three months after Windmills, had originally been a Freeman of the Merchant Taylors. The first recorded business address of Windmills was in St Martin's-le-Grand, but later he moved to 'Mark Lane End, next Tower Streete', which, as its name implies, is in the vicinity of the Tower of London. In due time, Windmills ascended to the hierarchy of the Clockmakers' Company, serving all the highest offices, from Junior Warden to Master, during the period 1699 to 1702. He appears to have died about 1723.

About 1700, Windmills entered into a partnership with his son Thomas, who had had a formal training under Clockmakers' Company auspices, having been apprenticed to his father for seven years from 17th January 1686 and having been admitted to the Freedom on 20th January 1695. After the partnership, clocks and watches tend to be signed simply 'Windmills'. Thomas Windmills became Master of the Clockmakers' Company in 1718 and, after his father died, seems to have gone into partnership with another craftsman, called Bennett, still working from Tower Street. Clocks and watches signed 'Windmills & Bennett' suggest the dates of this association were *c.*1725–9, and Thomas Windmills himself appears to have died *c.*1732.

Father and son of the Windmills family produced between them some fine clocks and watches of a wide variety of types, ranging from lantern clocks and spring-driven bracket clocks of different kinds, to long-case clocks, some of the highest beauty and technical achievement, while their watches include several styles as well as incorporating the technical developments that became current during their active lives. The exact circumstances of their working relationship with the monarchy is not recorded, but there is good reason to believe that it existed.

The evidence derives from a watch in the British Museum. The horological collection there includes a good representation of the craftsmanship of this talented family, a typical example being a fine watch with a sun-and-moon dial, one of the various arrangements tried during the period when it had become worthwhile to indicate minutes, but before the technicalities of concentric hour and minute hands had been worked out. However, the watch with royal associations is a 'wandering hour' watch in silver pair-cases by Joseph Windmills. This type of watch, in which the hour numerals pass in turn across an aperture in the dial, at

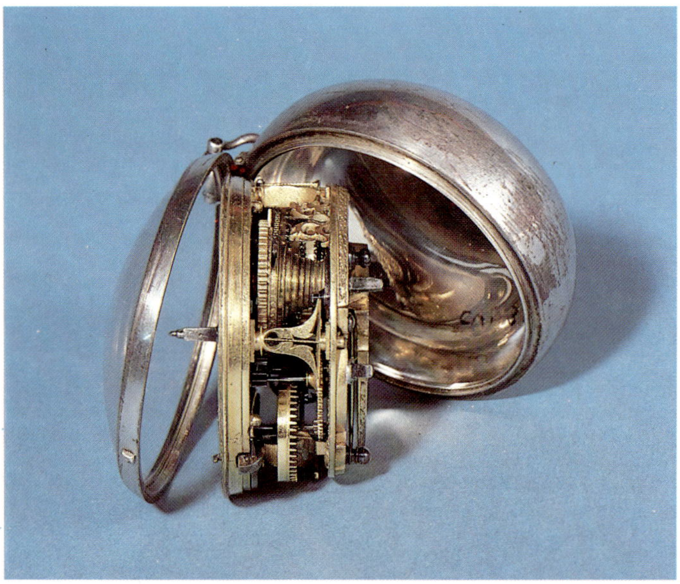

47. (Left) *Dial view of "wandering hour" watch by Joseph Windmills.* (British Museum)

48. (Centre left) *Movement of Joseph Windmills watch.* (British Museum)

49. (Bottom left) *The royal arms as portrayed on the back of the case of the Windmills watch.* (British Museum)

the same time indicating the minute against a scale calibrated around the edge of that aperture, is comparatively rarely found but was just such another experimental approach to the problem of indicating minutes, and all the finest makers produced examples of it.

This particular design of watch is unique in that, almost always, its decoration incorporates some royal reference. A typical example was described by H. Marryat in his little book *Watches*, which was privately printed in 1938; and an almost identical specimen, by the same maker, is reviewed in *Apollo Annual* for 1948, pp. 43–4. In both cases there is a miniature of Queen Anne incorporated into the lower half of the dial, although she is shown full-face in one and profile in the other, while her arms are worked into the decoration of the elaborately pierced and engraved balance cocks. The London maker concerned is John Bushman, whose working dates are given as 1687–*c*.1710. Such watches were current only for a short time, either side of the year 1700, and the consistency in the use of such decorative motifs must have had some basic purpose, but this remains undiscovered at present. Otherwise, use of 'royal' motifs on watches was sparing but not unknown. Marryat himself mentions a watch with a rotating hour disc synchronized with a conventional hour hand, by John Finch, which has royal arms on the cock, while in the Fitzwilliam Museum at Cambridge
there is a watch by Thomas Tompion, number 4329, 50
with a silver dial having a blued-steel centre, against which is set the arms in silver filigree. It is thought possible that this may have been a later addition, however.

The British Museum watch has none of these things. Its cock is of the usual broad-footed, solid-rimmed, winged variety, with a mask at the neck, the table and
foot pierced and engraved with foliage and strapwork. 47
The silver dial has Windmills's name in a cartouche 48 49
below centre, and between a cockle shell and a cherub's head, while the 'wandering hour' band is engraved with a running floral design between the hour apertures. Features of the movement include 'tulip' pillars, verge escapement and an endless-screw mainspring set-up beneath the barrel. The back plate is signed—'Jos. Windmills London'—but not numbered visibly; this maker usually scratch-marked the plate beneath the cock foot. The silver pair-cases are both numbered, a little indecipherably, but seemingly 0717,

50. *The royal arms on the dial of a watch by Thomas Tompion.* (Fitzwilliam Museum, Cambridge)

and the casemaker is identified by his mark 'WI.' This watch's main interest lies in its square-hinged outer case, its band and bezel engraved with floral running decoration and a mask, and its back magnificently engraved with a representation of the Royal Arms, incorporating the mottoes, *'Honi soit qui mal y pense'* and *'Le main tienday'*, this last being more usually represented as *'Je maintiendrai'*. Despite the shield being, it would seem, a composite of two of the three variants of the arms that were in use between 1689 and 1702—the top sinister quarter does not belong to the remainder of the blazon—this is almost certain to be 'engraver's licence'; and anyway this is no mere decoration but a clear enactment of ownership. Authenticity is self-evident.

There is probably a similarity, at least of treatment, between this Windmills watch and a Tompion quarter-repeating verge watch in silver pair-cases, and numbered 46, which passed through Christie's in July 1967; unfortunately, its present whereabouts are unknown, but the catalogue entry states that its inner case was chased with the royal arms, although not of which monarch. However, the fact that their borders were conventionally pierced and engraved with inhabited foliage does suggest that the cases were of a piece with the movement, and the front view, which is illustrated, looks fine. The same can hardly be said, however, of a long-case clock by John Barrow, London, illustrated on page 1209 of *Country Life*, the issue being that of 27th June 1947. This has a positively enormous cresting, representing the personal arms of William III. It makes the clock look completely top-heavy at a time when proportions of clock cases by good makers—and Barrow, if not one of the finest, was at least competent as well as a London practitioner—were always most carefully contrived. It is suggested that the clock might have been a gift from the King, rather than for a palace; but it must seem more likely that the cresting has been taken from elsewhere and 'married' to Barrow's work. The moral in such cases is, of course, to judge each object on its merits once the available supporting evidence, if indeed there is any, has been appraised. Thus, the Windmills watch feels 'right', the Tompion watch remains an unknown quantity, and the Barrow clock looks 'wrong'.

The only example of Windmills's workmanship now in royal possession is an 8-foot long-case clock at Windsor Castle, which is the private property of Her Majesty The Queen and, as such, excluded from this survey. So, they must remain somewhat shadowy figures in the present context. The next maker to warrant investigation falls perhaps more nearly into the category of 'maker of mechanical scientific instruments', since his best-known works are a small group of astronomical clocks, two at least possessing antecedents of the greatest possible interest.

Samuel Watson is likely to have been born *c.*1635, but where is not as yet known. He seems first to have worked in Coventry—he was Sheriff of that city in 1686—coming to London about 1691. He set up in Long Acre, and the Rate Books of the Parish of St Martin-in-the-Fields identify him there in 1692 and continue to place him in that street, albeit in several different houses, until 1712. Early in his life in the metropolis he was admitted Brother in the Clockmakers' Company—this on 29th September 1692, and essential if he was to work in the City.

It is always said that Samuel Watson was Mathematician in Ordinary to King Charles II. In fact, no trace of such an appointment has so far been found, nor indeed is there any evidence that such an office even existed at this time. About 1682, it seems that he sold a clock to that monarch; and the following year he was to obtain the order for another, that remains to this day in the Royal Collection and is generally considered to be his masterpiece. One record remaining of that first clock is to be found in the Camden Society's account of the Secret Services of Charles II and James II, in which it is mentioned that one Henry Guy, an accountant, paid 'to Wm. Chaffinch, for so much monie he paid Saml Watson, for a clock he sold his late Ma'tie, wch shows the rising and setting of the sun and moon and many other motions, £215'. It is recorded that the King placed this clock in his bedchamber where, at one time, he had no less than seven clocks, whose lack of synchronization periodically caused all sorts of pandemonium to break loose; there was yet another clock, in

51. (Above) *The Samuel Watson astronomical clock, as now seen in the Library in Windsor Castle.* (Royal Collection)

52. (Right) *An historic photograph showing the clock removed from the wall panelling: beside it stand two celebrated horologists, at left, the late Courtenay Ilbert, and at right, the late Alan Lloyd. Taken about 1947.* (Alan Lloyd Collection)

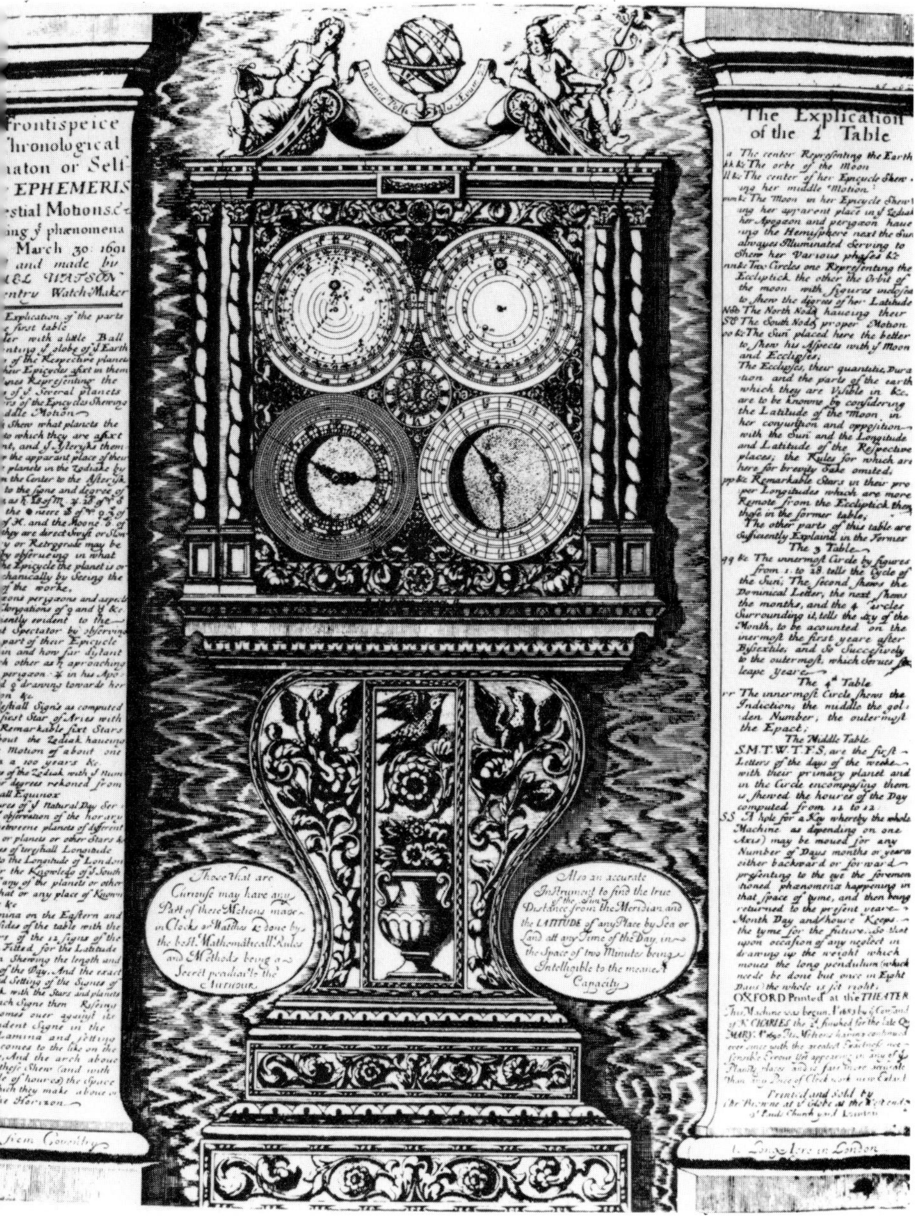

53. (Above) *The broadsheet of 1691 showing the clock in its original long case.* (Royal Collection)

54. (Right) *The case of this conventional longcase clock by Samuel Watson was made originally either for the royal astronomical clock, or as a companion to it.* (Herbert Art Gallery & Museum, Coventry)

His Majesty The King

TELEPHONE 2938 MAYFAIR.

Paid in December Quarter 1907.

To JUMP & SONS
93. MOUNT STREET
LONDON, W.

BY APPOINTMENT
TO H.M. THE KING

Makers of high class Watches & Clocks. Dealers in antique Clocks, examples by Breguet, Vulliamy, Jump & all the old Masters. Repairs Restorations.

REMOVED FROM OLD BOND STREET.

Restored the exceedingly complicated "William & Mary" clock (in very Delapidated & Decayed condition) — showing day of week - day of month - month of year - Roman indiction - the Golden Number, and the Epact. — Made all the going train, Wheels, Pinions etc all new. new Escapement Pallets Crutch. heavy Pendulum, Piece of all work. Extra large Fusee. Chain, Barrel Main Spring, and the necessary connections etc. etc. — Innumerable new screws, studs, fittings etc. collets & pipes to the old work. Every piece of the old work restored shaped lined & fitted afresh. every part made to act correctly & to perform the work as originally intended. etc etc etc (Estimate) 50 0 0

Made a Case for the above clock to approved plan all of brass moulded, & grooved to take stout plate glasses all round & at top with doors back & front. all wrought & fitted with screws & fittings to take to pieces to reglaze if necessary. 4 top Corner ornaments, & massive brass base. Also restored the faces & front of clock, painted the various parts to appear as sky with shaded blue & the various Zodiacal signs white. & heavy gilt Stars in metal, silvered all the metal dials. & waxed all the Engraving, figures, signs etc. The whole done to show the mechanical workings correctly (Estimate) 50 0 0

Carried forward £100 0 0

55. *Extracts from the invoice from Jump & Sons describing work carried out on the Samuel Watson astronomical clock in 1907.* (Alan Lloyd Collection)

the antechamber, which indicated not only the time but also the direction of the wind outside!

There is one other important contemporary and descriptive reference to this first of Watson's royal clocks. On 10th June 1685 a Mr Musgrave, of Oxford, gave an account to a meeting of the Royal Society

> of a piece of watchwork made by one Samuel Watson, a watch-maker at Coventry, shewing the rising, southing and setting of the sun, his declination and longitude, with the hour of the day; the rising, southing and setting of the moon, her conjunction and opposition to the sun, the sign and degree in which she is, the eclipses of the sun and moon, the day of the month in the Julian account; the day of the week; the golden number and epact; the Dominical Letter and cycle of the sun, with many other particulars. It was to be wound up once in eight days and was not subject to be out of order.
>
> Mr. Hooke supposed that it might be the same piece of watchwork that was in the King's bed-chamber; and was of the opinion, that it would not reach the exactness that was pretended.

In contemporary usage, 'watch' was ascribed to any timekeeper that lacked a striking-train.

Watson's first clock would certainly have caused something of a sensation, since clocks with astronomical motions other than the simple phases of the moon had been unknown for three hundred years in Britain, and indeed the only precedent—by a certain Richard of Wallingford—would have been long since forgotten. So there must have been pleasurable anticipation on all sides, when Watson returned to Coventry in 1683 to start work on this next royal commission, which was to be his *chef d'œuvre*.

Unfortunately, it took him a disproportionately long time to complete. It was not really ready until 1689, by which time his patron was dead, James II had abdicated and the incumbents were William and Mary. Very little interest was shown in his master clock, by anybody.

There survives in the British Library—King's Library MSS 277—an eighteenth-century copy of a contemporary account, from which it seems that an embittered Watson determined to raffle the clock, now rapidly becoming a white elephant. The plan was to sell one hundred tickets at £10 each, the first draw from which would reduce the number of participants to ten. The winner of a draw among these kept the clock; the remaining nine were each to have a watch valued at £10, presumably of Watson's manufacture. If this plan had matured, Watson's revenue would have amounted to £1,000 less £90—the cost of the watches—and any administrative overheads, which looks, at this distance in time, to have been fair recompense for six years' work.

It must have been to advertise this clock that Watson offered, in the *London Gazette*, 4th–8th September 1690,

56. *The glazed case supplied by Jump & Sons for the Samuel Watson astronomical clock was originally fitted with pineapple finials. These have been removed, but are still carefully preserved.* (Alan Lloyd Collection)

for the price of one shilling, an engraving of the front
view of the clock together with a printed explanation of 53
its various complexities. A subsequent edition of the print has been up-dated in minor detail, it being noted that Watson was 'Removed from Coventry to Long Acre in London'. Also a new printer had become involved.

However, the story had a happy ending. Edward Chamberlayne, in the eighteenth edition of *Anglia Notitia*, published in 1694, and commenting upon the high standards of clocks, watches and barometers obtainable in England, mentions in passing that 'The Queen hath a clock, made by Mr. Watson, late of Coventry, worth 1000l. in which are all the motions of the celestial bodies.' Originally the clock may have incorporated the cypher of Charles II, but appearing upon it now is certainly that of William and Mary; and how much Watson was paid for it, in the end, does not appear to be known. However, he seems to have been retained to look after it; a Calendar of Treasury Books for 1695 reveals: 'Samuell Watson for looking after a fine clock for four years £110'.

Before launching into a detailed description of this great work of art and science, now a feature of the Royal Collection in the Library of Windsor Castle, it is worth glancing for a moment at Watson's ordinary domestic output—although none of his work could ever be called really ordinary, and, happily, a great deal of it survives. There is a strong thread of scientific innovation running through many of his timepieces, both clocks and watches. Among the latter, for example, we find not only the comparatively commonplace quarter-repeater but the very much rarer and more sophisticated five-minute repeater, made only by a small handful of the finest makers. Another model is of that kind occasionally called a 'pulse watch' and said to have been made for a doctor's use although there seems no certain evidence on this point. The feature of such a watch which makes it rare at this period is a seconds dial; and associated with that feature is stop mechanism, operated by a lever projecting through the watch case, which brings the watch completely to a halt at will. This is the earliest ancestor of the present-day chronograph. But Watson also made more ordinary watches, as evidenced by an advertisement in the *London Gazette* on 18th October 1687. The notice reads: 'Lost the 15th instant on Cheshunt Common, a gold watch in a black Shagreen case with Gold Studs, tyed with a black Taffaty Ribon to a Steel Hooke, Engraven on the Inside Samuel Watson. Whoever gives notice of the same to Mr. Howell at the Penny Post Office in St Martin's Lane, Westminster, shall have a Guinea Reward.'

As for clocks, he made a number of small spring-driven carriage clocks—for want of a better term—
59 which, although cased in wood and bearing very
60 strong affinities with the design of bracket clock of the period, nevertheless had no pendulum but a balance pivoted on a platform above the movement in a manner reminiscent of much later carriage clocks. These clocks were less than 8 inches high and, incorporating other progressive features like pull-wind for the alarm train as well as for the quarter-repeating mechanism, were marvels of miniaturization at a time when such scaling-down often did not work very well. Associated with clocks of this kind, it would seem, was a clock now known only from its contemporary description, again in the *London Gazette*, of 27th–30th July 1696, from which these extracts are taken. 'Lost the 16th June last out of a house near Red Lion Square, a Repeating Table Clock in black ebony case and cap, with brass Furniture upon it . . . having two Pendulums, the longer moving behind and the shorter moving in a semi-circle on the upper part of the dial plate. . . . Whoever gives notice to Mr. Samuel Watson, Watchmaker, near the Royal Bagnio in Long Acre, shall have Two Guineas Reward.' The second 'pendulum' was, of course, a balance wheel; and other clocks incorporating alternative methods of controlling the action of the escapement are known, although immensely rare.

Finally there exists, among a variety of more-or-less complicated clocks by Watson, some with astronomical features of various kinds, one model which is so obscure that its purpose is still not properly understood. This is a single-train—that is, timepiece only—spring-driven clock in the conventional ebonized case with gilt ornaments and handle, the dial with aperture for mock pendulum and cherub spandrels. The mystery appears with the graduation of the chapter ring, which, while set up for a normal twelve-hour revolution of the hour hand, provides for the minute hand to revolve only once every two hours. The minute ring, in fact, is divided into sixty parts, which are numbered 1 to 60, for each half of the dial. Apart from the provision for a two-hourly revolution of the minute hand, the movement of this clock is quite conventional; but the intention behind it certainly cannot have been!

Watson's royal astronomical clock did not pass unnoticed in contemporary horological literature. There were only two writers in English on the subject, at this period, who were of any note, and they both mentioned it. John Smith, in *Horological Disquisitions*, in 1694, in an essay upon the preparation of tables to compensate for the equation of time, remarks, 'and fifthly, by Mr Samuel Watson, the curious contriver of that rare Celestial Orbitary, now in the present Queen Mary's possession'. The other pundit of the time, William Derham, writing in his *Artificial Clockmaker*, 1696, in his chapter upon celestial motions, notes 'and of late, that elaborate piece of Mr Watson, late of Coventry, now of London, in her late Majesty's closet'. Subsequently, this famous clock was seen and described by the German traveller and bibliophile Zacharias Conrad von Uffenbach when he visited London in 1710.

As seen today, Watson's magnificent clock has been substantially altered—and that, sadly, in comparatively recent times. Originally it was in a long case—as 55
indeed it appears in the contemporary print which has 56
already been mentioned. It was housed in its present square glass-sided bronze case in 1907, by the firm of Jump, successors to Vulliamy. At the same time, the one-second-beating pendulum was removed and a $\frac{2}{3}$-second substituted. This involved a new spring-driven going-train, for the clock was originally weight-driven.

It is just possible to obtain some idea of the original appearance, however, since Watson seems to have made another clock, without all the astronomical
complications, to pair with this one; and that is still in 54
its first case, which appears identical to that depicted in

57. *A second, and superficially different, astronomical clock by Samuel Watson.* (Clockmakers' Company, London)

the contemporary print. That clock, too, has a 20-inch dial, far too large for common domestic use. It has been argued that this was the original case of the royal clock and that it was disliked and refused by Queen Mary, who had the clock mounted in panelling in the wall instead, so causing Watson to make another and much simpler movement for the case; but there is no supporting evidence on this. The clock seemingly came from Hampton Court to Buckingham Palace, where it was stored for some fifty years prior to its renovation—if that is what you can call it—being finally installed at Windsor Castle in 1908. That is as far as the inventory record takes us.

Whatever may be the ethics of that particular 'restoration', there can be no doubt that the great joy of
51 this clock, its very complicated dial, remains unimpaired. Still with its indications formulated according to Ptolemaic theory, the main dial, some 20-inches square, is divided into four quarters, each containing a subsidiary dial. Without going into abstruse detail, the top left-hand dial shows the sun and planets revolving around the earth; the top right-hand dial is the lunar dial, the earth at its centre with the moon moving in its own epicycle and revolving upon its own axis so that its white side always faces the sun. At bottom left are indications of the year of the Solar Cycle (of twenty-eight years) and the Dominical Letter. This dial also incorporates a perpetual calendar—that is, with automatic correction for leap years. At bottom right, the Indiction (fifteen years) and the Golden Number or Metonic Cycle (nineteen years) are shown as well as the epact for each year. Finally, and right in the centre of the whole display, a dial shows the hour to the nearest quarter; its centre, which contains seven diamond-shaped plates each with a planetary sign for a day of the week, revolves to bring the correct sign into juxtaposition with XII on the hour dial, against which it is read. Abutting this small dial are two winding-squares, that alongside III taking the winding-key for the mainspring driving the whole mechanism, while above XII is another square enabling the entire astronomical display to be set forwards or backwards, or indeed to any desired date.

Before leaving Watson, brief mention must be made of his two other highly complicated clocks, both still surviving and both in a more original state. These are
57 spring-driven, in ebonized cases of architectural form and surmounted by, in one example, a single gilt statuette—of Mercury—and in the other, three such figures, including a centrally placed Mercury. The only obvious alterations carried out, perhaps at the same time, are the substitution of double-bob pendulums on spring suspensions for what it is considered might have been single-bob pendulums fixed rigidly to the escape arbors. Even so, the recoil escapements remain untouched; they are not verge conversions, and indeed these would be unlikely in clocks with such pretensions to precision.

These two clocks were made, it might seem, up to a decade apart; and it was a very significant decade indeed. The first clock—and the earlier—is in the
Collection belonging to the Clockmakers' Company and 58
still bases its astronomical information upon the Ptolemaic concept. Its probable date falls within the bracket 1680–90. The second clock probably dates

from *c.*1695, and its basic astronomical concept is the heliocentric principle of Copernicus. This clock is in the Science Museum, London. It is relevant that this second clock followed closely upon the publication, 1686–8, of Sir Isaac Newton's *Principia*; there is strong evidence to suggest that both these clocks at one time may have belonged to him. This matter has been discussed *in extenso* by H. Alan Lloyd in the *Horological Journal* for December 1948, pp. 750–59.

It is conceivable that, to the population who observed such wonderfully ingenious machines in Watson's own day, they must have appeared to possess all the near-magical qualities of our own micro-chip processors. Yet there were those who were not impressed; and, towards the end—as it must have been—of his life, Watson received an untypical rebuff from the Clockmakers' Company which is summarized in their Court Minutes for 3rd November 1712:

A proposal in writing of Mr. Samuel Watson's about an instrument to discover the hour of the day at sea and several other useful mathematical matters, which he therein offered to deliver and sell to the Company on certain conditions therein specified was read and considered. And the result was that this Court do not concern itself therein.

Watson might perhaps be described as a fine horological mathematician, in an age when all the best craftsmen—and there were many—had something extra to offer, apart from sheer mechanical skill. The greatest of these—because he never produced work

58. *The dial of a third astronomical clock by Samuel Watson. No others have been recorded.* (Science Museum, London)

that fell below the inordinately high standards he set himself—was Thomas Tompion; but it can well be argued that second in eminence only to him was Daniel Quare. At his best, Quare was at least the equal of anybody in the horological trade, and way ahead of most. Yet there exist pieces which do not conform to his best practice, and he was certainly the focus of much faking, especially by Continental makers. There are also watches signed 'Quaré' of high quality, such as could well have come from his workshop, and it has been hazarded that he added an accent deliberately on some of his export work as a merchandizing gimmick. This kind of muddled picture inevitably leaves many questions unanswered; but, in general terms, there can be no doubt that Quare was one of the great horological personalities of his day.

There is some little doubt about the exact circumstances of Quare's birth although it is widely thought to have taken place somewhere in Somerset about 1648. Born of a strict Quaker family, the details of his training as a clockmaker have not been recorded either; but he was admitted a Brother in the Clockmakers' Company, and described as 'A great Clockmaker', on 3rd April 1671.

In 1676, he married Mary, the daughter of Jeremiah Stevens, a maltster of High Wycombe, at which time he was living in St Martin's-le-Grand. An interesting sidelight is provided into the intelligibility of addresses appearing on horological wares at this time, for the dial of a thirty-hour Quare clock movement is signed, within a fine lambrequin, 'Daniel Quare in Martins Neare Alders Gate Londini fecit'.

Daniel Quare's Quaker leanings brought him frequently into conflict with 'the establishment' in his own locality, where he found himself unable to conform to the practices of the community. Thus, he was fined in 1678 for refusing to pay a rate for clergy maintenance, and again the following year, in respect of charges for the militia. In 1683, he offended by attending a proscribed meeting and again in 1689, by refusing to pay tithes and priest's maintenance. He was one of some fifty of the Society of Friends—the correct name of the Quaker fraternity—who were summoned to appear before a commission, appointed by James II in 1686, to plead for liberty of conscience. There is no doubt that his standing, so far as his own kind were concerned, was of the highest; he was even able to arrange for four Friends, one of them the celebrated George Whitehead, the great privilege of an interview with William III.

Daniel and Mary Quare had at least three daughters, including Ann and Elizabeth, as well as a son Jeremiah who does not appear to have followed in his father's footsteps in the craft. Yet curiously, a second Daniel—said to be 'son of Robert', and possibly a nephew—was

59. *A bracket clock by Samuel Watson, of conventional appearance.* (Sotheby's, London)

apprenticed to his famous namesake on 19th March 1707 for seven years. He never seems to have been admitted to the Freedom of the Clockmakers' Company, and there is no further trace of him.

Because his beliefs did not permit him to take the Oath of Allegiance, Quare was never able to be appointed Royal Clockmaker; however, he was given free access via the Back Stairs—'The Yeoman of the Guard lets me frequently go up without anybody for leave, as otherwise he would tho' persons of quality'—and his particular persuasions never seem to have been any major hindrance to his advancement. Indeed, when Elizabeth married Sylvanus Bevan in 1715, the list of wedding guests—and especially the 'near miss' by the Prince and Princess of Wales—could hardly have been more impressive. Rebecca Osgood, daughter of Salem Osgood, writing about the function two months afterwards, says:

As to ye wedding I don't know, but ye hast had an account of it before this, but I will give ye the best account I am capable of, being of ye invited gest. Y^e^ Prince and Princess and most of ye quality was invited, and they gave them some hopes of honouring them with there company till ye night before, and then they sent word y^t^ they could not come, nor none of ye quality which had places, because of ye Actt which obliges them to go into no meeting—but thare was severl of ye quality y^t^ had no places, ye Dutchess of Marlbourow was thare, and ye Lord Finch, ye Lady Cartwrite, ye Venetian Ambascior and his lady, and a lady that is governess to ye young Princesses, hous name I have forgot, and severl other persons of distinction. Thay desiered y^t^ ye meeting might be put off till one of ye clock, which was done. . . . Accordingly from thence we went to Skiner's Hall whare we dined thay gave a very splendid dinner as could be and ye quality was mightily pleased both with ye ceremony of ye marriage and thare entertainment as to ye young couple thay came of very well. Y^e^ bridegroom spoke very hansomly and ye bride better then could be expected before so great an ascembly. I had y^e^ honour to wate on them home at night.

60. *The unconventional movement, controlled by a balance rather than a pendulum, of Samuel Watson's bracket clock.* (Sotheby's, London)

Despite the belated discovery of the adverse Parliamentary ruling—it forbade attendance by the royal family at dissenting places of worship—the Princess did attend the subsequent dinner, which was for some three hundred guests and included also the Countess of Brocklinborough, the Count and Countess of Guicord and Francis de Fleurs.

One can imagine that Elizabeth's wedding must have constituted the peak of Quare's social career; but the marriages of his other children, previously, had not gone unnoticed. When Ann Quare married John Falconer in 1705, the guests included the Envoys of Venice, Florence, Hanover, Portugal, Sweden, Prussia and Denmark; and these probably represented good business connections as well as social assets. For example, there is in the Palazzo Pitti in Florence a typically magnificent month-duration long-case clock with equation work—with an explanation of the function of the latter engraved upon it in Italian—by Quare, who almost certainly received the order for it from the Grand Duke of Florence, this being transmitted by Quare's friend, the Envoy. Again, in 1712, both a son and a daughter married, and this time the guest-list included the Earl of Orrery, the Duke of Argyll, the Venetian Ambassador and the Count of Briançion. Other known friends of the Quares included William Penn, Henrietta, Countess of Stafford, and the Duke of Bolton.

Meantime, Daniel Quare was pursuing his activities in the Clockmakers' Company with his customary enthusiasm and energy. Elected to the Court of Assistants in 1697, he became Junior Warden in September 1705—his nearest rival was George Etherington, another maker of renown, who had to wait a further year before being preferred for that particular job—and he served the office of Master in 1708.

Probably Quare's best-known connection with the Clockmakers' Company relates to his developments in repeating-work in watches. In 1676 the Reverend Edward Barlow—a very talented mechanic, born near Warrington in 1636 and, although ordained, far more devoted to improving horological instruments—invented rack-striking for clocks, and it was a short step from this to its application in repeating work for watches. Barlow took such a step, and Tompion made a watch for him incorporating his new repeating system, about 1685. Barlow applied for Letters Patent to give him a monopoly in the making of repeating clocks and watches, but the Clockmakers' Company decided to resist his application and to back Daniel Quare, who had also been experimenting in the same area for some time. The Company accordingly petitioned the King in Council and, at the hearing of the case on 2nd March 1687, Barlow's bid was refused. Subsequently, the

61. *Repeating watch no. 611 by Daniel Quare: dial view.* (Ashmolean Museum, Oxford)

62. *Movement of the Daniel Quare repeating watch.* (Ashmolean Museum, Oxford)

63. *The pair-cases of Daniel Quare's repeating watch, showing medallion portrait of James II and the inscription in Latin.* (Ashmolean Museum, Oxford)

King held a trial of both repeating watches, giving preference to Quare's design on the grounds that a single push upon a pin projecting from the case sufficed to actuate the mechanism, while Barlow's system required separate actions to sound first the hours and then the quarters. The decision was duly promulgated in the *London Gazette*.

A watch said to be 'identical to' the Quare watch
61 preferred by James II—it seems likely that it might be
62 63 the actual watch—is preserved in the Ashmolean
Museum, Oxford. It has an interesting history, in that it first turns up in print in the *Morning Chronicle* for 11th December 1823, when it was in the possession of a certain John Stanton of Benwell, near Newcastle-upon-Tyne. In gold pair-cases, the outer bearing a medallion portrait of James II, the inner has a Latin inscription 'J.R.2nd. *Gloria deo excelsis—sino pretio redimi mini mala lege adlatum—bono Rege restituiture*,' this last being more usually represented as 'restituire'. The inscription is not easy to read, and several versions of it have appeared in print over the years, but the meaning appears to be 'Taken away wrongly by law, it is restored under our good King.' The movement is signed 'Daniel Quare London 611', and it is unique in that the repeating-work is operated by a push-piece at the one o'clock position on the band of the case. These details, both decorative and technical, lead, at the least, to the conclusion that the watch is very similar indeed to the one which was the subject of the royal trial. Quare, incidentally, was one of the first makers—if indeed not the first—to employ a cap fitting tightly over his watch movements as an added protection against dust.

Quare is known to have had several business addresses during his working life. He seems to have moved from St Martin's-le-Grand into Aldersgate proper, then to Lombard Street, finishing up at King's Arms in Exchange Alley, a tiny thoroughfare much favoured by the horological trade at the time. At some point in his later life, about 1718, he took Stephen Horseman into partnership, and timepieces were subsequently signed Quare & Horseman. In 1724 Quare died, at Croydon, and was buried, on 24th March, at the Quakers' cemetery at Bunhill Fields, Finsbury. All the best craftsmen in the trade attended Quare's funeral. Afterwards his business was carried on by Stephen Horseman, and even the serial numbering was maintained exactly as if he were still working. However, Horseman was no equal, on his own, to his former senior partner, and eventually, in 1733, he went bankrupt, when the business was sold up. It is usually held that Richard Peckover took over the goodwill, as he was certainly in Exchange Alley by 1735, and the serial numbering of his watches appears to run on from that of Quare & Horseman. He is recorded at least until 1754.

During his working life, several other craftsmen are known to have been associated, in one way or another, with Daniel Quare. The trade card of Thomas Grignion, to name but one, presents something of a problem since it is said to be inscribed 'Finisher to the late Mr. Daniel Quare, at the King's Arms and Dial, Covent Garden'; yet the standard works of reference give his date of birth only as 1713. He must have been a most precocious child! Another minor mystery is concerned with the large number—fourteen, at the last count—of apprentices who were bound to Daniel Quare during his working life. Chronologically, these are as follows:

John Becke	1673	John Zachary	1687
George Heady	1675	John Nolson	1689
Faith Leake	1677	William Johnson	1690
John Foster	1680	John Kirton	1696
John Marshall	1682	Stephen Horseman	1701
Robert Todd	1684	Joshua Appleby	1705
John Davis	1685	Daniel Quare	1707

It seems doubtful if one or two of these ever attained the Freedom of the Clockmakers' Company; and, with the sole exception of Stephen Horseman, who of course went into partnership with his master, all of them remained virtually unknown.

The same stricture cannot apply to Joseph Williamson, however, and it is a pity that more has not so far come to light about this gifted mathematician and craftsman. It is probable that he was born about 1672, if Baillie is correct in stating that he was apprenticed in 1686—for this formal training usually commenced at age fourteen—although he is not listed in the Clockmakers' Company's Register of Apprentices. He had business premises in Clements Lane, which runs between Lombard Street and King William Street. By 1721 he had reached the office of Junior Warden in the Company, being elected Master in September 1724. He died the following June, while still in office. Although he held no official appointment to the British monarch, he was appointed watchmaker to King Charles II of Spain. Virtually nothing is known about his family, but the fact that he had an apprentice called William Williamson turned over to him although originally bound to another maker, might suggest some family relationship.

Williamson's association with Quare was based on his particular specialization, the construction of motion-work to show the equation of time. The advantage of this correction factor being continuously available—and accurately shown—on a clock dial, rather than only after ascertaining it from a specially constructed astronomical table, was obvious. If a clock stopped, the only way of re-setting the hands correctly, in the days before any kind of universal time-signal, was to use a sundial. Of itself this was not enough, however, because on only four days in any year did the time as measured by a swinging pendulum exactly coincide with that cast by the sun's shadow; and the extreme differences between the two could be as great as sixteen minutes fast or slow. However, a clock with an equation dial which was directly connected to the dial showing mean time provided an easy solution: set the equation dial by sun time, and the mean time dial was automatically corrected.

Williamson's claim to have virtually invented equation work for clocks is set out in a letter he wrote for public assimilation, and which appeared in *Philosophical Transactions* at the end of 1719. He seems to have been goaded into this by the rival claim of a French maker; his communication starts:

> A letter of Mr. Joseph Williamson, Watchmaker, to the Publisher, wherein he asserts his Right to the curious and useful invention of making Clocks to keep time with the Sun's Apparent Motion. . . . And in the first place I must take notice of . . . a clock found in the Late King Charles the Second of Spain's Cabinet about the year 1699 or 1700 which sheweth both equal and apparent Time according to the Tables of Equation, and which went four hundred days without winding up. This I am well satisfied is a clock of my own making; for about six years before that time, I made one for Mr. Daniel Quare, for whom I then wrought mostly, . . . and went for 400 days. This clock Mr. Daniel Quare sold, soon after it was made to go, to the said King Charles II of Spain. . . . Soon after this clock was sent to Spain, I made others for Mr Quare which showed Apparent Time. . . . For one of those, and not the first, made with the rising and setting of the Sun, Mr Quare sold to the late King William and it was set up at Hampton Court in his lifetime, where it hath been ever since. . . . So that I think that I may justly claim the greatest right to this contrivance of making clocks to go with Apparent Time; and I have never heard of any such clock sold in England but was of my own making, though I have made them so long.

However, Williamson's case is by no means watertight. Although the fundamental element of the invention is a specially designed cam or eccentric, called the 'kidney-piece', there are at least three ways in which this can be applied to the clock mechanism in order to achieve the required effect. Tompion was certainly very early in the field with an Equation Clock—it will be described later in this chapter—and Williamson's connection with that machine, if indeed he had any, has not so far come to light. Nevertheless, he certainly can claim undisputed originality in one of the three systems, and the one most favoured by Quare; so he was undoubtedly a pioneer at the very least. The pros and cons of this matter have been argued at length by modern-day specialists such as the late H. Alan Lloyd and Professor Hans von Bertele, and their views

64. (Right) *The year-duration longcase clock by Daniel Quare, at Hampton Court Palace.* (Royal Collection)

65. (Far right) *Detail of the hood and dial of Quare's year-going clock.* (Royal Collection)

can be ascertained, *inter alia*, in the Christmas 1943 edition of *Horological Journal* and the December 1955 issue of *Antiquarian Horology*.

Quare's use of equation work is almost invariably allied to one of his monumental year-duration clocks, of long-case form and superb both in concept and execution. The equation dial and motion-work are generally accommodated in the trunk door, rather than as an adjunct of the principal dial, and there is transmission by connecting rod and endless worm with the main mechanism. Thus, it would have been easy for this additional feature to have been made separately by Williamson and incorporated by Quare after the bulk of the mechanical work was finished.

However, the first of Quare's royal clocks to be described does not work on this principle. This is the 64
one referred to by Williamson in his published letter; made for King William III and installed in his State Bedroom at Hampton Court Palace, there it has remained. This is an enormous clock, 10 feet high overall. The case is of oak, veneered with burr walnut, and standing upon an elaborate gilt brass base. Britten gives the measurements as plinth 22 inches, waist 48 inches, hood 24 inches, dome $10\frac{1}{2}$ inches, surmounted by a gilt-brass figure adding a further 12 inches. There are four other smaller gilt cherubs distributed at the four corners of the hood.

The dial plate of this remarkable clock is 16 inches by
14 inches, and, along the bottom of this and below the 65
main dial, there are three subsidiaries, the one in the middle being smaller than those in each corner. One shows the rising and setting of the sun, that in the middle has an index and a scale for latitude, while the third was for disconnecting the equation work as it is engraved on one side '*Tempus apparens*' i.e. sundial time, and on the other '*Tempus aequale*' or mean time. This alteration seems most likely to have been effected in 1836 when Vulliamy removed the original pendulum and escapement, replacing them with an up-to-date dead-beat installation. This is especially sad because the system of equation work in this particular clock depended upon the cam being used to change the effective length of the pendulum, thus causing the clock itself to run faster or slower according to the state of the sun at any particular moment. Thus, when the small subsidiary showed '*Tempus Apparens*', the main clock dial was actually registering sundial time.

There exists another year clock by Quare, formerly in the Ilbert Collection and now in the British Museum,

66. (Left) *Another year-going longcase clock, possibly with royal associations, by Daniel Quare.* (British Museum)

67. (Right) *Detail of the hood and dial of this second Daniel Quare year-going clock* (British Museum)

68. (Below) *Detail of the Equation Dial set into the trunk door of the same clock.* (British Museum)

which works on the principle previously described, 66 67 68
where the equation mechanism has been separated off and accommodated in the trunk door. This also is an enormous clock, very unlikely to have been made for any room less than 20 feet high; and since it incorporates the royal arms in its dial embellishments, seems likely to have been made for a palace, although there is no evidence on this point.

The next of Quare's royal clocks to be described has, 69
most unfortunately, also been modified, to the extent that its entire movement was replaced by Frodsham in 1862. This is a small travelling-clock—it is only $6\frac{1}{2}$ inches high—in a gilt-metal case of broken-arch form, the dial plate having two part-subsidiaries tucked into the top corners, which are now disconnected. The case sits on four moulded feet, and there is a top central fitting which probably incorporated a trunnion. In prime condition this clock would have been unique, and such unnecessary alterations must be the cause for much regret today.

69. (Right) *All that remains of a splendid small clock by Daniel Quare. 6½″ high, it was fitted with a modern movement in 1862.* (Royal Collection)

70. (Below right) *A conventional bracket clock, striking and repeating, by Daniel Quare, in Windsor Castle.* (Royal Collection)

There is one Daniel Quare bracket clock at Windsor
70 Castle, which stands 1 foot 5 inches high. In ebonized case with an inverted bell-top and cast handle, there is a metal fret in the door above the dial, backed by crimson silk, and the side panels are similarly treated; escutcheon plates *en suite* are located in the door frame on either side of the dial. Two subsidiaries are placed in the corners above the main dial, for strike/silent and regulation, and there is provision for pull-repeat. The clock sits upon four moulded metal feet, and there is a carved and gilt matching bracket. Sad to say, this clock also has a Frodsham movement.

Before leaving Quare, it is worth noting that he had a separate but equally outstanding reputation as a maker of free-standing pillar barometers, of a type and style which are peculiarly his own. He took out a patent in
71 respect of his development work, number 342 of 2nd
72 August 1695, and these portable barometers on their folding tripod stands are greatly sought after by collectors. His work in this field has been extensively examined by Nicholas Goodison, in *English Barometers 1680–1860*; and it appears from this that he must have made three barometers for William III, one of a quite unique design for wall mounting, an ivory pillar barometer on a tripod, and an angle barometer which even so possessed structural similarities with his typical pillar design. The last two of these barometers are at Hampton Court, while the first reposes in a private collection. His reputation was even further enhanced, in 1696, when no less a person than William Derham experimented with two of 'Mr. Quare's best portable barometers at the Monument . . .' in measuring the relative heights of a column of mercury at the top and bottom of this famous London landmark.

Finally, we come to Thomas Tompion, arguably the greatest clockmaker the world has ever seen and certainly the supreme figure in English antiquarian horology. Like Quare, Tompion also made barometers, but for special customers only, it might appear, since nothing like the quantity of Quare's output seems to have come from Tompion's workshop. He also made sundials and mathematical instruments, but similarly in very small quantities, to judge by surviving specimens; and it is for his clocks and watches that he will be always remembered.

The earliest records of Tompion's life are sparse indeed. He was born at Ickfield Green, which is a hamlet in the parish of Northill, in Bedfordshire, and baptized

71. (Above) *One of Daniel Quare's barometers at Hampton Court Palace.* (Royal Collection)

in the church there on 25th July 1639. His father, also Thomas, was a blacksmith; and his mother was called Margaret. Tompion's paternal grandfather, Robert, had also been a blacksmith, whose Will, proved on 4th August 1635, left all the tools of his trade to Tompion's father—but when in turn he died, in 1665, he passed down the 'Tooles wch are in my Shoppe' to his younger son, James. It may be that Thomas junior was no longer living in the neighbourhood by that time, or that he had no taste for blacksmithing.

In any event, the next certain information concerning the young Thomas Tompion comes thirty-two years later when, on 4th September 1671 and on payment of a fee of 30 shillings, he was admitted to the Clockmakers' Company as a 'Brother'. Here was yet another craftsman to be admitted as a 'Great Clockmaker'—that is to say, he must previously have specialized in iron clocks for churches and the like, and he might, indeed, have owed previous allegiance to some other Livery Company; but searches made in the records of the most likely ones have thrown no light on the subject whatever. A little later on, in fact on 6th April 1674, Tompion was admitted 'a ffree Clockmaker upon Redemption', which means that he had to purchase his entry—at a cost of 10 shillings—rather than by the more usual method of serving an apprenticeship; this might be seen as regularizing his situation, in so far as working within the City of London, and employing others in his workshop, was concerned; but it gives us no hint whatsoever as to how he himself obtained his training. Indeed, this thirty-odd years of darkness regarding Tompion's early life has remained completely impenetrable up to the present time.

He cannot be located with any certainty in London before 1674, when he was living in Water Lane (now called Whitefriars Street), which was then a modest thoroughfare running into Fleet Street. From then on, most of our knowledge of Tompion is derived from the diary of Robert Hooke, best known as the brilliant English experimental physicist, but equipped with as versatile a mind as could be imagined, even for those days when it was still possible to make an intellectual reputation in several different fields at the same time. Hooke, who was a bachelor, was variously Professor of Geometry at Gresham College, Curator of Experiments of the Royal Society, and Surveyor to the City of London as well as an architect of renown; into the bargain, he was an active and innovative exponent of horological theory, contributing two important inventions in this field that greatly improved the performance of clocks and watches, namely the anchor escapement with its associated long pendulum, for clocks, and, for watches, the incorporation of a spiral spring to regulate the balance. It was his inherent interest in horology that

72. (Right) *Another of Quare's barometers, also at Hampton Court Palace.* (Royal Collection)

73. *A rarely-encountered timepiece by Thomas Herbert. The crown and cypher on the back of the outer case of this coach watch suggest a royal provenance.* (Private collection)

brought him and Tompion together on common ground, for he cannot have been a very pleasant person. Robert Waller, FRS, in a biographical sketch, describes him as

> despicable, being very crooked. He was always very pale and lean, and laterly nothing but Skin and Bone, with a meagre aspect. . . . He wore his own Hair of a dark Brown colour, very long and hanging neglected over his Face uncut and lank. . . . He went stooping and very fast . . . slept little, seldom going to sleep till two, three or four a Clock in the Morning. His temper was Melancholy, Mistrustful and Jealous, which more increas'd upon him with his Years.

By contrast Tompion, to judge from his portrait by Sir
74 Godfrey Kneller which was engraved in mezzotint by J. Smith, appears well set up and smart, of a good presence and pleasant of feature. They must have made an odd-looking pair.

The two men first met in April 1674, when Hooke employed Tompion to make for him a quadrant of Hooke's own invention in which the Royal Society had become interested—in fact, the Society was paying for it. These two very different men seem quickly to have generated a mutual respect for one another, and Hooke, in his terse manner, notes 'Much discourse with him [Tompion] about watches. Told him the way of making an engine for finishing wheels, and a way how to make a dividing plate; about the forme of an arch; about another way of Teeth work; about pocket watches and many other things.'

Their relationship prospered, and others joined it. Flamsteed, the up-and-coming young astronomer of twenty-eight and apparently, on account of some illness as a boy, as crooked, ugly and irritable in demeanour as Hooke, came to see the quadrant; and when it was at last completed, on 5th July 1674, Tompion took it round to Gresham College to deliver it in person, only to find also present Sir Jonas Moore, the mathematician (1617–79) who was HM Surveyor of Ordnance, and of course a friend of Flamsteed, who was to be the first Astronomer Royal (see Appendix 1). Afterwards they all repaired to Blacklock's Coffee-house.

R. W. Symonds, whose definitive work *Thomas Tompion—His Life and Work* was first published in 1951, regards 1674 as a highly significant year in Tompion's burgeoning career, for it was the year in which he started to move from obscurity to recognition, meeting in the course thereof many of the leading scientists of the day, some of the nobility and, of course, the King. It was the following year, however, when events really started to favour him; and the first such did not even occur in Britain.

Christian Huygens, the Dutch physicist of genius, while pursuing his interest in developing a marine timekeeper, designed a watch in 1675 which he called a 'pendulum watch' because its balance was controlled by a spring. In fact, using a spring in this context—the effect of which was to regularize the operation of the balance and therefore of the escapement—was exactly analogous with the gravitational effects which produced that same uniformity of action in a pendulum. This device came to Hooke's knowledge as a result of Huygens's offering a share in the relevant patent rights to Henry Oldenburg, who was Secretary of the Royal Society; the information was conveyed to him by Robert Boyle, an old friend and celebrated chemist and natural philosopher.

Hooke was greatly aggrieved by this news, for there is no doubt but that he had developed a similar invention some years previously. An account of 1668 speaks of

> a pocket watch with a new pendulum invention. You might call it with a bridle, the time being regulated by a little spring of tempered wire, which at one end is attached to the balance-wheel, and at the other to the body of the watch. This works in such a way that if the movements of the balance-wheel are unequal, and if some irregularity of the toothed movement tends to increase the inequality, the wire keeps it in check, obliging it always to make the same journey.

This description relates to Hooke demonstrating his then-new watch before members of the Royal Society. He subsequently suppressed his invention, having apparently failed to make suitable arrangements for its production.

His natural tendency towards secretiveness always militated, in the end, to Hooke's disadvantage. His immediate reaction to the news was to order Tompion to begin making him a special watch—the details to be explained later—and simultaneously to institute a search in the Royal Society's Minute Book for a record of his demonstration in 1668. When he could not find it, he at once concluded that Oldenburg had omitted it deliberately, in conspiracy with Huygens.

On 7th April 1675 Hooke, accompanied by Tompion and Sir Jonas Moore, went to Whitehall Palace to show the new watch to King Charles II. There is no doubt it received royal approbation, in preference to that of Huygens; the King promised Hooke a patent and ordered a similar watch for his own personal use.

On 17th May the 'King's watch'—as it became known in Hooke's diary—was completed and delivered to the King, who 'Received the watch very kindly, it was locked up in his closet'. Its subsequent performance must have been erratic, however, and it was returned to Tompion for further adjustment. He seems to have been unconscionably long over this, and it became a matter of dispute between Tompion and Hooke, the latter always fearful that the King would lose patience and that Huygens and Oldenburg would profit thereby.

In the end, the watch was considered fit for further royal use on 26th August, when it had now been fitted with a cap over the balance inscribed 'R. Hooke inven. 1658 T. Tompion fecit 1675'. It was given over to the King's closet-keeper, one 'Mr Chiffins'. Subsequently, the Duke of York and Prince Rupert each ordered similar watches for themselves.

During that summer the watch seems to have performed well; on 15th September, Hooke reports, the King 'Cald me to him told me that my watch did very well that he had tried it the day before and found it true with his Pendulum clock to a minute'. By 5th October, however, with colder weather approaching, Hooke notes 'At Whitehall saw the King in the Gallery he spoke to me in the park that weather had alter'd watch.' There was, of course, no provision at that time for compensating for the expansion and contraction effects brought about by changes in temperature, and such was not to be incorporated for another century.

It was shortly after this that Hooke and Tompion quarrelled badly—over what, is not clear—and this was to signal the gradual drifting apart of these two great men. References to Tompion in Hooke's diary after becoming increasingly scurrilous become rarer and rarer, their meetings less and less frequent. However, a complete breakdown seems never to have occurred; some kind of relationship between them probably continued until Hooke's death in 1703.

It may be that Tompion's mounting fame offended Hooke's jealous nature; and it certainly entailed a lessening of his self-centred influence over the great clockmaker. The latter, in any event, was by now becoming involved more and more with the fitting out of the Royal Observatory at Greenwich, for which he was to make the twin two-seconds-beating wall-mounted regulator clocks, their 13-foot pendulums suspended above them. These are fitted with plaques inscribed to show Sir Jonas Moore's commissioning of them, and dated 1676.

In 1675 Tompion, at that time working somewhere or other in the length of Water Lane, and perhaps having been in the same premises since 1671, decided that the time had come to aspire to something more suited to his increasing reputation. He therefore took over the partly-vacant large corner house, still in Water Lane but with a valuable frontage into Fleet Street; and he was certainly installed there by October, when customers were already calling upon him. The move had caused him some temporary financial embarrassment, however, and he had to borrow money from Sir Jonas Moore to see him through.

Starting with four apprentices and one female servant, Tompion's rate of business expansion would be applauded even by present-day standards. By 1680 he had obtained a larger share of the house, with apparently several lodgers thrown in. Two years after that he was actively engaged on repairs and alterations to the premises. In 1693, his household consisted of his sister and seven servants, mainly his apprentices; while, two years later, by which time he must have been the busiest and most prosperous clockmaker in the country, his household had grown to nineteen, all told. This included Edward Banger, his former apprentice, who married Tompion's niece Margaret Kent and was subsequently taken into partnership by his master. With one exception, the other menfolk in the list of those in Tompion's house were either journeymen or apprentices, with a balance in favour of the latter. It was probably cheaper to 'train as you go', with plenty of cheap labour arising therefrom, than have to employ qualified artisans. It is interesting to note, too, that Tompion had far more of his share of apprentices than he was entitled to under the Clockmakers' Company ordinances; he managed this by a technical loophole, the practice known as 'turning over' an apprentice from one workmaster to another after the initial binding.

So, during the reign of William III, Tompion was at the height of his career, and the large premises at the sign of 'The Dial and Three Crowns'—perhaps this latter was to signify service under three sovereigns—a positive hive of industry. There is no doubt that Tompion's workshop was much larger than the average of those times, and probably he had some non-resident staff into the bargain; his main output must have been in the field of clocks and watches, but he also made sundials, alarms and barometers. Certain it is, too, that he manufactured for export; not only have many of his works turned up in continental Europe, but an instruction sheet issued by him appears in French, and there is a record of his obtaining a permit to go to Holland, in 1697. No details of this trip have survived, but there can be little doubt that it was of a business nature.

The trappings of fame, in Tompion's day, were much the same as they are now. Sir Godfrey Kneller, the fashionable Court painter, painted his portrait; this was subsequently engraved in mezzotint by J. Smith for more general dissemination, whereas today colour photographs would probably be more appropriate. His name became so much a household word that it occurred in the dialogue of a stage play. Perhaps the final accolade to his genius might be that he was extensively forged, and there is a well-known story to the effect that, when confronted with one of these spurious watches by a customer, he promptly smashed it with a hammer, handing another watch to the astonished owner with the words: 'Sir, here is a watch of my making.'

74. *Portrait of Thomas Tompion: a modern interpretation based on the mezzotint by John Smith, or possibly copied from a contemporary miniature.* (Clockmakers' Company, London)

It is an interesting reflection of the awe in which mechanical craftsmen like Tompion were held in the seventeenth century that, when St Paul's Cathedral, started in 1675, was at long last ready to be fitted out with a clock, there should have appeared in *The Post Boy* a notice reading: 'Mr. Tompion, the Famous Watch-maker, is making a fine Clock for the Cathedral Church of St. Paul's which is to go for 100 Years without winding up; and t's said the same will cost 3 or 4000 pounds, it being finer than that at Strasbourg.' This was not a solitary report, and the absurd exaggeration only serves to underline how little the man-in-the-street then understood about the limitations of clockwork, let alone the principles underlying it. In the event, of course, Langley Bradley supplied the clock for the cathedral at a cost of £300; but he was a generation younger than Tompion, and his royal associations were still to come.

The Clockmakers' Company seems to have constituted something of an occupational hazard, to be dealt with discreetly and with the minimum of personal inconvenience, so far as Tompion was concerned. He felt constrained by their apprentice regulations; he seems to have made a specious excuse—illness and preoccupation with repairs to his premises—the first time he was asked to serve in an official role, that of Steward, in 1684. It was not until he was sixty years old, in 1700, that he consented to accept appointment on the lowest rung of the ladder leading directly to election as Master, in other words, to become Junior Warden. In 1701, he became Renter Warden, the year after, Senior Warden, and finally—in 1703—he was elected Master.

There had been a notable addition to Tompion's staff in 1696, when George Graham, bound apprentice to Henry Aske in 1688, finished his due term and was invited to enter Tompion's service. The two became very friendly—not unexpectedly, since Graham was an inventor as well as a fine craftsman, and Tompion certainly favoured innovation although it was not his own particular strength. Eventually, Graham was to marry Tompion's other niece, Elizabeth, the daughter of his brother James.

Thus Tompion had, at the latter end of his working life, and not simultaneously, two partners, both of them related to him by marriage. Clocks and watches signed jointly by Thomas Tompion and Edward Banger seem approximately to span the years 1701 to about 1708; those signed Thomas Tompion and George Graham from 1710 to Tompion's death in 1713. There seems to have been a substantial quarrel between Tompion and Banger about 1708, from which time on the last-named disappears from the records without trace. During 1980 two watch movements, bearing his signature alone, came on the market, but otherwise Banger's subsequent activities remain an inexplicable mystery. The only positive indication of bad blood between them derives from Tompion's Will, wherein he refers to a legacy to his niece Margaret Banger being not 'Subject, or lyable to the Acts, Debts, forfeitures, Incumbrance, Intermedling Disposition or Controll of her said Now Husband'.

The Tompion and Graham partnership had a run of only three years, and that period was not without other pressures upon the ageing clockmaker. His nephew, also Thomas Tompion, was eventually to acquire the habits of the criminal and to be charged at the Old Bailey, initially with picking pockets and later with murder. He seems to have spent some time in Newgate Prison, while his wife 'Mol Tompion, a most notorious offender' was only reprieved from the death sentence on account of pregnancy. As for Tompion himself, declining health led him to favour the waters of Bath in the early years of the new century, and he was quickly integrated into the social life of that city. He was made an Honorary Freeman; and the Corporation benefited from the superb equation long-case clock which he supplied for the Pump Room, and the sundial he made to allow the clock to be checked by solar time.

It would seem from the foregoing that Tompion's business must have been largely under George Graham's control during the last two or three years of Tompion's life; and when he died, on 20th November 1713, Graham lost no time in advertising that he was carrying on business as usual, having inherited all the stock-in-trade as well as work-in-hand, both finished and unfinished. Another former associate of Tompion's, however, both as apprentice and subsequently journeyman, one William Webster, tried very hard to cash in on the situation, advertising that he had worked and lived with Tompion for a considerable time, and was 'fully acquainted with the Secrets of the said Art'.

Thomas Tompion was buried in Westminster Abbey on 25th November; and R. W. Symonds has pointed out that, in those days, this was not the great honour that it would be today. It was possible for anyone of means and modest distinction to purchase a burial place within the church, and it was then, as it is now, a matter entirely within the discretion of the Dean and Chapter. No one would argue that Tompion possessed both the distinction to qualify and the wealth to underwrite it.

The biggest enigma surrounding Tompion's working life is the total absence of any formal royal appointment. It has been held that he was excluded only on account of the post being held by Thomas Herbert, of Whitehall, a relatively unknown craftsman who effectively blocked the way to anybody else, being Royal Clockmaker respectively to James II, William III and Queen Anne. Yet, the absence of formal recognition clearly impeded him not the slightest; as Christopher Wren remarked to the Lord Chamberlain of the Household in 1711, 'It is well known that Mr. Tompion and others have been employed not only to make some clocks, but to take care of and look after those they did make . . . .' As for Herbert, admitted to the Freedom of the Clockmakers' Company in 1676 and active until about 1708, his surviving work includes a tortoiseshell-veneered bracket clock, formerly in the Wetherfield Collection, and a magnificent silver coach 73
watch, dating *c.*1693, having verge escapement and hour-striking action, in pierced and engraved inner case, with leather outer case bearing the royal monogram WR repeating and reversing, surmounted by a crown. In the 1680s he took over from Robert Lynch an apprentice called Evan Herbert, probably a relation, and in the record of that event he is described as the King's Clockmaker; otherwise little is known of

75. (Above) *The 'Record' Tompion longcase clock, now in Colonial Williamsburg.* (Percy Dawson)

76. (Above centre) *The 'Record' Tompion: detail of the dial and hood.* (Percy Dawson)

77. (Above right) *The 'Record' Tompion: profile view of hood.* (Percy Dawson)

78. (Right) *The 'Record' Tompion: detail of the base.* (Percy Dawson)

him, and he remains unrepresented in the Royal Collection at this time.

Tompion's most extravagant royal patron was undoubtedly William III; and when he died, he owed Tompion a not inconsiderable sum of money, no less than £564 15s, 'due to him for clocks and watches &c. presented by the late King to the Duke of Florence'—so ran Tompion's petition for payment which he presented to Queen Anne. Florence, incidentally—and particularly the Palazzo Pitti—seems to have constituted a ready market for the work of the finest London clockmakers, for to this day it contains one of Quare's 'palace quality' monumental long-case clocks, of one month duration of going, and with equation work incorporated in the trunk door. Surmounted by three urn finials, the magnificent burr-walnut case needs considerable surrounding space around and above it to be seen to advantage; the movement has bolt-and-shutter maintaining-power and strikes hours only. Tompion's work was in good company.

However, Queen Anne was not inclined to foot her brother-in-law's bills out of hand—'Her Majesty has no occasion for his [Tompion's] clocks and watches'—but it seems that eventually she agreed to a settlement of £126 4s 'in full of his bills for a new swing clock and for work done for Her Majesty from 1702 to 1708'. The former may conceivably have been the 'Barnard' Tompion, *q.v.*

So, the time has arrived to consider the royal commissions that Tompion executed; and, if a start is made with his long-case clocks, one characteristic immediately catches the attention. There is a startling similarity between the most magnificent and monumental creations that bear his name, and those made by Daniel Quare, even if only in the larger elements. Both makers, for example, seem to have favoured a height between 9 and 10 feet, and nearer the latter; both favoured gilt bases, of decorative form and substantial load-bearing capacity; both favoured hoods surmounted by gilt figures rather than the abstract forms of urns, flambeaux, pineapples and the like which were the normal fashion. At the least, it might be assumed that they used the same source for some of their cases, although there is as yet no evidence as to what that source might have been.

Tompion's royal commissions divide happily into three sections, long-case clocks, bracket or table clocks, and barometers. Taking them in that order, the first
75 long-case clock to be reviewed is unhappily no longer in
76 77 the Royal Collection. This is the clock popularly known
78 as the 'Record' Tompion; this title is a misnomer the
derivation of which is obscure but presumably relates to the then-excessive price which it fetched on the open market, many years ago now.

This particular clock is said to have been made for William III's bedchamber at Hampton Court—like Quare's remarkable year clock—and to have been removed because its ticking was found to be a nuisance. If this is true, it places the date of the clock during or after 1699, on account of enlargements that were being carried out at that location. The clock has a two-train movement and a three-months' duration of going, and is equipped with maintaining-power; but the most unusual feature is the provision of perpetual calendar work, that is, automatic provision for leap years, which, of all Tompion's clocks, is found only in this example and in the equation clock made for Queen Anne's husband, Prince George of Denmark, which will be described next.

The finely figured walnut case of the 'Record' Tompion is lavishly fitted with fire-gilt ornaments of the highest quality, the hood being surmounted by a figure of Minerva on a pedestal, the front of which bears the cypher of William III. Tompion's preference for trusses, gilded and decorative, at various points on his large royal clocks has been the subject of special study—superbly executed even though, often, well above eye level, the same designs can be found on several of his clocks, supporting the pedestal on top of the hood, or at the four corners of the trunk immediately below the hood. These large clocks also rest on gilt-metal bases of elaborate design and construction, with decorative motifs incorporating Cupids, swags and scroll feet. This clock, incidentally, conforms well with the usual proportions of a palace clock, being 10 feet 2 inches high, and with a dial 12 inches square.

The dial of this clock is one of the first on which Tompion employed a tiny cross in the outermost zone of the chapter ring to mark half-quarter hours. There are two calendar slots, the upper one indicating the name of each month and its number of days, while the lower shows the day of the month according to the perpetual calendar motion work.

The history of this clock is a sad one. Queen Victoria gave it to her cousin, the second Duke of Cambridge (1819–1904), and upon his death it was sold in Christie's auction rooms, for 125 guineas, to the late Percy Webster, a prominent dealer and authority on clocks and watches. Even so long ago as that, the amount paid for this clock was ridiculously small; seemingly, the catalogue made no mention that the clock was by Tompion, it being included in the sale only at the last moment as 'Lot 284. A Clock in tall walnutwood Case moulded with chased ormolu'. Webster sold the clock to a certain George Dunn, of Maidenhead, upon whose death in 1914 the clock was once again auctioned and again bought by Percy Webster, this time for 380 guineas. Next it found its

79. (Left) *The year-going Equation clock made by Thomas Tompion for William III: full length front view.* (Royal Collection)

80. (Right) *Detail of hood and dial of Tompion's royal Equation clock.* (Royal Collection)

81. (Right) *The dial of the Equation clock partially dismantled to reveal the motion work.* (Alan Lloyd Collection)

82. (Far right) *The movement of the Equation clock, from above. The 'kidney piece' can be clearly seen behind the dial arch.* (Alan Lloyd Collection)

85. (Right) *Detail of hood and dial of the Tompion and Banger Year Equation Clock.* (Royal Collection)

86. (Far right) *The partially dismantled dial of the Tompion and Banger Year Equation Clock, showing the motion work.* (Alan Lloyd Collection)

83. (Left) *The Tompion and Banger Year Equation clock with perpetual Calendar: full length front view.* (Royal Collection)

84. (Above) *The Tompion and Banger clock as seen in the Pictorial Inventory: a noticeable feature is the replacement of the ball finial surmounting the hood.* (Royal Collection)

87. (Far right) *The movement of the Tompion and Banger Clock showing some of the complications of the calendar work.* (Alan Lloyd Collection)

way to D. A. F. Wetherfield of Blackheath, one of the great collectors of clocks in the early part of the present century. His famous clock collection was sold by private treaty, when Wetherfield died in 1928, to the well-known Bond Street antique dealers Mallet & Son, acting in collaboration with Percy Webster and Arthur Vernay of New York. The clock was sold to an American collector, Francis P. Garvan, for £5,000 and was exhibited for several years at the Pennsylvania Museum. However, it returned to England in 1934 to become part of the collection of Mr J. S. Sykes, and when it was displayed at the 'Five Centuries of British Timekeeping' exhibition at London's Goldsmiths' Hall in October 1955, the catalogue noted 'fortunately, it has now returned permanently to England'. As it turned out, nothing could have been further from the truth. It subsequently went back to America for a very substantial price and is now reported to be languishing in a warehouse at Colonial Williamsburg, the authorities there being quite unable to find any suitable surroundings in which to show it to its proper advantage. There can be no doubt whatsoever that such an intrinsic part of the horological heritage of Britain should never have been permitted to leave its country of origin in the first place; but once having done so, the Review Committee on the Export of Works of Art apparently have no power to stop it happening again.

From one famous royal clock that escaped the Royal Collection to two others that, happily, remain intact therein. The first of these was also made for William III,
79 80 81 82 probably during the closing years of the seventeenth century, and is the earliest extant Equation Clock by the great clockmaker; as such, it inevitably enters the controversy concerning Joseph Williamson's claim to have invented equation work. The clock movement, with its year duration of going—in practice, between 380 and 390 days seems attainable—has no striking-train, since the sheer size of the weight needed to drive a clock of this type took up so much room within the trunk of the case that accommodation for a second such, necessary to provide motive power for striking-action, was out of the question. The escapement is inverted, that is to say its anchor pallets point upwards, and it is located at the base of the movement; the pendulum, as a result, swings behind the dial and in front of the weight.

The dial of this clock is its most eye-catching feature. Divided in twenty-four hours, its outer minute circle—which is inscribed 'Apparent Time'—moves backwards and forwards to record against the fixed hour circle, which is marked 'Equal Time', the phenomenon known as the equation of time, *q.v.* There are two apertures above the dial, the lower exposing an annual calendar ring while the upper shows the signs of the zodiac and the ecliptic circle for the sun's position. The lever actuating the bolt-and-shutter maintaining-power is located at the right-hand side of the dial, and the winding-square, which operation of this lever reveals, is sited within the chapter ring, at twelve o'clock. Such was the critical friction factor in year clocks—the long duration required wheelwork, pivots and the like of the finest quality and strength, as well as accuracy of construction, otherwise it could not be attained—that it was even considered desirable to counterpoise the minute hand, which has been done in this case, while seconds hands were dispensed with altogether.

The case of this clock, of beautifully figured walnut veneer, has a door in front of the dial as well as a sliding hood, suggesting a fashion change: hood doors were a desirable new feature. A unique characteristic at this time is the broken arch, required above the dial to show the calendar work; it contrasts strangely with the early convex moulding below the hood, and the fire-gilt ball finial surmounting it. This is a small clock by Tompion's 'royal' standards, being a mere 7 feet 3 inches to the finial pedestal, and with a 12-inch square dial, excluding the semi-arch.

The second Tompion clock to grace the Chamber 83 84 85 86 87
Floor Corridor in Buckingham Palace, is yet another year clock with equation work, but this time also with a perpetual calendar. It was made by Tompion and Banger about 1703, to the order of Prince George of Denmark, husband of Queen Anne. It is a larger clock than the other, being 8 feet 6 inches high excluding the figure surmounting it—now a French Cupid, which is undoubtedly a replacement—and four vase finials are missing; its walnut case is more elaborate, although one feature missing is the lenticle of pointed-arch shape at the bottom of the trunk door, so designed to permit easy judgement as to whether or not the pendulum, its bob clearly visible against the point, was in beat. Otherwise, the gilt-brass pierced frieze panels, the side frets, the trusses and all the more elaborate and decorative elements of these clocks are extensively represented, including a gilt cast base formed of swags of flowers with cherubs' heads between the open scroll feet. The dial in this instance has a concave-sided and flat-topped broken arch wherein is a fan-shaped aperture showing the days of the month, the months of the year, the signs of the zodiac and the sun's place in the ecliptic, as well as the number of years after leap year. There is also a provision—which seems to have undergone some alteration if the present dial be compared with an illustration of it printed about 1760—for showing the days of the month according to the Old Style as well as the New. Within the chapter ring itself is another fan-shaped opening displaying the

88. (Right) *An eight-day three-train longcase clock by Thomas Tompion, in Windsor Castle.* (Royal Collection)

day of the week, and the planet after which each day is named; while finally, below the chapter ring, is a square window to show the day of the month 'as in a Common Clock', the big difference being that, as a perpetual Calendar, it is always correct whether the month has thirty, thirty-one, twenty-eight or even twenty-nine days. The main dial rings operate exactly as in the other Equation Clock, the outer circle, '*Temp. apparens*', moving backwards and forwards to correct for the equation of time, against the inner circle, '*Temp. Aequale*'. Yet again, bolt-and-shutter maintaining-power is activated by a lever in a crescent-shaped opening at the right of the dial plate, the winding-square being at twelve o'clock as before.

Both the clocks described above have endured changes of environment over the years. George III personally selected them for the furnishing of the Queen's House, as Buckingham House came to be called, and they were brought in, probably from Kensington Palace, in 1762. Later, they were taken to St James's Palace and, fortunately, were rescued from the fire that occurred there in 1809. In more recent times, they have graced the northern section of the Bedchamber (second) Floor Corridor, on the East Front of Buckingham Palace, and both clocks were displayed, by special permission of King George V, at an exhibition of clocks by Thomas Tompion organized by a well-known City of London wine-merchant as well as the owner of a fine clock collection, one F. H. Green, acting in association with the clock-making and restoring firm See page 292 Watkins of Carey Street; this was staged at 13 Royal Exchange, in the City, at the latter end of 1933. They do not appear to have been seen in public since.

The other long-case clocks by Tompion in the Royal Collection pale somewhat by comparison with the
88 foregoing. At Windsor, for example, there is an eight-day clock standing 8 feet $6\frac{1}{2}$ inches high, the walnut long-case being, perhaps, the most interesting feature, since it also has gilt scrolling trusses to support the hood, which is surmounted by a gilt pineapple and two vase finials. The hood is also the location for pierced frets of repoussé gilt brass, backed by crimson silk. The movement originally had three trains, but the six-bell chime was removed by Vulliamy, who also fitted one of his diamond-cross-sectioned pendulum rods; yet the anchor escapement remains untouched. This clock has been mis-reported on various occasions as being of month duration, in an amboyna-wood case, and so on; it is worth recording that the movement serial number on the back plate is 275, indicating a date *c.*1698.

While this clock is a fine specimen despite Vulliamy's depredations, even he could not wreak any worse havoc on another Tompion long-case clock, of 'grandmother' height, being only 6 feet $4\frac{1}{2}$ inches tall. Believed, even in the 1920s, to be wholly authentic, and reproduced as such in *Practical Clock and Watchmaker*, issue dated 15th December 1928, neither the mahogany case nor the dial of this clock is original; nor is its provenance known. The eight-day striking movement bears the serial number 293, which could indicate a date *c.*1699.

It is now time to turn to the spring clocks, for table or bracket, made by Tompion under Royal Command. Again, the first—and arguably the most important of
89 all Tompion's clocks, no matter of what kind—no longer graces the Royal Collection. In Tompion's day, clocks with a year's duration of going were considered something remarkable, even for a weight-driven machine—and Tompion made at least four of these—while a similar achievement, only spring-driven, would have been thought little short of miraculous. Tompion seems to have been the only English clockmaker to succeed in making one.

It has been said that it was only William III's extravagance that made it possible for Tompion to indulge in these flamboyant masterpieces; and perhaps, like many other works of art through the ages, it has taken centuries for their true worth to be appreciated. Yet it appears that Tompion cannot claim all the kudos for himself. The making of long-duration timepieces of any kind in his day—over eight days, that is—was a difficult feat, in engineering terms, requiring a great deal of finesse in design and construction. Tompion certainly discussed the problems he encountered with others of his own kind, but more especially with Hooke, whose wide-ranging intellectual capabilities were probably better attuned to solving them than if he had been a narrow technician. In any event, it is possibly true to say that, in the greatest flights of achievement bearing Tompion's name, there can be detected the influence of others among the most eminent scientists of his day.

Everything about Tompion's year spring clock is sumptuous. Essentially on two levels, the main carcase of the case is of veneered ebony. Most of the ornaments are in silver, and the clock—like other Tompion royal masterpieces—sits on a highly decorative metal base which consists of gilt scroll feet, connected by silver swags to a gilt central mask head. The larger, lower level of the clock proper has shaped glazed panels front and back, at the front elaborately embellished with silver ornamentation. The next, smaller level which contains the dial, has, in addition to the silver ornament, four fire-gilt Doric columns, one at each

89. *Sometimes called the 'Silver King', the famous year-going spring-driven clock by Thomas Tompion, made originally for William III, has recently passed from Lord Mostyn into the custody of the British Museum. In this picture the ormolu spear, normally held in the outstretched right hand of Britannia, had been removed for safe keeping while the clock was sent away for overhaul. A comparable, but not identical, figure surmounts the 'Record' Tompion, see fig. 76.* (Christie's, London)

90. *This informal picture shows H.M. Queen Elizabeth The Queen Mother admiring Thomas Tompion's remarkable spring-driven year-duration clock, when it was privately exhibited just outside London in 1954.* (Southern Press)

corner. Above this rises the flat-topped dome, on the front of which appears an escutcheon containing the arms of William III, while at its front corners appear the lion and the unicorn, with the rose and thistle at the back, and the towering figure of Britannia surmounting the pedestal on top. The total effect is quite overwhelming.

Mechanically, the clock is no less of a miracle. Known to run for as long as thirteen months—a record of winding has been kept since 1793—it strikes the hours and has pull quarter-repeating action powered from an auxiliary spring. The larger lower level of the clock contains the two extremely strong mainsprings in their 4-inch diameter barrels, accompanied by their fusees and connecting-chains, also of extra-strong construction; Tompion usually used gut in this context, and he was clearly aware of the extraordinarily large energy source needed in this clock. The pendulum of the clock swings in front of the movement—another similarity with Tompion's large weight-driven year clocks—and is regulated by a worm and sector arrangement which raises or lowers it as necessary; the decorated bob can be seen swinging through the panel on the front of the clock base. Behind the pendulum appears the Tompion signature on an oval plaque which is effectively on the front plate of the mechanism; it is repeated on a silver cartouche within the dial centre. There are elaborate silver spandrels of unusual design, and a fan-shaped calendar slot which gives the day of the week and a planetary figure representing that day.

Unfortunately there are no definite records of the commissioning of this clock, which was probably made between 1695 and 1700. There is in the Lord Chamberlain's Accounts an item 'fine clock £600' which Tompion seemingly supplied in 1695 (PRO, Calendar of Treasury Books 1695) but no positive connection can be established from this; and indeed an eighteenth-century letter relates that the clock cost £1,500, and 'the person to repair it, if wanted, is Dutton, Fleet Street, London'. William III left the clock to the Lord Chamberlain of the Household, the Earl of Leicester, whose niece, Lady Sidney Sherard, gave it to Lady Yonge, through whom it descended to the present owner, Lord Mostyn. The beauty and importance of this clock, incorporating as it does everything quintessential in the finest practice of the clockmaking art at the end of the seventeenth century, cannot possibly be overstated.*

It is only to be expected that such an eminent craftsman as Tompion, whose output of timekeepers of all kinds was almost certainly the largest in London in his day, and who was greatly favoured by successive sovereigns into the bargain, would have produced some fine pieces whose royal associations, if they ever existed, can nowadays no longer be proven beyond reasonable doubt; fine clocks nonetheless, some of these will be discussed elsewhere in this book. His reputation of recent years, of course, has been even further enhanced as a result of the growth of public interest in antiquarian horology; and this interest has been reflected in more recent additions to the Royal Collection. On the twenty-fifth anniversary of King George V's accession to the throne, that is, in 1935, the Corporation of the City of London made a presentation of an exceptionally fine Tompion ebony-cased bracket
clock, bearing Tompion's serial number 388. This clock 91
had been made originally, it would seem, for one of the Hesse family of Denmark, whose arms appear on the dome. This two-train clock has five-bell pull quarter-repeating; and there are subsidiary dials for strike/

*In May 1982 it was publicly announced that Lord Mostyn intended to sell this most famous of Tompion's clocks, and that it would be auctioned on 14th July. Fears were immediately voiced that, like the 'Record' Tompion, it would leave these shores; but these proved unfounded as, even before the sale could be held, Lord Mostyn had reached agreement with the Government to permit its acquisition by the British Museum for a price which, after tax, is stated to have been half a million pounds.

91. *Bracket clock no. 388 by Thomas Tompion, which was presented to George V.* (Royal Collection)

92. *Tompion bracket clock no. 204, from the late Queen Mary's Collection.* (Museum of London)

silent and for regulation by raising or lowering the pendulum. The clock was completely overhauled by Daniel Parkes, a celebrated craftsman-restorer in Clerkenwell who continues to exercise his skills to the present day; it seems that, for some reason, the dial had been coated with red varnish, and when this was removed, its original brilliancy had obviously been well preserved. Incidentally, this clock was one of the highlights of the Tompion Exhibition at the Royal Exchange in 1933, to which reference has already been made.

The late Queen Mary was an enthusiastic collector of
92 works of art in her own right; and when she was widowed, she retained a second Tompion clock, which had been presented to Their Majesties on that same Silver Jubilee celebration in 1935, by the London Chamber of Commerce. This particular clock was exhibited at the Victoria and Albert Museum in 1954, in a special display of some of her many art treasures; subsequently, it was placed in the Museum of London on permanent loan from the Lord Chamberlain's Office, together with a great deal of other material from Queen Mary's London home during her later years, Marlborough House, and it is accessioned as part of her collection.

The clock itself is typical of one of Tompion's best-quality spring clocks. The eight-day movement is in an ebonized case with ormolu mounts and a basket top. There are the usual striking- and repeating-actions, a verge escapement, and the signed gilt dial with silvered chapters and aperture for a mock pendulum, has subsidiary dials in the upper corners, for strike/silent and regulation. The back plate is decoratively engraved in the usual fashion and includes the signature 'Thomas Tompion Londini Fecit' and the serial number 204. At one time this clock passed through the hands of the well-known dealer Percy Webster who, incidentally, was Master of the Clockmakers' Company in 1927.

It is always held that truth is stranger than fiction. There have been two curiously identical occurrences concerning two different Tompion spring clocks, of recent years, both of them being among the very finest and most desirable of Tompion's models, and one of the clocks certainly having royal antecedents. The first such curious happening took place with Tompion no. 222, whose particular claim to fame rests on its being the smallest Tompion spring striking clock so far recorded, standing only $6\frac{7}{16}$ inches high without the handle. The clock was bought in 1937 by the late Courtenay Ilbert, possibly the world's greatest ever clock- and watch-collector, who died in 1956 and whose collection was then acquired for the nation and is now housed in the British Museum.

The case of this tiny clock, as found in 1937, was of pearwood which had been japanned black. Twelve years later, in 1949, there turned up at Sotheby's a magnificent ebony case with silver fittings containing a movement that was clearly not the work of the great master, seemingly having been made about 1830 albeit adorned with a silver plaque inscribed 'Tompion'. When trial was made, there could be no doubt whatever that number 222 had originally graced this beautiful case—it was not of the customary design but of the 'lift off' type in which the movement fits on to a metal base to which the case can then be attached. Mr Ilbert bought the original case and brought the two parts together again; even so, the japanned case may well have been intended for use when the clock was travelling, to avoid any risk of damage to the other, more elaborate housing. At some later date, perhaps early in the nineteenth century, it had been decided to

93. (Above) *The silver-mounted gilt-brass clock case and dial of a clock of undoubted royal provenance, made by Thomas Tompion.* (Private collection)

94. (Left) *Side and back views, showing detail of the magnificent case of the Tompion clock—winding is through the side.* (Private collection)

Falling
Rising
Rain
Fair
Dry
Stormy

Falling
Raine
Change
able
Raine.
Faire.
Much
Raine.
Clear.
Stormy
Settled
Faire.

95. (Far left) *The Tompion barometer at Buckingham Palace.* (Royal Collection)

96. (Left) *The Tompion barometer at Hampton Court Palace.* (Royal Collection)

97. (Right) *A second Tompion barometer at Hampton Court Palace.* (Royal Collection)

make two clocks out of one, by fitting the spare case with a so-called 'Tompion' movement.

Much more recently, history seemed about to repeat
93 itself. In February 1971 there appeared at Christie's a
94 superb and unique small silver-mounted gilt-brass
clock case and dial, a cartouche on the latter being signed 'T. Tompion, Londini fecit'. With a height of only 8 inches and a dial of $4\frac{3}{4}$ inches square, this was yet another of Tompion's tiny products; and clearly the mechanism was of special significance, since at the top corners were blued-steel regulating-switches, that on the left for rise-and-fall of the pendulum, and on the right for alternative escapements, the incised letters P and B giving optional pendulum or balance. The dome on the rectangular case incorporated on either side the royal monogram WR repeated and reversing, surmounted by a crown. Uniquely, the clock case had three handles, the usual scrolled lifting-handle on top being allied to two vertically mounted carrying-handles at the sides. In other respects, the case had ogee mouldings surrounding the doors, sides and top, while the rear door, sides and top were mounted with pierced silver chased with scrolling foliage, trumpeting putti, masks and swags of flowers. Behind all this sumptuousness was a French *grande sonnerie* carriage-clock movement with platform lever escapement.

There were certain clues to be observed. Tompion's finest work post-dated the accession of William III in 1689; and when the latter went campaigning in Ireland and the Low Countries, there are records of 'folding' and 'travelling' equipment made for his use, although no specific reference to a clock. When this clock case came up for sale, however, there already existed a movement only, of a Tompion travelling-clock, with alternate balance and pendulum arrangements—the only one of its kind attributed to Tompion so far—which bore the date 1693, which was that of the Irish campaign and, incidentally, the only known example of Tompion dating one of his clocks. Could the two belong together?

Indeed they could; but on only one occasion to date, within the private confines of a celebrated London antiques shop, have they in fact been put together. The case and original dial—but with the French movement removed—were found exactly to fit with the Tompion movement once its non-original dial had been dis-

98. *The Tompion sundial at Kew, which is identical to another at Hampton Court Palace.* (Crown copyright)

mantled. In view of the several unusual features, such as winding-arrangements through a side panel, it is inconceivable that these two main elements were not once but one clock, and a magnificent masterpiece even for the great Tompion. The sad feature of this situation, however, is that, despite all efforts, so far it has not proved possible to unite them permanently, and they remain in separate hands. In view of the enormous importance of the object, the only proper solution, and one which should be aimed for in the longer term, is that the complete clock should find a permanent resting-place in some national collection, where it can be appreciated by everyone.

So much published material extols Tompion's many and manifest virtues that even the great man himself could not object if this chapter includes an anecdote that might perhaps set his feet firmly on the ground once again. It is taken from a delightful little book by a watchmaker, practising in New Bond Street in London, by the name of Adam Thomson. Published in 1842, its title is *Time and Time-Keepers*, and on page 76 thereof will be found the following:

> During the seventeenth century there existed a great taste for striking clocks .... Several by Thomas Tompion not only struck the quarters on eight bells but also struck the hour after each quarter. At twelve o'clock forty-four blows were struck, and 113 between twelve and one. Failures in the striking part of these clocks were attended with much inconvenience, as they would sometimes continue to strike without cessation, until the weight or spring had gone down, and they were frequently contrived to go for a month. A clock of Tompion's, upon this construction, caused much annoyance to H.R.H. The Duchess of Gloucester, soon after her marriage. This clock was fixed in an apartment adjoining the bed-chamber; the failure took place about two o'clock in the morning. It struck quarter after quarter, each followed by the hour, but as the clock continued to go properly, each quarter of an hour was followed by a silence of about two minutes which, if possible, rather aggravated the annoyance. As the case could not be opened, the clock continued to strike until eight.

Thomas Tompion must have been not only a brilliant craftsman but an amazing organizer—perhaps administrator would be a better term. There are bills in the records of the Lord Chamberlain's Office demonstrating how busy he was on other royal commissions—many of them elaborate watches, for presentation to governments and officials in places like Algiers, Tripoli and Tunis to quote examples from the period 1694-8—while at the same time, he was keeping up a phenomenal and varied output not only for royal consumption at home but indeed for any rich citizen who wished to avail himself of 'one of Mr. Tompion's timepieces'. Like Quare, he also made barometers, and there are three superb examples in the Royal Collection, 95
one at Buckingham Palace and two at Hampton Court; 96 97
curiously, these are the only unquestionably genuine barometers of his manufacture to have been discovered up to the present, although there is documentary evidence to show that he certainly made others, notably for Hooke and Robert Boyle, as well as the Hon.

Robert Harley. Unlike Quare, Tompion also made sundials, and there are fine examples of his royal work in
98 this field at old Kew Palace and in the gardens of Hampton Court. Finally, he and Graham made the first orrery—a mechanical model of the solar system—although the particular machine from which the name derives was a copy of their design, made by an instrument-maker called Rowley for his client, the Earl of Orrery.

Tompion also outshone Quare in the number of apprentices bound to him. Starting in 1673, no fewer than twenty-three were accredited, although the last was in 1699, by which time Tompion may have been starting to take a less active role in day-to-day affairs of business. The names and dates of his apprentices are as follows:

Michael Knight	1673	Edward Banger	1687
Robert Pattison	1676	Robert Creed	1689
John Webster	1676	George Harrison	1689
Benjamin Harris	1677	John Hilton	1690
William Morelley	1680	Robert Anderson	1691
Jeremiah Martin	1680	Robert Youell	1691
Benjamin Sacheverell	1680	William Swann	1692
Edward Boone	1681	Thomas Davis	1694
Charles Lloyd	1683	Nicholas Heather	1694
George Allatt	1683	William Thompson	1698
Joseph Audley	1683	Anthony Walraven	1699
Whitestone Littlemore	1684		

It is a curious thing that, in the case both of Quare and of Tompion, not one of their apprentices achieved any sort of subsequent eminence in the craft; perhaps the greatest artists cannot also be the best teachers. As for Tompion, on his death the goodwill and stock-in-trade of his business passed to George Graham, his partner of three years. If it was a strange enigma that Tompion made so many royal clocks yet never received a Royal Warrant, then what can be said of Graham? Here was a craftsman certainly as distinguished as his former master but perhaps a little more retiring, so that the same degree of fame to some extent eluded him—but a Fellow of the Royal Society, no less, and by far the most important clock- and watchmaker throughout the first half of the eighteenth century, for he lived until 1751. Yet not only did he also never receive a Royal Warrant but, so far as can be established, he never made any timepieces for the sovereigns during whose reigns he worked in London; and there is no representation of his craftsmanship in the Royal Collection today. It must seem a sad and serious omission.

Tompion's death in November 1713 was the end of an era in every sense of the word. The following year, on 1st August, a new sovereign was proclaimed—George I. Son of an Elector of Hanover, he was able to claim the British throne through his mother, who was a granddaughter of James I. His reign lasted thirteen years and must have created a constitutional shambles. Unable to speak any English, he had to depend wholly upon his Ministers, chief among them being Sir Robert Walpole, with whom he managed to communicate upon affairs of state in very indifferent Latin; most of his life, however, appears to have been devoted to pleasures of the grosser kind, and several of his German mistresses were ennobled with English titles.

4 The Hanovers sire a scientist king

It would be stretching credulity too far to assume that George I had any horological tastes or interests whatsoever. However, even he must have had to tell the time, so that royal clock- and watchmakers were indeed accredited to his Court; and naturally they were men of substance and capability.

The first to be considered here is Joseph Antram. Little enough is known about him; he was apprenticed to Charles Gretton on 17th January 1697 for a period of seven years, being eventually admitted to the Freedom of the Clockmakers' Company on 7th October 1706. He seems to have taken no further part in the Company's affairs, and the next we hear of him is contained in an account of the travels in London in 1710 of the German bibliographer Zacharias Conrad von Uffenbach (1683–1735). The following extract undoubtedly refers to him:

> On our way back we got down at St. Dunstan's Church, [Fleet Street], and went to a clockmaker's opposite to it, Herr Antram, a young and most polite Englishman who speaks French tolerably. We did not only see his watches, which are not at all bad, and he has in hand at the moment a most elegant watch for the Swedish Ambassador. But we were most anxious to have an inspection of his famous invention of a clock which is set in motion by light, without wheels or springs. It is like a great English striking clock, and it stands in the middle of his room with all four sides of glass, so that one can see that it is not like an ordinary clock. It may, indeed, have no springs but it is not entirely without wheels, or at least rollers. If my memory is not at fault, everything depends on one basis, as in the case of the so-called Cartesian candlesticks. The tin tube in which the light is placed has below it an embolum with a button, to which is fastened a chain or string; this is wound round several wheels to which the discs of the clock are fastened. When the light burns low, it ascends by means of the weight attached to the end of the cord, turns the rollers, and at the same time the hands on the dial marking the hours and minutes (which are fastened to the rollers). If the light is extinguished the minute hand stops immediately; but if it is lit once more, the clock goes again. So it is no wonder that Herr Antram maintains that the movement of these clocks is inaudible, because the discs and wheels need no indentations or teeth, but are merely rollers one slowly propelling the other.

Antram died in 1723 so that his effective working life was only a matter of seventeen years. There is some evidence that Benjamin Gray, who became clockmaker to George II (*q.v.*), was making movements for him, certainly around 1707. A number of very fine clocks of his have survived, a typical one being a large spring clock in ebony-veneered case, the dial incorporating complicated calendar indications which included month, date, day of the week and sign for the day. The verge escapement action was repeated at the front by means of a mock pendulum; and there were alternative quarter-chiming facilities utilizing one or six bells. This particular clock had originally belonged to Sophia, mother of George I. Another of his products which, to judge from the royal cypher incorporated into the arch, may also have formerly graced one of the palaces, is a magnificent three-train musical spring clock in a fine walnut case with ormolu mounts. Thought to date from *c.*1715, and of break-arch design, this timekeeper has the music indicator in the arch, with its controlling pointer sited accordingly; twelve tunes are listed, and the action consists of thirteen bells actuated by some twenty hammers, i.e. some of the bells are provided with two hammers to produce a fast, staccato effect. There is a mock pendulum aperture above the dial centre, two subsidiary dials providing strike/silent control and regulation, and below centre a window for the day of the month. Surmounting the whole structure is a fine Father Time.

Sadly, nothing remains of Joseph Antram's work in the Royal Collection today.

Another maker who was active in the Court at this time was Thomas Cartwright. Watchmaker to both

99. (Left) *The back plate of a watch movement by Thomas Cartwright, showing the unorthodox signature.* (Clockmakers' Company, London)

Queen Anne and George I, he seems to have started his apprenticeship on 4th December 1693 with Richard Watts, at some point along the line being turned over to Christopher Gould, and either never completed it at all or failed for some other reason to obtain his admission to the Freedom of the Clockmakers' Company. Britten states that he lived 'behind the Exchange'; and all the known timekeepers by him claim a royal association, sometimes in slightly unorthodox form. There is, for example, in the Clockmakers' Company Collection (cat. no. 89), a quite typical specimen, one of his watch
99 movements which is signed 'Thos. Cartwright Principi Horologs. London'. This particular item has a spectacular feature on the back plate in the shape of a silver-rimmed cock, the table being of crystal and the centre a gold cap with a garnet. On his clocks, however, he seems to have been content with describing himself as 'Watchmaker to the King'. Cartwright died in 1741, and, like Antram's, his work is not represented in the Royal Collection today: he was, however, a watchmaker, and fewer period watches than clocks have survived over the years.

A third clockmaker of some consequence around this time was Richard Vick. He seems to have had an unusual start to his career; bound apprentice to Richard Speakman on 31st January 1692 for seven years, the customary term, he was, at some point, turned over to a craftsman simply listed as Aslin—forename presumably unknown, but this was probably Francis Asselin, of French extraction, admitted to the Company in 1687—and then went on to take up his Freedom with the Haberdashers. He was only admitted to the Clockmakers' Company on 2nd April 1702. However, he went on to serve all the higher offices in the Company, becoming Master in 1729. His business premises were in the Strand; and he seems to have had a long career, for Baillie lists him as dying in 1750.

Vick was appointed Keeper of the Clocks in the King's Palace and, as such, provided some of them himself. He is also said—by Robertson & Walker—to have supplied a repeating watch for the King, although this cannot be traced. Of his surviving royal clocks, one is a quarter-chiming eight-day clock in a boulle case, standing 2 feet 2 inches high. The last-mentioned authority describes the ormolu ornaments on this clock as 'relating to Revelry'. Better known, however, is a long-case clock at Windsor Castle, said to date about 1740, although the 100
bell-shaped top to the hood, with its three flambeaux finials, could well be at least twenty years later. A two-train clock with strike/silent in the arch and a day-of-the-month calendar above VI, it is illustrated in Britten's 6th edition, 1932, as figure 794.

It is worth digressing for a moment at this point simply to notice, in passing, a royal craftsman in an allied trade—that of instrument maker—who seems momentarily to have impinged upon the horological scene. John Rowley, Instrument Maker and Master of Mechanics to George I, made the original Orrery, which is a machine for representing, by appropriate gearing, the various motions of the heavenly bodies. His machine was so called on account of its acquisition, about 1713, by the fourth Earl of Orrery, after whom it was named; but the inscription on the object itself gives credit for the original invention to George Graham in 1700. In fact, that earlier instrument is jointly signed by Tompion and Graham and is in the Museum of the History of Science, at Oxford, while Rowley's Orrery is to be found in the Science Museum in London. Upon the death of the Earl in August 1731, his large and exceedingly fine collection of scientific instruments, which he bequeathed to Christ Church, Oxford, was catalogued by Thomas Wright, of Fleet Street, who was Scientific Instrument Maker to George II, but who must not be confused with another Thomas Wright, of the Poultry, who became royal watchmaker later in the same century.

George I died on 11th June 1727, and he was succeeded by his only son, George Augustus, born in 1683, some eleven years before his father's unhappy marriage to Sophia Dorothea, heiress to the Duchy of Celle, had been dissolved. George II, unlike his father,

100. (Left) *The two-train longcase clock by Richard Vick at Windsor Castle.* (Royal Collection)

spoke English fluently even though he had lived in Hanover until 1714. Much influenced by the wise advice of his wife, Caroline of Anspach, George II became a good constitutional monarch, and it was not until the later part of his thirty-three year reign that some of the old regal power endeavoured to reassert itself, being finally manifested in his strong dislike for, and struggle against, William Pitt. This sovereign died at Kensington Palace on 25th October 1760.

Like the previous one, it cannot be said that the reign of George II produced very much of special interest in terms of royal horology. One craftsman only stands out from the common herd, and he did not appear on the scene until nearly half-way through the period concerned. For the moment the incumbents during the previous reign continued in office.

Two craftsmen did make fleeting appearances, however, of whom one was Godfrie Poy. Virtually nothing has come to light about this man: Baillie hails him as 'a fine maker' without filling out the picture in the slightest, apart from listing some mouth-watering objects ascribed to him. It is left to Britten to write up a 'choice, small pull-repeating and alarm clock . . . said to have been made for George II when Prince of Wales'. Where that item is now has not been recorded, but clocks and watches of Poy's make are not too uncommon, so that he had, it might seem, a reasonable output. His dates are given, by both Britten and Baillie, as 1718–50; and he is not to be confused with another clockmaker of the same name, save for the more conventional spelling of 'Godfrey', who seems to have been at work in the Haymarket in London, somewhat later in the eighteenth century.

The other craftsman is rather better documented, and very much more of an impresario, it would seem. This was Charles Clay, maker of 'machine watches'—and much else besides. A Yorkshireman from Flockton, in the West Riding and only a handful of miles from Wakefield, he first comes into prominence in 1716, when he petitioned the King for a Patent in respect of a repeating device for pocket watches, said to have taken him several years and much money to perfect. This immediately aroused the indignation of the Clockmakers' Company—and, in particular, of Daniel Quare, who had already fought off another similar encroachment thirty years before, in the case of Edward Barlow, *q.v.* There was a counter-petition. The whole matter turned out something of a 'cliff-hanger', with Clay's petition making favourable headway throughout all the early stages, even to the point where a Warrant had been prepared for the King's signature, granting him a Patent. The Company immediately petitioned the Lords of the Privy Council to be further heard on the matter and, in the end, a Committee of the whole Council reported unfavourably towards Clay, and the Patent was not granted. The Company recorded, ruefully, that their opposition in this affair had cost them £74 17s 11d. Three years later, in December 1719, Clay petitioned for a re-hearing so that the Company, once again, had to object; but this time, nothing seems to have come of it, and the subject was dropped.

Clay then passed out of the limelight for a while, meantime removing himself to London where, about 1720, he set up shop near St Mary-le-Strand Church. By 1723 he had been appointed Clockmaker to His Majesty's Board of Works, in which capacity he made a clock for the gatehouse of St James's Palace which was installed in 1731. It would not appear to have been a very sophisticated machine, to judge by contemporary references which show it to have had only one hand and a wooden dial made 'in a great number of small pieces, curiously dovetailed together'. The clock was removed in 1831, when the gateway was being repaired, and, since the roof was reported unsafe, it was not replaced. However, the local inhabitants missed it so much that they petitioned William IV for its return, whereupon the King asked the responsible authorities how it was that, if the roof was unsafe, it was yet considered a suitable occasional observation post from which a number of people could watch processions. After this, the clock is said to have been replaced, but with a new dial as well as the addition of a minute hand. This account does not at once appear to be reconcilable with the inscription B. L. Vulliamy attached to the movement which he installed in substitution for the earlier Hampton Court clock in 1835, *q.v.*; in any event, the gatehouse clock was finally taken away, and a completely new one fitted in its place in 1882.

It may be worth spending a moment to consider in detail the varying fortunes of the St James's Palace gatehouse clock, before returning to those of Charles Clay. Formerly the site of a leper hospital, the Palace was built by Henry VIII, and the gatehouse, apparently complete with clock although little is known about it, was finished in 1535. In those days, its one dial faced into the courtyard rather than outwards to the world at large; and this first clock seems to have given good service, as it is not heard of again until 1618, when it seems to have had to be repaired after being struck by lightning. As depicted in 1638, the clock had just such a diamond-shaped dial as might be expected for a turret clock of that time. During the late 1680s, a new clock for the gatehouse was supplied by Thomas Herbert—that shadowy royal clockmaker of whom so little is known—which had dials on both sides; and a belfry superstructure was added at the same time. This lasted until 1731, when Charles Clay installed his clock; this was replaced by Benjamin Vulliamy in 1799. This first Vulliamy clock survived until 1831, when it was removed while the roof was restored; in 1832 B. L. Vulliamy installed one of his own clocks in the gatehouse to replace his father's, which he then altered and set up at Hampton Court in 1835. Its slate dial still survives there. Finally, the second Vulliamy clock was replaced by Gillett & Johnston in 1882, and this clock remains there to the present day although it has been modernized by the addition of auto-winding units—this in 1976—and it was removed altogether for a short period during 1978, while the roof was being repaired.

101. *W. H. Pynes's* History of the Royal Residences . . . . *(1819) includes this aquatint in colour of the Cupola Room in Kensington Palace with, in the centre, Charles Clay's 'Temple of the Four Great Monarchies' clock.* (Guildhall Library, City of London)

In *The Weekly Journal* for 8th May 1736 there was a report that Charles Clay had exhibited a musical clock to the King and Queen, at Kensington Palace. Queen Caroline was so impressed that she ordered 50 guineas to be spent on tickets in a raffle to be held for the clock—this was a favourite way of disposing of such ultra-elaborate and highly-expensive items, for which there can hardly have been any clientele sufficiently wealthy to buy one outright. It does not seem to be recorded if the Queen was successful, nor is it known with absolute certainty which of a number of elaborate

THIS CLOCK

102. (Far left) *'The Temple of the Four Great Monarchies', Charles Clay's monumental musical clock: a general view, as now seen.* (Royal Collection)

103. (Left) *One of the two panels of Clay's clock not visible in the general view.* (Royal Collection)

104. (Below left) *The other panel hidden in the general view; the painting is by Amigoni, the figures in relief by Rysbrack.* (Royal Collection)

105. (Right) *The gilt-bronze group by L. F. Roubiliac which surmounts 'The Temple of the Four Great Monarchies'.* (Royal Collection)

106. (Below) *These figures, representing 'Europe' and 'Asia', recently rediscovered in Windsor Castle, once formed part of the decoration of Charles Clay's masterpiece.* (Royal Collection)

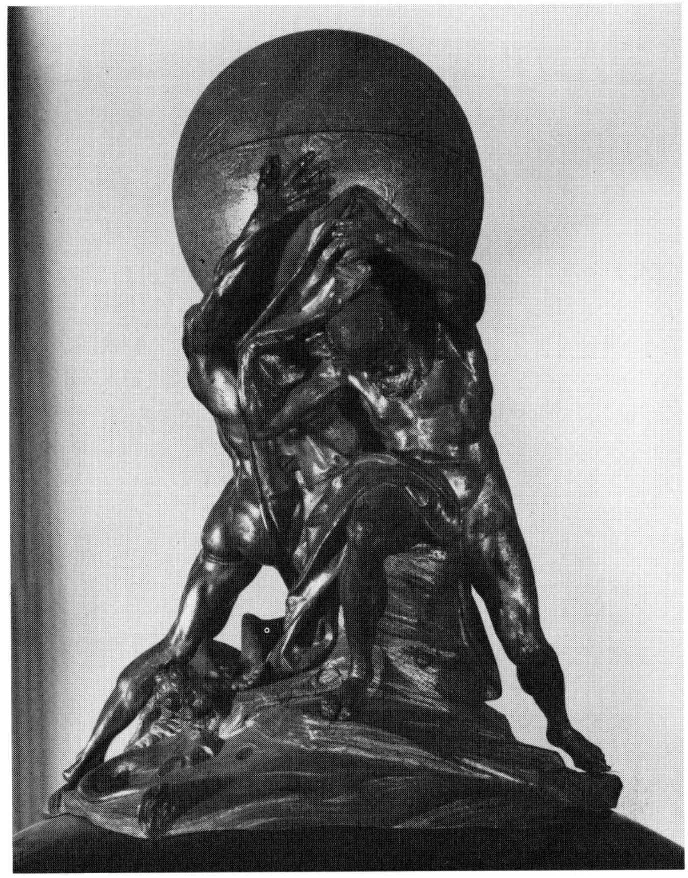

clocks by Clay was the prize. The Royal Collection does, nevertheless, include a Clay masterpiece—perhaps his greatest—albeit in a sadly distressed state: this was acquired by Augusta, Princess of Wales, in, or soon after, 1743.

This clock was called by Clay 'The Temple of the Four
102 Great Monarchies of the World'. The original base and
103 104 movement are now completely missing, but a news-
paper cutting of 31st December 1743 shows that it was still complete then and on exhibition, when it was described as 'begun by the late ingenious Mr. Charles Clay and finished by Mr. Pyke, Clock and Watchmaker in Bedford-Row, London'. It would, therefore, seem unlikely that the fate decreed by Clay himself, almost certainly for this particular clock, was ever carried out; for, in his obituary, which appeared in the *Gentleman's Magazine*, under date 25th February 1740, it was reported that 'three days before he died he ordered a Musical Machine, which had cost him about 20 years Time, and upwards of 2000L to bring to Perfection, to be beat to Pieces, and entirely destroyed, to prevent further Expence of the Time and Money of anyone who should attempt to finish it after his death'.

John Pyke, in Holborn before he moved to Bedford Row, apprenticed in 1710, admitted to the Freedom of the Clockmakers' Company in 1720, and died in 1762, is described by Baillie as 'eminent', and he must have been a remarkably competent man to take on anything as ambitious as one of Clay's clocks; the strange thing is
110 that his son, George Pyke, seems to have inherited a
111 predilection for such artistic complexities, for a magnificent musical and automata clock, with much of Clay's exuberant style about it, yet signed by him, is in the Museum of London. That clock is dated *c.*1760. Incidentally, yet another John Pyke, *fl.* 1747–*c.*1780, was signing his wares in the 1750s 'Clock and Watchmaker to the Prince of Wales'; he worked from Newgate Street.

How should one differentiate Clay from several other eighteenth-century makers of elaborate exhibition
107 clocks, like Jacob Lovelace for example? The answer
108 109 must be in the extraordinary quality of the artists and
musicians he persuaded to decorate his masterpieces, and to ensure that they emitted only the sweetest sounds appropriate to their particular themes. His associates in this context were all household names in their own right: such people as Jacopo Amigoni, John Michael Rysbrack, Louis François Roubiliac, George Frederick Handel and Francesco Geminiani. The Kensington Palace clock originally had music 'composed by the three great Masters Geminiani, Handel and Corelli, and properly adapted to the Machine by Mr. Geminiani'; Amigoni seems to have specialized in the dial-painting, while at the base of the dial is an applied

107. *For comparison, a complete example of a Charles Clay musical clock: general view.* (Partridge Fine Arts, London)

108. (Left) *Detail showing the dial panel, again with painting by Amigoni, and figures in relief by Rysbrack.* (Partridge Fine Arts, London)

group of figures representing the Liberal Arts, described as 'made of silver in Alto Relievo, by Mr. Rysbrack'. Rarely can the decoration and audible amenities of any clock have been so carefully carried out, which makes it all the more sad that the clock today is in such a very imperfect state.

Before leaving this imperfect masterpiece, it may be useful to summarize its defects and deficiencies. Mechanically, the clock was still complete and working at the beginning of the nineteenth century, so that Vulliamy, in July 1801, was paid £68 for putting it in order, this to include 'adjusting the Music of both the barrels and putting a great many pins in both', repairing the bellows of the organ, 'Cleaning and varnishing all the painting' and so forth. The clock was then in the Queen's House, that is to say, Buckingham Palace, but after cleaning it was returned to its original
101 home, Kensington Palace. An illustration by W. H. Pyne, in his *History of the Royal Residences*, which includes it in a view of the Cupola Room, shows that it was still in its original form; this was in 1819. Later in the same century, perhaps because of a second failure of the music, the clock was taken off exhibition and put into store; inevitably it suffered so that, when it was again brought into the light of day in the second half of the century, the base containing the organ was discarded, and the clock mechanism and dial were replaced by modern substitutes. Neither the new base nor the mechanism was worthy of the clock. As to the artistic elements, the only complete remnant of 105
Roubiliac's sculpture is his fine group representing Hercules taking the celestial globe off the shoulders of

109. (Below) *The organ from the complete Charles Clay clock: it contains 96 wooden pipes, upon which the $13\frac{1}{2}''$ diameter pin barrel plays ten tunes. The principle is similar to an ordinary musical box.* (Partridge Fine Arts, London)

Atlas which surmounts the whole edifice; but his 'four figures in bronze, being Emblems of the Four Monarchies' disappeared when the other depredations oc-
106 cured, and although two of these, depicting 'Europe' and 'Asia', have recently been discovered in a storeroom at Windsor Castle, they have lost their gilding, and their supports have been altered, making it impossible to replace them on the clock. Whatever Francesco Geminiani, a well-known Italian violinist and composer who lived and worked in Britain, principally in Ireland, between 1714 and 1740, may have contributed to the clock can only be hinted at from a manuscript of his, preserved in the British Library, which is entitled *Tunes for Clay's Musical Clock*—there are eleven of them in the set but no indication as to which of Clay's clocks they were intended for. Not even a hint remains of the work of Handel and Corelli; so that the only complete contributions, as the clock stands today, are the bas-reliefs in frosted silver by Rysbrack, and Amigoni's paintings. These still impart a sense of wonder in the onlooker, so that the effect of the original, unaltered creation must have been electrifying, to say the least.

One of the John Pykes—it is difficult to say which—
112 was responsible for another clock in the Royal
113 Collection and located at Windsor Castle, which is remarkable in a number of respects. Attributed to the middle period of the eighteenth century, this is a monumental two-train spring clock in a really massive case which is decorated all over with a somewhat random polychrome lacquered motif. Here is not the precise chinoiserie treatment to which one is accustomed in lacquered clock cases, but a truly English style. To cap it all, a cupola rises above the main structure of the case, which is similarly decorated and surmounted by an ormolu figure of a female winged trumpeter. The silvered dial of the clock with gilt spandrels, is likewise on a large scale with, outside the main chapter circle, a sequence of rings giving complex calendar information and including sunrise and sunset and signs of the zodiac. There is also a ring denoting the equation of time, with the customary words 'Watch faster' and 'Watch slower', associated with an indicating hand decorated with a sunburst. The glazed door at the rear of the clock, however, reveals an unusual anomaly. The movement employed to drive this great clock is hardly larger, if indeed at all, than that normally found in any conventional domestic spring clock of the period having outer dimensions probably less than a quarter the size of this one. There is one very large multi-toothed wheel planted outside the back plate of the clock and having a diameter that exceeds it, so that it projects beyond the main frame; this must be part of the complex calendar work, one element of

110. (Above) *A remarkable similarity of approach, by comparison with Charles Clay's clocks, is to be seen in this general view of a musical clock by George Pyke.* (Museum of London)

111. (Right) *The grouping of figures below the dial of the George Pyke clock is virtually identical to that favoured by Clay: unlike him, however, Pyke includes automata in the painting above.* (Museum of London)

which revolves once per year. Finally, there is locking-plate striking, presumably because the under-dial calendar gearing left no room for the much more usual rack and snail system. This clock was probably acquired by Queen Mary, although the exact circumstances are uncertain.

Even this is not the end of the story, so far as the Pyke family of clockmakers is concerned. At Royal Lodge, Windsor, Her Majesty Queen Elizabeth The Queen Mother has a fairly conventional two-train mahogany long-case clock with broken-arch top to the hood and dial. In the arch is a strike/silent subsidiary with the usual cast and gilt scrolling dolphin on either side. Below, the silvered chapter ring has five-minute
114 numerals but no half-hour marks. The spandrels feature an urn, and blued-steel hands are nicely made. There is the usual day-of-the-month calendar aperture above VI and a seconds ring below XII. The movement has a recoil anchor escapement, with pendulum having brass rod and bob. The signature on the clock dial, either side of VI on the chapter ring, reads "Jnº & Geo. Pyke, Bedford Row, London". This may be the first positive evidence that father and son were, at least for a while, in business together.

It seems that the craftsman who succeeded Joseph Antram as Royal Clockmaker was Francis Robinson. Here we are on slightly firmer ground, since he served his apprenticeship with no less a man than Henry Jones, *q.v.* Bound on 8th October 1685 for a term of seven years, Robinson was not, in the event, admitted to the Freedom until 7th April 1707. It is difficult to explain away a gap of fifteen years, but, at that time, it is always possible that he had originally joined another Livery Company and did not transfer until pressure was exerted on him to do so. Robinson served all the senior offices of the Clockmaker's Company and eventually, in June 1725, became Master when the incumbent, Joseph Williamson, died in office. However, Robinson remained only three months at the helm, for in September 1725 Peter Wise was elected to supersede him.

Robinson's working premises were in Inner Temple Lane—his clocks are frequently signed 'in $\mathrm{y^e}$ Temple'—and there used, formerly, to be one of his watch movements in the Clockmakers' Company Collection at Guildhall. This was disposed of following a thinning out of this fine accumulation in 1974–5. The only feature of special interest in this watch is that it was signed '$\mathrm{Fra^s}$ Robinson, London, $\mathrm{Ser^t}$ to his Royal Highness', which has been taken, probably correctly, to mean that his Appointment, originally, was to George II when Prince of Wales. This would agree with the hypothesis that he took over from Antram in 1723, even if it seems strange that he was not appointed to serve the reigning monarch, but rather his son. Today,

112. (Below) *A general view, from the front, of the monumental lacquer-cased two-train bracket clock by John Pyke in Windsor Castle.* (Royal Collection)

113. (Right) *The surprisingly small movement that drives the John Pyke clock.* (Royal Collection)

114. (Far right) *The dial of a conventional two-train longcase clock by John and George Pyke, Bedford Row.* (The Queen Mother's Collection)

sad to say, there is no trace of any work by Robinson in the Royal Collection.

Robinson remained the King's Clockmaker, according to the published records, until George II's death in 1760. Baillie, however, suggests a last recorded date of 1747 although quotes no source; this does not, of course, imply his death in that year, but even if it did, there must have been so much trade inter-play between the craftsman to be considered next, and both Robinson and his predecessor Antram, as to have insured no break in continuity of royal service, whether in clocks or watches. Indeed, a watchmaker's Day Book of this period has survived which has been identified as Benjamin Gray's, in which there are entries concerning the supply of movements to both Robinson and Antram.

On 30th March 1742 Benjamin Gray was appointed
115 Watchmaker in Ordinary at a yearly stipend of £150, in place of Thomas Cartwright deceased. This event may perhaps be seen as the start of a horological dynasty which extended to beyond the mid-point of the century following and which became—not necessarily for the best of reasons—possibly the most influential one that has ever held office.

Benjamin Gray—curiously, contemporary printed records generally spell his name Grey, although this was not the usage on his timekeepers—was born in 1676. His early training seems to be unknown—indeed, from his date of birth nothing further is heard of him for forty years, and he never seems, at any time, to have had any associations with the Clockmakers' Company. Since his only known working premises were in the City of Westminster, this is not so strange as it sounds—for, although the Company's official sphere of influence extended to 10 miles beyond the boundaries of the City of London proper, it seems hardly ever to have ventured outside them, certainly in so far as its official 'searches' were concerned.

The first mention of Gray in his working life is found in 1716, when he apparently took into service an apprentice named Thomas Richard Wacklin. The latter hailed, it would appear, from St Giles-in-the-Fields; and Gray was then at St Martin's-in-the-Fields. The premium paid for the apprenticeship was £20. By 1727 he is believed to have moved to Pall Mall; in 1738 he set up business at St James's Street West, at 'Ye Sun Dyall in Thatched House Court'. In 1752 Gray moved again, for the last time, to 74 Pall Mall. Before that, however—about 1730, it might seem—he had encountered a young Swiss, who had come to London from Paris in order to enlarge his horological experience and expertise, especially in relation to the cylinder escape-

115. *Portrait of Benjamin Gray.* (Clockmakers' Company, London)

ment. This friendship eventually blossomed forth into a business partnership, entered into in 1743; and, in 1746, Justin Vulliamy married his partner's only daughter, Mary.

Gray had one son, George, who was bound apprentice, under the auspices of the Clockmakers' Company, on 7th October 1728 and for seven years, to John Hoddle; or at least so it is supposed. Nothing further is ever heard of him, and he does not seem to have followed the craft in his father's footsteps.

Gray's own work is noted for its fine design and craftsmanship, although his output cannot have been prolific, to judge by surviving examples. He was possibly the first to make pedometers in London; and his watches are serialized by a code of letters, not so far deciphered.

In 1764, Benjamin Gray died, at the ripe old age of eighty-eight. It appears that the Royal Warrant originally granted in his name was extended, after he was
116 joined by Justin Vulliamy, to the partnership; and the premises at 74 Pall Mall, which were subsequently renumbered to become no. 68, remained the headquarters of the Vulliamy business for three generations. There was another address used by them—and usually described as 'the small back house'—which seems, from contemporary plans to have been no. 67 in the same thoroughfare.

The Royal Collection does not seem to have retained any pieces made by Gray prior to his partnership with Vulliamy; there are several fine clocks dating from after that time, however. The earliest of these is a rather
severe-looking, albeit elegant, bracket clock in an 11
ebonized case with inverted bell top, the sides fitted with brass latticed frets, and, on top, a carrying-handle. The overall height is 1 foot 9 inches, the width $10\frac{1}{2}$ inches and depth 7 inches. The dial is signed, in the arch, 'Benj. Gray: Just. Vulliamy. London' between two subsidiary dials, one for 'rise and fall', that is to say, for regulating the timekeeping by altering the effective length of the pendulum, and the other for strike/silent. The spandrels of the main dial are particularly finely chased, with a mask at the centre. The hands are delicate in design and beautifully made. The dial centre is engraved with an elaborate representation of the Royal Cypher of George II; and the clock probably dates to *c.*1750. It is said to have been the only repeating clock in the Royal Collection up to 1835, although this seems somewhat unlikely.

The second clock is quite different in appearance, although said essentially to date from only ten years
later. It is housed in a fine mahogany case with break- 118
arch top, the sides of which are almost entirely taken up with large brass fish-scale-pattern frets, set into projecting moulded rectangular frames; this, however, is from the period *c.*1780. Unlike the previous example, this is a three-train quarter-chiming clock; the principal dial arrangements, with two subsidiaries in the arch, are repeated. Additionally, there is a day-of-the-month calendar appearing through a square aperture just above VI, as well as a mock pendulum slot above the dial centre. The signatures on the dials of both clocks appear identical, whereas the spandrels are substantially different, the predominant motif in the second clock seeming to be a vase or urn. Both clocks have finely engraved back plates bearing the signatures of the partnership; the second clock was brought over from Osborne, Isle of Wight, in 1913.

To continue, for the moment, in the same craft stream, the other partner in this Anglo-Swiss *entente*, François Justin Vulliamy, was born in 1712, so that he was well over thirty years the junior in age. He came from an area of Switzerland renowned for its watches, the Pays de Vaud, although it is difficult to be more precise than this; Vulliamys were to be found all over that region, and it seems more than likely that Justin's forebears may have been engaged themselves in some aspect of horological manufacturing. It was one of Justin's grandsons, Theodore, in a note describing his grandfather's early life, who relates his interest in the

cylinder escapement; and, while it has also been mentioned that he married Mary Gray in 1746, he must have known her well for some years, since there is an entry in the Register of the French Chapel of the Savoy stating that they both stood as godparents for Marie, daughter of d'Esaie and Charlotte Fleureau, in 1739. Fleureau was another clockmaker, who is listed by Baillie as *c.*1710.

It seems that Justin Vulliamy was very proud of his Swiss birth and upbringing; he took the lead in establishing the Swiss Church in London in 1762 and remained President of that Church's Committee from its inauguration to his death. Still in existence in the present church building, in Endell Street, are the clock he presented to it, as well as a plaque upholding the 'Memory of its Founder, François Justin Vulliamy'.

116. (Left) *Portrait of Justin Vulliamy.* (Clockmakers' Company, London)

117. (Below left) *Two-train repeating bracket clock in ebonized case by Benjamin Gray and Justin Vulliamy.* (Royal Collection)

118. (Below) *Three-train mahogany-cased clock by Benjamin Gray and Justin Vulliamy.* (Royal Collection)

119. (Right) *Watch by Justin Vulliamy, in gold and enamelled pair-cases.* (Camerer Cuss, London)

120. (Far right) *The outer case of the Vulliamy watch with the Prince of Wales's cypher and crown.* (Camerer Cuss, London)

121. (Below) *Three-train clock in 'balloon' case veneered with tortoiseshell, by Justin Vulliamy.* (Royal Collection)

On work undertaken by the partnership it was, as has been shown, customary to use both their signatures, but after Gray's death, the usual style was 'Just. Vulliamy' or sometimes the full forename. After Justin's death, however, clocks tended simply to be signed 'Vulliamy', whether the work of son or grandson.

In the present context, and perhaps because, as items of personal jewellery and adornment rather than pieces of furniture, they have a more ephemeral existence than clocks, watches tend to be overlooked. A particularly fine royal watch by Justin Vulliamy exists, although no longer in the Royal Collection. This is in gold pair-cases, the outer carrying an oval medallion enamelled in red, white and blue with the Prince of Wales's cypher, from which flutes radiate to the band; the inner case is plain, the watch dating from *c.*1780. The movement, with typically fine cylinder, is serialized 'uon' in the Vulliamy fashion, and the white enamel dial has gold 'beetle and poker' hands set with diamonds. This habit of serializing watches by a coded sequence of letters—always combinations of three during the lives of Benjamin Gray and Justin Vulliamy—continued during the nineteenth century, when sequences of four letters started to appear, but since the cypher has not yet been broken, it has not proved possible to convert the letters into numbers, from which the firm's output might be gauged. 119 120

Mary and Justin Vulliamy had three children. The eldest, Benjamin, born on 27th August 1747, succeeded to the family business; a second son, Lewis, apparently became a sugar refiner; and there was a daughter, named Marie, born in 1750 and believed to have died young. She is not mentioned in Justin's Will, which was made in French in 1795, two years before he died on 1st December 1797.

More clocks by Justin Vulliamy have been recorded than by the partnership, and three superb specimens

from the Royal Collection will be described, all totally
121 dissimilar from one another. The first is a three-train quarter-chiming balloon clock, veneered in tortoiseshell which has been richly mounted with finely chased and gilt brass, the shaped base supported upon chased paw feet and, surmounting the whole, a vase. At the sides are openwork panels backed with silk, and the clock is said to date *c.*1770. It is interesting to note that the mounts for this clock are probably the work of Matthew Boulton (1728–1809), the great creator of decorative metalwork, in his Soho factory in Birmingham. Neither Gray nor Vulliamy hesitated to use the finest craftsmen available to enrich their work. Another was George Michael Moser, born in Switzerland in 1705 but working in London from 1720 to *c.*1780, who was an enamel painter and goldsmith—his repoussé work is extremely rare—of the highest reputation, and a Royal Academician into the bargain. Moser died in 1783; but during his working life he created many fabulous watch cases, both for the partnership and for each partner on his own, as well as fine enamel boxes and the like for George II and for George III.

Before leaving this first clock, it should be noted that the silvered dial is signed, untypically, in the fullest expression—i.e. 'Justin Vulliamy London'; formerly in the Great Library at Buckingham House, it went to Windsor Castle and was brought back again by Queen Mary in 1913. The second clock is signed, in similarly full style, on its back plate, which is otherwise decorated with engraved rococo ornament; the dial, however, bears the simple inscription 'Vulliamy London'.

This second clock was also, originally, in Bucking- 122
ham House (the Queen's House); it is illustrated and so 123

122. (Left) *Three-train bracket clock in bell-topped ebonized case with extensive ormolu mounts, by Justin Vulliamy.* (Royal Collection)

123. (Above) *The engraved back plate, with maker's signature, belonging to the previous clock.* (Royal Collection)

described in the Pictorial Inventory. Also three-train and quarter-chiming, it is a singularly handsome bell-top ebonized bracket clock, of architectural form, with superb rococo ormolu mounts which include double-scroll feet, the corners supported by female caryatids and inverted trusses, and the sides with openwork engraved panels mounted over red silk. Surmounting the whole structure is an ormolu male figure, in classical drapes, seated and holding a scroll. The gilt dial plate with fine spandrels is fitted with three white enamel dials; in the arch, two small subsidiaries for rise-and-fall and strike/silent, and below them the main dial, which has an outer ring of five-minute numerals typical of the period, and again beautifully made pierced hands. This clock was made for George III and is thought to date *c.*1765.

Like others before him, Justin Vulliamy could also turn his hand to barometers. Exhibited in the display entitled 'George III—Collector and Patron' which was mounted in the Queen's Gallery during 1974–5, was one made for George III about 1770. With a case of
125 carved and polished mahogany, it had a brass dial with silvered chapter ring, and with spandrels of chased and gilt bronze. It was a substantial instrument, being over 4 feet high. Its case has been attributed to John Bradburn, who died in 1781. On the drawing of this barometer in George IV's Pictorial Inventory there are annotations to the effect that, at one time, this formed part of the furniture in George III's bedroom, and subsequently, in his Library at Buckingham House.

Yet a third three-train clock by Justin Vulliamy is said to have been a favourite of Queen Victoria, on account of the exceptional legibility of its dial; and this clock resided on the chimney-piece of Her Majesty's dining-
124 room at Windsor Castle. In a broken-arch ebonized case, with gilt fish-scale panels at the sides and a carrying-handle on top, this was a later and more conventional clock than the two previously described. The white enamel dial with large five-minute numerals outside the main chapter circle is certainly easy to read, but the purist might cavil at the planting of the winding-squares, which cut into the numerals III and IX. The hands are finely executed, and there are two subsidiary dials in the arch, at the left for regulation by rise-and-fall, and the right for strike/silent. The gilt spandrels have, by the time of this clock—say *c.*1775—become rather simpler and more open in style, and somewhat coarser.

After Justin Vulliamy, two further generations of this famous clockmaking family were to hold the Royal Warrant, covering the period from 1797 to just beyond the mid-nineteenth century. Many other interesting events were taking place in the context of palace horology during the second half of the eighteenth century, however, and it is necessary to back-track to 1760 in order to take account of them.

124. *Three-train bracket clock by Justin Vulliamy in ebonized break-arch case, with gilt fish-scale panels at the sides.* (Royal Collection)

George II died, as has been seen, in October 1760, to be succeeded by his grandson—the eldest son of Frederick, Prince of Wales—as George III. The first Hanover who could truthfully claim to be a Briton born and bred, he was to reign for some sixty years and throughout a period of considerable political turbulence. He also had to suffer grave personal problems, such as periods of recurring insanity which even caused him to contemplate abdication; these eventually became so serious that the last decade of his life was to be totally impaired by them. Despite all these predicaments—and he has been often criticized as being neither a wise nor a constitutional monarch, who brought many of his misfortunes upon himself—he did enjoy, during his later years, a measure of popularity which was part sympathy for his crippling illness and part respect for his blameless personal life and his homely ways with his somewhat plain wife, Charlotte, Princess of Mecklenburg-Strelitz, whom he had mar-

125. (Left) *Barometer made by Justin Vulliamy, ca. 1770, for George III. Originally in the King's Bedroom and later in the Library of Buckingham House, the handsome case is attributed to John Bradburn.* (Royal Collection)

ried in 1761. Even Dr Johnson, never given to mincing words, described him as 'the finest gentleman I have ever seen . . .'. According to Thackeray, Johnson was regarded by the man-in-the-street as a kind of oracle so that, when 'the people heard the great author's good opinion of the new sovereign, whole generations rallied to the King'.

So far as the Royal Collection is concerned, George III exercised as profound an influence upon it as any British monarch, either before or since. The King developed an interest in scientific matters at an early age, which was to turn into a life-long devotion and bring in its train an accumulation of scientific instruments, clocks and the like which remains in existence to this day and which, often enough, combines practical usefulness with enduring beauty of workmanship and design. As early as 1760, with the original purpose, so it is said, of observing the transit of Venus, the King built his Observatory at Kew where he located his collection of scientific instruments. It was fortunate for succeeding generations, perhaps, that a certain Dr Stephen Demainbray, who had been the King's tutor, was subsequently to become his adviser in technical matters, for it was Demainbray's collection, started about 1740, which was later to form the nucleus of the King's collection, eventually consisting of over two thousand objects. This was presented to King's College, London, by Queen Victoria, and the greater part is now on display at the Science Museum in London. Some of the greatest treasures in this magnificent accumulation must be those from the hands of George Adams, of the Strand, who was the King's Mathematical Instrument Maker, and who enjoyed a world-wide reputation for the quality of his globes.

Especially was the King devoted to clocks and watches, and this manifested itself not only in the superb timekeepers he commissioned but also in the practical help and support he gave to working craftsmen of special skill and ability. That his interest was more than that of the dilettante, or even simply of the connoisseur of beautiful objects, but was of a much
more practical and fundamental nature, can be 126
demonstrated by the survival, in the Royal Archives, of a series of notes in the King's own hand, headed respectively 'Directions for mounting a Watch', 'Directions for unmounting a Watch' and 'Explanation of the Motion'. These not only bespeak the King's diligence in applying himself to the mastery of a subject which

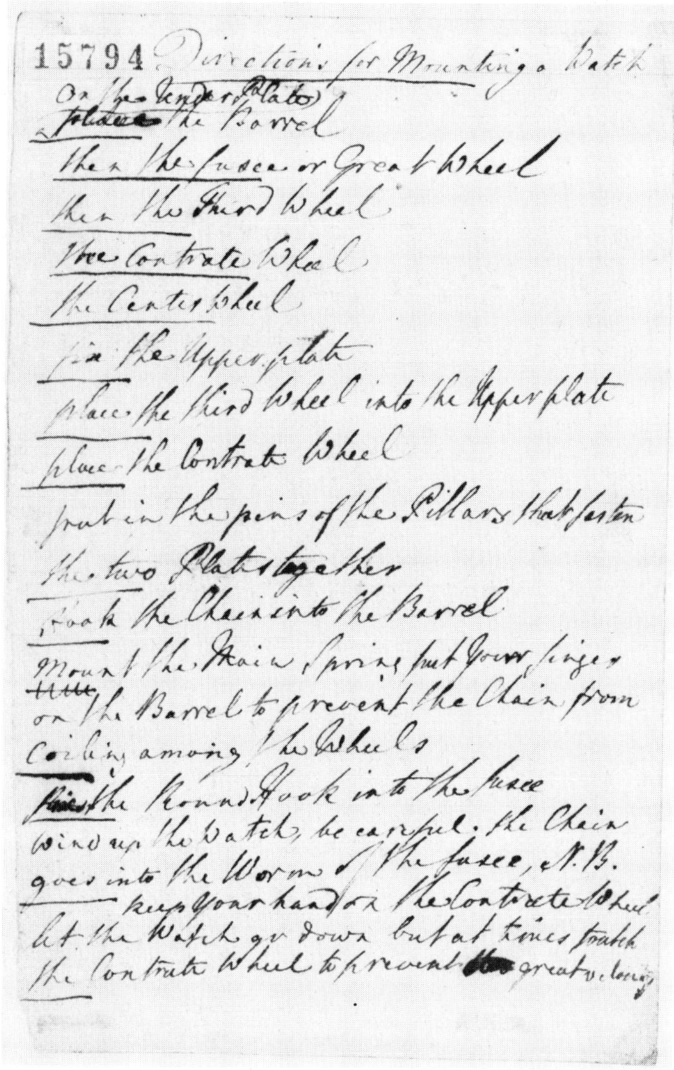
15794 Direction for Mounting a Watch
On the Under Plate
place the Barrel
then the fusee or Great Wheel
then the Third Wheel
the Contrate Wheel
the Center Wheel
fix the Upper plate
place the third Wheel into the Upper plate
place the Contrate Wheel
put in the pins of the Pillars that fasten
the two Plates together
hook the Chain into the Barrel
Mount the Main Spring put your finger
on the Barrel to prevent the Chain from
Coiling among the Wheels
fix the Round Hook into the fusee
wind up the Watch, be careful the Chain
goes into the Worm of the fusee, N.B.
keep your hand on the Contrate Wheel
let the Watch go down but at times touch
the Contrate Wheel to prevent the great velocity

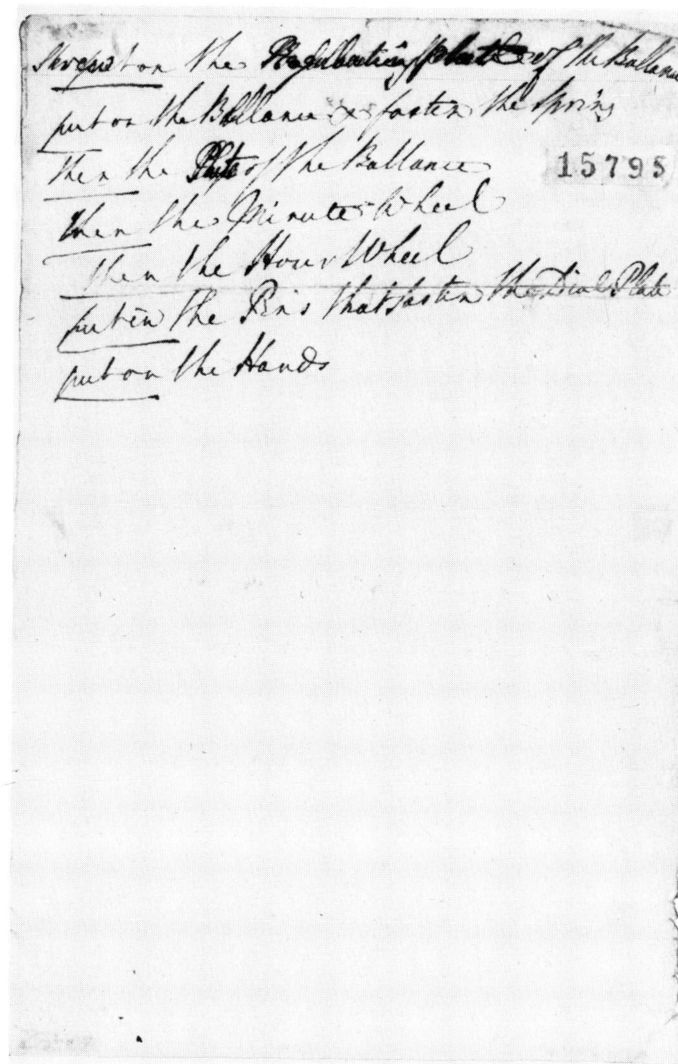
Screw on the Regulating plate of the Ballance
put on the Ballance & fasten the Spring
then the Plate of the Ballance 15795
then the Minute Wheel
then the Hour Wheel
put in the Pins that fasten the Dial Plate
put on the Hands

particularly interested him, but also show, by his correct use of the contemporary terminology, that he must have himself carried out the procedures he describes and become, from personal experience, aware of all the pitfalls that await the unwary or ignorant, when dealing with very small, fine machinery. It is perhaps not wholly irrelevant to note, at this point, the enormous and ever-increasing interest shown by peoples of all the developed countries of the world, in its horological heritage; throughout history, the amateur in horology has always had an important part to play. Were George III alive today, he would find many kindred spirits with whom to share at least this part of his scientific interests.

Just such a science-based clockmaker as would have particularly appealed to the King was one John Shelton. Eventually he was to become a famous London maker of regulators and precision timekeepers for observatories and the like; but he started out as an apprentice, bound to Henry Stanbury on 20th May 1712 for the nominal seven years. He was admitted to the Freedom

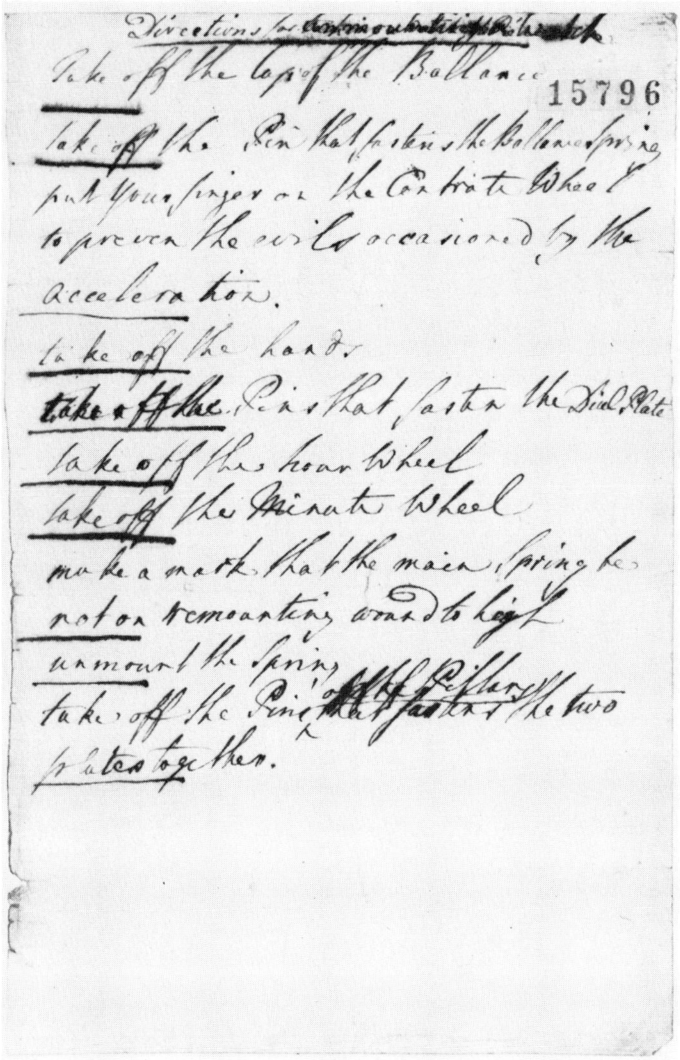

Directions for ...
Take off the Cock of the Ballance 15796
take off the Pin that fastens the Ballance Spring
put Your finger on the Contrate Wheel
to prevent the evils occasioned by the
acceleration.
take off the hands
take off the Pins that fasten the Dial Plate
take off the hour Wheel
take off the Minute Wheel
make a mark that the main Spring be
not on remounting wound to high
unmount the Spring
take off the Pins that fasten the two off the Pillars
plates together.

126. (Above) *Three sheets of notes in George III's handwriting, listing the sequence to be followed when assembling or dismantling a watch movement.* (Royal Archives)

127. (Left) *George III's Observatory at Kew: the building as now seen.* (Richmond Reference Library, London)

128. (Above right) *Detail of the Radcliffe Observatory at Oxford, reproduced from Wm. Combe's* History of Oxford *. . . 1814. Shelton's clock is said to have stood at the bottom of the staircase, but this clock case is empty.* (Guildhall Library, City of London)

on 17th January 1720 but for some reason does not appear to have been elected to the Livery until 1766, by which time he had already served the office of Steward and was 'fined for Assistant'—that is to say, he preferred to pay a fine rather than serve on the Clockmakers' Company Court of Assistants. These long-extended dates may, however, arise since Shelton was only the first of three generations of his family, all likewise called John, who followed in each other's footsteps in the craft, operating from premises in Shoe Lane, and it is difficult to distinguish between them in contemporary records. Shelton's clocks went into a
number of eighteenth-century observatories such as 128
the Radcliffe at Oxford, and George III, who gave a Shelton precision clock as a gift to Gottingen University, in Prussia, certainly used one or more in his own private observatory. It has sometimes been held that one or other of the two Shelton clocks that were included in the Wetherfield Collection, being described by W. E. Hurcomb in his account of that great accumulation but, strangely, being omitted by F. J.

Britten in his, were used in that connection; but there appears no concrete evidence on this point. However, a Minute Book of 1853, preserved at Armagh Observatory, in Northern Ireland, which lists certain items transferred there from the King's Private Observatory at Kew, includes: 'Shelton's mean-time clock' and 'Half-second journeyman clock by Shelton. It rings the minute and can be stopped at signal'. This last clock had already disappeared when a search was made for it thirty years ago. Another clock by Shelton, which also formerly belonged to George III, is at Lerwick Observatory, in the Shetlands. When last reported upon, some years ago now, it was maintaining a consistency of rate within one second *per diem*. 127

129. (Above) *Tortoiseshell and ormolu bracket clock, by James Newton (or Nenton): general view.* (Royal Collection)

130. (Right) *The same clock, from the back.* (Royal Collection)

Kew Observatory continued to fulfil a scientific role for more than two centuries after it was built. It was used variously as a meteorological station and as a research laboratory testing a variety of scientific apparatus; for a period, it provided the time-signals that regulated clocks in the Palace of Westminster and in Whitehall. It finally closed its doors to all these activities only on 31st December 1980. Clocks must inevitably have been part of its equipment during George III's life; but, sadly, knowledge on this point is almost wholly lacking. In the last chapter, a clock by Justin Vulliamy will be described, which may have been there; but no inventory survives in the Royal Archives. The only certainty, it appears, concerns a turret clock which is now installed in Osborne House, Queen Victoria's home on the Isle of Wight. This clock was made by John Smith, who is said to have died in 1779; working under Demainbray in connection with Kew Observatory, this craftsman had been apprenticed to Henry Hindley of York, whose highly individual style shows in Smith's work. The clock is said to have been completed in 1777, under the eagle eye of the King himself, and to have been fixed in a brick tower, purpose-built at Kew. The official account continues:

> The Pendulum having in the first instance been suspended under two Knife edges, which suspension failed, the present suspension and also the Escapement were made by B. Vulliamy A.D. 1780. The Clock as first made shewed the time on only one Face, by command of Her MAJESTY, QUEEN VICTORIA, it was altered by B. L. Vulliamy, and the necessary communication work was made, to shew the time upon four Faces; a new Deal Pendulum Rod was substituted for the original Iron Rod, and the Clock was fixed in the Tower at Osborne, A.D. 1849. The four dial works formed part of a Clock made by B. L. Vulliamy A.D. 1818 for the Pavilion, Brighton & removed to Buckingham Palace, A.D. 1849.

There were, in fact, two tower clocks at the Pavilion, one in the stables and one on the building proper; there does exist correspondence relating to their removal in 1848 (PRO. Works 19–1/2 and 19–8) when B. L. Vulliamy apparently had difficulty in obtaining access. Which one was concerned here, is not clear.

Before turning to the larger, scientifically-inclined clocks which George III commissioned, it might be
129 130 instructive first to examine some of the smaller and essentially domestic timekeepers which were made to his order. A particularly attractive one, utilizing tortoiseshell veneer enriched with ormolu, was made by James Newton, about 1762; and the only mystery about this clock, if it can be called such, concerns this maker. He appears to be virtually unknown, apart from this one object. He has been located in Red Lion Street, Clerkenwell—in other words, in the very heart of the clock- and watch-manufacturing area of London in those days—in 1760, but nothing else about him seems to have been recorded.

As to the clock, it is intended to be viewed 'in the round'. Its height is 1 foot $2\frac{1}{2}$ inches, width nearly 9 inches and depth $6\frac{3}{4}$ inches; and Clifford Smith has included a very detailed description of it which cannot be bettered. He calls it

> A BRACKET CLOCK, of tortoiseshell and ormolu with oval domed top and silver dial ornaments . . . . The panels at the back and sides are delicately chased with landscapes, trees, rocks and water, in open-work rococo borders; and the shaped trusses at the angles are mounted with exquisite open scroll designs in the manner of the finest goldsmith's work found on the snuff boxes of the time. The little panels on the dome are minutely chased with buildings and trees; and on the side near the base of the dome are a pair of chased oval handles. Around the enamel dial (which is some forty years later) are spandrels of open silverwork. The original movement had a crown wheel escapement [i.e. verge] with bob pendulum which has been replaced by an anchor escapement, and the repeating bells have been disconnected.

Recent examination of this clock has revealed certain hitherto unrecorded details. Whereas the spandrels surrounding the $3\frac{1}{2}$-inch-diameter dial are of finely chased silver, the dial edge is rather crude; and the dial itself, which is stylistically anomalous, turns out to be signed 'James Nenton' (*sic*). As for the alterations, they could well have been the work of one or other of the Vulliamys, for the anchor escapement is allied to a typical pendulum of their making. The records, however, seem to be deficient in these respects.

Apparently the King ordered this for Buckingham House; it was later moved to St James's Palace and rescued from the fire there in 1809. A somewhat similar clock, now in the Victoria and Albert Museum, has a movement by George Prior; this is said to date *c.*1765, and, apart from certain resemblances in detail, that clock has an ormolu crown above the dial. What, if any, significance attaches to this remains still to be discovered.

For a complete contrast, a pair of clocks—not identical, be it said, but obviously intended to be seen in proximity to one another as part of a larger decorative scheme, and undoubtedly meant to be set in front of mirrors, since they are almost as attractive when seen from the back as the front. They were originally the property of Queen Charlotte. The Queen's artistic tastes and interests must have been the perfect complement to her husband's scientific ones, both of them meeting at the junction where fine craftsmanship comes into play—and, like those of the King, her tastes were being refined and developed even from the time of her marriage at the tender age of seventeen.

The clocks in question are in exquisite cases of

Chelsea soft-paste porcelain from the Gold Anchor
131 period (*c*.1757–69), of rococo design and some 17
132 inches high, with a ground of claret colour with some gilding, and with figures of a shepherd and shepherdess modelled and painted in the manner of Boucher. The setting is the bosky grove or arbour so romantically evoked at this period, and these clock cases are regarded as masterpieces of English eighteenth-century porcelain. The clocks themselves, with single-train calendar movements and identical to one another, have to be inserted from the front—there is no rear access—and winding is through the dial. The maker was George Philip Strigel, who was Watchmaker to the Queen. Born in 1718, Strigel was made an honorary Freeman of the Clockmakers' Company on 2nd April 1781. This grade of entry was specially reserved for those whom the Company considered could help it to advance its interests, either because they wielded special influence or by virtue of their social position or for other such good and sufficient reasons. He was located in
133 Pimlico—in Stafford Row, near Buckingham Gate—and was, therefore, conveniently close at hand for the Queen's requirements. He died in 1798. These delightful objects, incidentally, are now gracing Her Majesty Queen Elizabeth The Queen Mother's London home at Clarence House, where, no doubt, they continue to give the greatest pleasure. In the same way, with their inspiration probably derived from the Louis XV style,

133. *Advertising watch paper of George Strigel, placing him in Ranelagh Street 'near Her Majesty's Palace'.* (Clockmakers' Company, London)

131. (Right) *The magnificent non-identical pair of clocks in Chelsea porcelain cases, with movements by George Philip Strigel.* (Royal Collection)

132. (Below right) *The same clocks, seen from the back.* (Royal Collection)

they must have charmed George IV, who bought them for £73 10s at Christie's (sold 11th May 1819, Lot 47), after Queen Charlotte's death.

Of an entirely different style again is a clock *c*.1771, in the design of which the King himself is believed to have had a hand, although no sketch of his survives. The case of this clock is of chased and gilt bronze with panels of 'blue john', or Derbyshire fluorspar, mounted at the corners with rams' heads and hung with laurel
garlands. On the top are four ewers and a vase. The 134
clock stands just over 19 inches high, 11 inches wide and $8\frac{1}{2}$ inches deep. The dial and movement were by Thomas Wright, and the clock case by Matthew Boulton, to whom reference has already been made. He worked from drawings supplied by Sir William Chambers (1726–96), with whom, as a young man, the King had studied architecture; in surviving correspondence Boulton informs his partner that Chambers was about to give him 'the King's design wch I will send down', but surviving preliminary and final drawings are all by Chambers.

As for the movement, this was originally of month duration with a pin-wheel escapement but was subsequently altered, probably in the early-nineteenth
century, by B. L. Vulliamy. Thomas Wright, the 135
clockmaker, had premises at 6 The Poultry; clocks by him are customarily signed 'Maker to the King', but he seems to have held the Appointment primarily in respect of watches. He was admitted to the Freedom of the Clockmakers' Company in 1770 and was, apparently, a Quaker. In 1783 he patented (no. 1354) a form of detent escapement and compensation balance. He died, in 1792, while on a visit to Birmingham, doubtless to see Boulton. It seems that he may have been somewhat dilatory in carrying out his part of the clock just described; at the first attempt his movement could not be made to fit the case, which had to be sent back to the Soho works for modification, and a further four months were wasted as a result.

Matthew Boulton is far too well known a figure to make any lengthy biographical note necessary here. So far as his work on clock cases is concerned, however—and indeed the same thing applies to others of the more ornate articles of his manufacture—he was by no means above borrowing his decorative ideas from almost any other source that came to hand: nowadays, it might be called plagiarism. His ormolu mounts, often

enough 'cribbed' from another artist, tended to be used over and over again, and exclusivity of design was an unknown concept where his wares were concerned. This nearly militated to his own disadvantage, when it was discovered that he had made several copies of the King's clock, which he fully intended selling to the highest bidder with all the commercial advantage implicit in such transactions. However, in the end wiser counsels prevailed. It was represented to him that the King might not be best pleased to find copies of a clock in the design of which he had himself taken part, being offered on the open market; nor would His Majesty take kindly to the debasing of his own purchase which would necessarily follow such further production of it. Even so, there does exist at the present time at least one copy of the royal clock case.

During the years 1760 and 1761, for some reason, the post of Royal Clockmaker is shown in official publications as vacant. From 1762, there seems to have been a complete reshuffle, the Watchmaker being named as George Lindsay—in office till 1777—while the Clockmaker was John Ellicott. He served until 1776. However, as will be seen elsewhere, there seem frequent inconsistencies between the periods of service of royal tradesmen as derived from different sources; the aim will be to try not to omit anybody, while not being too dogmatic about precise years in office.

For a maker of some distinction, very little seems to be known about George Lindsay. Baille records him first in 1743—by which time, presumably, he was well established in business—and he is known to have died in 1776. His watch papers carry the description 'G. Lindsay, watch maker to His Majesty and Her Royal Highness the Princess Dowager of Wales, at the Dial in the Strand'. The rest of our present knowledge is drawn from his surviving work, of which there is a fairly representative quantity. This ranges from the large and very fine organ clock, which was one of Courtenay Ilbert's favourites and is now in the British Museum, to a smattering of good ordinary watches, of which there is a fairly typical example in the Clockmakers' Company Collection. He seems to have enjoyed making musical

134. (Left) *'Blue John' clock by Matthew Boulton and Thomas Wright.* (Royal Collection)

135. (Below) *Advertising watch paper of Thomas Wright, Watchmaker to the King.* (Clockmakers' Company, London)

136. (Right) *George Lindsay's remarkable organ clock, showing the general view from the front, and beside it detail of the organ, seen through the open rear door.* (British Museum)

clocks, however. Ilbert's clock has an eight-day striking movement—this on a bell—with the organ element playing a selection of eight tunes, the chosen one being repeated three times automatically every three hours. Another musical clock of his make, this time in a fine mahogany long case, plays a selection of six tunes on twelve bells, but employing thirteen hammers, the extra hammer permitting a fast staccato effect on one bell. Despite his eminence, George Lindsay's work is unrepresented in the Royal Collection today.

John Ellicott is very much better documented. He was the son of a London watchmaker of the same name, who had come to the metropolis from Bodmin, in Cornwall, served an apprenticeship which started in 1687, been admitted to the Freedom of the Clockmakers' Company in 1696, elected to the Court of Assistants in 1726 and was still serving in the office of Warden when he died in June 1733. His home was in Allhallows, north of London Wall, while his business premises, at first, were in Austin Friars and later in Swithin's Alley, Royal Exchange. Baillie describes him as 'an ingenious watchmaker of great note', but, in the event, he never attained the eminence of his son. John Ellicott junior was born in 1706 and has been identified in Sweeting's Alley by 1728—Sweeting's is an alternative rendering of Swithin's—presumably in his father's workshop. Curiously, John junior never seems to have had any connection at all with the Clockmakers' Company, and the details of his training remain a mystery although it can be reasonably assumed that his father played some influential part in it. Chamberlain describes Ellicott as a scientific investigator; he certainly had a happy knack, probably helped by his undoubted brilliance, of getting to know the great scientists of his day. When he was elected, in 1738, to the privileged Fellowship of the Royal Society, his sponsors were Sir Hans Sloane, President of the Society and the Royal Physician, Martin Ffolkes the

137. (Above) *Portrait of John Ellicott, F.R.S.: the mezzotint is by Robert Dunkarton after a painting by Nathaniel Dance.* (Private Collection)

138. (Right) *Two-train bracket clock by John Ellicott in ebonized case with elaborate gilt-bronze mounts.* (Royal Collection)

antiquary, John Senex the celebrated globe-maker, and John Hadley the astronomer. In time, Ellicott was to become very friendly with James Ferguson, who frequently visited the Ellicott household at St John's, Hackney, where an observatory had been fitted out and experiments were made.

Ellicott's claim to horological fame rests on two developments. He paid particular attention to the cylinder escapement, bringing it to a state of perfection; his ruby cylinders are arguably the best of their kind ever made. There can be no question but that his craftsmanship was superb, and, in his more costly products, he went in for lavish decoration of cases,
138 some of them being genuine works of art, even their dials being enamelled on gold. The only clock of his make in today's Royal Collection is a two-train bracket clock in an ebonized case, with highly elaborate gilt-bronze ornamentation, standing 1 foot $8\frac{1}{2}$ inches high.

His other major contribution to horology was his unique compensation pendulum, in which the bob rests upon levers that are subject to movement from the superior expansion of a brass bar attached to the steel pendulum rod. He carried out some interesting experiments on the effects of two pendulums in close relationship with each other which must have laid the foundations for designs later put into such startling effect by A-L. Breguet, *q.v.* Several ideas of his were communicated through the medium of the Royal Society, appearing in its *Philosophical Transactions*; he was himself on the Council of that body for three years. Ellicott is said to have been a man of even temperament and cheerful disposition—clearly borne out by his
portrait, which was painted by Nathaniel Dance and 137
reproduced as a mezzotint by Robert Dunkarton—who took his pleasures in archery and whist; but it was his wife who, unintentionally, caused the greatest sensation in the household. She appeared to have died, and notices were sent out to that effect; but when examined by the Quaker Dr Fothergill, who had stopped to offer sympathy, she was found only to be in a trance. Even so, she remained thus for eighteen days; but later made

a complete recovery and lived many years after. Ellicott himself, however, dropped out of his chair, unexpectedly dead, in 1772.

Mention of Ellicott's compensation pendulum must inevitably lead to the first of George III's mainly scientific clocks, which is fitted with one. This is the monumental clock-driven barograph, the first of its kind, made by Alexander Cumming. This maker came to London from Scotland, where he is said to have been born in Edinburgh *c.*1732. He lived first in Clifford Street, off Bond Street, moving to Fleet Street in 1794. In 1766 he had published his well-known *The Elements of Clock and Watchwork, adapted to practice*; and in 1781 he was made an Honorary Freeman of the Clockmakers' Company. In 1763 he had been appointed one of the experts investigating John Harrison's explanation of his longitude watch known as H4. He was a Fellow of the Royal Society of Edinburgh—but not, as is sometimes said, of the more famous London one—and a magistrate; in fact, he had acquired all the appurtenances of a man of distinction, but more was yet to come.

The barograph briefly mentioned above was commissioned by George III; the transaction was finalized
141 with the payment, on 14th February 1765, of £1,178, a large amount in those days. Subsequently, Cumming received a retainer of £150 *per annum* for its maintenance. Not only is the machinery of the greatest sophistication—the clock case is of the highest quality, although its maker has not been recorded. With its carcase made of kingwood and mahogany, extensively mounted with chased gilt-bronze ornaments, it also has an interior fitting of carved ivory. The military trophies and other mounts are of such quality that the workmanship involved has been compared with that of the finest silversmiths of the time.

The mechanism consists, at the centre of the large
140 barograph dial, of a small month-duration regulator
142 143 clock, which has an escapement of Cumming's own design and, as already mentioned, an Ellicott compensated pendulum. The clock dial is surrounded by two removable parchment discs, the inner one revolving in six months and the outer in a year. In the trunk of the case, below the main dial, is the openwork dial of a siphon wheel barometer, graduated from 28 to 31 inches in hundredths of an inch. Barometric height is indicated by a pointer operated by a float, consisting of an ivory carriage supporting six ivory rods; two pairs of these rods, at their upper ends, carry pencils which record on the parchment discs. The ivory elements of the machinery, which are visible behind the glass panel in the trunk door, have their own artistic setting, within carved and fluted ivory Corinthian columns supporting a carved entablature, of the same material.

139. *Portrait of Alexander Cumming, F.R.S.* (Clockmakers' Company, London)

The Clockmakers' Company possesses a fine portrait of Cumming painted in oils by S. Drummond, ARA. 139
Apart from his own inventiveness and craftsmanship, Cumming has one other claim to fame: he was the uncle of John Grant, one of the finest of the London makers at the end of the eighteenth century. Grant, who died in 1810, was, in fact, apprenticed to Cumming and is often said to have succeeded him in the Fleet Street shop—but Cumming outlived him by four years. Even so, they may well have been in business together at some time or another, for Britten records seeing a watch signed 'Cumming & Grant, London'. In any event, Cumming eventually retired from the trade and settled in Pentonville, where he owned property. He died on 8th March 1814.

Apart from commissioning the finest English clockwork for the Royal Collection, George III did much, in a quiet, unpublicized way, to support and encourage the best workmen in the trade in London; and two examples here will suffice to illustrate his interest in them.

Thomas Mudge, son of a clergyman who later became a schoolmaster, was born in Exeter in 1715. He 144
seems to have been brought up in a cultured environment, and his father was sufficiently sympathetic to his talents and aspirations in the field of practical mechanics to bind him apprentice to no less a luminary in the horological world than George Graham—this for seven

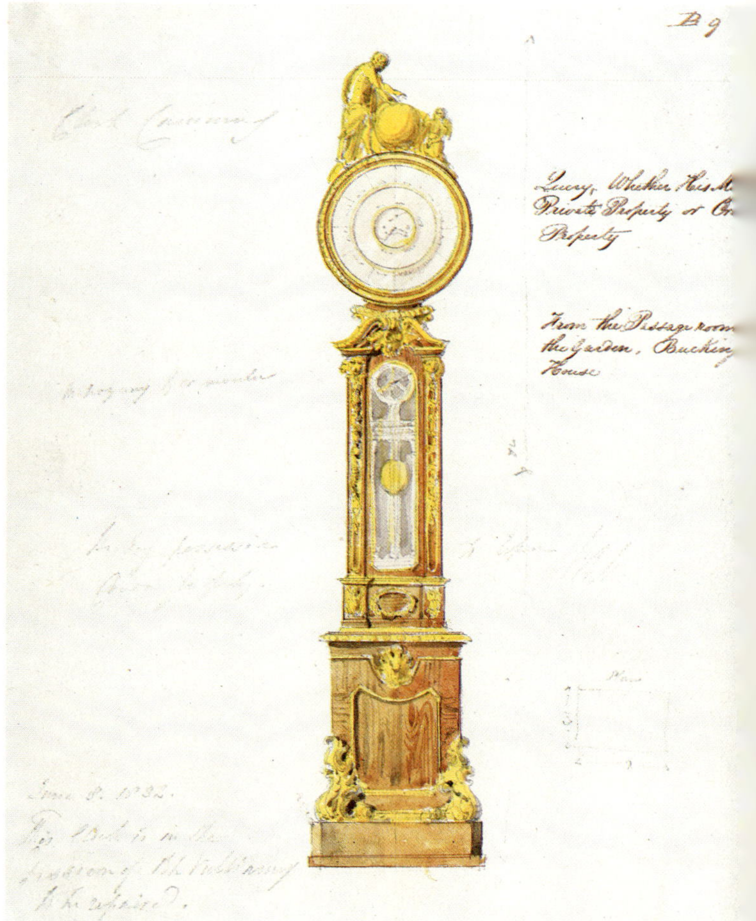

years from 4th May 1730. He was admitted to the Freedom of the Company on 15th January 1738, when he was a mere twenty-three years old. When Graham died, in 1751, Mudge took over his business and eventually took into partnership another of Graham's apprentices, William Dutton, forming the firm of Mudge & Dutton, but it has not yet been discovered exactly when this happened. Baillie states that watches signed with the two names do not appear before 1765. At any rate, in 1751 his premises, according to an advertisement in *The Daily Advertiser* for 18th November, were at the sign of the 'Dial and one Crown', opposite the 'Bolt and Tun' in Fleet Street.

However, Mudge's reputation as a superlative craftsman had been established even before Graham's death, and he seems to have had a permanent commission from Ferdinand, King of Spain, to supply any of his masterpieces that he pleased. It may have been as a result of this kind of popularity that he came to the notice of George III: the circumstances have not been uncovered up to the present. He will be remembered by horologists the world over for his invention of the lever escapement—the very heart of most mechanical watches worn today—and its application to two watches and as many clocks. He also

140. (Far left) *Full-length front view of Cumming's clock-driven barograph.* (Royal Collection)

141. (Left) *Cumming's barograph as depicted in the Pictorial Inventory.* (Royal Collection)

142. (Below) *Detail of the dial of Cumming's barograph.* (Royal Collection)

143. (Right) *Interior of Cumming's barograph, as seen through the trunk door, and showing ivory fittings and Ellicott pendulum bob.* (Royal Collection)

played a very considerable part in the formative years of the marine chronometer, through which he lived. Like Ellicott, he was one of the expert members of the Committee appointed in 1763 to assess Harrison's fourth timekeeper; and in 1771 he gave over his Fleet Street premises wholly to William Dutton and retired to Plymouth in order to find a quiet and undisturbed ambience in which to pursue his own thoughts and ideas about the solution to what was almost a national preoccupation—the design and production of an efficient marine timekeeper. The story of his efforts in this direction, with the design, manufacture and submission for test to the Board of Longitude of three timekeepers to his own very sophisticated and complex pattern is well known, as is also his son's attempt to reproduce them after Mudge senior's death in 1794. The fact is that the prototypes worked beautifully, the copies very poorly. Nobody could match the superb workmanship which Mudge bestowed upon his products, and that was sufficient to rule his designs in the marine context out of court. They had to be not only accurate in performance but reproducible in quantity by the average craftsman. Such a qualification was the very last that could conceivably be applied to Thomas Mudge, about whom a Select Committee of the House of Commons, assisted by a committee of men in science, philosophical instrument makers and watchmakers, which included Atwood, Ramsden, Troughton and De Luc, had said, in 1793: '[It is] admitted on all hands that Mr. Mudge was one of the first watchmakers that this country has produced.'

144. *Portrait of Thomas Mudge, by Nathaniel Dance.* (Clockmakers' Company, London)

It was by virtue of his work on the lever escapement that Mudge came to prominence in a royal context. He is thought to have developed the idea first about 1754, but whether as a model, a clock or perhaps only as a drawing, no one as yet knows. His most famous example, however, is in a watch, which has been described as 'perhaps the most historically important watch in the world'. This was acquired by George III—the circumstances of the acquisition do not seem to be known, nor indeed how much the King paid for it—and it is likely that he presented it to Queen Charlotte, although the only evidence for this is that the Queen complimented Mudge several times on the accurate performance of 'her watch'. This masterpiece remains in the Royal Collection to the present time and is kept at Windsor Castle.

The watch itself is large, with a movement all but 145 146 147
2 inches in diameter and the rest in proportion. The gold pair-cases carry the hallmark for 1769, indicating that Mudge constructed this object some time after the original lever idea had been developed by him. The cases bear a maker's mark PM, which is that of Peter Mounier, or Mouncer, of Frith Street, Soho, who registered it at the London Assay Office on 7th May 1761. A very full and complete technical analysis and report on this watch was published by Richard Good, FBHI, an expert restorer and now a member of staff of the British Museum, in a compendium entitled *Pioneers of Precision Timekeeping*, in 1965. That account, compiled shortly after the watch had been dismantled for the first thorough examination and overhaul for many years, gives a remarkable insight into Mudge's ingenuity and astonishing skill. It also touches upon such matters as the second Mudge lever watch, and the relations of this craftsman with his patron, Count von Bruhl, which would be superfluous in the present context but are to be recommended as compulsory reading for anyone wishing to delve more deeply into the history of this fundamental timekeeping invention.

The extraordinary thing about Mudge's principal contribution to horological history is his total disregard of it, at the time. There is no doubt that his version of the lever, like his chronometer model, would have been exceedingly difficult for any other craftsman—let alone one of only average skill—to make; and there were still minor technical improvements to come. Mudge's views

145. (Above) *Thomas Mudge's lever watch: general view.* (Royal Collection)

146. (Left) *Back plate of the movement of Mudge's lever watch.* (Royal Collection)

147. (Below) *The main elements of Mudge's lever watch, dismantled.* (Royal Collection)

are summed up in a letter he wrote to Count von Bruhl in August 1776, in which, after saying that he is too busy on his chronometers to make any more lever watches, he goes on:

> Another reason, and not a trifling one, is that although I think, if well executed, it has great merit, and will, in a pocket watch particularly, answer the purpose of timekeeping better than any other at present known; yet it has this disadvantage, that it requires a delicacy in the execution that you will find very few artists equal to, and fewer still that will give themselves the trouble to arrive at; which takes much from its merits. And as to the honour of the invention, I must confess I am not at all solicitous about it; whoever would rob me of it does me honour.

On the death of George Lindsay in 1776, George III made Thomas Mudge the Royal Watchmaker, at a fee of £150 a year, and this continued for the rest of his life. Indeed, it seems to have continued well beyond, for the official journals still publish Mudge's name in this incumbency up to 1820, which was long after he had died. It may be that the Appointment reverted to the parent firm, now with the Dutton sons Matthew and Thomas, which survived until 1824. It can hardly have gone to Thomas Mudge junior who, despite his horological entrepreneurship, was not himself a craftsman at all.

The other watchmaker in whom George III took more than a passing interest was also involved in the pioneering activity directed at finding a practical marine timekeeper. This was John Arnold, whose year
148 of birth has now been narrowed to 1735 or 1736; where, is not certain, although he is said to have come from Bodmin. Descended from a family of clockmaker/gunsmiths, he seems to have left the Bodmin area quite early in his working life and to have established himself at Launceston, Cornwall. Following some kind of domestic dispute, probably with his uncle, Arnold went to work in Holland where, if nothing else, he acquired fluent German, as spoken in the Low Countries. He spent about two years so occupied, returning then to his native land and working for another five years as a kind of travelling journeyman, in which he also practised the gunsmith's art. It has been conjectured by Dr Vaudrey Mercer, who has written the definitive work on the Arnolds, that John may have been the subject of a story recounted by E. J. Wood, in his remarkable *Curiosities of Clocks and Watches*, concerning the dismantling, cleaning and re-assembling of a watch on the top of the 404-feet-high spire of Salisbury Cathedral. This is said to have been undertaken by a watchmaker named Arnold, for a wager made at the 'Pheasant', in Salisbury; and the whole operation was to take less than an hour. However, the account of this feat starts with the words 'At the commencement of the same century . . .' to establish when it was carried out; and reference back to the preceding paragraph leads straight to the phrase 'Early in the present century . . .', which clearly means the nineteenth. John Arnold's life was wholly encompassed within the eighteenth.

Arnold's career really seems to have got under way when, early in 1762, and while working in St Albans, he had occasion to repair a repeating watch for a Mr William McGuire. This gentleman was so impressed that he put up the money for Arnold to move to London; and the next we hear of him is in May 1762, when he is recorded for the first time as paying rates on business premises in Devereux Court, in the Strand. He stayed there until 1769.

The next important step took place probably before 1764, when John Arnold was favoured with an audience of the King, at which he was granted permission to present a watch for the royal approbation and as a gift. In any event, in that year he did present the King with a tiny watch, having a half-quarter-repeating cylinder movement which was a mere one third of an inch in diameter, and which was mounted in a ring. This event caused such a stir at the time that it was reported *in extenso* not only in the *Gentleman's Magazine*, under date 4th June but also in the *Annual Register* for that year; and subsequently it was incorporated by E. J. Wood in his book mentioned above. The first-named of the two journals gave a part-by-part breakdown of the content of this watch movement, together with the weight of each component listed. Wood describes how Arnold had himself to make nearly all the tools he used in its manufacture; and by any standards it must certainly have been a quite remarkable achievement.

The King, who by now can have been no mean judge of fine clock- and watchwork, was so pleased with this mechanical marvel that he gave Arnold 500 guineas as a recognition of his skill. The Emperor of Russia, when he heard of this, offered Arnold 1,000 guineas to make one for him also, but Arnold refused so as not to risk depreciating the King's watch by duplicating it.

There is some confusion, in relation to this first watch, as to whether it had a ruby cylinder escapement or one of the more usual kind; but the probability is that it was the latter. Not so with the second such watch, however. The *Annual Register* for 1770 states: 'Mr. Arnold, watch-maker in St. James's Street, presented to his Majesty a small repeating watch in a ring, the cylinder of which he made of an oriental ruby. Its diameter is the 54th part of an inch, its length the 47th, and its weight the 200th part of a grain.'

The King was not the only member of the Royal Family whose interest was caught by these baubles: on the first occasion, another newspaper report has it that

148. *Portrait of John Arnold, engraved by Susan Esther Reid after a painting by R. Davy.* (Clockmakers' Company, London)

'Mr. Arnold, when he waited upon his Majesty . . . had the honour of being introduced to their Majesties, the Princess Dowager of Wales, and the Princess of Mecklenburgh, who were all graciously pleased to show their approbation to so excellent a piece of mechanism.' Later the same report intimates that orders for similar watches had been received from distinguished foreigners. Finally, we come to the archival detail. The following excerpts are taken from the relevant royal records:

1st October 1764	To paid Mr John Arnold for Repeating Watch in a Ring	£315
18th October 1766	To paid Mr Arnold for remounting Your Majesty's Ring Watch with Diamond Brilliants, etc.	£33.1.6
5th November 1767	Paid Mr Arnold, Watchmaker, by Your Majesty's Order upon Account	£100
— May 1770	To paid Mr Arnold for a Watch	£400
— August 1771	To Paid Mr Arnold for a ruby cylinder	£12.12.0

The first payment appears to correct Wood's account, in that the premium for the first watch was 300 rather than 500 guineas. The second watch, at £400, reflects the added work in making the cylinder of ruby, as well as other, perhaps decorative refinements. The last payment is something of a puzzle. Vaudrey Mercer suggests that, since the King had an intense practical interest in watchmaking, he commissioned a ruby cylinder, on its own, for the sheer pleasure of admiring the superior technical achievement implicit in its manufacture; for when in place in a watch movement, it would hardly be visible at all. Finally, there remains the payment on account in 1767; it has been conjectured that this was by way of an encouragement to Arnold to enter the 'longitude' arena, by producing a prototype marine timepiece. His first attempt in that particular role was finished in 1768 and shown to the Board of Longitude in 1770.

If this last speculation is correct—and indeed it may well be—then it quite clearly shows the King in a patronage situation with a very strong national flavour. It was very much in the country's best interests to solve the constantly recurring problem of accurately determining the longitude when out of sight of land, thereby avoiding unnecessary risks of shipwreck or starvation which this lack of navigational precision could entail. In supporting Arnold, too, the King had made a singularly wise choice; it is generally acknowledged today that, in the final analysis, Arnold's particular contribution, which effectively put chronometer manufacture on an efficient quantity-production basis, was the most important of all. There was no point in designing a precision timekeeper for marine use, however good its performance, if its technical complexity was such as to prohibit its production save by one or two supreme master-craftsmen. The demand for such a commodity was not in units or tens but certainly in hundreds and eventually thousands, and the more skilled people capable of making such instruments, the better.

A fringe activity of Arnold's—he had been accustomed to plying a whole variety of different trades during his days as a journeyman—was as a button-maker, and there is one listing of him in which he is so described. George III collected buttons, and Arnold seems to have obliged him in this capacity as well, although to what extent is not known. It would have been a somewhat more relaxing pursuit than watch-making; and the fact that Arnold spoke fluent German would have been seen as advantageous, even though George III himself was perfectly fluent in English.

Mention has already been made of Arnold in St James's Street, where he moved from Devereux Court in 1769. Shortly afterwards, his wife Margaret—the date and details of his marriage have not yet yielded themselves to researchers—presented him with a son,

149. (Left) *A typical gold watch by Daniel de St. Leu: dial view, with engraved outer case on the left.* (Clockmakers' Company, London)

150. (Below left) *Movement of the watch by Daniel de St. Leu, removed from the inner of the engraved pair-cases, which is seen on the right.* (Clockmakers' Company, London)

to be named John Roger Arnold and to follow in his famous father's footsteps. St. James's must have been a very convenient address for a craftsman in such favour at Court, but he stayed there only two years, moving in 1771 to 2 Adam Street, Adelphi Buildings, Strand. His workshop remained at that address until 1782, after which he rented a shop in Bank Buildings, 102 Cornhill. Meantime, however, he had gone to live—from 1779 to his death—at Well Hall, Eltham. He died on 25th August 1799, at the age of sixty-three, and was buried at Chislehurst.

It is sad to report that neither of George III's ring watches has endured in the Royal Collection to the present time; and their whereabouts today are unknown. Their size would be so remarkable as to ensure their existence being recorded in print, had they indeed survived intact; their inherent fragility must make this unlikely. There is, in the Usher Collection at Lincoln, a tiny ring watch which, it is claimed, belonged to George III and was made by John Arnold. However, when Dr Mercer examined this object, he found it to be unsigned and almost certainly of continental origin.

One watchmaker is particularly associated with the Queen at about this period. Daniel de St Leu is first 149
identified at 'The Golden Head' in Cloak Lane, in 1753. 150
This same address later became simply 17 Cloak Lane. In 1765 he was appointed Watchmaker to the Queen, a title which he held for the rest of his working life, for his watches are consistently signed 'Servt to Her Majesty'. His output tended to be elaborately embellished, and it is quite usual to find his watch cases encrusted with paste or even diamonds. A typical example of the highly decorated style he favoured is to be found in a triple-cased clock-watch—the striking watch returned to favour for a while in the later eighteenth century. In this watch, the outer case is clad in leather overlaid with gold scroll and pin work; the middle case is of agate, a rarely used material in watch cases, and this too is overlaid with gold openwork decoration. The inner case is covered in green translucent enamel with gold floral decoration in relief. This watch is for the Turkish market and had the conventional verge full-plate movement of no special or unusual quality. This maker supplied many timekeepers for the Eastern markets, and then the emphasis was usually external, with the machinery being quite ordinary. Later on in his working life, Daniel de St Leu moved to 38 Cornhill, where he was succeeded, about 1790, by Rivers & Son, who were operating from 1782 to 1815. Baillie indicates a final date for de St Leu—but not necessarily his death—as 1797.

It must be cause for regret that his work is unrepresented in the Royal Collection, for any inspection of Daniel de St Leu's watches would make their appeal to the feminine taste obvious—and clearly the Queen succumbed to it.

Two of the most famous clocks associated with George III must be the complex astronomical spring clocks attributed to Christopher Pinchbeck and Eardley Norton; these share several things in common, apart from their both having four dials.

Chronologically the first, although only by two or

three years, is the clock by Norton. It has an elaborately carved mahogany case with, on all four sides, silver cresting featuring the lion and the unicorn and, below
151 the dials, inset panels of openwork silver showing
152 confronting female sphinxes. Apart from the astronomical work, the clock has a three-train format with 'ting-tang' quarters. The four dials are of white enamel, and the principal time dial has a painted rural scene with figures at its centre. The information exhibited by the four dials was described as follows, by the *Gentleman's Magazine* for June 1765:

> The first and principal face shews the true and apparent time, with the rising and setting of the sun in several parts of the world, by a moving horizon;
> The second front shews the motion of the planets in their orbits, according to the system of Copernicus;
> The third, the age and different phases of the moon, with the time of the tide at 32 different sea-ports;
> The fourth, by a curious retrograde motion in a spiral, shews every day of the month and year, with the number and days of the week in proper emblems.
> The calculations and numbers for the wheels for the solar system were given by Dr. Bevis, and the designs for the dial plates, with the numbers and calculations and mode of performing, etc., by Mr. Ferguson.

The thirty-two different seaports are mostly in the British Isles; and the description quoted above also refers to the installation of the clock by Norton and Christopher Pinchbeck in the Queen's House, or Buckingham House as it was better known. Pinchbeck
was presumably mentioned because, being the holder 153
of a Royal Appointment, he may have had to commission the work; but there seems no doubt that it was Eardley Norton who built the clock. On 5th July 1765 he was paid the substantial sum of £1,042; the entry actually reads: 'To Paid M. Pinchbeck for a Clock made by M. Eardley Norton as p: Bill £1042-0-0'. This entry, from the Privy Purse bill-book, has survived, but unfortunately, the bill itself has not, so that no certain details can be adduced, for example, concerning the superb clock case, in every respect of a quality fit for this particular mechanism.

151. (Below) *Four-dialled astronomical clock by Eardley Norton: view of two of the dials.* (Royal Collection)

152. (Below right) *The other two dials of the Eardley Norton clock.* (Royal Collection)

watches. Some of these are not of the highest quality and indeed were once thought to be forgeries; but there are so many of them, often complete with fraudulent hallmarks suggesting that they may have been finished in Switzerland, that they might seem more likely to represent his trade abroad. His watches of wholly domestic manufacture are well up to the finest London practice, however.

The second of these four-dialled astronomical clocks was completed in 1768, and the signature—which appears on the planetarium dial—reads: 'C. Pinchbeck Suscepit I. Merigeot I. Monk Perfecerunt'. Various interpretations have been put on this, but the sense might seem to be that Pinchbeck commissioned and supervised the project, while the actual work was carried out by John Merigeot and John Monk. The 154 155

153. (Left) *The Eardley Norton clock as it was originally sited, in the Octagonal Library in Buckingham House. This view comes from W. H. Pyne's* History of the Royal Residences . . . *(1819).* (Guildhall Library, City of London)

154. (Right) *Four-dialled astronomical clock by Christopher Pinchbeck: view of two of the dials.* (Royal Collection)

155. (Below) *The other two dials of Christopher Pinchbeck's astronomical clock.* (Royal Collection)

There has been some speculation upon this last aspect of this object. The principal contender as case-maker is generally agreed to be John Bradburn, the King's cabinet-maker. Clifford Smith cites an existing bill for a clock bracket as evidence, but the sum involved—£35 15s—seems ridiculously small; while Geoffrey de Bellaigue, despite disputing this assumption, nevertheless agrees that Bradburn may well have been responsible. It seems possible that the cost of the case may have been included in the large sum paid for the clock. Photographs of the Eardley Norton clock give little impression of scale, and in fact it is comparatively small, being $17\frac{1}{4}$ inches high, $9\frac{5}{8}$ inches wide and $10\frac{1}{8}$ inches deep. It was formerly in the Octagonal Library in Buckingham House, where it is shown in the engraving by Pyne which was published on 1st February 1818. It is now in the Principal Corridor of the Palace.

Eardley Norton is regarded as an eminent clock-maker, who was at work between 1760 and 1794, or thereabouts, and had premises in St John Street, Clerkenwell. He took out one patent, in 1771, for a new kind of striking-mechanism for clocks and watches (pat. no. 987). He is best known for musical and astronomical clock- and watchwork but is also thought to have had a considerable export market for his

former, the son of a clockmaker, also called John, with premises in Christchurch, Spitalfields, was apprenticed to George Somersall on 7th March 1742 but subsequently turned over to his father. He was admitted to the Freedom on 7th November 1750 and elected to the Livery in 1766. John Monk, on the other hand, was the son of a carpenter called Gilbert Monk, of Berwick Street, Soho, and already dead at the time of the apprenticeship. John was bound to Stephen Goujon for seven years from 18th January 1762; but he never seems to have been admitted to the Freedom, which may simply mean that he chose to leave the City of London to work elsewhere. Although such claims have been made, there seems to be no good foundation for connecting these craftsmen with the Congreve skeleton clocks made by John Moxon, *q.v.*; consideration of the time-scale alone must make any such association unlikely.

As for Christopher Pinchbeck, he was a member of a well-known family active in the clock and watch trade, and with extensions also into toy-making as well as musical instruments. Toys here mean small personal items rather than playthings. The metal alloy still called by this family's surname—consisting principally of zinc and copper in varying proportions depending on the end-product—has been claimed as the personal invention of various individuals of this very talented *ménage*, who referred to it as the 'true metal' and gave fearful warnings against being deceived by 'false metals' made by others. However that may be, Christopher—the second generation of this forename—was born in 1710. Details of his training have not been recorded, but probably it was undertaken within the family circle. After his father's death in 1732, he went into business under the sign 'Pinchbeck's Head', in Fleet Street and not far from his father's old shop which was now being run by his younger brother Edward.

Pinchbeck's middle name should have been versatility—toys, clocks and watches, ingenious musical and automaton extravaganzas, designer and patentee of a device for keeping candles upright in their sticks, nothing was too large or too small for his consideration, providing it was profitable. He experimented with other premises, finally moving to Cockspur Street where he remained until his death in 1783. His 'mechanical wonders'—such as 'the celebrated and well-known Triangular Musical Machine the Panopticon'—were exhibited from time to time, and latterly in a 'repository' above the Cockspur Street shop. It is sad that, apart from the astronomical clock in the Royal Collection, not one of his really elaborate masterpieces has survived; the eighteenth century is remarkable, among much else, for the emergence of these great exhibition clocks with multi-functional movements, and some work of other makers in this *genre* is still to be seen, so that comparisons could have been interesting.

The astronomical concepts of the Pinchbeck clock are clearly based upon the earlier example, of Norton. It was seen by Lady Mary Coke before delivery and installation; in a letter dated 29th January 1768 she writes:

Lady Stafford called upon me at half an hour after eleven. She proposed our going first to Mr. Pinchback [*sic*] to see a very fine Clock that was just finisht for his Majesty. 'Twas well worth the seeing. The Clock is itself very curious, but too complicated a piece of workmanship to be easily described. The case is magnificent, the execution extremely fine, and the design partly His Majesty's and partly Mr. Chambers' his Architect.

The case of this clock, veneered in tortoiseshell and enriched with finely chased ormolu and silver mounts, was designed by Sir William Chambers, and a full-scale preliminary drawing by him is preserved in Sir John Soane's Museum. As has already been indicated, the King is also said to have had a hand in it, although to what extent is not known; there are notable differences of detail between the drawing and the clock itself, as well as an increase in scale, and conceivably some or all of these reflect his influence. The four dials show, respectively, the time of day and solar time; a small orrery showing the motions of six planets, being Mercury, Venus, Earth, Mars, Jupiter and Saturn as well as, untypically, a metallic thermometer divided on a scale 25 to 85 with numbers marking each complete decade; the tides at forty-three points, again mainly British ports, with a moon dial above and four subsidiaries in the corners for controlling striking and regulating the pendulum; and finally, a display showing days of the week, position of the sun in the zodiac, and days of the month with a planisphere showing the position of the stars.

The Pinchbeck clock is considerably larger than its counterpart by Eardley Norton, standing 2 feet 6 inches high, 16 inches wide and having a base diameter of 1 foot 8 inches. Clifford Smith describes it as having groups of Corinthian columns, on which each of the acanthus leaves that form the decoration has been cast and applied separately; the rich entablature is surmounted by a dome, round which are eight small draped tortoiseshell vases. It stands on a circular plinth on which are four larger vases of the same material adorned with ormolu festoons. The clock is normally displayed upon an ebonized and gilt wood fluted pedestal, in the Music Room in Buckingham Palace.

This seems an appropriate point to hark back to the fortunes and personalities of the Vulliamys. Benjamin,

Mary and Justin Vulliamy's eldest child, born in 1747, seems to have shown some early promise for, at the age of eleven, he won a Society of Arts premium for a drawing. In due course he went into his father's business, but the commercial side of the enterprise did not really appeal to him. 'He was too much a gentleman to make a good tradesman, too much engrossed with the improvement of Norland House'—so wrote his son Justin Theodore, referring to a complicated transaction in the early 1790s whereby Benjamin bought part of the Norland Estate in London's Notting Hill Gate, and later Norland House itself, together with stabling and outbuildings. One of these 'improvements' was held to be the first artesian well to be sunk in England; a depth of 261 feet was reached, and water flowed out at a rate of 46 gallons a minute. The output from this spring was leased to a group of three people operating under the pretentious name of the Notting Hill Waterworks, for one guinea per week; they in turn sold it to the populace at large for half-a-crown a ton or one half-penny per gallon. Benjamin and his family lived at Norland House right up to his death on Christmas Day 1811, and the family interests in that area lasted until 1838. It is known that, at some point, Benjamin had married a Swiss girl, Sarah de Gingins, but of their twelve children, six died in infancy.

Benjamin Vulliamy was the first of his family to be admitted to the Freedom of the Clockmakers' Company, and that by an unusual route. On 8th January 1781 'Resolved that a Special Court be summoned to meet on Monday the 5th of February next at 9 o'clock in the morning in order to admit a number of Gentlemen of the trade and profession into the Freedom of this Company.' In fact, Benjamin Vulliamy headed the list of those admitted, but not until 2nd April in that year—and in the rank of Honorary Freeman, which was specially reserved for those 'men whose practical knowledge of the Art would be valuable in the protection of the rights and privileges of the Craft, and whose social position would enable them to render useful service in defence of its interests . . .' as Samuel Atkins and William Overall so succinctly put it, in their definitive history of the Worshipful Company.

The numbering of clocks by the Vulliamy firm has always been something of a mystery, but it is likely that it started during Benjamin's lifetime, although perhaps not including regulators and special commissions; in any event clock production was still small during the 1790s although it increased after 1800. It is probably true to say, too, that Benjamin Vulliamy had too many other interests occupying his time to worry about 'bread and butter' production so that he is seen at his best only in the more elaborate and sophisticated creations.

Like the other principals in his family business both before and after him, Benjamin Vulliamy enjoyed a Royal Appointment, this being first promulgated in 1773. He received a fee from this incumbency of £150 *per annum*; and it can be reasonably adduced that he earned his reward, for his name is constantly cropping up in connection not only with new timepieces but also with the repair and maintenance of those already existing in the Royal Collection.

Benjamin Vulliamy's most advanced timekeepers were undoubtedly his regulator clocks. Of three he made for George III, two were destined for the Observatory at Kew, and all date from the period 1790– 156
1800. In figured Spanish mahogany cases, the two 158
observatory clocks have grasshopper escapements, not only of the highest accuracy but virtually friction-free, and gridiron compensation pendulums; both these components were the inventions of John 'Longitude' Harrison. Both clocks also employ a pair of friction wheels to support each pivot of the wheel train, one set higher than the other to counteract the directional

156. *Benjamin Vulliamy's regulator, showing 'grasshopper' escapement and friction rollers* (British Museum—on loan from H.M. The Queen)

pressure from the pivot, and sun-and-planet maintaining-power is used to keep them going consistently during winding up. One of these clocks is now on loan to the British Museum, while the other is in the Science Museum, having passed to George IV, William IV, the Dukes of Sussex and Cumberland, the son of the latter, and finally to B. L. Vulliamy's widow and his successors. The third clock, with pedimented top, has Graham's dead-beat escapement and mercurial compensation pendulum; the movement is numbered 830, 157
and it is located in Buckingham Palace. The heights of Vulliamy's regulators, incidentally, seem to vary between 6 feet 8 inches and 7 feet 2 inches, making them of quite modest proportions.

One royal commission of Benjamin Vulliamy's remains a mystery. It seems that he made a combination clock and wind-dial for George IV, at a cost of £600, for the Great Staircase of Carlton House; at a later date it was said to have been fixed up in the Library at Buckingham Palace. However that may be, Benjamin Lewis Vulliamy, his son, refers to it, in correspondence during the year 1845, as being in the possession of a Mr Saunders, an official at Brighton Pavilion and Windsor Castle. Nothing seems to have been heard of it since, although W. H. Pyne, in his '*History of the Royal Residences . . .*' (1819), describes and illustrates a wind-dial of unique appearance in this location. Whether or not it was Vulliamy's production is not stated. (See also fig. 165).

As to his more domestic timepieces for his royal patron, Benjamin Vulliamy's range is best explored by describing two typical examples. The first was specially made about 1790 for the King's use at Windsor Castle and consists of a satinwood clock cylinder, garlanded in laurels of gilt-bronze and with a finial above, resting upon a temple-like structure containing a Derby group 159
in biscuit porcelain, of 'Time clipping the wings of Cupid'. The temple, its Corinthian columns of boxwood with ormolu capitals, has a cornice and inner dome painted with arabesques, garlands and swags *en grisaille*; it has a mirror back and is approached by steps veneered with tulipwood. The two-train movement has an enamel dial with gilt numerals, and the back plate is

157. (Left) *Benjamin Vulliamy's regulator with Graham's dead-beat escapement and mercurial pendulum: general view.* (Royal Collection)

158. (Far right) *Benjamin Vulliamy's regulator for Kew Observatory.* (Science Museum)

159. (Right) *'Time clipping the wings of Cupid'—the pedestal clock by Benjamin Vulliamy on painted satinwood cylindrical plinth.* (Royal Collection)

60
5
10
15
20
25
30
35
40
45
50
55
Regulator

160. (Left) *Clock by Benjamin Vulliamy in white marble case with ormolu mounts and resting on a yellow scagliola pedestal.* (Royal Collection)

161. (Right) *Marble and ormolu clock by Benjamin Vulliamy incorporating a symbolical group in Derby biscuit china.* (Royal Collection)

signed 'Vulliamy, London'. The clock rests upon a painted satinwood pedestal, the decoration of which includes three oval reserves showing mythological scenes, the central one being 'Apollo in his chariot'. Although offering a very appropriate setting and support for the clock, it seems unlikely that it was supplied especially for it as the Windsor guide-book for 1792 describes the clock, when it was located in the Queen's Drawing Room, but not the pedestal. Clifford Smith states that the clock used to rest upon the mantelpiece in the '1855' Room in Buckingham Palace, and that Queen Mary united it with the pedestal when the clock was moved to the Blue Drawing Room. Pedestal and clock together rise to a height of 6 feet 10 inches and a width of 1 foot 11 inches, the height of the clock alone being 2 feet 8 inches.

The second clock is essentially of white marble with gilt-bronze ornaments, and having three Derby biscuit 161
porcelain figures, on the right Astronomy, on the left an angel pointing to the clock dial with the right hand while holding a wreath in the left, and in front an infant holding a sextant. These figures are said to have been modelled by Jean Jacques Spengler, one of the most skilful artists employed at the Derby factory. At the left, in ormolu, is the reversed capital of a Corinthian column, upon which rests a parchment engraved 'Design'd/for his/R.H.ye P./of WALES'. The two-train clock itself is set centrally within a broken column, giving a focal point to the group, around whom are spread ormolu mounts in the shape of books, a telescope and a globe, the whole resting upon a curved stepped marble base. There exists correspondence between Vulliamy and William Duesbury of Derby, who took over the manufactory on his father's death in 1786, in which there are several references to the biscuit porcelain figures, such as putti, charged at 10s 6d each, which the former commissioned for mounting on his clock cases; and this particular clock was made for George IV in 1788. The signature 'Vulliamy' is to be found on an ormolu ornament—a book—at the foot of the angel.

Like his more famous—or perhaps, in the horological context, infamous—son Benjamin Lewis Vulliamy, Benjamin carried out his share of repairs and restorations to royal clocks, but without, apparently,

feeling the compulsive need to substitute his own work for that of every other craftsman. Nevertheless, he did undertake some alterations. In an invoice amounting to £47 7s 6d and dated 5th June 1811, for instance, it is clear that he added the cushion and clustered columns in imitation of bamboo which give added height to the Chinese Drummer Boy clock. In 1808—his bill is dated 24th March—he overhauled the astronomical clock with three dials by Lépine. There is also a very handsome bracket clock, in tortoiseshell with ormolu embellishments, in which he has inserted a three-train movement of his own make, about 1800. This is a most outstanding clock, much in the French taste but with a 162
bell top, surmounted centrally by a garlanded two-handled covered cup with an acorn finial; at the level of the broken arch, there are no less than five such finials. The sides of the case are fitted with very large diapered and fretted panels, and carrying-handles, while the front angles of the case are chamfered and mounted with climbing ormolu foliage arising from scrolling feet. The area below the dial is similarly enriched with ormolu festoons, while the dial itself is certainly reminiscent of French practice, as also are the hands.

There are other clocks by Benjamin Vulliamy, still at

VULLIAMY
LONDON

162. (Left) *Three-train bracket clock in tortoiseshell-veneered case with ormolu mounts, about 1760: it now contains a movement by Benjamin Vulliamy, installed about 1800.* (Royal Collection)

163. (Right) *Portrait of Benjamin Vulliamy.* (Clockmakers' Company, London)

work in the royal residences—Clifford Smith mentions, for instance, 'a good example of a Georgian timepiece of about 1780', in an arched mahogany case with chased scroll cornerpieces; and a rather more elaborate one of about 1790 is of white marble, of architectural design with chased ormolu mounts. The top, which is
160 surmounted by an urn, has seated figures of lions on either side while, below the dial, is to be found an eagle, in the French style. A tall finely moulded scagliola pedestal decorated with ormolu and resting on a satinwood base conceals the length of the pendulum; and the whole structure is 6 feet 9 inches high.

There can be no doubt that Benjamin, of all the
163 generations of his family to serve the Crown, stood in particularly high regard, being frequently consulted by George III—especially in relation to the private observatory at Kew—and his work might seem, at least in so far as renovations and alterations are concerned, to have been carried out with thought and sensitivity, rather than with functional efficiency as the sole objective. The Vulliamys, as a firm, supplied many other objects than simply clocks—George III, for example, whose enthusiasm for contemporary art had led directly to the setting up and early support of the Royal Academy, gave that august body, at one point, a superb bronze oil-burning chandelier of 'thirty spouts', to improve the lighting of its premises. The cost of this object—the bill of May 1812 is still preserved—was £2,400; extras included a chain costing £79 4s and a bracket, at £10; some 17 gallons of sperm oil were supplied, at 10s 6d a gallon; and finally—it seems likely that the chandelier was first used at the Academy Banquet—'Men's time tending, lighting and trimming, 3 nights' cost £2 10s.

Labour was clearly the cheapest commodity of all in those days; and indeed, when talking of the cost of works of art, including clocks, large sums of money were certainly involved. The story of the Vulliamy family can be left, for the moment, with two reflections upon this aspect of their activities. When the Prince of Wales, as he then was, married—in April 1795—Parliament passed an Act enabling the King to settle an annuity upon his eldest son, and to pay any outstanding debts, the intention also being to stop any more accumulating in the future as well as to regulate 'the mode of expenditure of the said revenues'. Pious hope though this may have been, a Commission was immediately established to give effect to the Act, the first stage of which clearly required it to audit the then-existing situation. This revealed that many thousands of pounds were owed, to a large number of tradesmen, the largest bill being for £15,500 for furniture supplied by Daguerre to Carlton House. Among the clockmakers, Benjamin Vulliamy was owed £776, John Thwaites of Clerkenwell £59, Breguet of Paris £157, and Lépine of Paris claimed no less than £3,250 'for a clock', but this last was disallowed by the Commissioners. The work of sorting out all these claims and settling up those that were justified, was not completed until 1807. That this was not to be the end of extravagance, however, was soon self-evident. The year when the Regency was instituted—1811—saw an enormous outlay of money upon new furniture, in the latest fashion, for Carlton House: over twelve months, more than £10,000 was spent in this way, of which Vulliamy's bill, for £2,129, was one of the largest. At the time, such expenditure was doubtless seen by many as the height of outrageous folly—and, on a comparable scale, might well be so seen today—but, at this distance in time, most people must be grateful that it is possible to enjoy such sumptuous objects still, while the circumstances of their acquisition have quite properly faded into mostly-forgotten history.

5 George IV and the French Connection

So far as clocks are concerned, the Royal Collection contains more of native English origin than of any other nationality; of the remainder, there are many more French clocks to be found than those of other foreign countries. That this is so is due almost entirely to George IV's remarkable sympathy with and desire for French works of art of all kinds. This is not really surprising. His education, among other benefits, had made him completely fluent in French, even to the point of writing letters to his mother in that language; his reading was predisposed towards the literary, military and historical works emanating from that great country; and his friends were dedicated francophils, who steered him even further towards the culture of the Sun King. In the event, however, he has been more often likened to Louis XV, not only on account of his less acceptable ostentations—his many love affairs and his gambling—but also for his many fine qualities. He was a noted host, who possessed to a degree those virtues needed to put guests at their ease and to ensure that they enjoyed themselves; and he was a gifted exponent of those minor but nonetheless important arts, of good conversation and of impeccable taste in all material things. Like Louis XV, too, he was preoccupied with architecture and the continual improvement of his surroundings. This in turn implied attention to fine detail, innovation and a flair for using space to the best possible advantage. As a result of all these influences, the Royal Collection today includes what must certainly be one of the finest accumulations of French art ever to be brought together outside France itself.

The French have always tended to view clocks as furniture first, their time-measuring capabilities taking second place to their fitness for a particular location in terms of their relationship to and visual harmony with the surrounding décor and architecture. There are exceptions, of course, and the Royal Collection possesses examples; but there is no reason to suppose that George IV had any appreciation of the technicalities of clockwork, and it is more likely, in view of his father's devotion to it, that he largely disregarded it. His French clocks were works of art first, furniture second and timekeepers a very poor third. This was just as well, perhaps, since B. L. Vulliamy took every opportunity to substitute his own mechanisms for those originally supplied. He had the poorest opinion of French clockmaking, as witness a letter he wrote to Benjamin Jutsham on 18th December 1813 concerning a clock submitted to him for examination: 'I am sorry to inform you that the whole except [the] Case is what may be comprehended under the term of complete French Work. The fixing into the Case of the Clock is so bad that it is as unsteady as a Clock can be, the Communication from the Clock to the hands is very bad . . . .'

For convenience, the appellation 'George IV' will be used to identify this monarch not only when he was King (1820–30) but also when Prince of Wales, from 1762, and as Regent, after 1811. Even though the records of his purchases are far from complete, it is possible to form some idea of his *modus operandi*. It is clear that he relied heavily upon friends or members of his Household to act as his agents abroad; sometimes they were specifically dispatched to seek some particular item or to inspect one that was already on offer. On occasion, objects were sent to this country on approval; but if they were too bulky to make a possibly fruitless journey worthwhile, drawings were often provided instead. The King also bought French works of art in London, acting through dealers in the case of items offered at an auction. The extraordinary fact remains, too, that even war with France did not unduly obstruct his purchasing capabilities. Important shipments of clocks and bronzes were received at Carlton House from the famous French bronze-manufacturer

P–P. Thomire both in June 1812 and in July 1813; by the latter time, Wellington was already busy driving the French back into France across the Pyrenees.

French clocks are to be found in such an enormous profusion of styles that it is difficult to categorize them; and, in any event, there is only space to include a relatively small selection, but sufficient, it is hoped, to give some indication of the sheer quality of these objects that is to be found in the Royal Collection. So far as it can be done, therefore, the clocks will be grouped under self-explanatory headings, being of more value, in that presentation, than if they had been grouped chronologically, for example, in order of acquisition. Indeed, such an arrangement as this latter would itself have presented difficulties since the antecedents of some objects are not known with complete certainty.

Large free-standing clocks

The nearest approaches to the traditional English long-case clock that the French considered acceptable were variously called the pedestal clock (*pendule sur socle*) and the tall clock (*régulateur*). While it is true that the English form has remained unique among large domestic clocks of all countries in that its long trunk case clearly has a mainly utilitarian purpose, the French, in their turn, went to the greatest lengths to disguise the need for height in which to accommodate the drop of the weights and the swinging long pendulum — 39 inches for the seconds-beating version. Thus, the trunk of such clocks tends to be seen either as a vertical tapering plinth, whose real function is hidden by applied decoration of various kinds and often of great complexity, or to consist of decorated bulbous shapes to mislead the eye, which associates weights and their cords with straight lines.

There are many such clocks in the Royal Collection, but perhaps it might be appropriate to start with one of positively monumental proportions, even when compared with English practice. With an overall height that just rises above 9 feet, its other dimensions are equally massive: its greatest width is 2 feet 9 inches and depth, 17 inches.

The case of this large clock is made of oak, veneered with tulipwood, purplewood and mahogany, the whole
164 being extravagantly enriched with gilt-bronze mounts consisting of scrolls and swags of ormolu drapery on the upper part, while on the pedestal there are masks and scrollwork extending to the base, which terminates in four huge lion's feet. The seated female figure and three

164. *Monumental* pendule sur socle, *with case by François Duhamel.* (Royal Collection)

165. *View of the Grand Staircase at Carlton House, from W. H. Pyne's* History of the Royal Residences . . . *(1819). The clock case by Duhamel appears at bottom right; above, 'Atlas, bearing on his shoulders a circular map of Europe, as the face of a wind-dial, the pivot being placed on the meridian of London; by which contrivance the index denotes the point whence the wind proceeds, and also what part of land or sea it visits in its progress'. This remarkable device may have been the work of Benjamin Vulliamy.* (Guildhall Library, City of London)

putti are in patinated bronze. This case corresponds stylistically with the period 1735–40, but there is a curious contradiction in that it is stamped by the Paris cabinet-maker (*ébeniste*) François Duhamel, whose working life as master runs from 1750 to 1801. French furniture could not be stamped with the cabinet-maker's name until he had been made a master of his guild, and so, in this instance, it seems more likely that Duhamel added his stamp when the case passed through his hands at a later date, perhaps for repair or for sale, since he also acted as a dealer. The clock was said to have come originally from the Palace of Versailles although there are no French inventory marks to be found upon it so that, although such a provenance may well be correct, it is hard to verify.

This fine clock was purchased for George IV in June 1816, for the sum of £262 10s, Lord Yarmouth acting 16
as his agent. Its first resting-place was at the foot of the Grand Staircase in Carlton House; it appears thus in an engraving by W. H. Pyne which was published *c.*1818. Originally this clock had a dial and movement by Jean-Baptiste Farine, a clockmaker working in Paris in the third quarter of the eighteenth century and who died in 1777. Sadly these were replaced in 1821 by a movement—numbered 903—and dial supplied by B. L. Vulliamy, which incorporates calendar and lunar work. When removed to Buckingham Palace, the clock was sited in the East Gallery.

Despite Vulliamy's depredations, this is a truly magnificent clock, and, before leaving it, brief reference should be made to Duhamel, whose name is stamped inside the door of the clock case, even if his association with it may have been tenuous. He was born in 1723, was received into the Corporation of Master Cabinet-makers of Paris in 1750 and subsequently specialized in the making of clock cases from his premises in the Rue du Faubourg St-Antoine. In 1775, he took over the workshop of Antoine Foullet, but nothing further seems to be known about him after 1780. He died in 1801.

It is worth a short digression at this point, to consider the remarkable contribution to our knowledge of many of the royal residences at the beginning of the nineteenth century, which can be attributed to the efforts of William Henry Pyne, mentioned above. Born in 1769, he became a painter, exhibiting at the Royal Academy in 1790. Turning subsequently to writing, he began, in 1803, to publish *Microcosm, or a Picturesque Delineation of the Arts, Agriculture and Manufactures of Great Britain.* However, in this present context, his significance becomes apparent on account of his *The History of the Royal Residences of Windsor Castle, St. James's Palace, Carlton House, Kensington Palace, Hampton Court, Buckingham House and Frogmore* (London, 1819). This large and elegant three-volume work was illustrated by 100 highly finished coloured aquatints, engraved by W. J. Bennett, R. Reeve, D. Havell and J. Bailey. The sumptuousness of the production—a parallel edition had the illustrations reproduced in monochrome only—involved Pyne in such serious financial difficulties that he was imprisoned for debt in King's Bench Prison. On his release he abandoned all his artistic pretentions in favour of literature, writing works of gossip and anecdote under the pseudonym 'Ephraim Hardcastle'. He died in 1843.

Another pedestal clock which has been seen on several recent occasions in public also has received

unwelcome attention from Vulliamy. Much smaller by comparison with the last-mentioned, this is a mere 5 feet 6 inches high, 1 foot 3 inches wide and $10\frac{1}{2}$ inches
166 deep. The oak carcase is veneered with ebony and brass and inlaid with boulle marquetry of engraved pewter on tortoiseshell backed with a red foil. It is liberally enriched with gilt-bronze mounts, which are stamped with nineteen crowned Cs, representing the period 1745–9; though this might imply that the clock was made within those years, in fact all that it really signifies is the payment of a tax levied then on all bronzes in the hands of dealers and manufacturers, whether newly-made or old stock. Stylistically, the clock appears to derive from rather earlier in the eighteenth century, and the original movement and dial were by the well-known Paris clockmaker Pierre Gaudron. He became *maître-horloger* in 1691 and from 1695 had premises in the Faubourg St-Germain. Clockmaker to '*S.A.R. Mgr le duc d'Orléans Régent*', he retired in 1728 and died in 1745. The present movement and dial were substituted for the originals by Vulliamy in 1835 and bear his serial number 1287.

It is worth pausing for a moment to consider the enrichments of this superb clock in detail. The clock case rests on four sphinxes, in turn supported on a severely tapered therm-shaped pedestal. The lavish mounts include a head of Apollo with lyres, cornucopias and an imperial crown which surmounts the whole edifice. There is also a mask of Father Time with hour-glass and scythe. The pedestal rests on four scrolling feet, these in turn supported upon a shaped sub-plinth embellished with a central gilt boss and a gilt decorative moulding, with a boulle rectangular panel above.

This clock was bought in Paris for George IV, by François Benois, and delivered to Carlton House on 13th May 1820. It has been twice shown publicly in recent years, on both occasions in the Queen's Gallery at Buckingham Palace; the first time was in the exhibition 'George IV and the Arts of France' in 1966 (item number 28) while, more recently, it has appeared in 'Sèvres Porcelain from the Royal Collection' during 1979–80, in which it was item number 5. There is, incidentally, a pedestal clock of the same design, although the mounts are not stamped with the crowned C mark, in the Metropolitan Museum of Art, New York. This still retains its original movement by Jacques Thuret, who died in 1739 at the ripe old age, in

166. (Right) *Pedestal clock, the gilt-bronze mounts stamped with nineteen crowned 'C's, which originally contained a movement by Pierre Gaudron.* (Royal Collection)

167. (Right) *Pedestal clock, surmounted by Father Time, now containing Vulliamy movement no. 1306.* (Royal Collection)

those days, of seventy. The case of that clock has been attributed to André-Charles Boulle himself.

The significant feature in all clocks of this type has to be the ornate complexities of boulle decoration and ormolu mounts. The same motifs tend to recur with unfailing regularity, albeit by different hands and with differences of design and posture. There is, for example,
167 a large clock—the overall height is 8 feet 5 inches—in which the dome above the clock case is surmounted by Father Time wielding his scythe supported by rams' heads and ormolu swags of foliage, while the corners take the form of caryatid figures and in front there is a figure group representing the Fates. The rich inlay of the exterior is extended also to the inside of the case, where it is visible through a glazed panel below the dial. As for the pedestal, this is a monument to complexity, with contrasting effects of brass inlaid on tortoiseshell at the front, and the effect reversed, with tortoiseshell laid on brass, at the sides. Once again a mask of Apollo is joined with rams' heads and leaf ornamentation, the whole structure resting on no less than six beautifully chased paw feet. The eight-day quarter-chiming clock movement is one of Vulliamy's, bearing his serial number 1306.

Another clock in much the same general style but somewhat plainer and lacking the complexities of inlay
168 found in the previous one, nonetheless also has its clock case surmounted by a dome, on the top of which Father Time is found, complete with scythe and in company with the obligatory rams' heads and swags of foliage; on the front corners level with the base of the dome, Cupids play. This time, too, there are caryatids at the corners. Turning to the pedestal decoration, however, this consists mainly of a tapered panel of brass inlaid upon black shell, below a small mask encircled with vine foliage and associated with richly chased ormolu mouldings with leaf ornamentation. This pedestal rests upon four carved ball feet, the overall height of the clock being 8 feet 3 inches. Once believed to have had an astronomical movement, the existing one is a Vulliamy substitute, bearing his number 774. This fusee mechanism is hour-striking; and two subsidiaries below the main dial indicate, at left, the days of the month and, on the right, the days of the week, in French. Neither the original clockmaker nor accession details of this clock are known.

So far all the clocks described have been of the style
169 known as *pendule sur socle*. The so-called *régulateur* at least possessed the saving grace—in English eyes—of a continuous structure, like a long case, and there is as

168. (Left) *A similar clock with Vulliamy movement no. 774.* (Royal Collection)

fine an example as one could wish for in Windsor Castle. Standing just over $7\frac{1}{2}$ feet tall, the movement of this clock exhibits both solar and mean time, employing a gilt hand for the former and a blued-steel one for the latter. The month and day of the month appear through an aperture in the engraved silvered dial, which is signed *'Inventé en 1736 par Julien le Roy, de la Société des Arts'*. F. J. Britten states that the dead-beat escapement of this clock has independently-pivoted pallets, a deviation from the norm quite sufficient to justify the innovative dial signature, for this is a rarity even among English makers. However, it is not true. The clock, in fact, has Lepaute's escapement. The elaborate case of the clock is inlaid with mahogany and kingwood veneer and decorated with unusually large ormolu mounts featuring cherubs, lions' heads and fruit as well as the customary scrolls and swags, and there is a bevelled plate-glass panel of rococo shape in the centre of the trunk through which the pendulum bob can be seen. The base of the clock case is conspicuous for its fine parquetry panelling, and indeed everything about it reflects its antecedents, for it came from the *atelier* of Charles Cressent, who also made the case for the clock to be described next.

Almost its twin, and also at Windsor, this next clock was acquired by George III. Slightly taller, at 7 feet 10 inches, the superficial case detail is identical with the clock previously described save only in the pattern of parquetry in the base panel. In this one respect the two 170
cases are very different. Otherwise, this second clock has an inner gilt-bronze zone on the dial, which is engraved 'Ferdinand Berthoud A Paris' while the outer silvered zone is engraved 'Vulliamy London A.D. 1821'. The movement is, of course, a substitute for the original installed by the last-named and bearing his serial number 783. The clock case is attributed to Charles Cressent, the Parisian *ébeniste* (1685–1768), who seems to have made a number of versions of this model including the one previously described. This clock is shown in a picture by Zoffany entitled 'Interior of a room in Kew Palace, with portraits of Queen Charlotte, Prince of Wales and Duke of York'.

In typically French fashion, the last clock to be described in this present section is neither a pedestal clock nor a *régulateur*; but large it certainly is. The structure consists of an impressive gilt-bronze clock case, flanked by two standing female figures in patinated bronze, said to be emblematic of Literature and Art; at all events, one is holding a parchment, the other an open book, and both are represented in the act

169. (Left) Régulateur, *its dial inscribed 'Inventé en 1736 par Julien le Roy, de la Société des Arts'; the clock case by Charles Cressent.* (Royal Collection)

170. (Above) *A clock very similar to the previous one, its case also attributed to Charles Cressent. The picture by Zoffany shows the clock in Kew Palace.* (Royal Collection)

171. (Right) *Clock with case by De La Croix.* (Royal Collection)

of writing even though momentarily glancing at each other across the front of the clock case. The latter is clearly of eighteenth-century origin, being fitted with glass panels and surmounted by two Cupids in bronze holding the typically Gallic emblem, a cock. At the corners of the broken arch of the case are massive garlands of oak leaves suspended from rams' heads, a treatment particularly characteristic of the third quarter of the century, and the beginning of the *style Louis XVI.*

The clock is located in the East Gallery of Buckingham Palace, where it looks well with some superb
171 bronze seven-light candelabra by P-P. Thomire. Untypically, the creator of this clock case is known, for it is signed 'De La Croix, Fondeur, Cizeleur'. This could well be Pierre Delacroix, who, when he was declared bankrupt in 1771, had in his workshop *'une très grande Pendule de valleur de plus de 4000 livres . . .'* Whether this is the same clock cannot be known with certainty, but *'très grande'* is almost an understatement, for it stands some 9 feet 6 inches overall, the clock itself being 6 feet $1\frac{1}{4}$ inches and the base on which it rests something over 3 feet 4 inches. The latter, consisting of an ebonized carcase inset with gilt bronze panels chased with low-relief scenes said to represent Neptune, Minerva, Venus and Vulcan, and edged with leaf-pattern mouldings, may, in fact, be of nineteenth-century origin, as indeed is the present movement, numbered 1910, by Vulliamy, which was substituted for the now unknown original about 1851. The exact details of the acquisition of this clock are also unknown; according to hearsay, George IV won it in a wager, from Charles X of France.

Clocks for the wall

French domestic clocks made to occupy wall brackets, constructed *en suite* and of various decorative materials, are a well-established style—and quite unlike their English namesakes, so-called, but which often enough were never intended for a bracket at all. Curiously, the Royal Collection is not particularly well favoured so far as French clocks of this type are concerned; perhaps they did not appeal to George IV, or possibly they did not easily blend with his decorative schemes, for most of the smaller French clocks are for the mantelpiece, sideboard or table.

Nevertheless, there is one fine example of an eighteenth-century French bracket clock in Her Maj-
173 esty The Queen Mother's London home, Clarence House. Sited above a half-landing on the staircase leading out of the main ground floor corridor, it is veneered in green-stained horn upon which are superimposed ormolu mounts, the principal one, which extends across the front lower part of the clock,

172. (Above) *Cartel clock in the style of Delafosse.* (Royal Collection)

173. (Right) *Bracket clock by Dey à Paris.* (The Queen Mother's Collection)

consisting of a figure holding the Sun, and beside it a tablet upon which is engraved *'Un Seul Suffit'*. This clock is the work of 'Dey A Paris', whose name appears upon the dial. A father and son of this name are recorded. Laurent Dey, who executed his *chef d'œuvre*—that is to say, his submitted piece of practical work for qualification as *maître*—in 1745, shortly afterwards set up shop in Rue Saint-Antoine, where he is located from 1748 to 1772. His son, Nicholas-Laurent, *fils de maître* in 1765, worked on his father's premises from 1772 to 1789. This particular clock seems likely to have been the work of the father.

Another well-known French wall timekeeper is the cartel clock; and once again, this type is not especially 172
well represented in the Royal Collection. There is a somewhat untypical one, however, which was formerly in the South Lobby at Brighton Pavilion, being brought to Buckingham Palace from Windsor Castle in 1911. Its present movement was installed by Vulliamy in 1820, and there is no record of the maker of the original. The interest in this clock must always have centred upon the case, however. In the style of Jean-Charles Delafosse, who published his designs for some *'pendules de caractères'* in 1771 after his *Nouvelle Iconologie Historique* in 1768, the ormolu case is elaborately chased with fruit and flowers, with a mask at the base and a terminal of leaves and berries. It is a large clock of its kind, being 2 feet 3 inches high and over one foot wide.

Clocks with decorative porcelain casework

Historically, many of the great European porcelain factories have manufactured decorative elements—figures, flowers and so on—for incorporation into clock cases, and sometimes even the entire case can be of this fragile-seeming material. The workmanship is often of great beauty and complexity, which probably reaches its peak in the output from Sèvres, although Meissen and Chelsea come readily to mind in this same context. Since the Royal Collection boasts the finest holding of eighteenth-century Sèvres porcelain in the world, it would be strange indeed if it did not include one or two clocks.

The first to be described, however, is a little out of character; but it need not be ignored for all that. It
consists of a group of two Chinese figures, a boy and a 174
girl, with between them a basket. They rest upon a rocky base strewn with coral and algae. At the time of its purchase by George IV in Paris in October 1819, this creation had been 'improved' by the addition of an early nineteenth-century gilt-bronze clock case containing a movement by Lesieur, who seems to have had various premises in Paris, including Vieille Rue du Temple and Rue de la Verrerie, between 1806 and

about 1830. At the same time the figure of the boy was decorated with a gilt-bronze cap, which remains *in situ* even though the clock and case have now been removed.

This large and ambitious group—$16\frac{1}{4}$ inches high, $18\frac{3}{4}$ inches wide and nearly 12 inches deep—is known in two other versions, one being in the Musée National de Céramique in Sèvres, while the other passed anonymously through Christie's sale rooms in 1977; and they seem to have presented many problems in the firing, as there are references in the manufacturer's stock lists to defective examples. In October 1752, two in a biscuit state were valued at 100 *livres* each; in the inventory of January 1756 two such were described as glazed and the value doubled, although whether these were the same pair is not clear. There is documentary evidence of other versions in addition to these. The
175 combination of this group with a later metal clock case does not seem to have been questioned until fairly recently, for the whole structure is illustrated complete, not only in Robertson and Walker's *Royal Clocks* (at page 27) but also in Clifford Smith's *Buckingham Palace* (plate 341). The group devoid of the clock case has now been exhibited in the Queen's Gallery display devoted to the Sèvres porcelain in the Royal Collection, which opened in 1979.

The next clock is in the form of a lyre, a popular shape from the late eighteenth-century onward and made in marble, as well as gilt-bronze and porcelain. They were

174. (Far left) *'Chinese Boy and Girl' Sèvres basket.* (Royal Collection)

175. (Left) *The previous object prior to removal of the later addition of a clock.* (Royal Collection)

176. (Below left) *Lyre clock by Kinable, in Sèvres porcelain case.* (Royal Collection)

177. (Below) *The Sèvres lyre clock as illustrated in George IV's Pictorial Inventory.* (Royal Collection)

178. (Below right) *Lyre clock by Garrigues.* (The Queen Mother's Collection)

first produced at Sèvres in 1785 and remained fashionable well into the next century. This particular example was delivered on approval to George IV at Carlton House on 12th October 1818 by the Paris dealer Lafontaine; the King purchased it. There is a fine representation of this clock in his Pictorial Inventory, where it is inscribed: 'From the Middle Room, Attic Floor, Carlton House. Delivered to Mr Vulliamy July 21st 1828 and by him sent to Windsor Castle Nov. 20th 1828'.

The clock stands upon an oval base and four ball feet. It is decorated with gilt-bronze mounts taking the form of branches of laurel, garlands of flowers and an Apollo mask on a sunburst, while its overall height is $22\frac{3}{4}$ inches, width $10\frac{1}{2}$ inches and depth 6 inches. The porcelain carcase of the case is of soft paste, in dark blue ground, which was the most popular colour although some were made in turquoise blue, green and pink. The clock movement is by Kinable, whose name appears on the dial together with that of the dial-enameller 176
Dubuisson, who was active in Paris, at the Rue de la Huchette, in 1795 and is later recorded at Barnabites, Rue de la Calandre, from 1812 to about 1820. It appears that D. D. Kinable was the most enthusiastic

customer for Sèvres lyre clock cases at the end of the eighteenth century, buying thirteen of them between 1795 and 1797. This maker had premises at the Palais Royal, Galerie de Pierre in Paris, between 1794 and 1830; and presumably his contribution to the illusion of the lyre is the gridiron pendulum forming the 'strings', which, incidentally, is hung with a necklace of
177 large gilt-bronze beads. Both clock and Pictorial Inventory depiction of it figured in the Queen's Gallery exhibition already mentioned.

In passing, it is worth noting that there are several lyre clocks in the Royal Collection—Robertson &
179 Walker describe one of white marble with ormolu decoration, the dial signed 'Hanson, Windsor', which is dismissed disparagingly as 'no doubt modern and of French manufacture'—but the only one to compare in beauty with that just described is located at the Queen Mother's residence, Royal Lodge, Windsor. The blue porcelain case is not so deep in colour as the previous one, and the fittings not quite so elaborate. Otherwise, it
178 has a fine movement and an admirably executed dial, signed 'Garrigues A Paris'. This maker, forenamed Jean-Antoine, was *maître* 1782 and operated from Rue de Grenelle 1789–90 and subsequently from Rue du Chantre 1800–12. There are two additional hands running concentrically with those indicating hours and minutes, the longer stretching beyond the chapter numerals to an outer ring of oval miniatures of the signs of the zodiac, each accompanied by the name of a month and the number of days contained therein; on a second ring, inside the chapters, are numbered the days of the month, with a shorter hand to indicate these. The pendulum bob is formed by a circlet of gilt beads framing the dial.

Also in the Sèvres exhibition was the next clock, which is usually called the Sunflower Clock; and, when
180 it was bought for George IV in Paris in 1819 at a cost of 5,500 francs, it was said to have belonged to Madame de Pompadour. Essentially, the illusion is of a vase containing a bouquet of flowers, all made in Vincennes porcelain save for the flower stems, which are of green-lacquered brass wire. The clock, which is sited in the middle of this bouquet, is disguised so that its dial appears as the seeding-centre of a gilt-bronze sunflower. The vase is fitted with gilt-bronze handles and rests upon a drum of the same material, standing upon a terrace approached from the left by a flight of steps and incorporating in front a musical trophy and on either side a pair of twin-nozzled candelabra. All of these last-mentioned elements, apart from the terrace itself, are now recognized as later additions, made sometime between 1766 and the year of entry into the Royal Collection, 1819. It has also been suggested that, instead of the candelabra, there might have been

179. (Left) *Lyre clock signed Hanson, Windsor.* (Royal Collection)

180. (Right) *The Sèvres Sunflower Clock.* (Royal Collection)

groups in Vincennes porcelain standing upon the terrace beside the vase.

The vase itself has a flared mouth with gadrooned edge, and it is decorated on each side with carnations in relief, on three entwined stems tied in a bow with pink ribbon. The white ground is further enriched with gilding and jewelling on gold foils and painted with landscape scenes in four reserves. The height of the vase is $11\frac{3}{4}$ inches, the overall height of the entire structure $41\frac{1}{2}$ inches.

This clock can probably be identified with one advertised for sale in Paris in the issue of *Petites Affiches* for 29th December 1766, even though the vase is said to be of Meissen manufacture. At some time in the last century the vase became separated from the flowers and the clock, and they were only reunited again early in the present one. The back plate of the clock is signed 'Benoist Gerard A Paris', and this maker is recorded, at Quai Conty, in 1745. Tardy states that he was *maître-horloger* in 1705 and that he died in 1758 *'à 58 ans'*, which, even had he been a child prodigy, seems somewhat unlikely!

Another Sèvres clock-case style which found much favour was based on architectural fantasy—the broken column. This style was much copied in other materials, for example, marble; but the Sèvres versions were widely distributed, being used by several notable clockmakers to house their movements. There is a comparable specimen in the Wallace Collection which, apart from slightly different mounts, is of the same model as that in the Royal Collection, but with a movement by Germain Dubois; that clock can be dated to 1786.

Inevitably, it might seem, the existing dial and movement of the Sèvres broken-column clock in the Royal Collection are English replacements. It is known,
181 however, that the original movement was by Charles Dutertre. One of a substantial family of fine French clockmakers, mainly based in Paris, this was probably Nicholas Charles, who seems to have been born about 1715. *'Fils de maître'* in 1739, *'Juré'* in 1775, he worked from various premises, including Rue de Bucy près de la rue Dauphine (1741–3), Quai Conty (1748) and Quai de l'Ecole (1749–87). He died at Quai de Chaillot in 1793. As for the clock case, this is in Sèvres soft-paste porcelain, the ground being white and dark blue, embellished with gilded decorations and gilt-bronze mounts. The clock was bought by George IV for £16 5s 6d at an auction conducted by Squibbs, being delivered to Carlton House on 5th July 1816.

There are other clocks in the Royal Collection with porcelain case-work of note: at Windsor Castle, there is 182
an oriental blue porcelain vase clock, with finely chased ormolu mounts and scroll handles which terminate in masks, the whole resting upon a richly carved ormolu base. At Osborne, Queen Victoria's home on the Isle of Wight, there is, on the Grand Staircase, a porcelain clock incorporating the arms and cypher of Frederick 183
William II, King of Prussia (1744–97), as well as paintings of his palace and castle. Others could be cited, but perhaps those described would be judged among the most interesting and important.

181. (Right) *The Sèvres broken column clock, formerly with a Charles Dutertre movement, as seen in the Pictorial Inventory.* (Royal Collection)

182. (Below) *Blue porcelain vase clock.* (Royal Collection)

183. (Far right) *Porcelain clock case with the arms of Frederick William II of Prussia.* (Royal Collection)

Clocks with cases 'in the Chinese taste'

Chinoiserie manifests itself through many materials—lacquer, porcelain, ormolu and enamel to name but four. There are several notable foreign clocks in the Royal Collection with case ornamentation whose composition includes Chinese elements, and one of these, in a Sèvres porcelain setting, was reviewed in the previous section. Mainly these are of French manufacture although, of course, there was a strong Chinese influence in the decoration of lacquered long-case clocks in Britain during the eighteenth century; and, naturally, the Chinese themselves played a part.

One of the most important clocks falling within this category is usually known as 'The Kylin Clock', a kylin 184
being a fabulous animal much used in the decoration of Chinese pottery. This particular clock originally stood on the chimney-piece of the Saloon in Brighton

184. *The Kylin clock.* (Royal Collection)

185. (Left) *Detail of the previous clock.* (Royal Collection)

186. (Right) *The Kylin clock in its customary setting.* (Royal Collection)

Pavilion which, during its day, was together with Carlton House among the greatest centres for this style of décor in England. Even so, it will soon be apparent that the character of this clock is cosmopolitan, to say the least!

The materials from which the Kylin Clock case are made are mainly gilt-bronze and Chinese porcelain.
185 186 The clock movement—numbered 742, by B. L. Vulliamy, and dating from 1820—is fitted into the shoulders of a *famille verte* vase of late eighteenth-century origin, on its side and level with the heads of two seated kylins of Ch'ien Lung porcelain, of the period 1736–95. The whole arrangement is framed with tendrils of lotus and sunflower plants, entwined around and above, where they also envelop a group of Japanese porcelain figures. This spectacular composition rests upon a decorative gilt-bronze base inset with open-work Chinese porcelain panels similar to those forming the balustrades of pagodas. There is a further scrolling gilt-bronze base which is not part of the original structure. Another version of this clock, but lacking the gilt-bronze lotus and sunflower enrichments, is in a German museum. It is generally considered that the mounts to both these clocks are French, although Vulliamy probably added extra ornament to the Buckingham Palace clock when he fitted it out in 1820. This clock is a fine large object, standing just over 3 feet 3 inches high and 2 feet 9 inches wide.

A more conventional clock in the Chinese manner is that known as 'The Chinese Drummer Boy Clock'. Made
for the Chinese Drawing-Room at Carlton House about 187
1792, the case is mainly of gilt and enamelled bronze. The cylindrical clock case forms a drum, which hangs from the left hand of the drummer boy, who is seated upon a cushion beneath a canopy. In his right hand he holds a drum stick with which he prepares to strike the drum, meanwhile looking smilingly to his right. The clock and figure rest upon a rocky base, which in turn is supported on clustered simulated bamboo columns, the whole resting upon a second, larger cushion. These latter elements were added by Vulliamy in 1811, at a cost of £47 7s 6d; and the present dial and movement, by Charles Frodsham, and numbered 890, were inserted about 1870. This apart, from the rocky base upwards, the object is a coherent entity. The decoration of the pagoda-like canopy, for example, with fish-scale painting, was intended to match that of canopies over the niches either side of the Carlton House chimney-piece upon which it stood. Hung with bells and supported by rather stylized palms, it is surmounted by a speared fish, made to look like a weather-vane, upon a globe—'a freakish motif which was employed later for many of the decorative objects at the Brighton Pavilion', as Clifford Smith observes.

It used to be thought that the Chinese Drummer Boy clock was English, but recent evidence suggests that it must have been made in France. Vulliamy, in his bill of 1811, already mentioned, describes it as 'a French clock in a Chinese case', and in another bill, two years later, there is mentioned the original maker's name, 'Manière'. Most likely this would have been Charles-Guillaume Manière, who was based in Paris, and *maître* in 1778, with premises first at Rue des Prouvaires (1781), then Rue des Merciers (1789), Rue Christine (1806) and finally Rue Bertin-Poirée (1810–12). From Carlton House the clock was despatched to Brighton on 6th November 1819, where it remained until its final move to Buckingham Palace. Its overall height is 2 feet 5 inches, and it is $13\frac{1}{2}$ inches wide.

Another clock in roughly this tradition forms part of Her Majesty The Queen Mother's Collection at Clarence
House. A two-tiered pagoda houses the clock in the 188

187. (Left) *The Chinese Drummer Boy clock.* (Royal Collection)

188. (Below) *The Pagoda clock by D. F. Dubois.* (The Queen Mother's Collection)

189. (Right) *The Peacock clock.* (Royal Collection)

190. (Far right) *The barometer made as a companion to the previous clock.* (Royal Collection)

upper level, while the pendulum bob, in the shape of a sunburst behind a mask, can be seen through the lower. Surmounting the whole structure is a mandarin figure under an umbrella, while the edges of the lower canopy are hung with bells, these being held at each corner by a winged beast. The two canopies and the base are formed of a marble carcase, overlaid with ormolu fish-scale decoration, the same material being used for all the other mounts. The clock is by 'D. F. Dubois à Paris', probably David-Frédéric of that name, who was *maître* in 1780 and was located at Rue St-Honoré (1783–9) and Rue du Roule by 1830.

It is worth digressing at this point to consider a clock
189 and barometer in matching chinoiserie cases that grace
190 adjoining mantelpieces in the Grand Reception Room in Windsor Castle. Surmounting each case is a peacock, while the clock cylinder, supported and surrounded by foliage, has an enamelled Chinese figure on either side, a man on one and a woman on the other. The composition is further embellished with richly wrought ormolu scrolls and dragons, the hands on the dials are delineated as curiously twisted serpents, and each case sits upon a lapis lazuli slab base. The latter must command some notice as, were they solid stone, they must be priceless; but it seems likely that they are veneered on some other base material. As for the clock, it now boasts a movement by Vulliamy. Both objects were made to the order of George IV for the Pavilion at Brighton and removed to Windsor upon the accession of Queen Victoria.

French clocks in historical and mythological settings

A mythological theme which seems to have been particularly popular in France in the seventeenth and eighteenth centuries, and which, to judge by the purchases he made that incorporated representations of it, must also have found great favour with George IV, is the story known as 'The Rape of Europa'. In this, the god Zeus has been captivated by the beauty of Europa, the young daughter of the Phoenician king. He appears to her on the seashore in the guise of a bull. The animal seeming to be tame and docile, her attendants first garlanded it with flowers, and then Europa, unwisely daring, climbed upon its back. The bull at once plunged into the sea and swam with her to Crete. It is said that

VULLIAMY
LONDON

191. (Left) *The Rape of Europa clock: the case by Osmond.* (Royal Collection)

192. (Right) *The former clock, seen in its usual context.* (Royal Collection)

Europa bore Zeus three children, all of them considerately adopted by the King of Crete, who later married her.

There are two clocks in the Royal Collection which feature scenes from this legend. In both of them Europa surmounts the cylindrical clock case, which is born on the bull's back; and in both the two principal effects are obtained by contrasting gilt with patinated bronze. In each case two other figures, Europa's attendants, flank the bull, the composition being held together with garlands of flowers.

The first such clock was delivered to Carlton House on 23rd February 1811; and in 1817 B. L. Vulliamy obtained permission to replace the existing French dial
191 and movement with substitutes of his own make and
192 bearing his serial number 631. Sadly, the name of the original French clockmaker has been lost, but the craftsman responsible for the fine bronze case is known, since he had the foresight to stamp it on the scrolled foot under the right-hand figure. 'OSMOND' is likely to have been Robert Osmond, the bronze-founder, located in Rue Maclou in Paris in 1773; he worked for many well-known French clockmakers, including the Lepautes, Robert Robin and Charles Le Roy. This clock rests upon a *bombé*-shaped musical box, made of oak which is veneered in rosewood and overpainted in green lacquer, the whole enriched with a musical trophy, frets and floral mounts in gilt-bronze. The movement inside it plays eight tunes, and the case bears the half-effaced signature 'F. Goyer', a Paris *ébeniste* who was *maître* in 1740 and who is known to have specialized in lacquered clock cases. Furthermore, five of the gilt-bronze mounts on this musical case are struck with the crowned C mark for 1745–9. Incidentally, Tardy reproduces one of Goyer's signatures from a clock case, and although the initial of his first name appears to be 'F', this name was in fact Jean. The illustration makes the ambiguity clear: it could as easily be 'J'. Curiously, too, in this particular instance, it looks as if Goyer was not responsible for the lacquering, since Vulliamy's bill of 1811 includes an item for 'paint^{g} in Varnish the Base which contains the Chimes . . .'.

There is an amusing sidelight upon the chequered history of this clock. When it was first received from the hands of Lord Melbourne in 1811, the description given was 'Old fashioned French Clock with Bronze figure of a Cow and Or Molu Figures'. It is impossible to tell, from the brief description at this time, if the musical case was included; the absence of crowned C marks on Osmond's clock case may mean that the two parts were made independently. As to the mistake in the sex of the beast, this was further compounded subsequently, yet another description stating 'The Clock the Europa Cow'.

The second clock of this kind constituted Lot 80 in an
auction sale at Squibb's rooms, which took place on 193
24th April 1818; it was purchased for George IV by Lord Yarmouth, at a cost of £125. Then, the clock—like its companion piece—rested upon a musical case in tortoiseshell which is now kept at Windsor. Similarly, too, its original French dial and movement were replaced by Vulliamy, who installed his substitutes, serially numbered 1040, in 1829.

It seems at least possible that this second clock—or rather its case—could be the work of a noted Parisian bronze-founder called Jean-Joseph de Saint Germain, who was located in Rue St-Nicholas in 1773. Although the case bears no marks, it is identical to one which does bear his signature; and a clock of the same design is known to have been in the possession, in 1784, of Madame Victoire, who was Louis XV's fourth daughter. It came from her Grand Cabinet, situated on the ground floor of the Palace of Versailles, beneath the Salon de la Guerre.

The dramatic and artistic possibilities deriving from the classic concept of rape were not confined to that of
194 Europa. Another clock in the Royal Collection is usually known as 'The Rape of the Sabines Clock'. The people referred to in that title lived in ancient Italy, in the mountains beyond the Tiber; they were subjugated by the Romans and amalgamated with them in the first century BC. The scene that is depicted on this clock represents Romulus, on the right, who is about to hurl his javelin at Tatius, King of the Sabines, when a group of Sabine women, with infants in their arms, arrive on the scene and throw themselves between the fighters. In the foreground, Hersilia, wife of Romulus and daughter of Tatius, begs her father and husband on her knees to cease combat, while behind, another Sabine mother is poised in the act of hurling forward her child from her upraised arms.

The composition has been adapted from a famous painting by Jacques Louis David (1748–1825), which is in fact dated 1799. The picture, on account of the nakedness of those depicted in it, received a rather mixed reception. It is clear that this influenced the maker of the magnificent gilt-bronze clock case, P-P. Thomire, for he has used drapery, thrown over the shoulders of Romulus, and garments in the case of Tatius, to avoid offence.

This clock was despatched to Carlton House from Paris in June 1812. The maker of the original movement is unknown, the existing two-train mechanism being a substitute. The antique marble rectangular base of this clock, chased in ormolu, depicts the rape in a scene on the front, while at the sides are figures representing Fame, and the back is enriched with festoons. Several other versions of this fine clock case are recorded, including one in the Hermitage Museum in Leningrad.

The name of Pierre-Philippe Thomire recurs regularly in describing the French clocks in the Royal Collection, and he was perhaps one of the greatest sculptors and bronze-workers of his day. Born in Paris in 1751, he died there in 1843; he enjoyed an unparalleled reputation for the quality of his castings, and, despite political upheavals during his lifetime, he

193. (Left) *The second Rape of Europa clock: the case possibly by Saint Germain.* (Royal Collection)

194. (Below) *The Rape of the Sabines clock.* (Royal Collection)

195. *The Oath of the Horatii clock.* (Royal Collection)

seems never to have lost favour. It is known that in 1775 he was located in Rue St-Martin. He retired in 1823, and the business, now run by his two sons-in-law, became 'Thomire & Cie'.

As will have already become apparent, in the early part of the nineteenth century clock cases featuring scenes adapted from classical paintings or groups of sculpture were popular; and a great variety of them were to be had. 'Nothing can be imagined more elegant and striking than their numerous collections of ornamental clock-cases,' wrote John Scott, in 1814, with reference to the shops in the Palais Royal in Paris. He singled out the popularity of the model whose description now follows.

This clock is usually called 'The Oath of the Horatii Clock'. Again taken from a picture painted by J. L. David, this time in 1784, the base of this clock case is of green marble mounted on the front with gilt-bronze figures in low relief. This scene is supplementary, however, to that represented immediately above, on top of the block of marble. Here, the three Horatii brothers face their father across the altar—which houses the clock itself—vowing fidelity to one another before fighting the Curatii to determine the supremacy 195 of Rome or Alba. The father hands them their weapons: in the ensuing struggle, two of the Horatii and the three Curatii are killed. Looking at the scene on the base of the clock case, the surviving brother is welcomed back by his father, his two dying brothers being depicted on his left while, on the right, his sister, who was betrothed to one of the Curatii, turns away in anguish.

This clock was purchased by George IV from a Mr Ricordon in January 1809 and was formerly in the Large Crimson Drawing-Room at Carlton House. It seems almost inevitable that the dial and movement had to be renewed—if that is the right word—by B. L. Vulliamy, who condemned the original, of which all trace has now been lost, as 'very bad'. The existing mechanism bears Vulliamy's number 678, and the substitution took place in 1819, when a third, day-of-the-month, hand was removed. The dimensions of the clock are height 2 feet 2 inches, width 1 foot 11½ inches, depth 8½ inches.

A number of French clocks in the Royal Collection focus their decoration around the classical god Apollo, who embodied the ideal of male beauty in ancient Greece. Son of Zeus and Leto, and twin brother of Artemis, Apollo led the Muses as the god of music, song and poetry, of agriculture and of the pastoral life. He

196. *The Apollo Clock.* (Royal Collection)

197. (Left) *P.-P. Thomire clock case depicting Father Time, the clock cylinder on his shoulder, its movement by Jefferson.* (Royal Collection)

198. (Right) *The same clock, in the Blue Velvet Closet, Carlton House, as depicted in W. H. Pyne's* History of the Royal Residences . . . *(1819).* (Guildhall Library, City of London)

features in a great number of Greek myths and legends, and his utilization on French Empire clock cases might, given the prevailing fashions, almost be a foregone conclusion.

The best-known, as well as the most elaborate, of
196 these clocks is usually known simply as 'The Apollo Clock'. The magnificent clock case by P-P. Thomire shows Apollo driving his chariot—which is drawn by four horses—across the Heavens, represented as an arch which is partly curtained by clouds. The wheel of the chariot forms the clock dial while the arch itself, resting upon a marble base, is of a blued metal and chased with four signs of the zodiac in gilt-bronze, Pisces, Aries, Taurus and Aquarius. This clock was purchased by George IV in May 1810 from a certain Mr Boileau, and it is interesting to note that an identical clock was sold at the auction of the property of another French bronze-sculptor in 1829. The catalogue entry on that occasion remarked that Thomire's price for this model was 1,500 francs.

The inevitable happened again with this clock, although, for some reason or other, it must have survived intact rather longer than was customary. In any event, in August 1834 B. L. Vulliamy noted that 'The works of the Clock are good for nothing & the case is very dirty. The case is well worth cleaning & new works' [*sic*]. This was duly authorized, so that the clock now contains Vulliamy's movement number 1223 which was installed that same year.

Clock cases incorporating standing figures, sometimes leaning upon the clock cylinder, sometimes free-
197 standing and sometimes actually supporting the clock,
198 are typical of the simpler forms of statuary enjoyed by the French. In the Library of Windsor Castle is a fine large clock, the bronze case with ormolu mounts representing a winged figure of Time, complete with scythe, who carries the clock cylinder on his shoulder. This case is the work of P-P. Thomire, while the movement, said to date *c.*1820, is by Samuel Jefferson, who was Watchmaker to the Prince of Wales. His premises were at 35 Bruton Street, in London, and he seems to have been active from *c.*1805 to *c.*1840. The clock was acquired by George IV direct from Thomire in 1812.

Another model of Apollo Clock reflects this same fashion. It exists in a number of versions, and the Royal Collection itself contains two of them. The first, with its
carcase of yellow Siena marble, is mounted on the 199
right-hand side with the standing figure of Apollo in patinated bronze holding a staff—which rests upon the top of the clock—and a lyre. On the other side is a flaming torch. The tapering marble trunk containing the clock, which is in the centre of the arrangement, is supported at its lower corners by winged figures, and at its upper corners by masks, both in ormolu. This clock was probably acquired by George IV in April 1803, together with a matching pair of candelabra to form a *garniture de cheminée*, as part of a whole consignment of works of art purchased from the Parisian furniture-maker and dealer M-E. Lignereux. His bill describes the clock, which cost £85 sterling, as *'Une pendule á une figure dite l'Apollon, en bronze couleur antique avec divers ornemens tant en bronze doré aumat qu'en couleur antique marbre jaune de sienne'.* Contemporary accounts indicate that Lignereux's showroom in the Rue Vivienne was often thronged with English tourists at the time of this transaction, and, even though his prices were considered high, there was general enthusiasm for the excellent quality of his stock. Little could he have known that this clock, which once graced the Library Ante-Room of the Brighton Pavilion before being removed to Buckingham Palace, would receive the attention of B. L. Vulliamy—but it did, so that his movement number 744 was substituted for the original in 1820.

A second version of this clock, which stands on the chimney-piece in the Royal Closet in Buckingham Palace, was originally in the Golden Drawing Room at that is from Lignereux. Of the two others, one also has a Vulliamy movement—this is in private hands—while the second, in the Musée des Arts Décoratifs in Paris, has a movement by Le Sueur, *q.v.* The Fetherstonehaugh version still retains its original dial, which is signed 'Manière à Paris'—almost certainly C-G. Manière, *q.v.*, who, since he was both clockmaker and bronze-manufacturer, could possibly have been the original creator of this model and made all the versions, Lignereux simply being the retailer.

It is pleasing to report, however, that one very striking Apollo clock survives intact. This forms part of a suite, consisting of clock and thermometer, and both in malachite and ormolu cases supplied by P-P. Thomire; one element of this pair graces each of the two handsome marble mantelpieces in the State Supper Room of Buckingham Palace. Both items were purchased by Benois from Thomire & Cie in 1828, together with the malachite candelabra in the State Dining Room, for a total sum of £500, and the 202
thermometer, supplied by Mortimer & Hunt, London, is fitted in a case upon which a figure of Diana, goddess of hunting, is shown leaning against a tree, from which her quiver is hanging.

199. (Above) *Standing Apollo clock, supplied by M-E. Lignereux, with carcase of yellow marble.* (Royal Collection)

200. (Right) *A second version of the previous clock, the carcase of red marble.* (Royal Collection)

200 Carlton House. Not only is its case in red griotte marble, but the plinth is decorated with extra gilt mounts. This clock was also acquired by George IV, although the bill recording its purchase has not been preserved. It could well have been bought from Lignereux, like the previous one, and it also suffered the same fate, in that Vulliamy substituted his movement, numbered 680, for the original in 1819. At least three other versions of this same model have been identified by Geoffrey de Bellaigue (see Bibliography—Appendix IV), one having been originally in the collection of French works of art of an intimate friend of the Prince of Wales, Sir Harry Fetherstonehaugh (1754–1846), who obtained it from the same source as the yellow marble version,

The composition of the clock case is in a vertical plane, the standing figure of Apollo in ormolu, and holding a lyre, surmounting a vertical rectangular
01 plinth in malachite with ormolu mouldings and paw feet, into which is inset the clock cylinder. The clock movement is by a remarkable French maker, Louis Moinet; something of a scholar as well as an horologist, he was born at Bourges in 1768. Subsequently, he went to Paris where he became technical secretary to the famous Abraham-Louis Breguet, perhaps the greatest scientific horologist of all, who entrusted to him comprehensive notes of his work, with the intention that they be published. Breguet's output is well represented in the Royal Collection so that biographical and other notes about him will be found later in these pages; suffice it here to say that his intended treatise was not published before his death in 1823. Moinet later published, in 1848, his own *Nouveau traité général astronomique et civil d'horlogerie théorique et pratique . . .* which was held by Breguet's son to be a plagiarism of his father's work. Since twenty-five years had elapsed, however, this seems somewhat unlikely. Moinet had various technical developments to his own credit, including an optical method for checking the shape of the teeth of watch and clock wheels. He exhibited a chronometer of his own design at the Great Exhibition of 1851, in London; and finally he died in 1853, in an impoverished state, since the publication of his work and ensuing lawsuits had cost him dear.

It was quite common to order a suite of chimney-piece furniture—nowadays sometimes called a *'garniture de cheminée'*—throughout the nineteenth century, the clock being accompanied by a flanking pair of candelabra *en suite*, or, later, a pair of vases. Apart from the one just described, Thomire supplied several such sets to George IV, another being based upon a fine gilt-bronze clock panelled with lapis lazuli. The rectangular base of this clock, supported upon gilt-bronze paw feet, is mounted with foliate arabesques and rosettes, while, at the centre, is to be seen the Prince of Wales's feathers within a wreath, the whole on a lapis lazuli ground. The left side of the base is signed 'THOMIRE', and scattered upon the top of it are implements of sculpture and emblems of music and painting. Rising from the base is, at the right, a winged male figure with his right elbow resting on the top of an accompanying pedestal, while his left arm holds a shield panelled in lapis lazuli and mounted in its centre with a low-relief female figure in gilt-bronze who is brandishing a trumpet in her

201. (Right) *Another design of Standing Apollo clock, the movement by Moinet.* (Royal Collection)

left hand while she blows another one held in her right. The pedestal at left, and round-headed, contains the clock cylinder in the upper half and, below, a military trophy in low relief together with the inscription 'ARTIUM / GENIO'; the clock is now usually identified 203
by this imprint. As to the mechanism, it is inevitably a Vulliamy substitute, his movement being numbered 801. There is no record of the original clockmaker. Now at Windsor Castle, this fine clock travelled from Paris separately from its matching candelabra—and with no accompanying statue of Diana this time—and it was received at Carlton House in July 1813. Its overall height is 36 inches.

Mention having already been made of the goddess Diana, it might be fitting to conclude this section by describing a clock in which she is featured within a rather more elaborate setting. Standing 2 feet high, the scene is a temple, made of white marble, its domed 204
canopy supported by five fluted columns, and resting upon a circular marble base with beaded ormolu decoration, the whole upon four turned feet. Ormolu mounts grace the capitals and bases of the columns, and the cornice contains reserves of fruit and foliage in the same material. Within this temple, on a round pedestal raised upon four steps, stands a statue in ormolu of Diana accompanied by a hound. The domed canopy is surmounted by an urn, upon which sits a cherub who points to two time-bands which rotate beneath him, to indicate the hour and minute. The clock in this case is by Gavelle, probably Maurice-Jacques, *maître* 1780, who specialized in clocks housed in marble with gilt-bronze decoration. At the Rue aux Ours from 1781–9, by 1800 he had moved to Rue Salle au Comte and was located at Rue St-Martin from 1804 to 1820. He was apparently a pupil of the famous maker Robert Robin.

Some other extremities of French clock case design

Apart from those already mentioned, other well-known French bronze artists are represented in the Royal Collection. For example, a craftsman who simply signed himself 'Denière Fabr. de Bronze' is worthy of inspection. Here again a father and son were involved; the elder seems to be found first in Paris in 1779. Subsequently, the son, in partnership with Matelin, worked from Rue Turenne in 1812, and from Rue

202. (Left) *The companion thermometer to the previous clock.* (Royal Collection)

203. (Right) *The Artium Genio clock.* (Royal Collection)

ARTIUM
GENIO

204. (Left) *Diana in the Temple clock, the movement by Gavelle.* (Royal Collection)

205. (Above) *Empire clock by Denière, made for Sultan Mahmoud II.* (Royal Collection)

d'Orléans 1820–40. Some of their clocks were exhibited in the International Exhibition in London in 1862.

Clifford Smith describes two clocks from the Denière establishment, and thereby provokes a small mystery. The first, and certainly the more interesting, has an 205
upright rectangular form, of mahogany, which has been mounted with chased ormolu in bold French Empire style, with horizontal mouldings at plinth and cornice, and shaped columns at the corners. This clock was made for Sultan Mahmoud II of Turkey, going subsequently to the Haversham and Adrian-Hope collections. It was then purchased by Queen Mary, who gave it to the Royal Collection, for Buckingham Palace, in 1924. The second clock, which Clifford Smith states to be fully signed and located in the Carnarvon Room, has 'the frieze decorated with men and animals, and is surmounted by two seated classical figures.' However, there is no record of the existence of any such clock. The clock now in the Carnarvon Room is shown at fig. 206.

There are no signatures to be found anywhere on either case or movement, which is a standard round French locking-plate-strike model, of *c.* 1850. The case, of gilt-bronze, places the clock cylinder on a leaf-strewn sward, with classical male and female figures resting against it; the rectangular base below is fronted with a trophy of musical and hunting impedimenta. The dial, which is clearly in poor order, is bordered by a zodiac band. 206

A constantly recurring theme in the French clocks under review is that of apparent motion; set pieces we may see, but it is often as if they had been frozen for a split second of time and would at any moment recommence their activities. Such a feeling pervades the Apollo Clock—the chariot is barely stationary. Indeed, chariots are often employed on clock cases to

206. (Left) *The clock now in the Carnarvon Room in Buckingham Palace; case and movement are unsigned, and the latter dates c. 1850.* (Royal Collection)

207. (Below) *Chariot clock, drawn by a swan, and with two cupids.* (Royal Collection)

combine the qualities of classicism with the appearance of mobility. One of these, for instance, depicts a cupid standing in a Roman chariot, the wheel of which, as in the Apollo Clock, forms the dial; in another example, the chariot is drawn by a swan and driven by a cupid,
207 with another pushing the vehicle at the rear. This clock is on a marble base supported upon lion's paw feet; the present mechanism was installed by Charles Frodsham during the second half of the last century.

Another representation of time standing still, albeit momentarily, is contained in a clock by 'Manière A
208 Paris'. In this version, a circular Rosa marble pedestal
209 on a square base supports a globe, around which two bands revolve. The upper band is inscribed with Arabic minute figures, and a standing ormolu figure of Father Time, on the left, indicates these with the tip of his scythe. A second band, below this one, has the hours represented in Roman numerals, and these are read against one of the struts supporting the globe. To the right, the figure said to personify Astronomy holds in one hand an open book, while the other is stretched out towards Time as if in the act of restraining him. The imagery is quite dramatic; and Charles-Guillaume Manière has already been noticed as the maker of the movement in the Chinese Drummer Boy Clock. His work is found not only in cases of Louis XVI style such as the latter but also in Empire-style settings.

Once the realms of history and legend are left behind, however, it seems more usual for the groups of figures used on clock cases to reflect a state of near tranquillity. Two of this kind are on marble break-front bases which are decorated with almost identical ormolu rectangular mounts of scrolling foliage and cupids. In both cases, too, the clock itself is raised on a pedestal, the front of which also carries ormolu decoration in relief.

The pedestal panel of the first clock depicts a group of children dragging along a goat, upon whose back sits
an infant Bacchus. The female figures seated either side, 210
both with infants and the one at the left crowned and holding a trident, are in patinated bronze, while the

208. (Left) *Globe clock with revolving time bands, by Manière à Paris* (Royal Collection)

209. (Below) *The previous clock, discernible in the background of this view of the Lower Vestibule, Carlton House, from W. H. Pyne's* History of the Royal Residences . . . *(1819).* (Guildhall Library, City of London)

210. (Below right) *Seated Figures clock, now with Vulliamy movement no. 679.* (Royal Collection)

eagle with outspread wings and grasping a trailing festoon of flowers which surmounts the clock cylinder is of ormolu. Whoever may have made the original movement for this clock—possibly Lépine—it was renewed by Vulliamy in 1819, his serial number being 679. This clock formerly stood in the Ante-Chamber to the Throne Room at Carlton House.

The second of these clocks which is very similar in concept, is still mechanically intact, the dial being signed 'Lepine, Place des Victoires, Paris'. The pedestal supporting the clock cylinder in this version is somewhat taller than the previous one and contains two inset panels, one above the other. These are chased with infant figures. Seated either side of the clock are male and female figures in ormolu representing Philosophy and Study, after models supplied to the Sèvres factory in 1780 for reproduction in biscuit porcelain, by the sculptor L-S. Boizot. Finally, surmounting the clock is a crouching eagle, thunderbolts depending from his claws. Both clocks are supported on six cast and chased ormolu feet.

There is one unique feature about this second clock. Comparison with the drawing of it which appears in George IV's Pictorial Inventory shows quite clearly that the plinth supporting the clock cylinder has been deliberately heightened, and the original marble base replaced by another one with different ornaments. From that original base come the two bronze plaques, each chased with trumpeting satyr infants, sitting back to back, which now adorn the front and back of the

211. (Left) *Another style of Seated Figures clock, with subsequent alterations. The drawing in the Pictorial Inventory shows that the clock pedestal has been purposely heightened.* (Royal Collection)

212. (Above and right) *Nicholas Sotiau also made clocks in cases of this kind.* (Royal Collection)

extra metal cube which has been added below the clock cylinder. It is likely that these alterations were carried out in 1837, to make this clock correspond more closely with the one described immediately before it. Their heights agree, as does the decoration upon their bases; and it is known that, in the late nineteenth-century, both clocks were sited in the White Drawing Room at Buckingham Palace.

Three other clocks in the same general style have dials and two-train movements by Nicholas Sotiau. This maker was well-known in his day, becoming 212
maître in 1782. He established himself in Rue St-Honoré in Paris the following year and died in 1791 when only forty-two years old. Sotiau's clocks are known to have featured among the wares of the Parisian dealer Dominique Daguerre, through whom they were offered to George IV.

One of his clocks in the Royal Collection, which is in ormolu, has the clock cylinder decorated with wreaths and surmounted by an eagle clutching thunderbolts, being supported on either side by seated male and female figures in patinated bronze. The base, in this example, is of a dove-coloured marble, decorated with figures and foliage in well-chased ormolu. Originally in George IV's bedroom in the 1780s, this clock went to Windsor Castle in 1828, being eventually brought to the Bow Room in Buckingham Palace in 1913. A similar clock, but with the figures this time in biscuit porcelain rather than ormolu, stood on the chimney-piece in George IV's dressing-room at the same period.

Yet a third version, its clock cylinder surmounted by two satyrs and supported by female winged sphinxes, was in 'the small room'. There was once a fourth example, given to the King as a birthday present by Mrs Fitzherbert.

A small digression here might not be out of place. It must seem strange that a monarch with such studied and cultivated taste in French works of art, including clocks, should have received such objects as birthday presents; apart from the ever-present risk that he might not have liked the donor's choice, there must be, one might think, a slight flavour of 'taking coals to
214 Newcastle'. Conceivably Mrs Fitzherbert's clock did not find favour; but another such birthday present presumably did, since it is still in the Royal Collection. This is the clock which Britten shows as Figure 645; a rectangular base raised on four feet supports, on the left, a pedestal with an inset clock cylinder and surmounted by a globe, and, on the right, a draped classical female figure, its overall height being 36 inches. Both base and pedestal also incorporate panels depicting figures, in relief, while the ancillary decoration includes flaming torches at the angles of the pedestal, as well as decorative mouldings. This clock was presented to George IV as a birthday present by the Duchess of Gloucester, being received at Carlton House on 11th August 1817. At the time it was described as French, but it now possesses an eight-day two-train movement by Samuel Jefferson, *q.v.*

Sometimes, French clock decoration followed the form of the traditional still-life painting; nothing can move because it is either dead or inanimate. An interesting example of this style was formerly the property of Queen Mary. In ormolu throughout, the clock cylinder, which is festooned with oak leaves and surmounted with military trophies, sits upon a cush- 213
ion, which in turn rests upon a rectangular base enriched with gadrooning and acanthus-leaf mouldings, the whole upon four cast and chased bun feet. This charming clock is signed by 'Le Faucheur A Paris', a member once again of a clockmaking family. Alexandre Le Faucheur, *maître* in 1729, became *horloger du roi* in 1746. With premises at the Pont au Change in 1748, he was later at *'Au Meridien'*, Quai de l'Horloge, 1772–80. His son Jean Ignace actually served the French monarch as second *valet de chambre*, from 1777 to 1784, later setting up at the sign *'Au Roy de France'*, in Rue de la Verrerie.

Architecture, as represented by the broken column, with ancillary figures flanking it, was a favourite decorative theme during the eighteenth and nineteenth centuries, both in France and, later, in England. Vulliamy's excursions into this style will be dealt with elsewhere; here, there is a good French example, in chased ormolu, 10 inches wide and 1 foot $4\frac{1}{2}$ inches high, which is perhaps rather too precious for many people's tastes but should be reviewed nevertheless. The clock cylinder, its bezel surrounded with a festoon of leaves tied at the top with a bow of ribbon, is inset into the short fluted column, which is surmounted by an urn similarly festooned and covered with a domed lid enriched with fruit and leaf decoration. This sits on a stepped base with projecting feet and inset decorative

213. (Left) *Cushion clock, by Le Faucheur.* (Royal Collection)

214. (Right) *Clock given as a birthday present to George IV by the Duchess of Gloucester in 1817.* (Royal Collection)

JEFFERSON
BRUTON STREET

215. (Right) *Musical mantel clock, unsigned.* (The Queen Mother's Collection)

216. (Below right) *Detail of the previous clock: the front panel of the plinth hinges outwards to reveal the musical movement.* (The Queen Mother's Collection)

panels, while flanking the clock are two cherubs in contemplative attitudes.* The clock dial is signed 'Passement Hgr. du Roi, Paris', a maker whose activities are not wholly clear. He seems to have been more involved with the construction of complex astronomical instruments than simply with clocks, and it is said that he made *'une sphère mouvante'* for an Indian potentate, that took three years to complete, being shown to l'Académie Royale des Sciences in 1749. The mechanism in this was made by Roques, the sphere by Dauthiau, and the case-work was by the Caffieri family, father and son. Passement published several descriptions of his work, not only on his globe but also on his design of conical pendulum. Simple clocks of his manufacture are not commonly encountered.

Two French clocks belonging to Queen Elizabeth The Queen Mother ought to be included at this point. The first, which is at Clarence House, is on a rectangular marble base with projecting squared corners, heavily
215 enriched with ormolu swags and garlands of leaves. This rests upon four flat gilt feet. The base, with four gilt finials, supports a marble slab, surrounded by an ormolu gallery and with beaded decoration, which forms the foundation from which springs the clock cylinder, resting upon a marble pedestal flanked by columns, the whole elaborately decorated with entwined foliage and with, at the centre below the clock, a panel of ormolu decoration showing birds and foliage in open relief. The columns terminate in scroll mounts of extravagant form, which rest against the clock cylinder and the small pedestal which rises above it; and, surmounting the latter perhaps the most striking feature of this clock, a small wide-mouthed vase of ormolu flowers, quite beautifully executed.

The dial of this clock is unsigned, the gilt hands of beetle and poker form, and the clock movement has two trains. However, in the fairly deep base, the front of which is screened by a hinged open-work ormolu panel incorporating swags of foliage against a diapered
216 background, there is concealed a fine musical movement, wound through a similar hinged panel at the

*This clock, included for the sake of completeness, seems to have been temporarily misplaced in the Royal Collection. However, Clifford Smith illustrates it at Plate 347.

side, and with an action of twenty hammers on some eleven bells.

The second of the Queen Mother's clocks is of a well-established type, but a particularly fine specimen of it. Of familiar Empire form in consisting of two pairs of columns springing from a solid base, and supporting the clock, the whole is surmounted by a finely sculptured eagle. The pendulum bob, visible between
217 the columns, takes the form of a sunburst. The dial of this clock is signed 'Chopin A Paris', this probably being the firm of that name that was established in Rue aux Ours in 1806. By 1820, they had moved to Rue Beaubourg.

This section concludes by considering two fine French clocks, wholly different in style and appearance—coming, possibly, from opposite ends of the vast spectrum of decorative presentations which this artistic race employed, even for such a humdrum object as a timekeeper.

The first is generally known as 'The Rock Clock'. It was despatched to Brighton from London on 13th October 1819, six days after it had arrived in the capital from Paris, where it was purchased. It stood upon the
218 chimney-piece of the Music Room in Brighton Pavilion; and according to the accounts for the furnishing of the room, B. L. Vulliamy was paid £550 for this object, far more than he could hope to have been paid simply for replacing the original movement. It may be, therefore, that he served as agent for the acquisition of the clock in France, in which case part of this amount might represent commission. In any event, at that time it seems the movement was by 'Ragot à Paris'—this was probably Claude Ragot, *maître* 1785, who could be found in the Rue St-Denis during 1789–90; one of his gilt-bronze clocks is recorded as having been sold for 9,000 francs in 1913. In 1820 the present dial and movement were installed by Vulliamy, bearing his serial number 739. As to the clock case, it used to be ascribed to Antoine Sebastien Slodtz, who succeeded Meissonier in 1750, as designer to Louis XV; but there appears to be little if any foundation for such a provenance.

Whatever misfortunes may have befallen the movement, nobody will deny that the great beauty of this clock lies in the monumental gilt-bronze case, which
219 stands 4 feet high. The rectangular stepped base, with symmetrical quarter-round moulding, gives way to a palm tree amid rocks, around which is entwined a dragon. A figure at left confronts the beast with a spear—according to a written description of 1838, although the outstretched right hand is now empty—while yet another figure, said to be Mars, climbs the tree above the dragon, at right.

From this point upwards, the clock—which is built

217. *Empire clock by Chopin à Paris.* (The Queen Mother's Collection)

in two sections—could be a typical cartel clock of the period, with the irregular decorative surround containing the clock itself in its drum case being surmounted by a nude female figure and an infant, similarly naked; these are held to be Venus and Cupid. They flank 'the Peacock of Love', whose tail fans out behind them.

This massive case is further chased with stylized foliage and other motifs, and the human figures are treated in the round; in all, a quite remarkable piece of work which, in other respects, should perhaps have been included in the section on historical and mythological clock settings. However, the attributions above-quoted might seem to be founded in a vivid

218. (Left) *The Rock Clock, in its present surroundings.* (Royal Collection)

219. (Above) *The Rock Clock in close up.* (Royal Collection)

imagination, for the lower figures, certainly, have an Oriental quaintness which hardly seems to accord with European legend.

The second clock, in common with several already described and with at least one more still to be reviewed, came from the *atelier* of that most eminent of French makers, Jean-Antoine Lépine, so that this might be a good opportunity to consider what is known about that great craftsman. Born at Challex in 1720, Lépine served his apprenticeship in Saconex, leaving for Paris when he was twenty-four years old and going to work for André-Charles Caron, whose daughter, Madeleine-Françoise, he married in 1756. *Maître* in 1762, he succeeded Caron in 1766 in the Rue St-Denis. The business was transferred to Place Dauphine in 1772, to the Quai de l'Horloge in 1778, Rue aux Fossés St-Germain l'Auxerrois during 1781–7. He went into partnership with Claude-Pierre Raguet after the latter had married his daughter; both were *'horlogers du roi'.* From 1789 he was established at 12 Place des Victoires, subsequently retiring when his sight failed him. He died in the Rue St-Anne in 1814.

Lépine's particular contribution to technical horology lies in his innovations leading to a thinner watch. About 1760 the 'Lépine calibre' first appeared: this dispensed with one of the two movement plates within which the mechanism was deployed, in favour of separate bars, or cocks, screwed to the remaining plate. He also introduced the mainspring barrel supported at one end only—sometimes called a hanging barrel—which, in conjunction with a cylinder escapement, helped even further to reduce the hitherto inelegant thickness of all watches. The finest French makers were years ahead of every other country in this respect, and their watches had a degree of sophistication in their appearance unknown elsewhere at that time. Apart from these activities, Lépine still found time to make a number of clocks for Louis XVI, as well as for the Spanish Court.

The Lépine clock now to be described is usually
known as 'The Negress Head Clock'. Its exact time of 220
entry into the Royal Collection is not known with 221
absolute certainty, but it may have been bought by George IV in 1790; correspondence in 1796 mentions the acquisition from Lépine of several clocks in that year, apart from which, according to a note left by Vulliamy in 1846, the clock movement is signed by this great French maker on a part that is not normally visible, and numbered 1790. It would be contrary to normal practice, but clearly not impossible, for this to be a date; and it has not, as yet, been practicable to check these latter details. The musical movement in the base of the clock is signed 'L^{e} pine H^{er} du Roy A Paris 4195'. What is certain is that the clock must have been

acquired prior to 1807, the date of a bill from B. L. Vulliamy for its repair and partial regilding.

Surmounting the structure is the compelling bust of the Nubian Negress in patinated bronze, her ornamental head-dress with its plume of feathers and the drapery with garland of flowers across her shoulders in gilt-bronze to provide contrast. A bow and quiver of arrows across her back are in a similar finish. This figure rests upon a musical case of white marble embellished with gilt-bronze mouldings, stepped at the base and of break-front design. This case is inset with panels of chased gilt-bronze in relief, showing dancing cherubs at the centre, while at the sides a stylized vase is set amid foliage, flowers and fruit; this, in turn, stands upon a stepped plinth of white and black marble, supported upon six gilt feet. Flanking the Negress Head and seated upon the front corners of the musical case are two discreetly draped winged cherubs holding flower garlands.

The head itself contains the clock, the time being indicated by Roman figures, seen in the left eye, which represent the hours, and Arabic figures, in the right one, to show minutes, divided into two-minute intervals. These indications derive from internal rotating drums. The eyes are normally closed. Ten minutes before the hour the eyelids slide away, revealing the time, and then close again two minutes after the hour has passed; but they can be re-opened at any time by pulling the Negress's right ear-ring. Her left ear-ring brings into action the sixteen-pipe organ housed in the base, which can play eight tunes.

This is probably one of the most spectacular clocks in the Royal Collection. Formerly in the Bow Room at Carlton House, it was later moved to the 1844 Room in Buckingham Palace, and it is now in Windsor Castle. The details of Vulliamy's bill for repairs, etc. are worth noting:

Dec. 24 1807 — Vulliamy & Son, 74 Pall Mall.

For taking to pieces a French spring clock, name Lepine à Paris, that shows the hours and minutes through the eyes of an African Princess, making new and additional work to the hour and minute motion in order to make them show the time correctly (which they never have done since the clock was made), and repairing the clock part and cleaning it. . . . £12 12s. 0d.

For cleaning the machine organ and tuning the pipes £2 18s. 0d.

For taking the case entirely to pieces, cleaning all the gilt ornaments, making them look like new and regilding in the best manner in dead gold the two Cupids, and putting it together again compleat. . . . £7 10s. 0d.

220. (Above) *The Negress Head clock, a general view with, opposite, detail of the eyes, shown opened to reveal the time.* (Royal Collection)

221. (Right) *The Negress Head clock, as illustrated in the Pictorial Inventory.* (Royal Collection)

Although the additional motion work supplied by Vulliamy is not specified, it might be seen that he had been fairly modest in his attentions to this timepiece—which is just as well, for a clock of this kind was rather outside Lépine's normal production; indeed it appears to be the only one he made. Other versions are known, by different makers but including two by Jean-Baptiste-André Furet, *fils de maître* 1746, who died in 1807. Three clocks with his machinery in 1784, included a Negress Head clock similar to this one, a singing bird-cage clock and a globe clock showing time in every country in the world.

Clocks with complicated or unconventional mechanisms

In some of the foreign clocks that have been reviewed, a musical action—usually on bells, but occasionally on a mechanical organ—has been installed. While this certainly adds to the complexity of the machine, in most cases the musical action is a quite separate entity from the time-measuring movement, which simply triggers the former at predetermined intervals. The musical case occupies the base of the clock, too, so that it can be a much later addition to the whole, carried out to enhance the interest of the clock within a specific setting.

In the present context, however, complicated clocks will be defined as those in which the main mechanism performs, by means of extra gearing and dials, and sometimes with another power source built in to complement that already existing, additional functions

222. (Above) *Astronomical mantel clock by Lépine: general front view.* (Royal Collection)

to those simple time-indicating ones which form the principal *raison d'être* of the common clock. Most often such clocks have a scientific basis, connected perhaps with astronomy and the predicting of positions of the stars and planets; or they may be complicated by the inclusion of special technology to improve the time-measuring performance, again quite often to enhance the accuracy of astronomical observations. English makers through the ages made many such clocks, of varying degrees of sophistication depending upon their period and the scientific and technical achievement of the craftsmen who designed and made them; such clocks are represented in the Royal Collection and will be considered elsewhere in this book. This section is only concerned with complicated foreign-made clocks, and more particularly French ones; also, it does not include the one or two formerly complicated foreign clocks in which the original movements have been subsequently replaced by English ones.

The name Jean-Antoine Lépine has already occurred several times: he was clearly a favourite clockmaker in George IV's estimation, and a number of clocks were bought from him. The one about to be described may be 222
one of several purchased in 1790, for which a total of £3,250 was asked. By July 1799, some £2,850 of this amount was still outstanding.

Following a break-front module, this large astronomical mantel clock—it is 2 feet $1\frac{1}{2}$ inches high and 2 feet 4 inches wide—is constructed in white marble, heavily enriched with chased and gilt-bronze 225

mounts. Incorporating three dials, the principal and central one, raised above those flanking it and within an arch supported by columns, is surmounted by a celestial globe on each side of which beautifully modelled figures of Cupids, in a simulated cloud setting, busy themselves with mathematical instruments. This dial indicates hours and minutes, together with sweep centre seconds and a fourth hand intended to show the equation of time. To the left of it and at a lower level is a smaller dial of hard-paste porcelain painted with jewel enamelling and richly gilt. This shows the year, the month, day of the month, and sign of the zodiac. Level with this dial but to the right of the clock, a similarly decorated dial shows the age of the moon and the days of the week. Below each of the three dials shaped reserves are inset with chased ormolu mounts, with foliate and ribbon motifs and, centrally, a male figure shown half-length. The plinth is decorated with rectangular reserves, inset, and chased with rosettes and scrolls at either side, while, in the central panel,

225. (Below) *The Lépine clock as depicted in George IV's Pictorial Inventory.* (Royal Collection)

223. (Top) *One of the dials by Coteau, from the previous clock.* (Royal Collection)

224. (Above) *Another Coteau dial from the Lépine clock.* (Royal Collection)

figures of infants at play have been nicely modelled. This rests upon eight shaped feet, which in turn are supported by a solid marble base with beaded moulding.

The principal dial, unlike the others, is white enamelled, and bears the well-known signature 'Lepine Hgr DU ROI Place des Victoires, N° 12'. The corresponding movement is inscribed 'Lepine horologer du Roi, Paris N° 4175'. There is also what appears to be a partly effaced signature of the dial painter, which seems to read 'B [?] CHON'. One wonders if this might have been Béchot, *émailleur de cadrans*, who was eventually

226. (Left) *The Lépine astronomical mantel clock as it appears in the context of the Blue Velvet Room, Carlton House. The coloured aquatint is reproduced from W. H. Pyne's* History of the Royal Residences *. . . (1819).* (Guildhall Library, City of London)

227. (Below) *Astronomical clock by F. L. Godon.* (Royal Collection)

located in Rue de la Huchette in Paris in 1812. One of the special delights of this clock, however, is the two
223 smaller dials. Possibly of Sèvres porcelain, they are
224 signed 'Coteau', probably identifiable with the miniaturist Jean Coteau (*c.*1738—after 1812). He was Swiss, from Geneva, living in Paris, and worked for the Sèvres manufactory *c.*1780–4. The technique of jewel enamelling was first used on Sèvres porcelain about 1778, and Coteau helped to perfect it. There exists another clock on which the signs of the zodiac are identical to those on this one, which is not only signed by Coteau but dated 1786.

B. L. Vulliamy repaired this clock at one juncture, his bill being dated 24th March 1808. Happily he does not
226 seem unduly to have 'improved' it. The clock was originally in the Royal Closet at Carlton House; it now graces the Blue Drawing Room in Buckingham Palace.

A less complicated but nonetheless interesting mantel clock bears the signature 'F. L. Godon Rel° de Camara de S.M.C.'. This maker was presumably François-Louis Godon, *maître* 1787, and established in the Rue de Valois-St-Honoré during 1789–90. He was, among other things, clockmaker to the Court of Spain. Again of marble with ormolu mounts, the design of this
227 clock shows a figure of a young girl kneeling on a draped stool, and bending forward over the clock, at the same time leaning her left elbow upon a gilt bird-cage which is resting thereon. On the other side, a figure of Cupid standing on a rocky mound holds a dove which he is about to place in the cage. This has been said to symbolize 'The Return of Love'. The bezel of the clock dial is festooned with flowers, and around the pedestal are finely chased ormolu panels providing a border of foliage with figures of infants blowing trumpets. Below four miniature steps there is a lower plinth decorated with a black and white mosaic composition. The whole rests upon six cast and chased gilt feet.

The finely executed dial of this clock was painted by Dubuisson, *émailleur en cadrans et boîtes de montres*, who worked in Rue de la Huchette in 1795, removing later to Barnabites, Rue de la Calandre, 1812–20. In the outermost ring it displays the days of the month in jewelled settings, and next, but still outside the chapter numerals, come in the upper half the days of the week, while in the lower half is a series of hieroglyphs believed to be Arabic but not fully understood. Finally, the Arabic chapters and, inside those, there is a seconds circle. The clock has two trains, being hour-striking.

An unconventional French clock is to be found in the
228 Principal Corridor in Buckingham Palace. Described as

228. (Right) *Empire mahogany and glass panelled clock, unsigned.* (Royal Collection)

an Empire Period free-standing mahogany-cased timekeeper—Clifford Smith believed it was an exhibition piece, made for display in a clockmaker's showroom—it has glass panels at front and sides, and measures overall 7 feet 6 inches high by 1 foot 6 inches wide and 10 inches deep, although projecting mouldings at top and bottom add marginally to these dimensions. The eight-day spring movement is neither signed nor numbered, but clearly French. With a dead-beat escapement, the 12-inch gilded dial with engine-turned centre, blued-steel moon hands and a centre-seconds hand, itself acts as the bob of a grid-iron pendulum. Although not of the customary design, it is thought that this does afford some degree of temperature compensation. The whole assembly terminates in a knife-edge suspension attached to the backboard of the case; similarly, a very long crutch rod gives impulse to the pendulum through a crutch pin with beat screws. Winding is carried out from the back of the movement, access being gained by turning movement and pendulum to the front on its top swivel just below the suspension.

It seems appropriate to save the most complicated of such clocks until last: there are two of special
231 importance. First comes a clock purchased by George IV in 1824 for 300 guineas and which has for some years graced the Library in Windsor Castle. It was shown in public, at the exhibition 'Pendulum to Atom', which was held at Goldsmiths' Hall in London in 1958.

This is an orrery clock made by the firm of Raingo
229 Frères in Paris; Raingo himself—his only recorded initial is Z, and the mind boggles at the possibilities that this conjures up—although thought to have been of French extraction, is believed to have fled from France for political reasons in early life and to have set to work in Gand, in Belgium, where he remained, at least for some time. He is recorded as being clockmaker to the Duc de Chartres in 1823. When—even if—he actually returned to Paris is not clear; he certainly made one very fine orrery clock signed as from Gand, and seeming to date *c.*1810. Antide Janvier is said to have supplied movements for some of his clocks, the complicated ones, that is; and during the decade 1820–30, Raingo Frères are known to have produced a series—say ten or a dozen—related, if not identical, astronomical clocks in the same style as this earlier one. The firm was also well-known for quite conventional domestic clocks, but that not need concern us here. Suffice it to say that it has been identified, at various times, as located in Rue de Cléry, Rue Vieille du Temple (1829), Rue de Saintonge (1840–50), as well as to have exhibited in the International Exhibition in London in 1862. Several horological patents are also to its credit.

The Raingo orrery clocks all follow the same general

229. (Above) *General view of the Orrery clock by Raingo.* (Royal Collection)

230. (Right) *Detail, viewed from above, of the Raingo clock.* (Royal Collection)

AOUT
SEPTEMBRE
OCTOBRE
NOVEMBRE

231. *The Raingo clock as illustrated in the Pictorial Inventory.* (Royal Collection)

style, varying only in detail. This style consists of a circular base, which supports four columns and an entablature. The clock is suspended between two of the former while the orrery surmounts the latter. The construction materials used for this architectural framework are, in the case of the specimen in the Royal Collection, amboyna wood, enriched with gilt-bronze ornamentation. Some specimens have, in addition, a musical movement in the base; at least one has standing figures around the edge of the 'temple' representing the four Seasons.

The purpose of these clocks is said to have been for domestic instruction; and since the motion of the orrery, when connected to the clock for conventional everyday use, would be imperceptible, it is so arranged that disconnection and speeded-up manual operation, by turning a small ivory handle, is easily accomplished. When such a demonstration is completed, all that is necessary to return the orrery to its proper relationship with the clock is so to set it that the pointer for the calendar ring indicates the correct day of the month. Incidentally, while the clock element of the mechanism—including striking-action when fitted—needs winding up every eight days, the orrery only requires this attention once every four years.

Starting with the dial of the clock, the only unconventional feature is a double-ended calendar hand; one end points to the day of the week, the other to a symbolic representation of the planet from which the French name for that day is derived. Thus, Tuesday, i.e. *mardi*, falls opposite an embodiment of the planet
Mars. Now taking a viewpoint from above the clock, an 230
outer fixed ring shows the symbols representing the signs of the zodiac; inside that, a calendar ring shows the day and the month against a moving pointer beneath the leap year dial. This is part of the constantly moving mechanical superstructure and indicates which of the years in the four-year cycle is current. The winding-square for the orrery is reached by means of a hole in this dial. Diametrically opposite is the larger component, which demonstrates the earth, moon and sun in their correct moving relationships to one another, below which is a dial indicating the age of the moon. It is worth noting that the clock utilizes a grid-iron type pendulum to compensate for the effects of changes in temperature and that the whole edifice is normally housed beneath a fitted glass dome.

At the very beginning of this chapter, it was stated that, of all foreign clocks in the Royal Collection, the French were predominant in numbers—and quality, inevitably, on account of the impeccable taste in such things of George IV, whether as Prince of Wales, as Prince Regent or finally as King. This is not to say, however, that there are no other foreign clocks worthy of notice, and it seems appropriate to complete this section with an early complicated clock of German origin and considerable importance.

It is not entirely clear how this particular clock entered the Royal Collection, but it has certainly been there for more than a century since it features on page 411 of the Appendix to E. J. Wood's *Curiosities of Clocks and Watches from the Earliest Times*, which was published in 1866. There it is described as follows:

Her Majesty The Queen has a large astrological clock of the seventeenth century, the framework being covered with turtleshell and silver appliqué scrolls and silver bands. The pedestal is quadrangular with shaped sides. This square clock has four twisted columns of Venetian glass in imitation of amethyst, and on each side is a silver obelisk of repoussé masks and scrolls, with an eagle at the top. There are dials on all the four sides, that on the front has a deep silver revolving-plate, with a calendar for every day of the year, and two smaller dials denoting the hour and the signs of the zodiac. The pendulum has a figure of Time. On the back are astrological dials. On the

232. (Above) *Jacob Mayr's astronomical clock: a print showing the clock's original state.* (Royal Collection)

233. (Above right) *The movement of the previous clock, seen from the front.* (Royal Collection)

234. (Right) *The back of the movement of Jacob Mayr's astronomical clock.* (Royal Collection)

pediment are two silver seated figures. Above is a sort of temple with two twisted ruby glass columns, two silver figures in niches, and ruby vases at the corner, surmounted by a gilt figure of Atlas supporting a globe. The height is three feet ten inches and a half. The maker was 'Jacob Mayr Junger, Augsburg'.

At the time that this clock was made—other sources place the date more finitely as *c.*1675—there was a considerable intellectual overlap between astronomy and astrology. Jacob Mayr the Younger seems to have been at work during the period 1672–1714 in Augsburg and is said to have died in the latter year; several makers, presumably related, bore the same name and were working in Augsburg around this time, hence the need for some distinguishing qualification.

The reason for quoting *in extenso* the description of the clock given by Wood, is to benefit from the first-hand knowledge of someone who actually saw the clock *case* in being; for it is sad to report that what remains of it is in pieces, and so much has gone missing over the years that there appears very little likelihood of its ever being restored. There is an old engraving of the clock in a complete state which helps to conjure up an impression of this remarkable creation; and it was
232 certainly still complete at the beginning of the present century for a photograph of it is reproduced in Robertson and Walker's *Royal Clocks*. Unfortunately, it has not proved possible to trace the negative of that illustration.

As to the movement of this remarkable clock, it now reposes in the British Museum, where it is on per-
233 manent loan from Her Majesty The Queen and is on
234 display in the Clock Gallery. Mechanically, the clock runs for thirty hours, strikes hours and quarters and has also an alarm train. The hour-striking facility provides alternatives on a twelve-hour or twenty-four-hour basis, the selection being made by one of a small group of four subsidiary dials. Besides the time, the other indications include: annual calendar with saints' days, hours of daylight and darkness throughout the year, and, on lower dials, alarm-setting and the position of the sun in the zodiac. Dials each side of the movement show the last hour and quarter struck, while the other principal dial gives astronomical and lunar information. Apart from setting the hour-striking system, the rest of the group of four subsidiary dials indicate the Golden Number, the Epact, the Dominical Letter and days of the week. There is also provision for strike/silent control. The going-train occupies the central part of the posted frame movement and is flanked by the striking-trains arranged at right angles to it.

As if all this were not enough, it seems that there was in the base of the clock case a musical action; this is not on display, and it may perhaps not be original, for it does not seem to be coherent with the rest of the clock. With all the in-built ingenuity to be found in complicated clocks of this period, it is sad to have to remember that sufficient progress had not, by that time, been made with the improvement of the basic time-measuring machinery to make any of it usefully accurate.

Clocks and watches by A-L. Breguet

Every student of fine clocks knows that the work of
Abraham-Louis Breguet (1747–1823) is a law unto 239
itself, setting standards of workmanship and attaining scientifically-based performances in precision time-measurement that, in their consistency, were equalled by nobody and, in their sheer achievement, excelled by none. Not for Breguet the clock as a piece of elaborate furniture, or the watch as an interesting toy; his products performed superbly, looked both elegant and functional, were sufficiently expensive that his clientele tended to be upper class and wealthy, and stood so apart from the run-of-the-mill work of his contemporaries as to ensure that they would eventually exert a considerable influence on the fashion in such objects. The Royal Collection, thanks again to the catholic taste of George IV in all matters of quality—which shows that it did not have to be disguised behind swags of gilt-bronze flowers and statuesque sculpture to attract his discerning eye—possesses three quite outstanding clocks by Breguet, and there are records of other timekeepers by him that have now passed out of the hands of the Royal Family, although originally commissioned by them.

As for Breguet himself, he was born at Neuchâtel, in Switzerland, of French Protestant refugee parents, in 1747. His father died when he was eleven years old, and shortly afterwards his mother remarried; her second husband, a cousin of her first, was a watchmaker of some repute who, apart from his business in Switzerland, also had an office in Paris. When he was about fifteen, his stepfather sent the young Breguet to Versailles—which at that time was a principal centre of the arts in France, enjoying substantial royal patronage—to be apprenticed to a watchmaker. Even during this time his remarkable talents came to the notice of the King, so that when, apprenticeship completed and married to the daughter of a substantial Parisian family in 1775, he set up shop in Quai d'Horloge in that city, he was already operating in the most promising milieu; and, in a mere handful of years, he was top of his profession.

Although concrete evidence is lacking, there is good reason to suppose that, in order to broaden his experience, Breguet not only spent some time in the workshop of—and perhaps even worked for—the eminent French chronometer-maker Ferdinand Berthoud but subsequently spent some while in London, where he had a friend as well as business agent in Louis Recordon. He is known to have had a close association with John Arnold, one of the great English chronometer pioneers; indeed, they sent their sons to each other for instruction.

From the start it is clear that Breguet had decided that the repetitive making of standard designs of timekeepers was not for him; he set his sights upon creating elegant but fanciful objects, custom-built for each customer, and with the highest possible standard of craftsmanship and inventiveness employed in order that each should be thoroughly functional and reliable. However, to finance this kind of entrepreneurial endeavour, he had to fall back on the more common designs then prevalent to keep his business viable; in the main these were based on *ébauches* imported from Switzerland, which Brequet finished and cased, and for which he supplied escapements.

While there are no records extant prior to 1787, it is known that the Duc d'Orléans, in 1780, and Marie Antoinette in 1782, possessed *'perpetuelles'*, Breguet's name for his design of self-winding watches.

By 1786 Breguet was prepared to start manufacture of *perpetuelles* in quantity; this was a lengthy and costly business. Despite entering, in 1787, into a partnership specifically designed to bring more capital into the firm, enough watches were not being finished and sold to keep it healthy. Breguet himself was spending too much time travelling, supervising the making of *ébauches* in Switzerland and taking orders—he did business with the Court in England in 1787, and again in 1790 and 1791—to be able to apply himself properly to the production of his unique wares. Also, to the disgust of his partner, Breguet was spending too much time cultivating the aristocracy and the Court and developing his ideas for individual and exceptional watches for his rich clients, to the detriment of their ordinary, if more financially rewarding, output.

With the Revolution clearly gathering momentum, life suddenly became increasingly dangerous for Breguet. His relations with the Court and with the titled gentry made him suspect, so that, in August 1793, it became expedient for him to flee to Switzerland, on the pretext of normal business. However, things were little better there: he was regarded as a traitor to the cause, on account of his illegal flight from Paris, and this was aggravated by the presence of his son, who had thereby avoided conscription. Nevertheless, Breguet set up on a small scale, with workshops in Neuchâtel and Locle. During his absence from Paris, his foreman there had carried on as long as he could; but eventually Breguet was proclaimed a traitor and his property confiscated and sold up.

However, when, in April 1795, Breguet eventually returned to Paris, his position was unexpectedly strengthened. With a city and an economy in chaos, there was a sudden demand for reliable timekeepers for the army and navy, as well as for scientific use, and it was decided to reinstate and reorganize the watchmaking centre at Versailles. Only Breguet had all the necessary skills to do this; but he felt strongly that he had been victimized by the Revolution. As a Swiss national, he considered himself a neutral and the appropriation of his home, possessions and business wholly improper. It shows something of the reputation that Breguet enjoyed in Paris at this time that he was able, as a condition of taking on the Versailles project, to insist upon the return and complete reinstatement of his premises at Quai d'Horloge, at public expense; and, after much argument, during which Breguet remained adamant, this is exactly what he got.

From that point onwards Breguet never looked back; the establishment of his international fame was simply a matter of time. His clients included most of the crowned heads of Europe as well as the great aristocratic families, including notably the Duke of Wellington and Napoleon. His honours included membership of the Académie des Sciences, and he was made a Chevalier de la Légion d'Honneur. The detailed notes he had made throughout his working life were handed by him to Louis Moinet, *q.v.*, to form the basis of a treatise on horology, but this was never done, and the notes still languish in the archives of the House of Breguet. Increasing deafness did not unduly hinder him in his last years, and he was still very active and serving as a juror in the 1823 Exhibition, when he died. At seventy-seven, he had enjoyed a satisfying life, ending up wealthy, highly esteemed by his contemporaries—and with a long list of technical innovations to his credit—as well as the founder of a remarkable business whose clients must have been among the most exclusive in the world.

One of his most remarkable clocks was purchased by George IV, and, notwithstanding its relatively plain exterior, it cost the King no less than £1,000. Delivered on 19th September 1825, it was accompanied by a memorandum from the Breguets, father and son, compiled the previous year, from which it is clear that they considered it a regulator of the greatest excellence. Also supplied was a pen-and-wash drawing of the clock.

In essence, this timekeeper consists of twin move-
ments, each complete with its own dial and pin-wheel 235
escapement, driven by a single 8-pound weight, the 236
ends of whose line are fixed one to each barrel. The

235. (Left) *Twin-pendulum regulator by Breguet, general view.* (Royal Collection)

236. (Above) *Detail showing the twin dials of the previous clock.* (Royal Collection)

related pendulums are suspended one behind the other, the method of compensation being zinc and steel rods, maintained in compression by special springs to eliminate too much freedom. The principle which Breguet was establishing in this clock was the sympathy that can be derived between pendulums in such proximity, so that gross error is shared between them—that is, halved in its effect upon the timekeeping. Since a regulator of this quality, in which the mechanism is installed upon a massive and immovable anchorage, is anyway capable of maintaining a rate of one-tenth of a second *per diem*, a twin-pendulum refinement virtually eliminates it altogether. It follows, too, that external influences affecting the rate of going of the clock will have their overall effect reduced by the reciprocal effect upon the two pendulums.

Externally, the clock can be seen to be fitted with a glazed mahogany case with gilt-bronze mouldings, standing just over 6 feet 8 inches high, with a width of $19\frac{1}{2}$ inches and a depth of $11\frac{1}{2}$ inches. The two dials supply differing information, that at the left having separate chapters for the minutes and seconds and an aperture for the hours above, while the right-hand dial has concentric hours, minutes and equation of time with seconds below, and between them an aperture for the date. It is interesting to note that the seconds hand on the right rotates anti-clockwise; the purpose was to ensure a reversal of the effect upon the twin pendulums of the other movement, thus equalizing out all the relevant forces.

The clock has an unusual duration—three weeks—and an even more unorthodox feature in the small box in the base, connected with a chimney running up the back of the clock case. By burning charcoal in this facility, it was possible to ensure that the temperature of the clock never fell too low. Both clock dials are signed, the style being: 'Breguet et Fils, H^{ger} de la Marine Royale, No. 3671'.

The second Breguet clock in the Royal Collection, seen in public when loaned for exhibition at the London Antique Dealers' Fair in 1957, is of that rare type called a *'pendule sympathique'*. On June 26th 1795 Breguet wrote to his son:

> I have invented a means of setting a watch to time, and regulating it, without anyone having to do it. The most coarsely made watch, provided it doesn't stop, will serve its owner as though he had a *garde temps*. This is how it works: you have to have a second clock or a marine [chronometer] arranged to receive the watch. The cost of this addition is a day's work for a workman and the same for the watch.
>
> Then every night on going to bed, you put the watch into the clock. In the morning, or one hour later, it will be exactly to time with the clock. It is not even necessary to open the watch. There will be nothing visible externally to show where it has been touched. I expect from this the greatest promotion of our fame and fortune.

The royal *'Sympathique'* clock, numbered 666 and designed to accommodate watch number 507, was sold to the Prince Regent, as George IV then was, in 1814
237 for the sum of 11,500 francs. He wore the watch,
238 which is of gold; the serial number given to it is said to be erroneous (for 507 had already been allotted to a *sympathique* watch sold with its companion clock to the Ministry of Foreign Affairs for 35,000 francs), and correctly it should have borne the number 721. However that may be, the clock is enclosed in a mahogany case with gilt mouldings and mounts. The mechanism consists of a constant-force escapement, which drives a two-armed compensation balance with recessed timing-screws, controlled by a gold helical balance spring with terminal curves. The silver engine-turned dial has a subsidiary dial at VI to show seconds and a disc at the centre to set the time of release of the setting-action. At the base is a lever for winding, while surmounting the clock is a cradle to receive the watch. There is also a carrying-handle.

The watch has a ruby cylinder escapement, a three-armed plain balance with parachute suspension, and a blued-steel spiral balance spring with regulator. Built into the watch—this was what Breguet meant by 'The cost of this addition is a day's work'—is motion work which, when released by the clock, will automatically set the hands to the clock's time as well as applying any correction to the watch's regulator necessitated by the degree of inaccuracy registered at the moment of synchronization. Contact between clock and watch mechanism is by means of a pin, which passes from behind the clock dial through the watch cradle and into the watch itself.

Famous clocks like the *'Sympathique'* and the double-pendulum regulator acquire a mystique all their own, so that those who have ever been associated with them will renew acquaintance whenever possible. In the middle of the present century the then head of Maison Breguet, Monsieur G. Brown, wrote to the well-known London horological dealer and bookseller Malcolm Gardner the following frustrated little note:

> Paris, le 2 Juin 1953
>
> *Je ne me souviens plus qui m'avait dit en 1950 que la Pendule Sympathique nº 666 était chez Frodsham pour être nettoyée, mais je crois me rappeler qu'une plaquette devait être éditée à cette occasion, comme il a été fait pour le Régulateur double nº 3671. Si cette petite brochure a été faite, j'aimerais beaucoup l'avoir pour connaître les détails de la pendule et de la montre. Il y a bien des années, j'étais allé à Buckingham Palace pour la voir, mais le Roi George V revenait d'une cérémonie et entrait dans son bureau au moment ou j'allais y entrer moi-même; je n'ai pu la voir pour cette raison et l'ai toujours regretté.*

The *'petite brochure'* mentioned above does not seem to have been produced, for scrawled in the margin in Malcolm Gardner's inimitable hand is an enigmatic *'Non'*.

Such technically sophisticated complexity as is represented by the *'Sympathique'* has been described by present-day authorities as 'Breguet's most advanced flight of mis-applied ingenuity', the main argument being that the watches supplied for use with this system

237. (Above) *Breguet 'Sympathique' no. 666, front view.* (Royal Collection)

238. (Above right) *Side view of the previous clock.* (Royal Collection)

239. (Right) *Lithograph portrait of A-L. Breguet.* (Clockmakers' Company, London)

were of ordinary quality only, since, unless they registered sufficient inaccuracy in performance, the object of the exercise would be totally defeated. In the present instance, watch number 507 had a plain—i.e. uncompensated for the effects of changes in temperature—balance, so that error was almost built into it, whereas Breguet was well able to provide watches with far greater pretensions to accuracy. The extension of this argument suggests that in reality Breguet was only interested in demonstrating his genius for devising sophisticated solutions to academic problems in applied mechanics, principally for self-glorification and to bolster his already prodigious reputation at home and abroad. When the enormously varied range of Breguet's production is considered it becomes clear that there may well be much truth in such judgements.

The third Breguet clock in the Royal Collection is perhaps even more obscure in its concept than either of
240 the foregoing. Known as 'the Metronome Clock', Vulliamy described it, in 1846, as 'a very complicated machine more curious than useful except as a time-piece'; and, possibly because he did not really understand it, he seems to have left it severely alone.

The exact circumstances in which this particular clock entered the Royal Collection have not been discovered. In the Pictorial Inventory it is labelled 'His Majesty's Private Property'; and it is known that the clock was originally in the Ante-Room to the Attic Floor of Carlton House. The simple case consists of an ormolu moulded frame housing five glass panels, the top secured by four small acorn finials. Two dials are positioned one above the other, the lower being 7 inches in diameter, of white porcelain with Arabic numerals and incorporating below 12, a 3-inch diameter seconds dial. Curiously, there was also a centre-seconds hand. Above this main dial is a silvered brass dial of $4\frac{3}{4}$ inches diameter, with an outer zone divided 0–60, an inner zone divided 0–4, with two concentrically-pivoted hands of appropriate lengths to register on them. Between the two zones at the top of this dial is engraved the word 'Chronometer', while the principal dial is signed 'Breguet' in black. There appears to be no serial number.

Mechanically, the clock has an eight-day going-barrel arrangement, with a pin-wheel escapement; the
241 11-inch pendulum is suspended on a knife edge 'with overhead bimetallic compensation terminating in two brass ball weights $\frac{5}{8}$ inch diameter'. This is taken from the official description, which goes on:

A second pendulum consisting of a $1\frac{1}{4}''$ brass ball suspended by chain can be brought into engagement with the crutch of the movement by pulling a small knob situated between the dials. This action also disengages the primary pendulum and may be raised or lowered by means of the small pointer in the centre of the top dial. When not in use the ball is located in a clip on the back plate of the movement. Very little seems to be known about the Metronome side of the clock which is also spring driven with going barrel and it would appear that the cadence may be set by means of (1) either adjusting the length of the secondary pendulum (2) moving longer pointer on top dial or (3) sliding bar calibrated 0–4 situated immediately to the right and between the two dials, or possibly a combination of all three. A second sliding bar to the left of the two dials selects either a bell (timbre) or a wooden box (toque) to reproduce the sound of the beat.

This clock spent many years in store at Buckingham Palace, where the author has been privileged to examine it so far as is possible without dismantling; and, probably as a result of a long period of disuse, it is at present out of order and badly in need of overhaul, as well as of organized research into all its many and varied complications. It appears to be complete save for one minor breakage behind the dial plate, where a lever terminates in a ragged hole which may, however, have only accommodated a limiting-pin working in an aperture in the plate. This cannot be determined until the dial is removed. Even so, the clock incorporates some typically ingenious features, which could not possibly have originated from any other maker than Breguet. There is a strong element of the innovative and experimental about it, but whether it really served a useful function—indeed, whether it even performed reliably all the functions it was designed to do, whatever they may have been—remain areas for speculation, up to the present.

Even so, certain components of the clock's make-up should be described, simply to illustrate the sophistication of its concept. The mechanism is powered by large twin going-barrels, presumably one for each pendulum variant. The main escapement is a pin-wheel, of the kind in which alternate pins are planted either side of the vertical wheel; on the same arbor is a second, apparent, 'escape wheel' which performs some function when the chain pendulum is operating, but this could not be made to work. Its design is radical in the extreme, consisting seemingly of two rims with inwards-facing teeth yet all made as one integral unit. The twin pendulums are mounted one behind the other on a platform which can be made to slide horizontally in key-ways by the use of a plunger, the knob of which protrudes through the front of the clock centrally between the twin dials. The engaging and disengaging of each pendulum from the single crutch is brilliantly devised: the crutch fork passes wide of either side of the chain pendulum 'rod', converging upon itself only to branch out into a cycloidal form that happily embraces the standard rod. As the pendulum platform is moved towards the rear, this rod disengages, but, at the same time, the chain rod, already trapped since the fork passes either side of it, is drawn into the narrowing zone behind the cycloid and is in turn engaged by the crutch. The chain of this second pendulum is, in reality, a watch-size fusee chain, from which is suspended a heavy bronze ball weight an inch or more in diameter—it is surprising that it bears it so easily—and the reason for this is quickly seen. The periodicity of this 'metronome' pendulum is varied by the simple expedient of winding up the fusee chain on a large grooved wheel immediately above it, this being done by means of a very substantially constructed rack and pinion directly behind the dial plate, and brought into use by means of the larger of the two 'hands' on the so-called 'Chronometer' dial. These hands are not in-

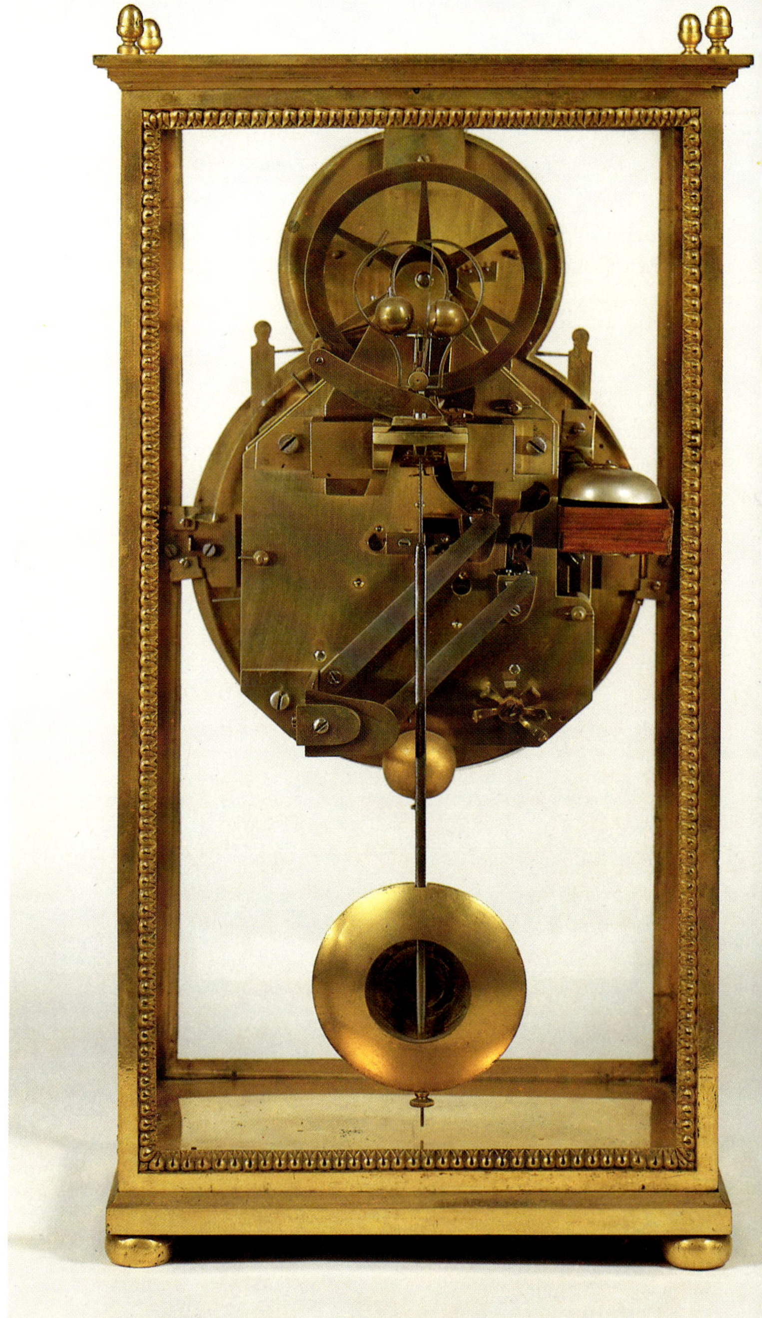

240. (Left) *Breguet's so-called Metronome Clock, from the front.* (Royal Collection)

241. (Above) *Back view of the foregoing clock, showing the complexities of the interchangeable pendulums.* (Royal Collection)

242. (Right) *A side view of the Metronome Clock, showing bell and box.* (Royal Collection)

Note: There is another version of Breguet's Metronome Clock, with more decoration and possibly a little later in date, in the Conservatoire des Arts et Métiers, in Paris. The workings of this clock are described in the Catalogue du Musée—Section JB *(1949), under item 27 on page 157, and a front view of the clock is shown at fig. 56.*

dicators, apparently, but are used to set up the rate of the metronome beats, the outer calibrated sector, on which the large hand registers, running from 0 to 60, with the calibrations changing between 30 and 45 from single divisions to halves, and between 45 and 60 to quarters. Correspondingly, the inner ring, for the smaller hand, is calibrated 0, 1, 2, 4, which presumably indicates whole divisions, halves and quarters. There is yet another controller concerned with the metronomic function, the vertically sliding calibrated lever to the right above the main dial, but how these three regulators interact remains very far from clear. The corresponding sliding lever to the left above the main
242 dial—from which, incidentally, the centre seconds hand is now missing—changes the sounding of the beat from a bell to a small open-topped wooden box like the tray of a matchbox, only square; the two components are mounted one above the other on a common axle, the lever bringing either within range of a small hammer, at will.

There are a number of other features visible in a fairly compact machine—twin fly governors, for instance, on a common arbor, as well as what appears to be a small pin barrel—but until the mechanism is dismantled, their functions cannot properly be established, and it is unwise to speculate too far where such complexity in mechanical detail is concerned. There remains one highly visual feature on the top of the main pendulum suspension, however, which must not be overlooked. This is the two large inward-facing and intersecting bimetallic compensation coils, each of about two-thirds of a single turn and terminating in brass ball weights at the inner ends. There is almost an element of Harrison's ideas in this component, which also incorporates calibrated adjustment facilities.

A little speculation as to the possible purposes of such a complex machine may, however, just be permissible. The alternatives offered—of a bell or a 'box' for sounding the beats—suggest a composite observer's and musician's clock, for examples of the former invariably employ a small bell, to enable the astronomer to carry out his count-down without removing his eye from the transit instrument, while a metronome, in its conventional form, usually uses a wooden sounding-board upon which to beat time. This type of metronome was perfected by Johann Nepomuk Mälzel (1772–1838) in 1816, but previously there had been a so-called Bell Metronome, which was an attachment to a clock by which a bell could be made to ring at every second, third, fourth or sixth beat of the pendulum. Details of the acquisition of the Metronome Clock are unfortunately unknown, the reference to Carlton House in the Pictorial Inventory clearly suggesting that George IV was its purchaser. However, despite his known musical proclivities, the clock, elegant though it is, does not appear to conform at all to that monarch's well-established taste in French clocks and might seem to relate more closely to his father's tastes and affinities, for George III had both music and astronomy to a high degree and was fascinated by horology as well. It would, too, be quite characteristic of Breguet—who went to some lengths to identify his best clients' peculiar needs and then to satisfy them—to devise such a special machine for use in several different contexts, each of them important to the particular buyer he had in mind, but probably not to anybody else. It may even be that he had heard of Mälzel's work, and endeavoured to emulate it. Yet one puzzle remains. It is not possible, in the case of the Metronome Clock, to operate both pendulums simultaneously, so that, once the standard clock pendulum is disengaged, the time-measuring facility would appear to be lost altogether in favour of the metronome beat. Knowing Breguet's remarkable faculty for solving just such technical problems as this, however—and since it would be highly inconvenient to have to re-set the clock mechanism all over again, every time the metronome function had been used—the writer would not be in the slightest bit surprised to learn that, when this clock is fully investigated, Breguet had made ingenious provision for just this eventuality. Finally, the existence on the clock of such an elaborate compensation system bespeaks the scientific instrument rather than the everyday timekeeper, and such a precision feature is quite irrelevant to the purely 'musical' side of the clock, suggesting that there is much more to it than simply an instrument of social and artistic convenience.

There is another clock by Breguet at present in royal hands, and this is the private property of Her Majesty Queen Elizabeth The Queen Mother. One of his carriage clocks in the famous 'hump-backed' silver cases with silver chain carrying handles, it is numbered 2806. Half-quarter repeating by means of a gold chain extending from the base, the engine-turned silver dial has subsidiary seconds, alarm and moon-phase rings, with the maker's signature upon an inset gold plaque, and the day, date, month and year indicators within a gilt engine-turned mask set with gold plaques for the number 2806. The clock is 6 inches high, with a Breguet-type silver key and chain, and leather travelling case supplied by Jump. The escapement, incidentally, is a jewelled straight-line lever with compensated three-armed balance.

The last Breguet clock with royal associations to be reviewed here has, sadly, left the Royal Collection and
243 when last seen—in 1964—was passing through one of the major London auction rooms. Numbered 1252 and possessing Certificate number 2896, this clock was sold to the then Prince Regent in August 1814, for the sum of 6,900 francs. The clock itself possesses all the appurtenances of one of Breguet's precision timekeepers—a constant force escapement, coupled with a *tourbillon*, which has a two-minute periodicity. Superficially, the body of the clock takes the form of a gilt-metal bell-shaped structure—it seems, from the Certificate, that this was originally ebonized wood, which perhaps proved insufficiently strong for the purpose—the base being decorated with a bead and leaf design. At a reclining angle on the outside of this hollow cone is the round engine-turned silver dial with gold hands, mounted within a rectangular gilt-metal frame; and surmounting the whole is the *tourbillon* supported by a steel bridge, the carriage of which incorporates two steel indices indicating the seconds on a silver ring which also carries the inscription '*Echappement libre à force constante réuni au Regulateur à Tourbillon*'. The clock is seated upon a gilt-metal ring with a bayonet fitting for the glass-domed cover, the whole being then mounted upon a square marble base.

243. *Three views of the Breguet constant force tourbillon clock no. 1252.* (Sotheby's, London)

In common with all Breguet's particularly sophisticated creations, this one includes all sorts of highly technical components; and, of course, Breguet invented the *tourbillon*, one of his major contributions to the art and science of time-measurement. Since its purpose, however, was to compensate for the positional errors that occurred in watches on account of their portable qualities, its relevance in a static clock may be open to question; and it must provide evidence for those who believe that Breguet deliberately revelled in over-complexity.

The highly-placed interest in his work which Breguet was able to engender extended, as far as the British monarchy was concerned, far beyond the objects hitherto described. If anything, his watches were even more sought after than his clocks; and if, as has happened, most of these have now passed out of the Royal Collection, their connection with it has, thanks to the existence of the Breguet business records, not been lost to view. In addition, several of these watches were absorbed into the specialist collection of Breguet's work formed by the late Sir David Salomons.

When the double-pendulum clock was delivered to George IV in 1825, the relevant invoice, dated 3rd October, totalled £1,115. Since the clock had cost exactly £1,000, it follows that the balance—£115—must have related to something else; and this was watch number 4420, valued in its native currency at 2,900 francs. This was a very flat watch in engine-turned gold case with silver band, the dial having separate chapters for hours and minutes, being also in silver. The hands were gold. The movement had a ruby cylinder escapement with parachute. Winding was accomplished when the back of the case was twisted, revealing the hole into which the key was inserted.

The technical concept behind the double-pendulum clock was capable of extension to watches also: this is mentioned in an undated treatise in Breguet's own hand. Breguet's theory of the dynamics of oscillating bodies concluded that, in clocks, the whole mass of the frame was in continuous, if microscopic, motion with the vibration of the pendulum; exactly the same principle applied to the frame of a watch movement in relation to its vibrating balance. He therefore set about making watches with two independent systems working in opposing directions, with the intention of equalizing and cancelling the movement of the plates.

Such a watch was number 2788, which was sold to the Prince Regent for the use of King George III on 2nd October 1818, the price being 7,200 francs. In gold engine-turned case 60 millimetres in diameter, the mechanism consists of two complete lever movements with separate barrels and trains, and twin two-armed compensation balances with recessed timing-screws, free-sprung spiral balance springs and parachute suspensions. The silver engine-turned dial has two sets of chapters, the left-hand with blued-steel moon hands and a sweep seconds covering the entire main dial, while the right-hand has gold moon hands and a small subsidiary seconds dial with gold hand all to itself. As for the twin pendulums, the concept is that the balances, vibrating as close to one another as feasible, divide gross error between them, effectively halving it.

The earliest watch purchased from Breguet for royal use seems to be numbered 83. This was sold to the Prince of Wales—as he then was—for 2,760 francs on '22 Ventose 1805', the Breguet Certificate being numbered 2404. The Republic altered, among other things, the calendar arrangements in France, so that the year started on 22nd September and contained twelve equal months of thirty days each, together with five or six complementary or republican days to make up the total, in the end, to a normal year. Each month was then divided into three 'weeks' of ten days, and these days were, of course, given fresh unfamiliar names. Finally, even the years themselves were restyled to date from the Revolution, so that, for instance, '*L'an VII*' finished on 21st September 1798. For all practical purposes this calendar was discontinued on 1st January 1806 (*'L'an XV'*), although references are found to *'L'an XVI'* (1807) and *'L'an XVII'* (1808). So, 22 Ventose 1805 appears to equal 21st March in that year.

As to the watch, its particular speciality was that it could be made to repeat not only the time—it was a ten-minute repeater, incidentally—but also the date. In gold case with engine-turned back and fluted band, the gold dial is fitted out with steel hands and calendar work; the movement has a ruby cylinder escapement and parachute. The repeating work is actuated by 'pendant piston' around which is a rotatable collar. Turning this to the right until it clicks will produce repetition of the time; on turning two 'clicks' to the left, the date can be repeated, in both systems the tens being sounded *'au toc'* and the units on a gong. Turning the collar yet further to the left locks the mechanism up. Ingenious as this watch sounds, seemingly another version has been recorded, in which the time is repeated when the watch is face up and the date when face down.

There is, in fact, another claimant to the title of
244 'earliest royal Breguet watch'; and its intrinsic significance merits its inclusion here. Of the type Breguet called a 'perpetuelle'—that is to say, it was self-winding—it bears the serial number 19, and the firm's records indicate that it was ready for sale by 1793, the movement having been finished by Boisson and the case completed by Mermillot. However, the sale details are blank; yet the back of the case bears the Prince of Wales' plumes above the Garter, which encloses the Prince's cypher. As for the watch itself, it is in an engine-turned gold case, the silver engine-turned dial having subsidiaries for seconds and up-and-down indication, with blued-steel hands. The automatic movement incorporates quarter-repetition; and the lever escapement, with helical steel spring and regulator, is fitted with a three-armed compensation balance. It is a pity that the early history of this watch is not better documented.

The next watch to be considered was bought for George IV by Messrs Rundell, Bridge & Rundell, who were the royal silversmiths at that time, with premises at 32 Ludgate Hill. The date was 27th May 1827, although for some reason the Breguet Certificate was not issued until 22nd June 1831. The purchase price

244. *Breguet 'Perpetuelle' watch no. 19, with putative royal associations. Aspects seen are the dial, the back of the case with its royal insignia, the under-dial mechanism, and the back of the movement.* (Private collection)

was '380 *livres* sterling'. The watch itself—the Certificate is endorsed 'First class piece'—is a miracle of sophistication, typical of Breguet's best work. In a gold engine-turned case, the movement is basically a half-quarter repeater with calendar work and equation of time, having lever escapement and compensated balance. The engine-turned silver dial also contains a subsidiary for regulation. Normally, the watch appears to be in a hunting-case; but the front cover can be removed and a glass substituted. Furthermore, a matching gold pair-case converts the watch into a '*montre à tact*'. It is interesting to note that, at one point, the original pair-case became lost, and the House of Breguet made a new one to exactly the same specification as the old; this was in 1831, and it seems to have been an expensive project since the pair-case cost 1,100 francs, while certain '*petites défectuosités*' had to be rectified at the same time, which cost another 25 francs. After the King's death, the watch had come into the hands of Mr Bridge, a partner in the firm of silversmiths mentioned earlier; he had to carry out these renovations but at the same time had his own arms engraved upon it.

One other royal watch by Breguet should be mentioned, since it went on from its original owner, George IV, eventually to find a place in the choice collection of Sir John Prestige, which was dispersed in the 1960s. Numbered 4548, this watch was sold to the King on 4th July 1827 for the sum of 7,600 francs and carries Certificate number 2367. A self-winding *montre à tact* with lever escapement, and compensation balance with *suspension élastique*, it has an engine-turned silver dial with the chapter ring planted eccentrically to the right-hand side, and the subsidiary seconds thereon at nine o'clock. An aperture beyond the chapters on the left displays day of the month, at the top there is a regulator scale, balanced at the bottom by an up-and-down sector. There is a winding-hole in the dial, since an automatic watch will only self-wind when it is carried; otherwise it will eventually run down and stop. The gold engine-turned case has the rotating *à tact* hand on the back, and the band fitted with platinum touch-pieces. There is a record that the watch was sold in 1908 for £400: in 1963 it made £3,100. It so happens that the Duke of Wellington—the 'Iron Duke'—had an identical watch to this one, which has until recently remained with his descendants.

So much for the major works of art in time-measurement which Breguet contributed to Britain's Royal Family of his day. There were minor ones as well—watch number 4321, for instance, was bought by the Duke of York on 7th November 1825 for £200. This was in a sophisticated gold engine-turned pair-case—inelegant save in Breguet's treatment—with silver engine-turned dial upon which the chapter ring was placed eccentrically towards the lower edge. There were apertures for date and regulation, but no seconds indication. The lever escapement was accompanied by a two-armed compensation balance, overcoil spring and parachute. A push-piece at one o'clock disengaged the outer case of the watch.

Breguet's reputation—and that of the firm he founded—certainly did not die with him, as often happened with other craftsmen. Among his many gifts, amounting as they did to sheer genius, was also one of organization and the best utilization of the talents of others; so that, when he died, he left behind a tradition of quality, ingenuity and craftsmanship which still survives. So it is not surprising to find, as this chapter closes, that Queen Victoria's favourite watch also was a Breguet. But since it came new, on 17th July 1838, and bearing the serial number 5102, it was certainly never made in Breguet's lifetime. Extremely small, it was keyless and fitted with a lever escapement—and, needless to say, Breguet would also have approved the price, which was 4,250 francs. Neither would he be likely to find fault with the prices his watches and clocks realize on the antiques market today; very few other makers can compete with him on even remotely equal terms, a sufficient enough tribute to the lasting appeal of his craftsmanship as well as the brilliance of his designs.

A medley of French mantel clocks

The huge variety of forms which French antique clock cases assume must inevitably mean that any review which is unwise enough to attempt to categorize them will be left, at the end, with some that defy systematic listing. The following clocks from the Royal Collection bear little obvious relationship to one another but should not, for that reason alone, be ignored. They simply illustrate how very richly the whole French idiom is represented therein.

Mantel clocks before the time of Louis XV are rare anyway; far more common was the pedestal, the bracket or the wall as the supporting medium, rather than the chimney-piece. So the existence of several early examples of this particular manifestation of the house clock must be of interest.

245 The first such clock has a case of roughly balloon form, with a mask at each side and an area of boulle work around the clock cylinder, which is surmounted by a cherub holding up drapery. Below the clock, which has a two-train movement, a reclining figure of Time holds a balance in his right hand, the whole resting upon a stepped base enriched with engraved ormolu mouldings. This in turn sits upon a plinth of ebony inlaid with scrolling motifs, with an ormolu mask at the centre of the front and chimera feet at the corners. The plinth is of later date than the remainder, which is of Louis XIV period. This clock was illustrated by Britten at fig. 616.

An almost identical clock case, but lacking side masks, and with the surmounting cherub holding a scythe rather than drapery, appeared in a London saleroom in February 1981. In that instance, its three-train quarter-chiming movement was by Gaudron, of Paris. This was probably Pierre Gaudron (*fl.* 1695–1745) who was '*Horloger de S.A.R. Mgr. le duc d'Orléans Régent*'.

The clocks just described have their chapter numerals painted upon individual enamel plaques, the custom with clocks of that period. The next example has a one-piece enamel dial which is distinguished by its boldness, deriving from the large five-minute numerals which encircle the chapter ring, and the contrast between the short, stubby hour hand and the slender, long pointer which indicates minutes. The ormolu case of this clock is in a florid rococo style, with, rising above the clock dial, a stylized shell-shaped canopy while below, the main decorative element is a mask in a setting of diaper work backed by crimson silk. Of Louis XV provenance, the maker of this clock is indicated by the signature on the dial 'Gudin A Paris'. There seem to have been several makers of this name working in Paris about this time—say, the mid-eighteenth century—and it is not possible to identify with real certainty the one concerned. This clock is illustrated by Britten at fig. 618.

A clock in Louis XVI style and of considerable attraction was acquired by George IV in June 1792 for the sum of 100 guineas, the vendor being John Sheringham, a decorator and wallpaper-hanger who had been employed both at Brighton Pavilion and at Carlton House for several years around that time. The clock case of marble rests upon an ormolu base, and represents a bacchante reclining upon a *tambour de* 246
basque containing the movement and dial. The female figure is based upon a life-size model of a naiad by Clodion, which he executed in 1783 as part of the sculptural decoration for a bath house. Unfortunately, the clock now contains Vulliamy movement number 1345, inserted during the last century together with an engine-turned dial of silvered metal.

A delightful small ormolu mantel clock at Royal Lodge, the Windsor residence of Her Majesty The Queen

245. *Louis XIV mantel clock, maker unknown. The present movement, numbered 1222, was supplied by Vulliamy c. 1834. The so-called* 'tête de poupée' *clock case corresponds exactly to an original design drawn by André-Charles Boulle, and preserved in the Musée des Arts Décoratifs in Paris, save only for differences in the surmounting figure of Cupid.* (Royal Collection)

Mother, has one specially attractive feature. The chapter numerals upon the enamel dial are painted in bright blue rather than the more customary black.
247 More simple in concept than some of the other clocks described, the cylinder rests upon a concave-sided hollow structure with scrolling corners, and with a festoon to decorate the aperture at the front through which the pendulum bob can be observed. This then rests upon an architectural base of square fluted corners with a shaped rococo moulding between them. The sides of the cylinder have lions' masks and tassels, while surmounting all is a covered two-handled urn and finial. The clock dial bears the signature 'Baltazard A Paris', but this, too, is a common name among French clockmakers over several centuries.

The Queen Mother also possesses, at the same location, another small mantel clock of attractive form. Again with a white marble base upon four ormolu feet, but now of curved break-front form, on the front there are three panels in relief of which the longest, in the centre, shows cherubs at play, the other two being
simple rectangles of cruciform composition. The clock 248
cylinder is supported upon a marble pedestal shaped to follow the lines of the base, and enriched with ormolu

beading and festooning. Lying upon the clock cylinder is, at left, a winged cherub who is engaged in conversation with a female figure, leaning upon it from the right. Discarded below is a torch, as well as bow and arrows. Sadly, once again, the name upon the dial—'Chomas A Paris'—is unidentifiable.

Another clock using winged cherubs in its decoration has an overall height of nearly 1 foot 6 inches. On a flat moulded base intended to accommodate a glass protective dome, this clock is wholly in ormolu and encapsulates the last vestiges of the eighteenth century in its concept. The base is shaped to form seats
249 either side of a broken column, the corners terminating in pineapple finials. The clock drum is inset into the column, which continues above it, being surmounted by a globe around which a serpent is entwined, and with an assortment of mathematical instruments. Seated either side of the clock are two winged cherubs, that on the left holding a laurel wreath while the boy on the right points to a sundial he is holding. A garland bridges the area between the seats, across the base of the column below the clock dial.

The last of this type of smaller mantel clock to be considered is described by Robertson and Walker as 'a charming little timepiece'. Just under one foot high, it consists of a white marble D-ended base resting on six cast feet and enriched with conventional reserves of 250
chased ormolu having a central mask motif. Above the base, an architectural pedestal rises upon which the clock cylinder rests, with seated on each side and facing away from one another, two female figures holding the ends of a festoon which appears to support the clock. The curious feature of these ladies is that their draperies tail off into acanthus scrolls. Surmounting the clock drum is a wreath of foliage in which a pair of turtle doves rests; a sufficiently fanciful whimsy of a clock from the nineteenth century to illustrate the changing moods and fashions that were taking place.

246. (Left) *Bacchante clock, after Clodion.* (Royal Collection)

247. (Below) *Mantel clock by Baltazard à Paris* (The Queen Mother's Collection)

248. (Below right) *Marble and ormolu clock by Chomas à Paris.* (The Queen Mother's Collection)

249. (Above) *Ormolu clock, with cherubs and globe.* (Royal Collection)

250. (Right) *Clock with turtle doves.* (Royal Collection)

6 Powered precision and Victorian prowess

It is easy to assume, given the ascendancy of the London craft over provincial practice, that most, if not all, native English clocks in use by the Royal Family today were made in the metropolis. Such is not the case, and it may be of interest to review a group of the more important of those clocks that derive from other areas of the British Isles.

Her Majesty Queen Elizabeth The Queen Mother, with her Scottish ancestry, might be expected to have several clocks from north of the border; and one of these, not seen in public for many years now, is of such exceptional interest as to make a subject for specialized study on its own.

This is the monumental automaton and musical clock by John Smith of Pittenweem, which place is a port on the Firth of Forth. Another John Smith—he who wrote *Old Scottish Clockmakers* in the present century—illustrated this clock extensively in the
251 second edition of his standard work, which was published in 1921; and shortly afterwards the clock itself was given by the citizens of Glasgow as a present to HRH The Duke of York and the Lady Elizabeth Bowes-Lyon, on the occasion of their marriage, on 26th April 1923. It is now accommodated in Clarence House, the Queen Mother's London home.

Apart from the intrinsic complexity and unconventional appearance of this object, there are several other features to be considered. Smith signs his clock,
254 around the dial arch, as 'John Smith Pittenweem North Britain'. Associated with this same signature upon the back plate of the movement is the number '1804', which has hitherto been taken to indicate the date of manufacture. Such is not normal practice, of course, and numbers in this context are almost invariably intended to denote the manufacturer's serial, for identification purposes in his records. Even in the present instance there is now reason to doubt if this is intended to date the clock; apart from the unquestionably late eighteenth-century appearance of the various dials, there is, in the arch above the automaton display which fills the whole of the left-hand side of the case, a blazon of the royal arms, showing the inclusion of quartering for France; this was superseded in 1801.

Very little seems to be known about John Smith himself. He issued an advertisement in 1775 in which he describes himself as 'bred in the trade and never been out of the country', and, in those circumstances, much of his work has to be viewed as quite remarkable. The clock under review is not his only extra-complicated product; another in much the same *genre*, albeit in a rather different case, contained a large eight-day clock, so we are told, as well as a chime of sixteen bells and, in all, five trains, being the going, quarter-chiming, hour-striking, music—one of eight tunes every three hours—and the last to change the tune. That clock was taken to Edinburgh and exhibited, at one shilling a head, in Balfour's Coffee-house, after which it seems to have disappeared until a journalist, writing in 1891, stated that, at one stage, it had been brought to London to show to King George III, but unfortunately the King had gone blind before being able to inspect it. It was therefore taken back to Scotland and eventually disposed of to a landed proprietor in the west of Fife—or so the article says, but there is no verification whatever of this story. The clock itself then turned up in Dalkeith Palace, where John Smith, the writer, was able to examine it: he thought it most likely to have been purchased by an ancestor of the Duke of Buccleuch immediately after it had been exhibited in Edinburgh in 1775, and to have been in Dalkeith Palace ever since.

However, in 1808 John Smith went to Edinburgh again, this time with two clocks, one a spring clock 4 feet 10 inches high and the other weight-driven and

251. (Above) *Musical automaton clock by John Smith of Pittenweem, showing main dial. See also Frontispiece.* (The Queen Mother's Collection)

towering up to 9 feet. The latter must have been most impressive, with its four dials, complicated striking and music—a twenty-four-bell carillon set up to play eight different tunes—and enthusiastic friends apparently advised him to take both the clocks to London, as being the place most likely to recognize his talents and reward his labour.

Seemingly he had the honour of showing the clocks to the Royal Family at that time; and he also had them valued by experts, who set figures of £900 on the table clock and £472 on the long-case. It is thought that he must have made a little money by exhibiting his handiwork, but no purchasers were to be found so that, in the end, he had to return to Edinburgh where he tried to fix up a lottery for the two clocks, which he had had to bring back with him. To make it more attractive he added extra prizes—six eight-day clocks and an assortment of six watches in gold or silver cases—hoping to sell some three thousand tickets at half-a-guinea apiece. Despite keeping the subscription lists open for six months, it seems the operation fell far short of Smith's expectations, and when everything had been settled up, he barely cleared £500 for himself, not as much as the value set upon the two clocks on their own.

Both these clocks were later traced—one to a Colonel Harvey, in Clackmannan, while the other, now in Clarence House, unexpectedly turned up at Christie's in January 1900, where it was observed and reported upon by the Reverend H. L. Nelthropp, MA, a Past Master of the Clockmakers' Company and himself an enthusiastic collector who, incidentally, presented his collection to that body in his lifetime. The clock went eventually to a William B. Smith, of 156 Vincent Street, Glasgow, prior to its presentation to the then Duke and Duchess of York; as for that other Smith, the maker of

252. (Below) *The automata dial, on the left-hand face of the clock by John Smith.* (The Queen Mother's Collection)

this remarkable object, little more is known of him. He died in 1814, being buried in the old churchyard in his home town: his tombstone was barely decipherable in 1921, when inspected by John Smith the writer, and has doubtless now disappeared altogether.

ntis Anybody who can make a clock like this one, however, needs no other memorial. The clock case, of carved and gilded oak and standing 4 feet 10 inches high, is 2 feet wide; this in turn rests upon a plain oak pedestal 3 feet 8 inches high, making an overall height of 8 feet 6 inches. A plinth of alternating thistles and roses forms the lowest level of the clock case proper, from which spring slender Corinthian columns at the angles, supporting an entablature of broken-arch form, with open-work designs of leaves and foliage filling in the corners. Above this is a frieze of egg and lozenge decoration leading up to an open-strutted superstructure, with a gallery of alternating fleur-de-lys and Maltese crosses, and itself surmounted by an orb upon

254. (Above) *The movement of the John Smith clock: the musical section on the left and above, the automata on the right.* (The Queen Mother's Collection)

253. (Below) *The musical control dial on the right-hand face of the foregoing clock.* (The Queen Mother's Collection)

which stands a lion, holding in its paws a sword and a mace.

The front of the clock contains the main dial which, apart from the time, has subsidiaries showing the month, date of the month and day of the week, as well as a control for music, chiming and silence. There is also a seconds ring, and a lunar phases display and tidal dial in the arch, the latter indication relating, presumably, to the seaport of Pittenweem. The right-hand 253
side of the clock is completely filled with a dial displaying the musical capabilities; the conventional white-painted disc is set into a landscape with figures and buildings, and a windmill with rotating sails. Some sixteen tune titles are arranged in two concentric rings, each of eight, with a double-pointed indicator stretching diametrically to show a tune in the outer ring on one side and the inner ring on the opposite one. There

are also no less than five winding- and regulating-squares visible on this face.

The *carillon* of sixteen bells associated with this display is acted upon by thirty-two hammers. A tune in the inner ring is played at each hour, instead of a quarter chime, before the hour itself is struck upon the large hour bell; each tune operates for three successive hours before the pin barrel changes to the next one. The airs specified in the outer circle are played every third hour, to form a March as an accompaniment to the Procession displayed upon the automaton dial on the opposite—that is, left-hand—side of the clock. It is also interesting to note that the quarter-chimes, used for the first three quarters of each hour, do not fall into any of the generally encountered formats and apparently vary as often as does the music, so that there are eight different versions of the quarter changes.

Finally to the left-hand face of this extraordinary clock. Here, processions of figures on two different levels pass across apertures in the beautifully painted exterior
252 of a mansion—perhaps part of a palace. The scene painting of this clock, incidentally, is attributed to Alexander Nasmyth (1758–1840), who started life painting carriage panels but eventually made his name with landscapes and portraits. At street level a royal carriage with its attendants waits. Mounted guards, also automata, can be seen in sentry boxes, and foot guards in niches above them. There is almost an element of surrealism in the curiously contrived perspective, and when the scene was working—fifteen members of the Royal Family of the time passing across the upper level and probably as many members of the Household on the lower one—it must have been quite astonishingly effective. In fact, this clock may well be the finest surviving example—if only because it is so complete—of that exceedingly rare breed, the exhibition clock, which was so greatly admired in the eighteenth and nineteenth centuries. Others which come to mind include the Jacob Lovelace clock, Henry Bridges 'Microcosm', and only one or two more; neither of the two mentioned are anything like complete. Clocks of this kind were the lineal ancestors of that remarkable series of Guinness Clocks, of modern times; and as such it is surely desirable for John Smith's clock to be completely overhauled to restore it to pristine condition. Then, if the Queen Mother could bear to part with it for a while, perhaps it might once again be given the public display for which it was originally intended, possibly in the Queen's Gallery in Buckingham Palace, or in the British Museum. There must be many hundreds of students of horological history who would jump at the opportunity to see it.

A momentary digression might be appropriate—with Scotland and its craftsmen in mind—to notice an attractive orrery in the Library at Windsor Castle. This is mounted upon a gilt-brass tripod standing upon a
circular moulded ebony base, the moving parts con- 25
tained within an engraved glass globe and operated manually with an external key. A tiny clock has been incorporated into what was originally an ingenious demonstration model illustrating the movements of the planets relative to one another. A small circular medallion states: 'Made 1806, Presented 1822, Timepiece added 1851'. There does not appear to be any maker's name upon this contrivance, but documentary evidence shows it to have been presented to George III by the Reverend George Tough, of Ayton, in Berwickshire. He seems to have had a penchant for such things, and something of his work is described in the *Edinburgh Philosophical Journal*, volume II, 1819, as well as, rather later, in the *Edinburgh Evening Courant*, 21st April 1837.

255. (Below) *Orrery by the Rev. George Tough in the Windsor Castle Library.* (Royal Collection)

The Queen Mother has, of course, other Scottish clocks bearing well-known makers' names, even if of more recent vintage—the work of Crichton, as of Hamilton & Inches, both of Edinburgh, are among those to be seen in Clarence House; but a particularly nice provincially-made long-case clock, having a two-train movement and the lacquered case surmounted by three ball-and-spire finials, is the work of Benjamin Lockwood, of Swaffham, a Norfolk village, about 14 miles from King's Lynn. At the same London location, there are also four balloon clocks of varying sizes, two of them signed. In the Library is an especially fine example, the case of walnut with side carrying-handles and some marquetry and brass inlay in a panel below the dial; the style suggests a date *c.*1810. A second clock bears the

256. (Left) *Painted satinwood balloon clock on term-shaped pedestal, the dial signed 'Upjohn, New Bond Street'.* (The Queen Mother's Collection)

257. (Below) *Bracket clock in ebonized case, by William Evill, Bath.* (The Queen Mother's Collection)

signature of Chater & Livermore, of London, who are listed as active during the period 1787 to 1808. The third balloon clock, in the Drawing Room, is altogether
256 a much more ambitious object. Standing upon a therm-shaped pedestal *en suite*, which is raised at the front only on paw feet, this clock rises to an overall height of about 7 feet 6 inches. The case and pedestal are in satinwood painted with decorative motifs in a style reminiscent of turn-of-the-century work, and surmounted by a ball-and-spire finial on a plinth. The two-train movement is fitted with a regulator dial which carries the signature 'Upjohn/New Bond Street/London', but there are several London makers bearing this surname active around the end of the eighteenth century, so that it is difficult to identify this one with certainty. The fourth balloon clock, on a bracket in a side corridor, is notable for its small size, being only 14 inches high. The painted satinwood case houses a modern movement.

Two provincial clocks of special note are to be found at Royal Lodge, which is the Windsor home of the Queen Mother. The first, a two-train spring clock in ebonized case, happily still retains its verge escapement
257 and decorated back plate. This clock is the work of William Evill of Bath, and his signature appears upon a fan-shaped plaque in the centre of the dial below XII. This maker must have felt that he had a difficult name to live down for, in the *Bath Chronicle* for 18th November 1762, he advertises his wares as follows:

> To be sold, wholesale and retail, by William Evill, at his shop opposite the White-Lyon, Bath .... All sorts of Gold, Silver and Pinchbeck watches, which are made by a very good workman and I will warrant every watch good that I sell at Four Guineas and upwards and will engage to keep them in good repair for Seven years, or longer if required, the first year gratis and 2/6d a year afterwards. The Golden Cup, 21 The Market Place.

This clock has a day-of-the-month calendar aperture above VI, strike/silent dial in the arch, and several pleasant decorative features. The case door has wooden pierced spandrel pieces either side of the break-arch, while there are effective, yet simple, gilded metal festoons adorning its bell-top.

A somewhat more spectacular clock is the fine
258 mahogany long-case by Wyke & Green of Liverpool. In style it is almost identical to the one simply signed John Wyke, which is illustrated at plates XVI and XVII of G. F. C. Gordon's *Clockmaking Past and Present*, as revised by A. V. May in 1949, save that the city of origin is spelled correctly and not as 'Livarpool'. The Wyke family, of Prescot and Liverpool, went in as much for making the tools of the clockmaking trade as for making the actual clocks, and a famous tool catalogue

258. (Left) *Longcase clock by Wyke and Green, Liverpool: full-length front view showing typical 'brick course' feature at the angles of the plinth.* (The Queen Mother's Collection)

259. (Above) *Detail of dial and hood of the previous clock, showing lunar work in the arch.* (The Queen Mother's Collection)

of theirs, setting out and illustrating all the various kinds of tools they could supply, was published about 1770. John Wyke himself started life in Prescot, went to Liverpool about 1766 where he joined up with Green—about whom little seems to be known—and they continued certainly into the first few years of the nineteenth century, from premises at Wyke's Court, in Dale Street.

The clock under review is of substantial size—perhaps 9 feet overall—and the lines of the case, although following closely that instanced by Gordon, are, if anything, somewhat more ornate. The bases and trunks appear identical; both have the curious effect superimposed upon the angles of the former, in which carved 'brick courses' relieve what might otherwise be a simple chamfer. At the level of the trunk door—which is identical in both clocks, although the corners of the panel in the base below it differ, being simply made concave in the Queen Mother's clock—the forward angles in both examples are carved as fluted columns, complete with capitals and bases, and extending over perhaps five-sixths of the available height. The first real difference appears above the trunk door and below the moulding which supports the hood: Gordon's clock has a plain ogee moulding here, whereas the Queen Mother's clock has a carved arcaded frieze. As to the hoods of these two clocks, it is noticeable that Gordon's has lost all three of its finials, and that belonging to the Queen Mother has retained them—and very decorative they are, being carved ungilded wood and of rather exotic form. In both clocks
the angles of the hood are occupied by square columns, 259
fluted and with Corinthian capitals and bases of gilt metal; in the royal example, the scrolling 'horns' terminate in gilt paterae. The two-train clock movements with lunar work in the arches are probably identical, as, too, are dial ornaments such as spandrels. However, the dial centre of the John Wyke clock has a chequered pattern engraved upon it, while that of Wyke & Green has a matted background with some simple scrolling foliage on it. Seconds rings below XII feature on both clocks. Gordon comments of the clock he illustrates—and the same applies to the royal example—'The case is one typical of the district. . . . The base of the case is somewhat unusual, but by no means unique, since many were made so in Lancashire and Cheshire. Probably one of the most remarkable features about this case is the immense amount of detail in all the mouldings.'

There are always mysteries to tantalize the mind in connection with royal clockmakers. Who, for instance, was 'Samuel Samson, maker to His Majesty' located by Britten in Westminster, 1778–1805, and said to have made musical clocks? If he was good enough to do that, one would have expected much more to be known about him. Be that as it may, before leaving the last decades of the eighteenth century, notice must be taken of some royal tavern clocks that do have a real existence! It is now generally recognized that the appellation once universally adopted to describe clocks of this type—they always used to be called 'Act of Parliament' clocks—is a complete misnomer. The Act of Parliament referred to in such cases was passed in

260. *Tavern clock by Matthew Hill, Devonshire Street.* (The Queen Mother's Collection)

1797 and was concerned with a tax to be imposed on clocks and watches; this was so unpopular that it had a very short life indeed. However, the clocks that were associated for generations with this Act turn out invariably to have been made years, and more often decades, before it came into force. Nowadays, it has been clearly established from contemporary prints and such-like sources that clocks of this kind, with their large and legible dials, were intended for taverns and coffee-houses, indeed wherever the public at large gathered for social intercourse and might have need to refer to a public timekeeper.

Tavern clocks consist essentially of a dial, from below which extends a trunk that accommodates the pendulum and the drop of the weights. The concept could not be more simple, but the execution is often anything but that—and the best examples of such clocks nowadays are greatly sought after. One of the features that is said to offer a clue to dating is the shape of the dial surround, for, often, such clocks are not signed. Dials can be round, octagonal or in a variety of shield shapes.

At Royal Lodge, Windsor, there is a particularly fine tavern clock, beautifully sited at the head of a staircase. This one is signed and is the work of Matthew Hill, of Devonshire Street, London, who appears in the lists as being at work from 1744 to *c*.1790 and, at some 26
unspecified time, to have moved his shop from Devonshire Street to Charlotte Street. The dial surround is in one of the shield shapes, with a broken arch at the top, and the two lower corners formed into concave curves. The case is decorated in the chinoiserie manner with black and gilt lacquer, which extends even into the dial centre. The chapter circle, painted as a white ring upon such a ground, stands out well, and the large but simple gilt hands, the minute one extending back into a substantial 'tail' terminating in a crescent presumably to give counterpoise, are most effective.

The shield shape of the dial of this clock is held to indicate a date between 1745 and 1775; and it is interesting to note another tavern clock by this same maker, which is illustrated by Cescinsky and Webster, in *English Domestic Clocks*, at figure 400 on page 340. This is an entirely different clock, with a round white dial which has no five-minute numerals; the trunk bears some similarity in outline to the previous one, although the door therein is rectangular with the top edge slightly curved, as against a broken-arched top to Her Majesty's clock. Also there are shaped 'wings' extending beyond the lines of the trunk in apparent support of the round dial. Black and gold chinoiserie lacquer decoration is continued, but there is no similarity between the two clocks so far as the ornamental detail is concerned. Round dials of this type are supposed to span a period from 1750 to 1840, but from other considerations it is reasonable to suppose that the clock at Royal Lodge is several decades the earlier of the two.

By a strange coincidence, the Queen Mother possesses another tavern clock, of identical outline to that at Royal Lodge, at her remote home in the Castle of Mey. This particular clock was seen, all too briefly, in the television programme shown in honour of Her Majesty's eightieth birthday; and it hangs in the Hall of the Castle. It is signed in much the same fashion, and in the same place, as its London counterpart, only this time the maker is Joshua Hewlett of Bristol. This maker was apprenticed to his father in June 1741; and he was living in Wine Street in that city in 1750, when there was a theft from his house of two rings, said to be worth 10 shillings and silver buttons to the value of 3 shillings. He subsequently moved to Corn Street. He is also recorded as a maker of long-case clocks. The Queen

Mother's clock has some interesting and unusual trunk decoration, showing Time rewarding a labourer and chastising an idle man; there is an inscription beneath this which reads 'Redeeming the time'.

There is, as it happens, a tavern clock with a round white dial in the Royal Collection, too. This is illustrated in Britten's sixth edition, figure 892 and page 651, as well as being mentioned in Robertson and Walker, on page 17. It seems to have been in the Footmen's room at
261 Windsor Castle at the beginning of this century. As for the clock, it has several interesting features, notably the undecorated shaped trunk with its curved waist and long narrow rectangular door; there are no five-minute figures on the chapter circle, which is otherwise distinguished by the use of the Roman IV in place of the much more usual IIII. It is always said that the latter came into general use in order to prevent illiterate people from confusion with VI, which is not so unlikely as might at first appear when it is remembered that the curvature of the dial causes IV to be shown nearly upside down. In any event, this clock has been located at Windsor recently; it is unsigned, and in an oak case, measuring 4 feet 2 inches overall and 2 feet wide across the dial.

There may once have been confusion between IV and VI, but there were other numbers on tavern clock dials which occasionally gave rise to trouble—at least with the dial painter! At Snowshill Manor, a National Trust property in Gloucestershire, perhaps a dozen miles from Cheltenham, there is an unsigned tavern clock on the chapter circle of which the number XI appears twice—the first time in substitution for IX! Even so, it is surprising how few people notice it.

If the presence of tavern clocks in the royal residences may surprise the casual observer, then how much more may be his wonder at the existence of skeleton clocks in the self-same august surroundings? The great majority of these were factory-made in mid-Victorian times by such firms as Smith & Sons, of St John's Square, Clerkenwell. A wide range of elaborate frames—a better word than plates, because these settings for skeleton clocks had a functional as well as a decorative role to play—were available, often based on the outlines of well-known buildings, especially churches like Lichfield Cathedral and York Minster, and all tastes could therefore be catered for. There is even a skeleton clock model which is framed in an outline of the Brighton Pavilion, although it dates from long after the passing of George IV.

Yet the fact is that both tavern and skeleton clocks had perfectly honourable beginnings, and although perhaps the majority of specimens normally met with are of no great consequence, in both cases there are notable exceptions. The interest of the tavern clocks in the Royal Collection has already been demonstrated, and the skeleton clocks included are of no less importance and appeal. Both—and there are two royal skeleton clocks of major significance—are in Buckingham Palace, both were designed by Sir William Congreve, and both were made by John Moxon. They were acquired for Carlton House, where they were originally placed in the Library.

Congreve (1772–1828) enjoys a somewhat romantic reputation as a pioneer of rocketry in Britain. In fact, he was the eldest son of the comptroller of the Royal Laboratory at Woolwich, sometime officer in the Royal Artillery, became an equerry to the Prince Regent in 1811 and succeeded his father at Woolwich, from 1814 to 1828. During this same period, he was a Member of Parliament, saw service abroad and eventually succeeded as second baronet in 1814. Clearly a man of many parts, he also had time to experiment in things horological, where he is probably

261. *Tavern clock, unsigned: a different version of this type of clock.* (Royal Collection)

best known as the inventor of the 'rolling ball' clock. The rolling ball as a time standard had been considered, but not pursued, in the seventeenth century; Congreve seems to have rediscovered it, devising a different design altogether from that previously conceived. There is no evidence of his having any knowledge of what had gone before. His prototype, weight-driven—and the only one to be powered in this way—is in the Rotunda at Woolwich; it bears the inscription 'The first Experiment of a new Principle for the Measurement of Time, invented by Wm. Congreve Esq; is humbly presented to His Highness the Prince of Wales, 1808.'

Congreve patented his 'rolling ball' principle—number 3164, dated 24th August 1808—and Moxon
265 made these clocks for him: one passed through
266 Christie's in October 1959. Yet is seems likely that Congreve's invention may have been perfected some years prior to the granting of his patent. There exists a spring-driven rolling ball clock signed by Robert Bryson, of Edinburgh, which appears to be dated 1803, although this last feature might be only a serial number. Even so, it is stylistically a very early example of the type; and Bryson (1778–1852) was to receive a Royal Warrant from Queen Victoria in 1834 (vide Appendix Three). Contemporary correspondence, however, makes it clear that Bryson's clock owed its existence to Congreve's invention. The subject is dealt with in detail in '*Antiquarian Horology*' Vol. I, no. 11, June 1956, p. 164.

The two Congreve skeleton clocks in the Royal Collection are, however, of a different, but equally radical, design albeit much altered over the years. The first, disposed between no less than four frames of
262 raftered construction, separated by nicely turned brass pillars, has two spring-driven trains, complete with fusees, the structure topped by an hour-striking bell. Originally this eight-day clock had another Congreve patented component, his 'Extreme detached escapement'—this is engraved on the lintel of the front frame, above the dial; on the lowest member of the same frame is to be found 'Invented by Wm. Congreve Esq' and lower down still 'J. Moxon Fecit'.

Congreve was very proud of his escapement, and drawings of it exist; but unfortunately, in practice, this particular example seems to have given nothing but trouble. Benjamin Jutsham, who was for more than thirty years Inspector of Household Deliveries to George IV, as Prince, Regent and King, maintained meticulous records of the movements of furniture, clocks and so forth in and out of Carlton House; sadly, these also include deliveries of fine clocks from the Royal Collection to Vulliamy for repair, so often to be returned with brand new movements. On 24th August 1808 Jutsham recorded: 'Delivered to Mr. Congreve, the curious clock for the measurement of time, with a

262. (Left) *Skeleton clock by John Moxon.* (Royal Collection)

263. (Right) *The second skeleton by John Moxon.* (Royal Collection)

264. (Below right) *A rare watch movement by John Moxon.* (Clockmakers' Company, London)

pedestal from the Library at Carlton House, to be regulated'. The next year Jutsham noted:

27th May 1809. The pedestal painted to imitate lapis lazuli with stand for the clock, and glass shade to be fitted to the Congreve clock.

Some years later, from the Buckingham Palace Outfit Bills, 1837:

Work done by order of the Lord Chamberlain's Office by Benjamin Louis [*sic*] Vulliamy, Clockmaker, 68 Pall Mall. Dec.30. Repaired and made perform properly a spring Clock made by Moxon with extreme detached escapement upon Sir William Congreve's principle, that goes mounted in a large double skeleton frame, a most complicated and troublesome machine; and new silvered the work that had been silvered before, and lacquered the skeleton plates and all the large parts, and lacquering spirit levels . . . £4.

The deployment of the various elements in the movement of this clock are unusual and worthy of note. The two trains, placed one behind the other, are built up vertically, the spring barrels being at the bottom and the fusees at the top. Because of this strange arrangement, the going-train is wound from the front while the striking-train is wound from the rear. Very high numbered trains are employed, as can be seen from the multi-toothed pinions.

Even Vulliamy's best efforts were insufficient to bring this clock to order, it seems, and mediocre timekeeping continued. In the end, drastic action was almost inevitable, and Congreve's escapement was bodily removed. In its place there was substituted an Earnshaw chronometer escapement, constructed by Charles Frodsham & Co, and there is a legend to this effect engraved upon the base of the platform. At the same time the original dial, which must have given an uninterrupted view of the mechanism, was replaced by a solid disc of no particular merit, and Victorian fleur-de-lys hands.

This first clock, like the next to be described, originally had double overlapping chapter rings rather than a solid dial; this is clear not only from a drawing of the second clock, made by Congreve and included in George IV's Pictorial Inventory, but also because the
263 plugged holes into which these rings were screwed are apparent upon the frames of both clocks. The second

clock is in a gilt-wood long-case format with inset panels and having a glass-panelled trunk door through which the pendulum can be seen. The framing of the movement is similar to the first, and the present dial is again of little distinction. Engraved in a circle upon it, much in the manner of a subsidiary seconds ring, is the inscription 'Reconstructed by Chas. Frodsham & Co. Anno Domini MDCCCLXXIX'. Presumably this must indicate a major innovation such as a new escapement, but no documentary evidence survives to show precisely what was done, either in the Royal Archives or elsewhere, so that it is impossible to say, at this distance in time, exactly what the original mechanical make-up of this clock might have been. As now found, the clock is a striking regulator, the dead-beat escapement fitted with jewelled pallets; nevertheless, under the present dial can be found the legend 'Invented by William Congreve, Esq. J. Moxon fecit'. The weight—only one is employed— falls behind the pendulum, and a mirror is set between them, so that the former is invisible, being in its own compartment. The drawing of this clock shows that the glass dome over the bell was formerly surmounted by an imperial crown, but this, too, seems to have disappeared.

As for Moxon, he remains a shadowy craftsman, with very little being known about him; and virtually no work bearing his signature seems to have survived, suggesting that he probably worked principally for
264 others. A gold pair-cased watch, with the London hallmark 1813, bears on its movement the signature 'MOXON 3218 Clock Maker to H.R.H. the Prince Regent, LONDON'; one could wish for a little more flesh on these scanty bones.

It was indeed a curious quirk of fate that brought about the contemporaneous activities of two royal collectors with such entirely different tastes, like George III and his son—for, of course, George IV was already assembling his enormous accumulation of *objets d'art* throughout several decades before his father's death—and the need for some degree of contiguity and co-existence between them was not helped by their entirely different temperaments and aesthetic sensibilities. That this was a good thing, in the long term, for the Royal Collection cannot be doubted, however; whatever the effects, at the time, upon the royal personages themselves and their contemporaries, today's situation would be much the poorer without the massive contribution that father and son were, between them, to make to the heritage which the Collection encapsulates.

The year 1820 was an eventful one, in which George IV at last ascended the throne. At this point,
267 therefore, it seems appropriate to consider a most unusual clock which is generally believed to date from about that year. This is described as an astronomical wall clock, although the style is very unfamiliar for that period. The clock case is of mahogany inlaid with rosewood and presents a flat vertical rectangular fascia into which are inset two circular dials, one above the other. This is flanked by slender stylized turned and reeded columns, topped by finials much like those on the hood of the long-case clock by Wyke & Green already discussed. A third such finial is placed centrally in this instance too; and each might be described as consisting of an upturned fluted cup, from the centre of which rises a turned stem surmounted by an acorn. The top of this case is designed as a concave-sided flat-topped arch, bordered with a beading of interlocked links. The figuring of the wood on the front of this clock is especially fine.

Of the two dials, the lower is the larger. It displays sidereal time and the procession of the stars round the North Pole. This dial is driven by a small pinion extending from the main movement above, and meshing with the teeth around its outer edge, these being hidden by the apron of the surrounding fascia. The smaller main dial, in the arch of the case, simply shows hours and minutes. The clock rests upon four ball feet, on a simple bracket which is perhaps not contemporary with it. Curious though it might seem, nothing appears to be known about the circumstances of acquisition of this clock. Even more curiously, within the last year another version of it, very similar indeed in general characteristics, has come to light; a picture of this can be seen in the autumn 1980 issue of
Antiquarian Horology, page 254. This clock rests on a 268
vaulted bracket *en suite*, giving a rather more finished effect; while the top of the case consists of a simple arch with a twisted moulding, into which is set a third, very small, dial that appears to be that of a barometer. There can be no doubt whatever that both clocks came from the same manufacturing source, and one could wish that more was known about it.

The story of George IV's acquisitions of French clocks has already been told in the preceding chapter. He was succeeded by his brother, William IV, who was George III's third son, in 1830. William IV was as unlike his brother as both were unlike their father—timid, resistant to change, and apolitical, he nearly antagonized his contemporaries by impeding the progress of the Reform Bill of 1832 and only just recovered the situation in time. Thereafter he played little part in the day-to-day activities of government; nor, for present purposes, can he be ranked among those monarchs whose influence upon the Royal Collection was of any significance, particularly in the horological sense; those rare instances when he impinged upon it having already been mentioned in dealing, for example, with the travelling clock-watch by David Bouguet. A relatively unknown maker, Pierre Frederick Gougy, of Tavistock Street, Westminster, who patented a form of chronograph motion work—patent number 8308 of 11th December 1839—made one of the few royal clocks dating from this time, a bracket clock at Windsor Castle, said to date *c*.1830, which, sad to say, seems now to have disappeared without trace.

William IV died without issue in 1837, so that the next sovereign was his niece, Queen Victoria. During her reign, and subsequently, more clock and watch-makers had royal connections of one sort or another than heretofore; several of these stood out as giants among the rest of their fraternity, however.

The Vulliamy family have been mentioned many times already; and the seeming depredations wreaked upon the royal clocks by the last of that line, Benjamin Lewis, have figured frequently in these pages. Born on
269 25th January 1780, and the third generation in the family clockmaking firm, he entered the business at an early age. His father was often consulted concerning the observatory built by George III at Kew; and, for his

265. (Left) *Sir William Congreve's prototype Rolling Ball clock of 1808.* (The Rotunda Museum of Artillery, Woolwich)

266. (Above) *An apparently earlier version of the Rolling Ball clock, by Robert Bryson of Edinburgh: there is documentary evidence that Congreve had described his invention to him.* (Alan Lloyd Collection)

part, the son was similarly employed in helping with the alterations and additions being made to Carlton House early in the nineteenth century. This brought him, early in life, into contact with the younger members of the Royal Family, and his correspondence with some of the Princes, which still exists, demonstrates the affectionate esteem in which he was held. The position of the Vulliamys' shop, too, could not have been bettered: number 68 Pall Mall lay mid-way between the Queen's House and Carlton House. Clifford Smith relates that, from about 1806 onwards, B. L. Vulliamy was so constantly employed by George IV, then the Prince of Wales, not only on clock-work of various kinds but also on a whole range of other operations, that he became somewhat contemptuously nicknamed 'The Prince's furniture man'. These peripheral activities included acting as purchasing-agent in the acquisition of works of art, and also acting as a kind of foreman and clerk of works in connection with the making and repair of metalwork of all kinds—bronzes, inkstands, candelabra, the mounts of vases, cabinets, chimney-pieces and the like, many of which can still be identified. A typical such operation, in 1807, concerned the supply of gilt ornaments for four chimney-pieces, where they were 'to be handed over to Mr. Vulliamy to be looked over and brought into use'. Again, Vulliamy's detailed accounts exist for such matters as 'Taking entirely to pieces the Great Chandelier in the Gold Room . . . repairing the gilt metalwork . . . sending to Messrs. Parker & Perry's and fixing it up in their shop for the purpose of having the glass fitted previous to its being hung at Carlton House.' The cost of this task, in 1807, amounted to £50; and Parker & Perry, who described themselves as Glass Manufacturers to the Prince of Wales, supplied all the lustres of cut glass used in the chandeliers at Carlton House, which now grace the State Rooms at Buckingham Palace.

B. L. Vulliamy was admitted to the Freedom of the Worshipful Company of Clockmakers by Redemption—that is to say, he paid a 'fine' for the privilege—on 4th December 1809. He was elected to the Livery the following month—on 8th January 1810—and chosen for the Court of Assistants in April of that same year, at the very early age of thirty. Twice during the next forty-four years he served the various stages of Wardenship—between 1815 and 1820, and again between 1843 and 1846—while, in all, he became Master no less than five times, in 1821, 1823, 1825, 1827 and again in 1847. So revered within his craft was he during his lifetime that, on 2nd July 1849, the Clockmakers' Company made a presentation of plate to him, on which was engraved a lengthy inscription, terminating with the words '. . . in token of the high sense they [the Company's Court of Assistants] entertain of the eminent services rendered by him as a member of the Court during the long period of Forty Years with a degree of zeal and ability which have greatly advanced the interests and character of the Corporation'. When Vulliamy died, at the age of seventy-four on 8th January 1854, he bequeathed to the Company a group of three family portraits as well as another picture.

The Dictionary of National Biography (lviii, 396 et seq) and *The Record of Old Westminsters* (ii, 953) show conclusively what a multi-talented family the Vulliamys were. B. L. Vulliamy had sent both his sons to Westminster School, and the eldest, also called Benjamin Lewis, was to go on to Oxford before joining his father in the family business. The younger son George John, however, decided to follow in the footsteps of an uncle, his father's younger brother Lewis, and become an architect, in the pursuance of which he was articled to the famous engineering concern Joseph Bramah & Sons, and after that spent five years in Sir Charles Barry's office. The list of commissions, and work carried out in the public service, by uncle and nephew make impressive reading; but then so does a similar catalogue of the important public clocks supplied by B. L. Vulliamy. This would include examples at the Plymouth victualling yard, in churches in Norwood, Leytonstone and Stratford, and at St. Mary's Church, Oxford as well as for the University Press in that city. Vulliamy also supplied clocks for St. Martin's-le-Grand Post Office, as well as, somewhat further afield, for the

267. *Astronomical wall clock, unsigned.* (Royal Collection)

268. *A very similar clock to the previous one, and clearly by the same maker.* (Hoffman, Market Harborough)

cathedral in Calcutta; his turret clock for Windsor Castle has been mentioned elsewhere. Aside from work, he amassed a valuable collection of antique watches. His widespread interests were reflected in his Fellowships of the Astronomical Society, the Geographical Society and the Zoological Society; and he was in addition an Associate of the Institution of Civil Engineers, to whom he left his library of some 270 volumes on horology and the allied mechanical arts. During his lifetime, he had made many other gifts, to societies of various kinds as well as to the Clockmakers' Company Collection.

Vulliamy's reputation as a clock- and watchmaker rests upon the sheer quality and reliability of his products—which, to this day, grace many a government office and public building of every kind, not to mention the royal palaces—and he is not noted for any great inventive ability. It has been said in his defence that he was first and foremost a craftsman, and not in any sense an antiquary; that in his day, appreciation of fine antique mechanism, and the study of antiquarian horology, did not even exist; that some of his 'substitutions' were done at the direct order of others, more concerned with accurate time-measurement than with the preservation of out-dated machinery; and that he did attempt to preserve old movements that, in his judgement, were worthy of it, as witness his gifts to the Clockmakers' Company museum. Probably much of this is true; but someone who wielded such influence in high places as Vulliamy undoubtedly did, should perhaps have tried to educate those in authority to a greater appreciation of the consequences of the 'improvements' they were ordering him to carry out. Also, none of the original movements which he replaced—either at his own instigation or on the order of others—seems to have survived, and it is difficult to credit that the intrinsic importance of at least some of them can have been altogether lost on a person with all his knowledge and capabilities. It would indeed be interesting to know what did happen to all these discarded pieces of machinery—were they simply scrapped, or did Vulliamy find some other means of disposing of them? If any remained intact, it is likely that they would have been identified by now.

It is not completely true to say that Vulliamy initiated nothing new. He is credited with being the first to use a two-seconds-beating pendulum in turret clocks—although Tompion had, of course, used this feature in the Greenwich Observatory regulators—and one of these, at Christ Church, Oxford, is said to have run for six months without re-setting, with an aggregate error over the whole period of only thirty-five seconds. This is of the right order, even though not as good as the generally-accepted optimum rate for a mechanical clock, which is about one-tenth of a second per day; the Vulliamy rate works out at just under one-fifth of a second.

When Sir Charles Barry was considering the structure of the clock tower to house Big Ben, it is known that, having regard to his experience of turret clocks, he consulted Vulliamy; indeed, the clockmaker even submitted a design for the clock which he subsequently withdrew, somewhat mortified by the proposal to hold a competition in connection with it. Apparently, he later built and installed a prototype of his Westminster design, at Somerleyton Hall, Suffolk. There is said to have been mortal hostility between B. L. Vulliamy and

E. B. Denison, commissioned by the government to draw up a specification for the Westminster clock in conjunction with the Astronomer Royal, when the latter criticized Vulliamy's designs for the enterprise as being fit only for a village!

When B. L. Vulliamy died, there died with him the Royal Appointment held by him and his forebears continuously for 112 years. The firm also went out of existence. There had been at this time one other craftsman in the family, a certain Justin Theodore Vulliamy. Britten believes that he was Benjamin Lewis Vulliamy's brother. In any event, he seems to have been a Liveryman of the Clockmakers' Company in 1813 and a Warden during 1820–3; but neither of the watches listed by Baillie as being his work can be given such an attribution with any real certainty, and Britten maintains that he had no connection with the horological trades. The answer may lie in the listings in *The Royal Kalendar* during the 1820s, where he is shown among the royal tradesmen as 'Or Molu manufacturer and Gilder in Metal'. He probably died before his more illustrious brother, but he may well have played some part in the work on decorative metal

269. (Left) *Wax portrait of B. L. Vulliamy.* (Clockmakers' Company, London)

270. (Below) *Public clock above the State Entrance to the Quadrangle, Windsor Castle.* (Author)

271. *The large flat-bed three-train movement of the previous clock; detail of the minute-hand setting-dial, showing Vulliamy's inscription and serial number 1000; and Vulliamy's own design of pin-wheel escapement, described by Saunier in his* Treatise on Modern Horology. (Author)

ornamentation that went on, as a more or less continuous process, in the royal palaces during the early years of the last century.

The varied and never-ending restoration, repair and renewal work on the royal clocks, carried out by B. L. Vulliamy over nearly fifty years, has been a thread common to most of the foregoing chapters, and running through the clocks from all periods that have been reviewed. Yet he did supply some significant clocks that were wholly his own manufacture. His turret clock for Windsor Castle—in replacement for an obsolete Joseph Knibb original—has already been
270 mentioned; he installed it in 1829. This was perhaps
271 not quite like his usual practice of replacing the movements of fine domestic timekeepers—a public clock falls into a different category, in that it must keep good time. This was Vulliamy's principal reason for all his substitutions, so far as domestic timekeepers were concerned: the original movements were castigated as 'worn out', 'never was a good clock' and so forth, but great precision is perhaps less essential in the private than the public context, even in palaces.

How should one appraise the contributions of the last two generations of the Vulliamy family to the Royal Collection? Most typical of all Vulliamy mantel clocks is the 'architectural' format, with a broken column in white marble into which the clock cylinder is inset. Its plinth is generally of gilt metal, and putti in biscuit porcelain from the Derby works stand either side on the stepped marble base, usually with assorted mathematical or astronomical or navigational instruments, books and other ornamental devices spread around. One of these latter is often made the site for the Vulliamy signature. Such clocks exist in the Royal Collection and are by no means uncommon outside it. But the Vulliamys, father and son, being the expert metal-workers they undoubtedly were, could just as easily work 'in the French style' and one such clock, in the conventional guise showing two figures in classical
272 drapes standing either side of a clock cylinder supported on sphinxes that sit, in turn, on a marble pedestal with inset relief panel, the whole upon a marble base, is superficially convincing. However, the pedestal panel shows putti preoccupied with some highly technical activity—rather than frolicking in the French taste—while the figure at right, which is holding up an ormolu tablet and pointing to it with the left hand, is said to be demonstrating the function of the fusee!

Perhaps more respected—and justifiably so—are the Vulliamy regulator clocks, some details of which have already been described. The so-called Standard
273 Clock, at Windsor Castle, which is housed in a well-figured mahogany long-case with architectural hood, there being pillars either side of the dial as well as set into the angles of the trunk, is in fact the work of Justin Vulliamy, although it has sometimes been credited to his son. The enamel dial, of conventional form with five-minute numerals and pierced hands, and the gilt spandrels, as well as the lack of a movement number, bespeak the eighteenth century; yet this was a popular Vulliamy style, and an almost identical clock, also having two trains and jewelled pallets, but with a one-piece silvered dial, and formerly in the Wetherfield Collection, is said to date *c.*1820. B. L. Vulliamy, too, could make regulators at least as well as his father and grandfather: this is amply demonstrated by one now in the Science Museum in London and said to date *c.*1832. This has all the classic features of the high-precision timekeeper of its day—Graham's dead-beat escapement and mercurial compensation pendulum, high-numbered wheels and pinions, Harrison's maintaining-power, and so on. This was the type of clock which, as

272. (Above) *The figure holding the tablet, in this Vulliamy clock, is said to be demonstrating the function of the fusee.* (Royal Collection)

273. (Right) *Justin Vulliamy's Standard Clock at Windsor Castle.* (Royal Collection)

mentioned earlier, was capable, under reasonable conditions, of maintaining a rate of one-tenth of a second per day.

The so-called 'architectural' long-case seems to have been much favoured by all the Vulliamys, both to house movements of regulator accuracy as well as for those of more modest pretensions. A fine example of the latter, formerly the property of H.R.H. the late Princess Alice, Countess of Athlone, and removed from Kensington 274
Palace, was sold towards the end of 1981. Of well-figured but faded mahogany, with panelled plinth, its rectangular trunk door was flanked by fluted quarter columns, and the pedimented hood included brass-capped columns at the angles. The 12-inch square silvered dial, signed 'Vulliamy London 549', incorporated subsidiary seconds below XII with strike/silent above, and a calendar aperture over VI, while the five-pillared movement was fitted with rack striking and an anchor escapement having a wood rod pendulum. At the same time as the Vulliamy was sold, there appeared another of Princess Alice's clocks, a Regency mahogany bracket clock of unusual construction in that the quarter-striking on two bells was accomplished with two snails but only one rack. However, it is mainly worth mentioning because its maker's signature, 'Recordon London', hints at a remote connection with E. J. Dent through Louis Recordon's successor, Peter Des Granges, who was one of Dent's suppliers.

A fitting conclusion to this account of the Vulliamys' work in royal service might be to look at one more clock. Superficially this might seem yet another instance where a Vulliamy movement has been inserted into someone else's case, but at least this is not a substitution. In the Presence Chamber in Windsor 275
Castle, there is a complete marble chimney-piece incorporating, as its central feature, a clock case, the whole work being that of the sculptor John Bacon, RA (1740–99). This artist, once apprenticed as a modeller in a porcelain factory, became a student at the Royal Academy on its foundation in 1768, eventually turning—as did his son of the same name, following in his footsteps—to the execution of monuments for Westminster Abbey and St Paul's Cathedral. There is something of the feeling of such work in this monumental structure, and various interpretations of the artist's intentions have been postulated. Without going into detail, the flavour can perhaps be caught from the Latin tag which runs beneath the clock *'Quae lenta accedit quam velox praeterit hora ut capias patiens esto sed esto vigil'* which has been translated into English thus:

> Slow comes the hour, its passing speed how great!
> Waiting to seize it—Vigilantly wait.

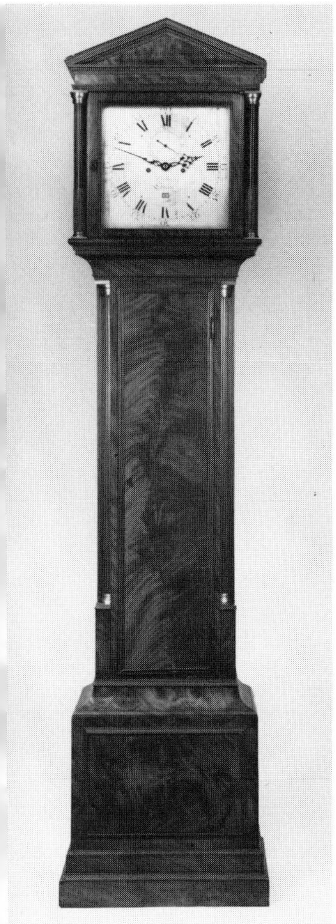

Horological giants such as the Vulliamy family were never common, but probably more of them thrived in Victorian times than either before or since; and at least two other such firms will be discussed later. Nevertheless, the royal service also had room for lesser mortals provided they were good and competent workmen; and quite a number of less well-known craftsmen passed, albeit momentarily, across the horological horizon in palaces and royal residences throughout the land, at various times during the last century.

Such a one was Sigismund Rentzsch, who first appears among the accredited royal tradesmen in 1821. Britten describes him as 'a clever mechanician and excellent workman', but very little seems to be known about him, and his work is only very rarely encountered nowadays. Customarily signing himself 'Watchmaker to the King and Royal Family', he worked from premises at 2 St George Street, St James's Square. He is said to have devised a peculiar chronometer escapement, and he certainly patented—number 3663, dated 13th March 1813—a 'hydrostatic or pneumatic chronometer', as Bennet Woodcroft summarizes it in his *Alphabetical Index of Patentees of Inventions* (1854). This was apparently a device which

274. (Above left) *Longcase clock, in the architectural style by Vulliamy, once owned by H.R.H. the late Princess Alice, Countess of Athlone.* (Christie's, London)

275. (Above) *The marble chimneypiece by John Bacon, R.A., in Windsor Castle: the clock is a Vulliamy product.* (Royal Collection)

276. (Right) *A regulator clock by Sigismund Rentzsch: general view.* (British Museum)

277. (Centre right) *Detail showing construction of the pendulum bob of the regulator clock by Rentzsch.* (British Museum)

278. (Far right) *Detail of the dial of the previous clock.* (British Museum)

attempted to measure time from the speed of mixing of
276 two fluids of differing gravities under pressure. There is,
277 278 in the Ilbert Collection in the British Museum, a regulator clock of his make, of curious construction in that the glass rod pendulum swings from front to rear, and the mercurial compensation is divided between a number of inverted small tubes of that metal located on top of the hemispherical lead bob. This is said to date *c.*1800, although Rentzsch is usually placed in the standard works of reference as flourishing between 1813 and 1842. All his surviving watches—and a few are scattered among museum collections—seem to have unusual features of one sort or another; and it appears, from the signatures on these, that he later had premises at Queen Street, Golden Square. It may be that his last recorded date, as mentioned above, is inaccurate—or that his firm continued under his name after his demise—for he continues to be listed among the royal tradesmen until 1857. In view of the quality of Rentzsch's existing work, scarce though it is, it is a matter for regret that there is no specimen of it in the Royal Collection.

It will be recollected that one of the great London craftsmen favoured by George III had been John Arnold, who was a pioneer in the field of practical chronometry, at the end of the eighteenth century, and who had certainly played a very large part in designing a marine chronometer that was both sufficiently simple to be capable of quantity production yet performed sufficiently accurately for navigational needs. Arnold had died in 1799, leaving the family firm to be carried on by his son John Roger Arnold. Jumping forward to 1830, we find that John Roger, the son, has taken into
partnership in his business one Edward John Dent. Born 279
in 1790 and apprenticed to a tallow-chandler, Dent had learned the trade of watchmaking while living in lodgings with a married couple called Rippon. Richard Rippon was a watchmaker, and, upon his death, Dent married his widow, his two stepsons take his surname, and Dent himself goes to work for some makers of repeating-actions for watches, called Callam. From 1815 to 1829 he worked for Vulliamy & Son, and he also spent some time with Barraud & Son, probably both on repeaters and helping with their chronometer work. When the opportunity arose for him to join John Roger Arnold, still one of the leading chronometer-makers in the metropolis, he jumped at it.

The partnership lasted ten years, and towards the

end of it, in 1839, the firm of Arnold & Dent was added to the list of approved royal tradesmen. Strangely, they continue to be so listed until 1843, although Dent moved away in 1840, setting up shop only two doors away from his former partner, at 82 Strand. The situation is further confused by the street-directory entries of the time: in 1839, *Kelly's Post Office Directory* shows: 'Arnold & Dent, Chronometer, Clock and Watchmakers to the Queen'. A similar entry appears in 1840, but by 1841 this has become:

Arnold, J. R. Watch & Chronometer Maker. 84 Strand.
Dent, E. J. Chronometer Maker and Watchmaker to the Queen. 82 Strand.

How Dent contrived to switch the Appointment to himself alone is unclear: it hardly seems likely that it had been granted originally to the partnership because of his involvement in it. The partnership had obtained the sponsorship of G. B. Airy, the Astronomer Royal, in this regard, and he spoke flatteringly of them. Yet when, on the dissolution of their joint enterprise, Dent again approached Airy to supply a testimonial for a similar Appointment for himself alone, he was refused, Airy saying that he could not distinguish between the merits of the partners in a firm and that, while supporting the latter on its corporate capabilities, he could not do the same for each of the individuals constituting it. Dent's Royal Appointment seems finally to have been granted in 1841, when he writes to a Mr Brocking on 8th April: 'It is with great satisfaction that I acquaint you that I succeed beyond my expectation in my business as well as patronage. I had the honour yesterday of being appointed by Special Authority "Chronometer Maker to Her Majesty the Queen", and which will give me considerable standing in business.'

E. J. Dent continues to be listed annually as a royal tradesman until his death in 1853, the year before B. L. Vulliamy died, thus relinquishing his grasp on a similar appointment. Like Vulliamy, Dent too was the representative of a craft family, only in his case he was first of that line, while Vulliamy was the last of his.

In February 1852 E. J. Dent had been given the order for the great clock for the Houses of Parliament—the long and involved story of that project is too well known to be explored yet again in these pages—and one of his successors, his stepson Frederick Dent, expected to take it over automatically. He did succeed to his stepfather's Royal Appointment, which in his case ran from 1854 to 1875, although he died in 1860; but he was not so fortunate over the Houses of Parliament contract, despite the fact that manufacture of the clock had been under way for some time, and it was only after much argument, legal as well as technical, that he was eventually allowed to proceed. Delays in completing the

279. *Lithograph portrait of E. J. Dent.* (Clockmakers' Company, London)

clock tower itself meant that, in the end, the clock could not be installed until May 1859. That event of itself led to yet further difficulties with which this book is not concerned.

Frederick Dent and his wife continued to prosper until 1858 when she suddenly became ill and, at the age of only forty-six, died. Frederick himself, distraught at the loss and with problems concerning the great clock at Westminster on his mind, gradually slid into alcoholism, dying on 25th April 1860. His intestacy was the subject of several lawsuits before being resolved. Frederick's brother Richard, E. J. Dent's younger stepson, had inherited the other part of the family business. At this stage, all that it is necessary to record is that Richard married Marianna Fredericka Cowslade in 1850 and that in the ensuing six years they had three children. The business prospered, mainly due to the practical abilities of Marianna who was to take it over completely upon the death of her husband, which occurred in 1856. Richard's death certificate read 'Softening of the brain, Convulsions, about a year', and it was rumoured that, towards the end of his life, he had had to be kept imprisoned in a top room in their house in Cockspur Street, an unpleasant and sad demise for a previously happy man of only thirty-nine. Nevertheless, he had been granted a Royal Appointment two years before he died.

The litigation that followed Frederick Dent's death produced a settlement in one very important respect: his business was taken over by his mother, Mrs Elizabeth Dent, formerly Rippon. She also seems to have inherited the Royal Appointment, which was still legally in the name of Frederick and was so published in official journals. In 1864 the firm adopted her initials into its business style, becoming 'E. Dent & Co. Watch & Chronometer Makers, To Her Majesty and H.R.H. The Prince of Wales'.

At this point it is interesting to consider where the Royal Appointments may have affected the fortunes of the Dents. Frederick Dent, apart from his connection with 'Big Ben', as it came to be known, had constructed a special design of chronograph, used to determine the time of Transits, for the Royal Observatory at Greenwich, as well as the Standard Astronomical Clock for the Royal Observatory in Edinburgh. He also made a turret clock for the Palace of Balmoral—this in 1857—which indicated time on four dials, each 6 feet in diameter. Elizabeth Dent was granted the contract to maintain Big Ben, the parties thereto being specified as 'The Queen's Most Excellent Majesty, The First Commissioner of Her Majesty's Public Works and Buildings and Elizabeth Dent'—quite an accomplishment for a woman, in those days. The annual fee for this work, 100 guineas a year, has been computed as equalling about £2,000 in 1977, and since to fulfil the contract entailed employing two men for about three days a week, it cannot possibly have shown any profit. In terms of prestige and status, however, it must have reaped substantial dividends.

Elizabeth Dent died of gastro-enteritis, at the ripe old age of seventy-six, on 21st May 1865. The firm then passed into the hands of Thomas Buckney senior and Amelia Lydia Sophia Gardner, who had been directors of the business previously. Still trading as E. Dent & Co, it was granted, in 1863, the Appointment of Watch and Clockmakers to HRH The Prince of Wales, by special warrant. They already held Appointments to the Queen and Prince Albert as well as to the Emperor of Russia. Thomas Buckney died on 18th July 1872. His son, Thomas Buckney junior, born in 1838, had become superintendent of the manufacturing division of E. Dent & Co in 1864 and a partner in 1872, just a fortnight before his father's death. He then became acting senior partner, a post which was to become substantive on the death of his aunt, Amelia Lydia Sophia Gardner, in 1881. From 1864 until his death in 1900, he was virtually in charge of the firm. In 1884, Thomas Buckney, trading as E. Dent & Co, had been granted the Appointment of Chronometer, Clock and Watchmaker to Her Majesty, Queen Victoria.

So much for the successors of Frederick Dent—but what of his brother Richard? His death in 1856 brought to the fore his competent wife, Marianna Fredericka Dent, who, since Richard had died intestate, was granted administration of his estate, valued at about £16,000. With three young children to look after, she determined to carry the business on, but re-styling it M. F. Dent, a name that was to be retained for sixty-five years, until its final amalgamation with E. Dent & Co Ltd.

Under Marianna Dent the business prospered. Originally at 33 Cockspur Street, the lease of number 34 next door was also taken up when it became vacant. Marianna married again, four years after Richard's death, her second husband being a solicitor named Samuel Ward Tucker. They were both in their thirties and successful; and they were granted a Royal Appointment in 1862. Marianna died of liver disease at the early age of forty-one, in 1869, and her husband, Samuel Ward Tucker, of heart disease and other ailments, in 1877. Marianna Dent had had seven children altogether, and upon her husband's death the family business came into the control of three of them in equal partnership—Edward John Dent, who was now the fourth member of the family to bear that combination of names, together with his sisters Maria Louisa and Amelia Maria. Edward John Dent died in 1899 of chronic alcoholism—not unknown in that family—leaving instructions that his third share of the firm be under the supervision of his two sisters until his youngest son was twenty-two or until either of his two sons had exercised an option to 'buy himself in' to his father's share. Amelia Maria Dent made similar provisions in her Will, in favour of her nephews and nieces when of age. In the event, a time came, in about 1920, when the business could have been taken over by these last, save that none of them was interested in carrying it on; so it was agreed to merge with E. Dent & Co Ltd, thus reuniting the two firms after a separation of sixty-seven years. As for Maria Louisa Dent, she outlived them all—born in 1853, she lived to be ninety-four, dying only in 1947.

The foregoing account of another of the great Victorian horological families serves to demonstrate, if nothing else, how very interlocked these businesses were—the Arnolds, the Dents and the Vulliamys—and there is still one more to come, the Frodshams; and this serves to take us full circle, back again to John Roger Arnold and B. L. Vulliamy.

John Roger Arnold, it will be remembered, had severed his business partnership with E. J. Dent in 1839, and relations between them became very strained indeed at this time. Dent set himself up in business only two doors away from his former partner, an unthinkable state of affairs today; indeed partnership agreements invariably forbid such an eventuality within a specified period, usually of years. Arnold had then to contend with the illness and death of his wife Jane on 3rd September 1840, followed almost immediately—on the 29th of that same month—by the legal dissolution of the partnership. Possibly as a result of such a prolonged period of worry, his health started to decline, and, having gone for a time to Bath in an effort to recuperate, he seems to have had a stroke, for he died there on 26th February 1843. He was then aged seventy-four.

A great deal of business agitation followed this occurrence: Arnold had been a contractor to the Government, mainly in the person of the Astronomer Royal, for years, for the purpose of chronometer maintenance, repair and rating; and most of this work was eventually, after desultory haggling, passed on to Dent. He was, however, thwarted in his ambition to take over the whole Arnold business, lock, stock and barrel. In fact, it was bought by Charles Frodsham; and for a while, such was the goodwill locked up in the very name of Arnold that trading went on under their joint names, Arnold & Frodsham. But who was this newcomer?

Charles Frodsham was the fourth generation of a family of craftsmen horologists that started with a certain William Frodsham, who was born in 1728, was made an Honorary Freeman of the Clockmakers' Company in 1781 and worked from Kingsgate Street, off Red Lion Square in Clerkenwell. His son, also William, predeceased him so that the business went to a grandson, John. He subsequently went into partnership under the style Frodsham & Baker, and his firm eventually passed to his sons, becoming a separate entity from the particular commercial thread being followed here.

Another of the first William Frodsham's grandsons was, however, William James Frodsham. Born in 1778, he entered into business with William Parkinson, setting up as Parkinson & Frodsham, of Exchange Alley, in 1801. All the Frodshams were good Clockmakers' Company men, and William James was admitted to the Freedom on 11th October 1802, then to the Livery, in 1811. He was chosen for the Court of Assistants in 1824, served the office of Warden during the period 1833–5 and was twice elected Master, in 1836 and again the following year. A Fellow of the Royal Society—one of only a handful of clockmakers to be so signally honoured—he presented a paper to that body in 1838, concerned with the isochronism of pendulums. He died in 1850, some eight years after his partner William Parkinson; and presumably he was a man of considerable substance, since he left a sum of £1,000 to the Clockmakers' Company, to be known as the Parkinson and Frodsham Fund and to be used for charitable purposes.

William James Frodsham trained four sons at the bench, of whom the third was Charles Frodsham. Born in 1810, he started up in business on his own account at an early age, at 7 Finsbury Pavement, having first been apprenticed to his father in 1824. For some reason, he was not admitted to the Freedom of the Company until 1845, but doubtless this was a commercial expedient connected with his buying up the Arnold concern. By 1850 he had started to serve his first term in the various levels of Warden, becoming Master in 1855. He started again, as Junior Warden, in 1859, becoming Master for the second time in 1862.

In horological terms, Charles Frodsham was undoubtedly the most eminent member of that great craft family. In addition to his business interests, he found time for extensive experimentation. In 1846 he received the Telford Medal for a paper he presented to the Institution of Civil Engineers, of which he became an Associate: the subject was *A History of the Marine Chronometer with the Laws of Isochronism*. He was also a Fellow of the Royal Astronomical Society and, for some years, a Vice-President of the British Horological Institute.

Following the death of B. L. Vulliamy in 1854, Charles Frodsham took over that business. During the same decade and the one that followed, he gained a steady stream of medal awards for the excellence of his chronometers, including a First Class at the Great Exhibition of 1851, a Gold Medal at Paris in 1855, Medal of Honour at the International Exhibition of 1862, and a similar award in Paris in 1867. In 1862 he also published a small book entitled *A Few Facts Connected with the Elements of Watch and Clock Making*, which was intended to be the prelude to the publication of an exhaustive treatise covering his practice and experiments over some thirty years; but sadly this never appeared, nor is the present whereabouts of any manuscript known.

In 1855, and presumably as a direct result of taking over the Vulliamy business, Charles Frodsham became 'Chronometer and Clockmaker by Special Appointment to Her Majesty The Queen and Their Royal Highnesses, the Prince and Princess of Wales'. He also held appointments to the Admiralty, to the Russian Government and to various colonial observatories. His work commanded very high prices, and a price list of 1885 quotes a gold-cased pocket chronometer at about £100 and a lever watch at £80. Complicated watches with multi-functional capabilities in those days cost up to £500.

Stories survive of the inherent kindness of Charles Frodsham, the best being that in which he is said to have noticed one of his artisans appearing listless in his work. Handing him a pill box, which was in fact filled with gold sovereigns, he said, 'I believe you need a holiday; go to the country and take some of my pills!'

Charles Frodsham died in 1871, after which his business was carried on by his son Harrison Mill Frodsham (1855–1927) in association with A. E. Rutherford, to whom one of his daughters was married. This is the only one of these great London-based horological enterprises of the last century to survive in recognizable form to the present time, the firm of Dents in Pall Mall having disappeared by merger only within the last few years. With the gradual inclination towards the new technology of the electronic age and away from traditional mechanical methods of time-measurement, the future must look bleak for those schooled in the craft tradition unless they can find the means to adapt to the changing conditions or diversify, or both.

By the second half of the nineteenth century, of course, the horological craft had become a great deal more standardized than at any previous time; quality could be preserved, but now, with the increasing use of interchangeable components, at the expense of the unique in design: this could no longer be easily accommodated when raw movements all came from the same handful of factories and only the fitting and finishing was done by the concern whose name eventually appeared on the dial. It is also fair to say that the same opportunities were not open to these later horologists in the royal service as had been available to their predecessors: there were no new palaces to furnish. Nevertheless, there are plenty of clocks in daily use in the various residences with movements by the Dents, the Frodshams and other great Victorian horological firms; it would take an enormous, and arguably unjustifiable, amount of research to evaluate them all, and suffice it to mention simply one of the biggest of their commissions. In 1857, Frederick Dent supplied, at a cost of £350 15s, the turret clock and bells for Balmoral Castle.

So much for those singular and significant personalities of the horological world who may be said to have made their own special contribution to the craft of the nineteenth century, as well as to the Royal Collection. Strangely, there were others active in the same field—that of royal service—who seem to have been mere shadows and to have left little impression behind them. Such a one was James Ogston, who became a royal tradesman in 1852 when the number of horologists so employed seems, for some reason unknown at this distance in time, to have been raised from three to four. He remained thus in harness until 1857.

Ogston is first identified by Britten in 1826, when he took out a patent—number 5314, dated 6th January in that year—jointly with James Thomas Bell, covering the construction of certain watches with two spring barrels. Bell is also an elusive personality; but together these two eventually joined up, for a time, with John Dwerryhouse, who is of somewhat more substance. Again quoting Britten, it seems that the first partnership consisted of Dwerryhouse, Ogston & Co, located at 27 Davies Street, off Berkeley Square, during the years 1835–42. Whether the '& Co' might indeed have been J. T. Bell all the time, is not clear, but the style changed from 1840, then becoming Dwerryhouse, Ogston & Bell. Later the firm moved shop to 131 Mount Street, after which all traces disappear.

In 1858 there occurs, for the first time in the authorized lists of royal tradesmen, the name of John Bennett. Born in 1814, and an extremely controversial character in his day, he was originally intended for an ecclesiastical career; however, when his father died, **280**
Bennett entered the family business, which was the manufacture of clocks, watches and jewellery. This had been established by his grandfather early in the eighteenth century, in Greenwich, but Bennett soon moved it into the City and in 1846 set up shop in Cheapside. In 1862 he was elected to the City of London's Court of Common Council, its local government body.

Bennett might perhaps be described as the first tycoon in the clock and watch trade, employing business methods that were anathema to others in the same line of manufactures as himself—although they would be regarded as commonplace today—and succeeding where they had failed. He never hesitated to harness to his own needs the power of publicity and, when such a business 'tool' was still used only discreetly, to give it full throttle. Thus, when rebuilding his factory in 1852, he heralded it with expensive advertising—all of £750-worth—on the back of the Catalogue for the Great Exhibition, a device which repaid him handsomely.

As a Sheriff of the City of London and Middlesex in 1872, Bennett received a knighthood in commemoration of a royal visit to the City. A great advocate of the advantages of machine tools and mass-production, he had given a series of public lectures, during 1856–8, in which the principal theme was his insistence on the supremacy of Swiss methods, which employed cheap

280. *Portrait of Sir John Bennett, from 'The Figaro', 1873.* (Guildhall Library, City of London)

female labour and machinery, together with standardization and interchangeability of parts. By comparison, the craft methods still customary in London seemed to him laborious and out-of-date. This at once antagonized all his contemporaries in the Clerkenwell trade, and it has even been said that the British Horological Institute was brought into being, in 1858, to protect their interests from 'new brooms' like Bennett. It is one of those contradictions so beloved of the British that he became one of the first members of the BHI's Council, but he never lived down the bitterness his advocacy of modern production methods had engendered, nor were his rivals ever generous enough to admit that he was right all the time. In 1877 he was three times voted Alderman of the Ward of Cheap, but each time the Court of Alderman vetoed his election. No reasons for such a rebuff are ever given. Sir John Bennett retired from the active management of his business in 1889, after which it became a limited company; he himself died in 1897, at the age of eighty-three, and his Will gave some hint of an unconventional life-style, at least for those days. The family firm he had so greatly revitalized continued in existence until 1940, when, shortly after the notification of its impending closure, enemy action terminated its existence once and for all.

Continental influences upon the clock and watch trade started to make themselves felt, among the exclusive circle of royal tradesmen, for the first time in the early 1860s. For a start, Aubert & Klaftenberger were appointed as a fifth grantee, from 1862—from 1852 there had been four, before that only three, and prior to 1839 only two, being one each for clocks and watches. D. F. Aubert started in Geneva about 1820 and subsequently went into a London partnership with C. J. Klaftenberger, their premises, from 1835 onwards, being at 157 Regent Street. What the make-up of this firm at the time of its royal Appointment may have been, is not recorded; but after 1885 it became simply A. A. Klaftenberger. In common with Charles Frodsham and E. J. Dent, Aubert & Klaftenberger had exhibited at the Great Exhibition in 1851: their exhibit included a selection of lever and duplex watches in gold cases, a similarly cased pocket chronometer as well as a two-day marine version, a gold-cased half-quarter-repeating and complicated lever watch, and a regulator with *remontoir*. The catalogue for the 1862 Exhibition reveals only Charles J. Klaftenberger at the Regent Street premises; his partner now appears as Aubert & Linton, at 252 Regent Street.

An interesting example of an association item—its history more important, perhaps, than its intrinsic interest—was sold in New York towards the end of 1981. Described as a 'Presentation enamelled gold watch, half-hunting cased and quarter-repeating', it was signed 'Klaftenberger no. 8564, Watchmaker to The Queen and H.R.H. The Prince Consort, 157 Regent Street, London'. The very high quality straight-line lever bar-type movement was jewelled to the centre wheel, and even the repeating-train hammer pivots ran in jewelled bearings. The gold case was enhanced by a polychrome enamel monogram and royal ducal coronet; but the inscription inside it brought that touch of pathos which gave the object its real importance. This inscription ran: 'To/DEAR LEOPOLD/IN/ the name of his devoted parents/ALBERT & VICTORIA.R/from his unhappy mama/V.R./Xmas 1864'. Leopold, the fourth and youngest son of Queen Victoria, lived only to the age of thirty-one, and was in poor health throughout his life; and the Prince Consort had already died three years prior to the date of this gift.

Two years after Aubert & Klaftenberger comes the first appearance among the royal tradesmen of Le Roy & Son. This was the London branch of one of two

281. *Trade card of Le Roy & Sons.* (Private collection)

282. *Leaflet of Lund & Blockley, Bombay.* (Private collection)

LUND & BLOCKLEY, CLOCK SPECIALISTS, BOMBAY.

TIMES OF ALL NATIONS

AGENTS FOR PULSYNETIC ELECTRIC CLOCKS.

AS SUPPLIED TO G. I. P. RY G. P. O., BOMBAY AND MADRAS. W. I. T. C., &c., &c.

As we receive frequent enquiries in regard to the difference in time between Bombay and various parts of the world, we quote below the hours and minutes difference between Bombay Standard Time and Solar Time at the cities mentioned.

TABLE OF VARIOUS CITIES SHOWING HOURS AND MINUTES FAST OR SLOW OF BOMBAY STANDARD TIME.

		Hrs.	Mins.			Hrs.	Mins.			Hrs.	Mins.
Adelaide	*fast* ...	3	.44	Hamburg	*slow* ...	4	.50	Philadelphia	*slow* ...	10	.31
Alexandria	*slow* ...	3	.22	Jerusalem	*slow* ...	3	.9	Pietermaritzburg	*slow*	3	.30
Amsterdam	*slow* ...	5	.11	London	*slow* ...	5	.30	Rangoon	*fast* ...	0	.55
Athens	*slow* ...	3	.55	Madrid	*slow* ...	5	.45	Rome	*slow* ...	4	.40
Berlin	*slow* ...	4	.36	Melbourne	*fast* ...	4	.10	Shanghai	*fast* ...	2	.35
Boston, U.S.	*slow* ...	10	.12	Milan	*slow* ...	4	.53	Singapore	*fast* ...	1	.25
Brussels	*slow* ...	5	.13	Montreal	*slow* ...	10	.24	Suez	*slow* ...	3	.20
Cairo	*slow* ...	3	.25	Munich	*slow* ...	4	.44	Sydney	*fast* ...	4	.35
Calcutta	*fast* ...	0	.24	Naples	*slow* ...	4	.33	Venice	*slow* ...	4	.25
Cape Town	*slow* ...	4	.16	New York	*slow* ...	10	.26	Washington	*slow* ...	10	.38
Chicago	*slow* ...	11	.21	Paris	*slow* ..	5	.21	Wellington, N.Z.	*fast*	6	.9
Colombo	*slow* ...	0	.11	Pekin	*fast* ...	2	.16				
Geneva	*slow* ...	5	.5	Petrograd	*slow* ...	3	.29				

The above illustration is of a clock hand-made by Mr. Lund over sixty years ago and is still in use. The original may be seen in our window.

LUND & BLOCKLEY,
CLOCK SPECIALISTS,
150/2, ESPLANADE ROAD, - - - BOMBAY.

concerns based in Paris, both using the same name and both with addresses in Palais Royal but wholly unconnected with one another, and neither having any connection whatever with the great chronometrists of the past, Julien and Pierre Le Roy. The story is a long and confused one, and this is not the place to recount it; but Charles Allix, in *Carriage Clocks—Their History and Development*, explores it in detail. A trade 281
card for the London concern is laden with details of its accomplishments, ranging from a list of its Appointments to European and other royalty, to the variety of medal awards it had gained at exhibitions in Paris, London and Dublin. The London address is shown as 211 & 213 Regent Street, which helps to date this relic; from 1866 to 1875 the firm had only one shop in this street, number 211, after which it acquired number 213, but later, in 1885, it removed completely to Bond Street.

Towards the end of the last century—from 1885—a new departure was made with the appointment of horological tradesmen in certain provincial areas where there were royal connections, as well as in the main centres in Scotland. This added no fewer than seven grantees to the list, located in Liverpool, Windsor, Cowes (Isle of Wight), Aldershot, Aberdeen, Glasgow and Edinburgh. As for London, the firm of Lund & Blockley, of 42 Pall Mall, makes a fleeting appearance on the scene, being listed for one year only, 1887. Watches by this partnership are not uncommonly encountered to this day, and they are very often inscribed 'Lund & Blockley To the Queen' on the dial; yet, when next heard of, the firm was ensconced in 282
Bombay, where it remains to the present time. However, it did not suffer that commonplace Victorian retribution, banishment to the Colonies, but simply went bankrupt, an occurrence which instantly voided its Warrant. The details will be found in Appendix 3. How the Indian branch managed to survive this disaster has not so far been discovered.

Imprudent uses of the Royal Warrant certainly seem to have proliferated during the nineteenth century. So discreet a recognition as an Appointment should perforce be its own reward, but after Queen Victoria's death, some existing Warrants were actually endorsed with permission to adopt the style of 'Maker to the late Queen', rather than simply allowing her Appointments to lapse, as would have been customary. Thus Dents then described themselves as 'Watchmaker to her Late Majesty'. Thomas Russell & Son, of Liverpool, more economical in their dial painting, simply claimed to have been 'Makers to Queen Victoria'. There were many other makers in the latter half of the century who claimed, in somewhat grandiose terms, to be grantees of Royal Appointments, such as 'F. W. Benson By

Special Warrant to H.M. The Queen and H.R.H. The Prince of Wales', this about 1880, and 'C. F. Hancock. Successor of Storr & Mortimer's, by Appointment to H.M. Queen Adelaide, and H.I.M. the Emperor of Russia'—a kind of grantee once removed. A similar example can be cited in respect of 'Rivers & Son, Cornhill, Successors to Daniel de St. Leu, Watchmaker to Her Majesty'. But worse was to come from Hancock's, who eventually claimed themselves to be 'By Appointment to the Principal Sovereigns and Courts of Europe'. The only other nineteenth-century maker who could perhaps rival this all-embracing claim—and he was a lot earlier, so possibly he set the style—was James Gorham, of Kensington, 'Maker to the Royal Family'. As to multiple claims stipulating the grantors, these were legion. One of the earliest must surely have been James Tregent, said to be of French extraction and first listed by Baillie in 1759, who has been identified at 35 Strand in 1775, moving to 29 Cranbourne Street, off Leicester Square, in 1780 and being admitted an Honorary Freeman of the Clockmakers' Company in 1781. His customary signature claims himself to be 'Maker to Their Royal Highnesses The Prince of Wales, Duke of Kent and Duke of Sussex'. Tregent is generally considered a fine maker, and he should perhaps have known better—although
his contemporary, Henry Favre, relatively unknown 283
yet went in for similar self-aggrandizement, by signing 284
himself 'Watchmaker to their Royal Highnesses the Prince of Wales, the Dukes of York and Cumberland'. Baillie, incidentally, places Favre as *c.*1800–24—and assigns him to the Prince Regent—but clearly he started in the previous century. John S. Matheson, working in Leith about 1880 and winner of the Reid and Auld Prize (value 3 sovereigns) for his device for winding up chronometers without reversing their suspensions, proudly signed himself 'Chronometer Maker to H.R.H. The Duke of Edinburgh and the Royal Navy'. Finally, the impertinence of the mid-nineteenth-century Spaniard J. R. Losada, of 105 Regent Street, cannot be beaten. With no Royal Warrant at all, he nevertheless signs himself 'Watchmaker to all the Crowned Heads of Europe'.

Mention of Leith recalls the large number of provincial clock- and watchmakers who, over the years, have served members of the Royal Family if indeed not actually the reigning sovereign. It would be a mammoth task, even if possible, to discover them all; but a casual search brings to light such men as John Scott, of Princes Street, Edinburgh, apprenticed 1779 and discharged his indentures 1785, died 1798, who was Watch- and Clockmaker to His Royal Highness the Prince of Wales. Then there is John Russell, of Falkirk, who is listed as active during the years 1783–1817.
There is a wheel barometer of his special design in 285
Buckingham Palace, which is signed by him as 'Invt. et

283. (Below) *The back of the movement of a watch by Henry Favre, the dustcap showing the multiple 'royal' signature.* (Strike One, Ltd.)

284. (Below right) *Advertising watch paper of Henry Favre.* (Clockmakers' Company, London)

285. (Left) *Wheel barometer by John Russell of Falkirk.* (Royal Collection)

Fect', and also 'Watchmaker to his Royal Highness The Prince Regent'. *The Edinburgh Evening Courant* for 6th July 1812 states of this maker: 'On Monday, Mr. Russell of Falkirk, watchmaker to his Royal Highness the Prince Regent, waited on his Royal Highness at Carlton House, when he had the honour of delivering a superb gold chronometer of his making, according to his R.H. gracious order. His Royal Highness, with his usual condescension, was pleased to declare his satisfaction with this specimen of Mr. Russell's workmanship'. (An account then follows of various other mainly non-horological objects, such as a gold-mounted box and a silver Crookstone dollar but also 'a very ancient watch of curious workmanship', not further described in detail, which he also presented.) 'His Royal Highness conversed for some time with Mr. Russell with great affability, and showed him a great many curious clocks and watches.' Both these makers owed allegiance to the same royal personage, and it is probably true that George IV, throughout his life, was as liberal with the distribution of his Appointments as any other sovereign, before or since.

Inevitably, the wares purveyed by the later holders of Royal Warrants in this trade prove less interesting to the antiquarian horologist researching the royal context. These firms did not have the unrivalled opportunities that fell to their predecessors in the eighteenth century, of furnishing new palaces and catering for the specialist requirements of two successive monarchs who had intense, albeit entirely different, interests in the subject. From individuals like O. J. Hamley or Caleb Elisha, both of Duke Street, St James's, and both appointed Watchmaker to HRH The Duke of York, in the first half of the century, to later concerns of the calibre of J. C. Vickery, in Regent Street, or Hunt & Roskell, in Bond Street, it is probably true to say that while quality of products was of the highest, intrinsic interest remained usually low. This last-named was, in any event, a firm of jewellers and silversmiths who sold clocks and watches as part of their retail operation; for this was the same period that was seeing the emergence of the giants of that type, Asprey's, Garrard's, Cartier's, the Goldsmiths' & Silversmiths' Company, and it was the retail clock and watch trade at this time which pioneered the techniques of mail-order selling. The nineteenth century saw the mechanical side of clocks and watches reach an all-time pinnacle of achievement, resulting in standards of precision time-measurement never attained before and never bettered—mechanically—since. Appearances certainly

286. (Right) *Queen Mary's Dolls' House at Windsor Castle: view of the Hall, showing longcase clock.* (Royal Collection)

suffered—the fussy, over-decorated Victorian clock case, at its worst, can be unimaginably dreadful—but in one sense, this is only history repeating itself. Only at very few points in the world-wide annals of clocks and watches have efficient mechanisms been allied to elegant yet functional cases; examples from such periods and places reach the highest prices of all in today's collectors' market.

Yet despite the threat of mass-production and cheap imports, the occasional firm of craftsmen survived to produce the different clock or watch, that singular object that is a perfect marrying of art, craft and function, as well as being still custom-built for the rich, knowledgeable and discerning client. Such a one was J. & H. Jump. Richard Thomas Jump, son of a watchmaker and the inventor of a special gauge used in connection with making wheels and pinions, had been apprenticed to B. L. Vulliamy in 1825, his brother Joseph following suit in 1827. When, in 1854, Vulliamy died, and Charles Frodsham took over his business, Joseph Jump went into business with another brother, Alfred, at 1a Old Bond Street, where they made many fine, elegant clocks in styles very reminiscent of Breguet's practice. There is an ebonized bracket clock of this firm's make, at Sandringham; and it was, of course, concerned with overhauling and housing the Samuel Watson astronomical clock in the Library at Windsor Castle.

Discerning clients are a *sine qua non* for the true craftsman. While the scope of this book, so far as the objects described therein, has been set as covering the period 1300 to 1900, it would be wrong to omit any mention of the several members of the Royal Family during the present century who have interested themselves in clocks and watches, generally as works of art rather than for their mechanical content, and have, to a greater or lesser degree, collected those particular examples that attracted them.

The doyenne of royal collectors of works of art during the last hundred years must be Queen Mary. She has already been mentioned a handful of times—in connection with a Tompion bracket clock and the large and complicated clock in lacquered case by Pyke, to name but two instances— and there were several other clocks among the exhibition of her treasures that was mounted at the Victoria and Albert Museum in 1954. One was a tiny 'singing birdcage' clock, undoubtedly of Swiss manufacture; another a French mantel clock. Indeed, any peregrination of, say, the State Apartments in Windsor Castle, produces ample examples of her taste and remarkable capabilities as a collector, and not least her generosity in giving many works of art to the Royal Collection. A particular object with which she must always be connected is the giant dolls' house, nowadays kept at Windsor Castle and open to public inspection. There are a number of clocks in this creation, but perhaps it is not generally known that they all have movements, which were supplied by 286
Cartier Ltd. Again on a small scale, Her Majesty bought, in 1934, from a London dealer, a watch that must rank as one of the smallest ever made, being only 8·75 millimetres in diameter and weighing less than half an ounce. A lever watch in a gold case, this was the product of a celebrated Swiss watchmaking concern at the beginning of the last century, Piguet et Meylan. It is said to date *c.*1820, although this might seem a little 287
early for this type of escapement. Another watch which Queen Mary greatly favoured was given to her at the age of six by the Dowager Duchess of Inverness; it had originally belonged to the Duke of Sussex, the sixth son of George III. This was only slight larger than the other, and also cased in gold.

Queen Mary's influence on the Royal Collection, although entirely different from, say, that of George III or George IV, must never be underestimated. When George V and his Queen—whose principal forename, Victoria, had been rendered unusable for fear of confusion with her more eminent namesake—moved unwillingly into Buckingham Palace, it was in a sad state of neglect, with the outer fabric requiring no less than 6,000 tons of Portland stone to make it presentable, while, inside, there was a haphazard accumulation of paintings and antiques, all badly in need of attention and proper organization. Queen Mary catalogued, restored, re-arranged and created proper settings for all these objects as well as tracking down anything that seemed to have gone astray, thereby acquiring not only an eagle eye for quality in *objets d'arts* but also a reputation as a most determined adversary when obstacles were placed in the way of any of her aspirations for the Royal Collection. It may well be largely due to her single-minded approach to such matters that the antiquities to be found in the royal residences today are, in the main, in such good order; and it has become increasingly recognized, of more recent years, that it must be in everybody's interests to keep them that way.

When the effects of the late Princess Royal were submitted to auction by Christie's on 28th June 1966, it became clear that she had had an interesting taste in fine antique watches, in addition to her enjoyment of 288
many other categories of small works of art. The most important was a superb gold and enamelled watch and

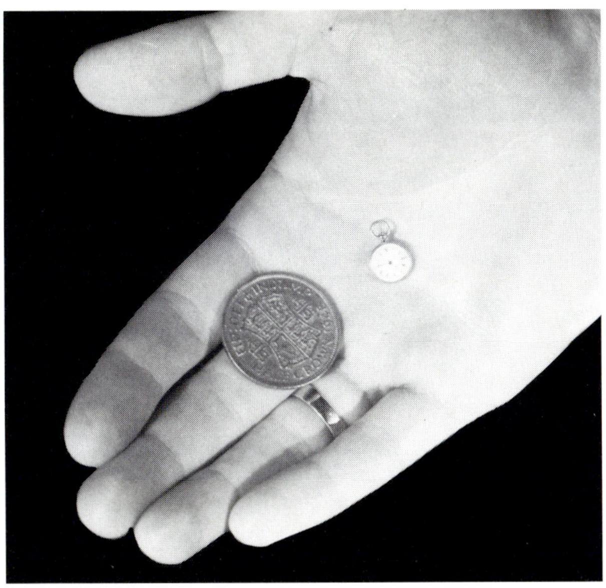

287. (Above) *Miniature watch by Piguet et Meylan, once owned by Queen Mary.* (Crown copyright: Science Museum, London)

288. (Right) *Watch by Daniel Grignion, with accompanying chatelaine, is shown in the centre of this photograph: to the left, a watch by Henry Moze, and to the right, another by J. Jackson, both having gold repoussé outer cases. All three watches once belonged to H.R.H. the late Princess Royal.* (Christie's, London)

chatelaine, the former with movement by Daniel Grignion (1684–1763), who worked at first on his own but later with his son Thomas in partnership. The decoration of the gold watch case, including colourful versions of the Roman Charity— as auctioneers always call it—and the conventional country scenes with a figure walking by a stream near a farmhouse, and the band embellished with vignettes of buildings in landscapes, was signed by 'Les deux frères Huaut', famed for this kind of work in the last quarter of the seventeenth century. It seems likely, therefore, that this watch case had been fitted later with a movement by Grignion, which was said to date from the second quarter of the eighteenth century. The watch was then enclosed in an outer case decorated *en suite* with the chatelaine, which consisted of three rococo medallions with enamelled scenes. In the same sale were several other good watches—a nineteenth-century Swiss form watch, for instance, in the shape of a melon, anonymous, as well as two watches in gold outer cases decorated with scenes in repoussé work, one having a quarter-repeating movement by Henry Moze, of London, whose sole claim to fame may be that he was declared bankrupt in 1743. Her Royal Highness possessed several small travelling-clocks usually in silver-gilt with blue enamel, four of which originated from Asprey's. Finally, there was a Butterfield-pattern silver pocket sundial with the usual adjustable bird gnomon, and the base engraved with the latitude of thirty-two European towns, the work of Nicholas Bion of Paris, whose active life spanned the last quarter of the seventeenth century and the first quarter of the eighteenth.

By far the best of HRH The Princess Royal's watches, however, was sold during her lifetime, by Christie's, on 15th March 1957. This was an extraordinary gold, enamel and rock-crystal pair-cased watch, having a verge movement by Josiah Roberts of London and numbered 923. Details of this movement include square baluster pillars, as well as a pierced and engraved cock with mask and broad foot. The inner case has an enamelled scene of the meeting of Dido and Aeneas on the back, a landscape scene inside, and
panels showing landscapes on the band. The white 289
enamel dial has provision for winding through, 290
between III and IV, as well as five-minute numerals in the outer ring, and gilt hands in the Continental style. The interest must centre, however, on the incredible rock-crystal outer case, in which this transparent mineral has been shaped and fitted into an irregular rococo gold bezel to act as protection for the enamelled back of the inner case. There are, furthermore, crystal panels on the band of this outer case, to reveal the enamelled landscapes on the band of the inner; as such things go, it is little short of miraculous. Josiah Roberts, to complete the picture, has been located in Bishopsgate Street during the last decade of the eighteenth century.

289. (Below left) *Magnificent gold, enamel and rock crystal pair-cased watch by Josiah Roberts, of London, given as a wedding present to H.R.H. the late Princess Royal. This view shows the dial and outer case.* (Sotheby's, London)

290. (Below) *The back of the inner case of the previous watch, viewed through the rock crystal back of the outer case.* (Sotheby's, London)

This watch came again on the market when the celebrated Belin Collection was sold by Sotheby's, on 29th November 1979. In the Catalogue entry, it was recalled that the watch had been given as a wedding present to HRH The Princess Royal on 28th February 1922, by the Princess Julius de Lippe, granddaughter of the Grand Duchess of Mecklenburg-Strelitz, having originally belonged to Princess Mary, Duchess of Gloucester, the daughter of George III. Later, it was given by George, Duke of Cambridge, to his sister Augusta, Grand Duchess of Mecklenburg-Strelitz, when she celebrated her golden wedding in 1903.

Very much more recently—in fact, in July 1979—the Trustees of the late Princess Royal have sold a clock that belonged to her; and since this is by Joseph Knibb,
291 it should be recorded here. The $6\frac{1}{4}$-inch square dial of this clock is inscribed across the base, beneath the silvered chapter ring, 'Joseph Knibb, London'; the centre is matted, and the cherub spandrels have engraved acanthus motifs connecting them. Above is a strike/silent lever. The movement, somewhat restored, has baluster pillars of which the central one has been removed, and the original verge escapement has been converted to anchor. The repeating-train has been removed and now gives only a single blow at the half-hour. The decorated back plate is engraved 'Joseph Knibb Londini Fecit'. The ebonized bell-top case has the conventional gilt carrying-handle and mounts, and the clock rests upon a separate base which utilizes the original gilt feet. No indication is given as to how Her Royal Highness came by this particular clock—and, if such an adjective can ever be used of a clock by any of the Knibb family, it is only one of their ordinary products, which has not been improved by alteration.

291. *Bracket clock by Joseph Knibb, which formerly belonged to H.R.H. the late Princess Royal.* (Christie's, London)

To bring this section up to the present day, who better than Her Majesty The Queen Mother? Unlike the other two members of the Royal Family whose interests have just been described, the Queen Mother really does enjoy fine clocks as a subject in themselves, although naturally surrounded by other interesting and colourful works of art of all kinds in her official residences. Mention has already been made of some of Her Majesty's clocks—the Pittenweem clock by John Smith, and the long-case clock by Wyke & Green of Liverpool, to name two fine specimens—and now would seem the moment to describe some later examples. A typical one is a small long-case regulator clock, no more than 6 feet in height, with dead-beat
292 escapement, in an arched top case of finely figured
293 rosewood, plain save for a shallow fluted frieze just below the hood. The wooden pendulum rod is fitted with a solid brass bob, the circular silvered dial is of the regulator type with subsidiary rings, above and below centre, for seconds and hours, while the minutes are shown by a full-length centre hand against the outermost edge of the main dial. The clock has a going-train only—almost an indispensable condition for this kind of timekeeper, as striking and chiming simply introduce more frictional elements into the system. The maker, who has been mentioned already elsewhere, is 'Gorham, Maker to the Queen, Kensington' and this clock
dates, clearly, from before the time when he claimed 295
even greater popularity in royal circles. Britten places James Gorham in 5 Kensington High Street during the period *c.*1815–54.

To avoid any possibility of giving a wrong impression, it should be said here that Gorham was far from being an ordinary run-of-the-mill maker; the evidence of this is to be seen in a remarkable astronomical skeleton clock, discussed by Dr F. A. B. Ward in an article 'A Mean and Sidereal Time Clock' which appeared in the *Horological Journal*, volume LXXXVII, number 1058, November 1946, pp. 466–7. The clock itself came up for sale by Christie's

292. (Left) *Full-length view of the regulator clock by James Gorham.* (The Queen Mother's Collection)

293. (Above) *Detail of the dial and hood of the previous clock.* (The Queen Mother's Collection)

on 7th February 1979, when it made some £19,000. The whole concept of this clock was highly original, 294 employing clock-driven celestial and terrestrial globes made for Gorham by G. & J. Cary of 86 St James's Street, members of a well-known family of globe-makers. As to the validity of its design, Dr Ward writes that the clock 'employs a simple, but relatively inaccurate, gearing which gives an error of 0·157 seconds per day, the sidereal time given by the clock being ahead of true sidereal time by this amount each day'. Since this clock was probably intended for domestic, as opposed to scientific use, the margin of error can hardly be considered critical, although it may well have concerned the clock's first owner, the mathematician John

294. (Right) *Astronomical skeleton clock by James Gorham.* (Christie's, London)

295. (Below) *Advertising watch paper of James Gorham.* (Clockmakers' Company, London)

Herapath (1790–1868), from whose descendants it has been passed down to the present day.

Two smaller clocks from Her Majesty's collection will serve to balance the somewhat larger clock just described, as well as to complete this review; both are at present in Royal Lodge, Windsor. The first is a conventional, but nonetheless good-quality, turn-of-the-century bracket clock in an ebonized case of broken-arch form, with carrying-handle on top and fish-scale frets at the sides. In the corners of the case 296
below the dial are open-work gilt-brass spandrels backed by crimson silk. The white enamel dial with Roman hour numerals and no five-minute figures has pierced gilt hands typical of the period *c*.1800, and gilt bracket feet. The two-train movement is signed 'Johnson, Gray's Inn Passage', and Britten places this maker—John Johnson, of 9 Gray's Inn Passage—as active 1770–99. This must be one of his later clocks; and the next clock is much later.

This is a pleasant Victorian mantel clock, not too large, and again in an ebonized case, the top broken-arched and surmounted by a pedestal tapering to a

296. *Bracket clock by Johnson, Gray's Inn Passage.* (The Queen Mother's Collection)

297. *Bracket clock by Payne & Co., 163 New Bond Street.* (The Queen Mother's Collection)

basket-of-fruit finial. Two other gilt finials grace the front corners of the broken arch, with caryatids in the angles below them, a border of gilt ornament below the glazed door in the front of the clock, and scrolling gilt feet. The arch of the dial contains a subsidiary for
297 strike/silent, while the gilt spandrels are of the winged cherub design that usually enriches seventeenth-century clocks, a perfect example of the Victorians' love of reproducing past glories, but often in an 'improved' form, which, happily, has not happened in this case, the general impression being quite restrained. The two-train movement with pierced steel hands is signed 'Payne & Co. 163 New Bond Street, London. No. 3531'. Britten places William Payne at this address during the period 1830–50, although, in fact, they remained there well into the present century; and it might be said that this very pleasing little clock stands at the threshold dividing the old-fashioned craft-based clock-manufacture from the machine-made, quantity-produced, over-decorated and under-designed clock which has become identified in the lay mind with the archetypal Victorian timekeeper.

7 Royal pretensions—to be or not to be?

From time to time, auctioneers handling the sale of works of art will feature a clock or watch which has pretensions to an association with royalty; after the physical attributes and artistic merits of the object have been catalogued, the provenance starts with that time-worn cliché 'Family tradition has it that . . .'. Lest any auctioneer feels that he has been unfairly treated in the foregoing statement, let it be at once admitted that such attributions are just as commonplace elsewhere: public and private collections, special exhibitions and the like have all contributed to this state of affairs. Even the Royal Collection itself is not immune from possessing objects whose hitherto-accepted origins must be open to doubt, in the light of the modern analytical approach to such things.

The cumulative effect of unproven attributions is insidious; a single example will suffice to illustrate this. In 1937, a Loan Exhibition of Royal Treasures, as it is usually described, was mounted as a special attraction for visitors to the Coronation of King George VI. The well-known art journal *The Connoisseur* noted that it consisted solely of 'treasures formerly owned by Royal Personages and of gifts bestowed by them'. The display included a wide array of objects ranging from pictures, furniture, costumes and jewellery to clocks and watches. Charitable as were its aims, this exhibition nevertheless included many objects which would certainly have been rejected had they been subject to any kind of informed and critical selection process.

In recent years several of the watches included in that exhibition have come on the market at London auction rooms—such items will be found in the pages that follow—and, quite naturally and properly, the related catalogue entries have noted their presence in that earlier event, thereby bestowing an aura of authenticity upon them which may not always have been entirely deserved.

It is not the purpose of this present chapter to deride often long-cherished beliefs: many of the objects concerned are intrinsically of great interest, occasionally almost unique, so that their true provenance may be regarded as only a secondary issue anyway. Were there to be any real evidence of fraudulent intent behind any doubtful royal attribution, the situation might well be different; any such indication is the exception rather than the rule.

The following pages, therefore, set out to do two things. First, three objects which have all been held to have had royal associations dating back to the sixteenth century—one of these, indeed, forms part of the present-day Royal Collection and is said to have been acquired as authentic by Queen Victoria—will be investigated in some depth. Secondly, as large a selection as space will permit—although taken almost at random and from a wide variety of sources—of objects claiming to have had some kind of royal background, will be reviewed. As an adjunct to this last, there has been collected together at Appendix Two all the timepieces with royal attributions—whether real or imaginary—to appear in a handful of catalogues published in the nineteenth century in connection with some of the most important auction sales and public exhibitions of antiquities held during that period, as well as, for comparison, entries of a similar type in the 1937 exhibition. Many—perhaps most—of the objects listed or described will, however, long since have been lost sight of, so that, in the absence of the 'corpse', no final conclusion as to provenance can be possible. The sheer scale of the phenomenon, however, will be self-evident.

Nowadays, attitudes to such objects, when they come within the purview of those expert in the appropriate disciplines within our national institutions, have notably hardened, so that what might have been displayed, once upon a time, with a tentative—or even substantive—royal attribution, tends not to appear at all these days unless it survives exposure to a much more clinical and impartial assessment than ever used to be the case.

It is a matter of wholly fortuitous good fortune that the first three objects to be discussed have all, in recent months, been subjected to expert assessment by Hugh Tait, Deputy Keeper in the Department of Mediaeval and Later Antiquities at the British Museum. They illustrate very well the scrupulous care which has to be exercised, when endeavouring to authenticate any claim connected with antiquities for the purpose of display—especially to a public which, thanks mainly to what are now called 'heritage interests', is far better informed than heretofore. It also applies when establishing a market value or, perhaps, when permitting or restraining the export from Great Britain of any really fine works of art. It may well prove to be the unseen influence of such official bodies as the Review Committee for the Export of Works of Art that has brought about this much more analytical and objective approach to establishing the truth about claims of origin in this field.

The first object belongs to the Worshipful Company

298. (Below) *The so-called Mary, Queen of Scots Skull Watch: general front view, with outer case.* (Clockmakers' Company, London)

299. (Above right) *The Skull Watch, opened to show the dial.* (Clockmaker's Company, London)

300. (Right) *The movement of the Skull Watch.* (Clockmakers' Company, London)

of Clockmakers, who display it among their Collection, which is open to the public. Until fairly recently, it was only on loan to them, having before that been privately owned by the purchaser who first acquired it from the Dick Lauder family, among whom so many of its origins seem to lie.

Known for decades as 'the Mary, Queen of Scots, Skull Watch', this object takes the form of a silver skull, which is pierced and engraved all over with religious
298 and mythological scenes as well as quotations in Latin from the works of Horace. Watches of this kind, often called *memento mori* watches and supposedly a product of the morbid curiosity about death which preoccupied generations in the past, are by no means uncommon in the seventeenth century and later; what particularly sets this example apart from all others is its large size. Without its close-fitting protective leather outer case, it measures no less than $3\frac{1}{2}$ inches by $2\frac{1}{2}$ inches and is correspondingly heavy.

The watch dial and movement are hidden inside the skull, and access is obtained by pulling down the jaw bone, which is hinged at the back. The mechanism has
299 been greatly altered over the years, having now been
300 converted to lever escapement, although it also includes a striking-train which is probably original. The silver dial has two hands and is engraved with a scene representing Saturn swallowing his children. The signature on the movement is 'Moysant Blois'.

Preliminary investigations quickly revealed that this was not to be the story of one watch but of three, all reputed to have belonged to the Scottish Queen. The earliest account of any such watch comes from the records of the Society of Antiquaries, at Burlington House in London's Piccadilly, and is dated 14th November 1822.

On that day, a certain Henry Wansey, who was a Fellow of the Society, exhibited three drawings of a watch, along with a detailed description of its Latin inscriptions and minutely engraved scenes. He also added his own observations. These were as follows:

(a) The watch was made of 'silver, thickly gilt'.
(b) It was 'in the possession of a person at Salisbury; and is said to have been pledged to a pawnbroker of Edinburgh about eighty years ago by a decayed branch of the family of Sir Robert Melville, Mary's private secretary'.
(c) It bore 'the inscription: EX DONO FR.R.FR AD MARIAM KEG SCOTORVM ET FR. The arms of France and Scotland, on separate shields, are engraved on the sides of the jaws'.
(d) 'In its top is a square hole, conjectured to have been intended for the insertion of a small crucifix.'

The drawings which Mr Wansey showed are happily still preserved by the Society and will be referred to again later in this account.

Chronologically, the next reference to appear is dated 1840 and once again has some connection with the Society of Antiquaries in that it is taken from a work 302
entitled *Historical and Literary Curiosities*, by another Fellow, the (even then) late Charles John Smith. The excerpt, which consists of a line-engraving by Smith together with two printed pages of text, is entitled *A memento-mori Watch presented by Mary Stuart, Queen of Scots, to her Maid of Honour Mary Seaton.* This is the first appearance in print of the watch now owned by the Clockmakers' Company and formerly in the possession of Sir Thomas Dick Lauder. Despite the fact that there is nothing on the watch itself to provide any link with either Mary, Queen of Scots, or Mary Seaton, this legend is published as historical fact. C. J. Smith died, as it happened, in 1838—two years before his work was published—but the engraved illustration bears his signature and is said to be taken from the work of the late Mr Hugh Irvine, so that it must seem likely that the watch was in existence before, say, 1835. However, comparison of the illustration and text description of this watch with that represented in Wansey's drawing of 1822 shows that they do not relate to the same object—apart from which, the latter was then in Salisbury, and the former with the family of Dick Lauder.

In 1849, there is a reference back—in *Archaeologia* (p. 9)—to the Wansey watch, in which the vital inscription is quoted accurately, but with an inaccurate addition, viz. 'with the date 1560', an error that was subsequently repeated by later writers.

Yet a third so-called 'Mary, Queen of Scots, skull watch' makes its first appearance in 1865. Harking back once again to the *Proceedings of the Society of Antiquaries* (p. 123), we find that on 4th May 'John Browne, Esq. exhibited a watch', which he then incorrectly identified as the one in the Wansey drawings of 1822. A comparison between the two reveals many differences, for example:

(a) The inscription now reads: 'EX DONO FR^{S}R FR. AD MARIA S^{T} ^{de} SCOTORUM FR. REGINA.'

While this inscription is not very intelligible, it corresponds exactly with that on the third skull watch, which, unlike the one in Wansey's drawings, still exists and of which details will be given later on.

(b) The two shields are not on the jaws, as in the 1822 drawings, but on the sides of the skull, and the cartouches containing the coats-of-arms are of rococo form, an impossibility before the middle of the eighteenth century.

301. *The companion Skull Watch, formerly in the Belin Collection.* (Sotheby's, London)

(c) The profile of the skull is entirely different and the jaws are not solid, as on the drawings.
(d) The word *'tuque'* is incorrectly written as *'inque'*, at the back of the skull of John Browne's watch.
(e) In 1822 it was 'conjectured' that a crucifix might be screwed into the top of the skull; by 1865, it has become a fact.
(f) The dividing line between the Crucifixion scene and the Garden of Eden scene runs from front to back, whereas, in the 1822 drawing, it runs across the skull from one side to the other.
(g) The engraved compartment of pseudo-Gothic form enclosing the Figure of Time, which is above the hinge at the back of the skull, is not mentioned at all in 1822, either in the drawings or the accompanying description.

It is to be noted that, on the Dick Lauder/Clockmakers' Company watch, the Figure of Time is similarly engraved within a like compartment at the rear, but most of the handle of the scythe has not been engraved; this indicates the error of a mere copyist rather than that of an original artist, since it occurs after the foliate scrolls pass in front of the scythe.

Since the third watch now comes more fully into the picture, it merits some descriptive account before further consideration of the documentary records. Superficially, this watch is a facsimile of the Dick Lauder watch—or *vice versa*—save only that it is silver-gilt 301
rather than silver and that, in addition to the integral carrying-eye and chain depending from the top of the skull of the latter, there projects a vertical threaded bolt ostensibly to take a small tortoiseshell and silver crucifix which, however, looks completely out of place and period when *in situ*. The workmanship of this ancillary does not compare, either, with that of the watch itself. There are a number of differences in fine detail, which were brought out during the course of the investigation, but the only other difference of great substance is the absence altogether, on the Dick Lauder watch, of any presentation inscription of the type seen on the silver-gilt version and in the account and drawings of the Wansey watch.

Returning now to the chronological review of recorded references, the next in order—the very nature of the work makes it almost inevitable—comes from E. J. Wood's *Curiosities of Clocks and Watches*, which was published in 1866. Here, a long account of the Dick 303
Lauder watch appears on pp. 236–9, and there is an illustration of it on the title page. Incorrectly, Wood

302. (Above) *The drawing of the Skull Watch by C. J. Smith, from* Historical and Literary Curiosities, *1852.* (Guildhall Library, City of London)

303. (Below) *The title page of E. J. Wood's* Curiosities of Clocks and Watches, *1866.* (Clockmakers' Company, London)

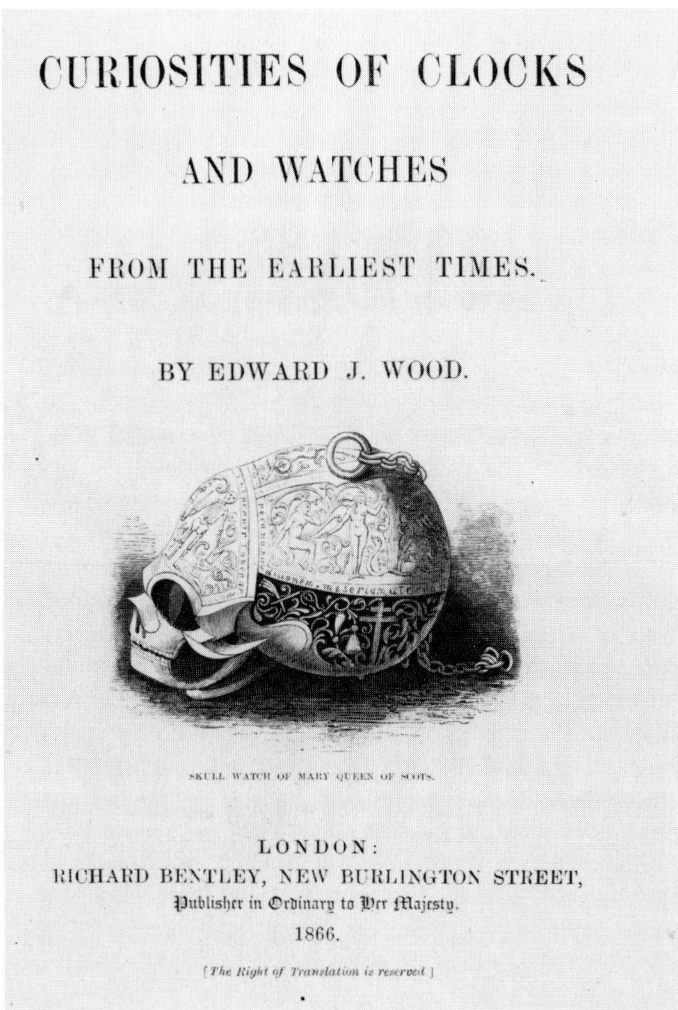
CURIOSITIES OF CLOCKS

AND WATCHES

FROM THE EARLIEST TIMES.

BY EDWARD J. WOOD.

SKULL WATCH OF MARY QUEEN OF SCOTS.

LONDON:
RICHARD BENTLEY, NEW BURLINGTON STREET,
Publisher in Ordinary to Her Majesty.
1866.

[*The Right of Translation is reserved.*]

states that this watch can be identified with Wansey's version of 1822.

There is then a gap of over thirty years, to the first appearance of what has come to be regarded as one of the great books on antiquarian horology, and, in later revised, even rewritten, editions, remains to this day a standard work. This is F. J. Britten's *Former Clock and Watchmakers and their Work*, which was first published in 1894, the next—and subsequent—editions adopting the more familiar style *Old Clocks and Watches and their Makers*. In this first edition, however, is illustrated, at figure 31, the engraved scene of the Nativity which occurs on both existing watches yet is not mentioned either in the drawings or description of 1822. Both contain the curious error: *'GLORIA ECCLESIS . . .'* instead of *'Gloria in excelsis Deo . . .'*. A much later edition of this work, the sixth, which had been revised and brought up-to-date by F. W. Britten, son of the author, and which is considered the best of all the versions of the original work—since seventh and subsequent editions were, to all intents and purposes, entirely new books by fresh authors—referred, when it appeared in 1932, to the silver-gilt watch 'formerly in the possession of Miss Browne, now in the private collection of Mr. Percy Webster' (p. 139).

Percy Webster (1862–1938) was one of London's great horological dealers in his day, his influence extending over forty years, and being succeeded in business by his son Malcolm. He seems to have acquired, even during his own lifetime and certainly since his death, a somewhat apocryphal reputation for unjustifiable over-restoration. He certainly applied his precepts in such things to his own personal collection, however; and this was undoubtedly one of the finest of its kind in private hands. It was finally dispersed in 1954, and the catalogue issued by Sotheby & Co for the second of the sales concerned—on 19th October—described the silver-gilt watch at Lot 137. By now, it has acquired a movement signed 'Jehan Moisant a Bloys', whereas in 1865, when it belonged to John Browne, the maker's name was given as 'C. Bloies'. The dial, too, is now silver with an alarm disc, whereas it had once a modern substitution signed 'Moore, London'. It is significant that, in a substantially illustrated catalogue for the Webster sale, Sotheby's omitted to include a picture of the skull watch; yet they did illustrate it, when it once again came up for sale as part of the Belin Collection, dispersed on 29th November 1979 and of which it formed Lot 53. This time, however, the compiler of the catalogue added 'The style of construction and engraving would seem to indicate a date between 1790 and 1830 and it is probable that this watch was made as a romantic manifestation of the earlier legend.'

Hugh Tait adds two further comments to what has been set out above, both of them particularly germane to this strange rigmarole. Although the 1822 documents include no measurements, the three drawings seem to indicate that the watch was probably the normal small-scale form watch made as a skull—these are a well-recognized type—whereas the two existing watches are both excessively large and heavy. Secondly, although the engraving on these two watches is not identical and there are detailed differences in its quality, it does seem to be closely related, sufficiently so to suggest a common origin, especially in the repetition of iconographic irregularities such as the combination of St John and the kneeling Mary Magdalen—instead of the Virgin Mary—at the foot of the Cross, and the inclusion of a bird and a barking dog in the scene of 'The Temptation'. Nevertheless, the style of the engraving is certainly not of a sufficiently high quality to grace a Court object of the late sixteenth–early seventeenth centuries. There remains the possibility—which is quite incapable of being proved—that the third watch, said to have been in Salisbury in 1822, gave rise to the creation of the two versions at present known to exist; and the theory that they were created as evocations of the past and that their specific attribution to Mary, Queen of Scots, came later, remains the most attractive on the basis of the evidence presented.

The second object with traditional associations with the Scottish Queen is a sand-glass in the British Museum collection. This formerly belonged to Courtenay Ilbert, whose massive accumulation of clocks, watches 304
and other timekeepers was purchased for the nation by the late Mr Gilbert Edgar; before that, according to the Catalogue prepared by Christie's in 1958 for the sale of the Ilbert clocks—an historic sale because, in fact, it never took place—the sand-glass had formed part of the Herbert Elkington Collection. Nevertheless, there lurks in the author's mind an account given him personally by Courtenay Ilbert, to the effect that the glass had come from a safe, bombed during the war but known to have contained horological relics, and the contents of which had been bought 'sight unseen', as the auctioneers say. If any other details were given, however, they cannot now be recollected.

The above-mentioned catalogue entry reads verbatim as follows:

Lot 92 THE MARY QUEEN OF SCOTS SAND GLASS—$3\frac{1}{2}$ in. high—in leather cylindrical case tooled and gilt with monogram. The ebony case with moulded borders, turned and baluster pillar supports containing four hour glasses for hour, three-quarters hour, half-hour and quarter-hour, with recessed panels to the top and base, painted in colours with 305
the arms of Scotland and France, in cylindrical 306
leather case with cover, the borders tooled with scrolls and bands, the top with the monogram representing 'M' for Mary entwined with the Greek 'F', representing King Francis II of France, who was the first husband of the Queen.

This sand glass is believed to have been originally the personal property of Mary, Queen of Scots or at least connected with her. A similar monogram is found on a

304. *The so-called Mary, Queen of Scots sandglass: general view with outer case.* (British Museum)

305. *One end of the sandglass, showing supposed royal arms.* (British Museum)

306. *The opposite end of the sandglass, with the supposed arms of France.* (British Museum)

307 *small cannon reputed to have belonged to the Scottish Queen, illustrated in 'The Relics of the Royal House of Stuart' by Gibbs & Shelton, p. 11.* *

From the Collection of the late Herbert Elkington, Esq.

Exhibited: 'Masterpieces of British Art and Craftsmanship', 1954, No. 126; 'Five Centuries of British Timekeeping', 1955, Section [*sic*], p. 41; Goldsmiths' Hall, 1958.

This object has never been displayed publicly by the British Museum—a cause of some chagrin to the late Mr Edgar, who had a high opinion of it. Of itself, it is a thing of great interest and some beauty; nevertheless, it also encapsulates several anomalies and strange features which, taken together, preclude any real likelihood of a provenance along the lines of that indicated above.

It is possible to arrive at a 'latest date' for the sand-glass, by reference to another object in the British Museum collections. This is the signet ring that belonged to Mary, and Hugh Tait, in describing the characteristics of the ring in the relevant Catalogue—*Jewellery through 7,000 Years*, British Museum Publications, 1976, pp. 248–9, item no. 422—writes:

The Greek letters which compose the cypher stand for the names Francis (Francis II of France, to whom she was married, aged sixteen, in 1558) and Mary. Since after her marriage she no longer bore the arms of Scotland alone and after the death of Francis in 1560 she would no longer have used the cypher with his name, it has been assumed that the ring was made in France, shortly before 1558. . . .

The same argument must apply to the sand-glass; yet the coat-of-arms thereon turns out, on investigation, to be the Scottish version as used between 1603 and 1707; it was certainly not in existence prior to the earlier date. Furthermore the lion in the first quarter is facing the wrong way, an unbelievable error. Finally, of course, the Irish harp does not occur as a quartering before 1603 and was never associated with Mary, Queen of Scots, anyway.

It would appear to follow from all this that the cypher of Mary and Francis stamped on the leather carrying-case is a deliberate forgery, even though such a cypher was used between 1558 and 1560, as mentioned above. In any event, the tooled decoration is rudimentary—'coarse' is probably a better word—and hardly of the quality it would be reasonable to expect in a truly 'royal' object. The most likely explanation appears to be that both hour-glass and case originated

* The correct title of this work is simply *The Royal House of Stuart*, and the contributors include William Gibb and John Skelton. *Vide* Appendix Two, and the exhibition having the same title held in London in 1888.

not earlier than the beginning of the eighteenth century, and that they were subsequently fraudulently enriched; without the embellishments, they would be perfectly feasible as genuine artefacts from that period. It might be revealing, were it possible to remove the suspect features on the sand-glass for examination, but so far no method of doing this has been devised without the risk of consequent damage being unacceptably high.

There is another timekeeper said to have belonged to Mary, Queen of Scots, with which it will be convenient to deal briefly at this point. Geoffrey Harmsworth, describing the watches in the Usher Art Gallery, in Lincoln, for the magazine *Everybody's*, some years ago now—the magazine itself is long since defunct—wrote:

> Historically, the most notable watch in the Usher Collection
> 308 is one that belonged to Mary, Queen of Scots. Made at Blois, between 1570 and 1580, by Pierre Duhamel, it has a white enamelled dial, with only one hand and no glass. Watch glasses were not introduced until about 1600. The inner case is of plain 22-carat gold with black shagreen outer case studded with gold pins and engraved with the monogram of the ill-fated Queen.

307. *The cypher on a cannon believed to have belonged to Mary, Queen of Scots: illustration from William Gibb's* The Royal House of Stuart, *1890.* (Guildhall Library, City of London)

Stylistically, this watch would now be placed unhesitatingly in the seventeenth century although, when Mr Harmsworth wrote his article, it may be that knowledge was not so far advanced. In any event, Pierre Duhamel—a noted French maker of the most decorative watches, examples of his work being in several public collections including that in the British Museum—has now been identified in Blois about 1650 and is said to have gone to Geneva in 1663. Both this one and another watch in the Usher Collection, incidentally, seem to have emanated from an earlier accumulation formed by the Reverend Hawkins, when that was dispersed in 1895.

The most important of these supposed sixteenth-century royal relics, and the one to be described next, is comparable with the sand-glass in that it has virtually no documented antecedent history, certainly not of any antiquity; yet, since it forms part of the present-day Royal Collection, it can still qualify as an authentic royal timepiece, but for an entirely different reason! This is, of course, the so-called Anne Boleyn Wedding
309 Clock.

This clock seems to have put in its first appearance in print, in the Catalogue of the Auction Sale of the contents of Horace Walpole's home at Strawberry Hill, in 1842—relevant verbatim extracts will be found in Appendix Two. Walpole had settled at this house near Twickenham, which he turned into 'a little Gothic Castle', in 1747; and this sale, extending over no less than twenty-four days, must have been the veritable Mentmore of the last century. The clock, put up as Lot 48 on day seventeen—which was 13th May—was purchased for the sum of £110 5s on behalf of Her Majesty Queen Victoria and has graced the Royal Collection ever since, being normally accommodated at Windsor Castle.

When the manuscript *Strawberry Hill Accounts—a Record of Expenditure in Building, Furnishing, &c. kept by Mr. Horace Walpole from 1747 to 1795* was eventually printed, as recently as 1927, with notes and index by Dr Paget Toynbee, a full-page plate of the Library taken from a contemporary print showed the clock in position in a niche in one corner of the room, to the left of the fireplace and completely dwarfed by the imposing Gothic-style bookcases. There is, however, no mention whatever of the clock in the text. Such earlier provenance as is available, so it would appear, comes from the Sale catalogue, where the clock is said to have been given to Horace Walpole by Lady Elizabeth Germaine.

Lady Germain—the *Dictionary of National Biography* prefers to omit the final 'e'—was born in 1680, the daughter of Charles, second Earl of Berkeley, and died in 1769. Familiarly known as 'Lady Betty', she was the second wife of Sir John Germain (1650–1718), a soldier of fortune who left her a large inheritance, which included the Arundel cameos. Germain himself was reputedly the son of William II, Prince of Orange, and accompanied William III to England, serving under him in Ireland and Flanders. Created a baronet in 1698, his first wife, Lady Mary Mordaunt, left him much property.

Little except, perhaps, opportunity can be derived from these antecedents—opportunity occasioned by historic contact with the monarchy of England, not only through Germain but through the Berkeleys, and probably even through Lady Mordaunt, whose surname is that of the earls of Peterborough or possibly related to Sir John Mordaunt, who had been a Privy Councillor in 1526. The clock could have passed down any of these lines.

It is perhaps not quite true to say that the clock has no published antecedents prior to 1842; but what there are derive from Walpole himself and are tantalizingly uninformative, almost as if he were hiding something! For example, in 1774 he first produced and published a catalogue of the contents of his home, for the greater edification of the general public. Ten years later there appeared an enlarged version, which is entitled *A description of the Villa of Mr. Horace Walpole . . . at Strawberry-Hill near Twickenham, Middlesex. With an*
314 *Inventory of the Furniture, Pictures, Curiosities &c.* Dealing with the Library—the work is conveniently divided by rooms or other manageable spaces—there is a print illustrating vividly the Gothic nature of the décor and appurtenances; this same print is reproduced in the 1927 edition of the Strawberry Hill Accounts edited by Dr Paget Toynbee, already mentioned. The clock can just be discerned in a niche between the bookcases, and the accompanying text has this to say of it:

308. *Watch said to have belonged to Mary, Queen of Scots, and made by Pierre Duhamel.* (Usher Gallery, Lincoln)

A clock of silver gilt, richly chased, engraved and ornamented with fleur de lys, little heads &c, on the top sits a lion holding the arms of England, which are also on the sides. This was a present from Henry 8th. to Anne Boleyn; and since, from Lady Elizabeth Germaine to Mr. Walpole. On the weights are the initial letters of Henry and Anne, within true lovers knots; at top, Dieu et mon Droit; at bottom, The most happy . . . One of the weights, agreeably to the indelicacy of that monarch's gallantry, is in a shape very conformable to the last motto. The pedestal is adorned with small heads of bronze gilt of the age of Henry 8th, but which did not belong to the clock.

The last sentence must suggest that some tampering with the fabric had already been detected; but what is to be made of another Walpole reference? This is taken from a letter written by him from Strawberry Hill on 14th October 1760. It is addressed to George Montagu and recounts an unexpected and not entirely welcome visit from the Duke of York. Speaking of this distinguished intruder, Walpole writes:

He was, as he always is, extremely good-humoured; and I, as I am not always, extremely respectful. He stayed two hours, nobody with him but Morrison; I showed him all my castle, the pictures of the Pretender's sons, and that type of the Reformation, Harry the Eighth's *measure*, moulded into a weight to the clock he gave Anne Boleyn—but observe my luck; he would have the sanctum sanctorum in the library opened. . . .

This extract comes from Mrs Paget Toynbee's *Letters of Horace Walpole*, volume III (Oxford, 1903), and there are suggestions from some authorities that Walpole was making an obliquely phallic reference to Henry VIII, with the emphasis he placed on the word 'measure' in relation to the physical appearance of at least one of the weights. That there is some kind of mystery surrounding the weights cannot be doubted, however, as will be seen shortly when they come to be described.

Determined to extract the greatest possible value out of the Strawberry Hill catalogue—thereby attracting more potential buyers and higher prices—the compilers supplied, by way of a 'curtain-raiser', an introductory text which highlighted some of the more mouth-watering objects which were to be dispersed. Page xiv of this refers to the clock in the following 317
terms:

The gallantry of Henry the Eighth is conspicuously set forth

309. (Above) *The so-called Anne Boleyn Wedding Clock.* (Royal Collection)

310. (Right) *The side doors of the Anne Boleyn clock, arranged to show the different engraved decorations to be found on each surface.* (Royal Collection)

311. (Below) *The movement of the clock, viewed from the back.* (Royal Collection)

312. (Left) *The movement, viewed from the front.* (Royal Collection)

313. (Above) *The weights of the clock, showing differences in the engraved decoration and overall shape.* (Royal Collection)

314. (Left) *View of the Library at Strawberry Hill, showing the Anne Boleyn clock hanging in a niche in the left-hand corner of the room: this appears opposite page 33 in the edition printed by Thomas Kirgate in 1784 of* A Description of the Villa of Mr. Horace Walpole at Strawberry Hill . . . with an Inventory of the Furniture, Pictures, Curiosities, etc. (Guildhall Library, City of London)

in the little clock of silver gilt (drawn below), which he presented to Anne Boleyn on the morning of his marriage. It is richly chased and engraved and ornamented with fleur de lys, &c. On the top sits a lion bearing the arms of England. The weights, which are gilt, are curiously chased with the initials of Henry and Anne within true-lovers'-knots. One bears the inscription, 'The most happye', the other, the royal motto. This love token was, doubtless, meant as an emblem of enduring affection. It remains the same, after an interval of more than three centuries; but four years only after it was given, the object of Henry's *eternal* love was sacrificed on the scaffold. The clock still goes on; it should have stopped forever when Anne Boleyn died!

A small illustration of the clock and another, supposed to represent the initials above the lovers' knots and that curious saw 'The most happye', accompany this text, and further reference to these will be made later. The
316 next printed reference to the clock also takes the form of an illustration, this time very much larger since it forms the frontispiece to a book on horology which, curious though it must seem, was written and published in France. This little-known work, by one Pierre Dubois, is entitled *Histoire de l'horlogerie depuis son origine jusqu'à nos jours* . . . and was published in Paris in 1849; of Dubois virtually nothing is known beyond the fact that he wrote several works on horology between 1845 and 1858, including one about the famous collection of Prince Soltykoff. In the present instance, the frontispiece is the only manifestation of the clock; admittedly the caption does make it free-standing, yet one might have expected some mention in the main text as well.

From that time forward, the clock is frequently referred to both in serious and popular works on horology; and, sadly, with each re-telling the descriptions and illustrations vary in salient detail to the 315
point where, even making every allowance for artistic not to mention literary licence, it has sometimes to be questioned whether it is always the same clock that is being depicted. One or two examples will suffice to illustrate this state of affairs.

In 1873, the Reverend H. L. Nelthropp, sometime Master of the Clockmakers' Company, published his little book, *A Treatise on Watch-Work, Past and Present*. On page 69 he describes the clock as follows:

PORTABLE CLOCK, presented by Henry the Eighth to Anne Boleyn on their marriage, now at Windsor Castle, the property of her Majesty Queen Victoria. It is thus described by Horace Walpole: 'A clock of silver-gilt (brass), richly chased, engraved, and ornamented with fleur de lys, ... On the weights are the initial letters of Henry and Anne . . . at the bottom 'The most happye'. One of the weights, agreeably to the indelicacy of that monarch's gallantry, is in a shape very conformable to the last motto' [whatever that may be supposed to mean]. The movement is quite modern.

James Kendal, writing in his *A History of Watches and other Timekeepers* in 1892, at pages 57–8, states

There is in possession of Her Majesty at Windsor Castle the case of a clock which was given by Henry VIII to Anne Boleyn . . . but the original movement has been unfortunately replaced by a modern one. . . . The Rev. H. L. Nelthropp and other writers speak of it as a portable clock. I have not been able to see it; but whatever it may be now, the mention of the weights seems to negative the idea that it was originally driven by springs.

On the matter of the age of the movement, no less an authority than F. J. Britten changed his mind from edition to edition. In 1894, in his foundation book *Former Clock and Watchmakers and their Work*, he wrote:'The present movement in it is a modern one.'

Retitled *Old Clocks and Watches and their Makers*, he had decided, by the fifth edition, of 1922: 'Though not modern, it is certainly later than the middle of the sixteenth century.' Finally, in the sixth edition, he had decided: 'Though not modern, it is certainly not earlier than the end of the seventeenth century.'

So much for documentary background. Before turning to considerations of the clock itself, in relation to these as well as on its own account—always supposing that we are dealing with one and the same timekeeper—there is one other curious circumstance to be touched upon. It has been rumoured that some considerable time elapsed between 13th May 1842—the day on which this clock actually came under the hammer and was knocked down to the Queen—and the time when it was formally delivered to its new owner; and that during that time it reposed in the Vulliamy workshops. While it would certainly be convenient if this were so—it might indeed explain a lot of the disturbing features about the clock's present make-up—a search of the relevant archives reveals no precise record as to when it was actually handed over to its royal owner.

It is now time to examine the clock which has recently been in the custody of the British Museum for critical appraisal. It will be convenient to consider case, movement and weights separately, if only because it is difficult to relate each of the several anomalies that will be mentioned to all of these basic components of the clock. This is one of the major puzzles so far as this particular object is concerned.

The case

1. The Sale Catalogue of 1842 states that this is silver gilt; and this same error is repeated from time to time up to and including the 1937 Loan Exhibition of Royal Treasures Catalogue (*q.v.*). Nelthropp states that it is 'silver gilt (brass)'—whatever that is intended to mean—and, in fairness, the 1937 Catalogue only uses the term 'silver gilt' in the heading: in the descriptive text the clock is represented as 'gilt'.

However, the clock case is of gilt metal, which should not, normally, be confused with silver gilt. Furthermore, certain elements of it might appear to be electrotypes, a wholly nineteenth-century technique; since small parts of the case are still lacking, it is conceivable that these replaced other deficient features.

2. Starting from the top, the lion and shield it is holding are of entirely different quality and colour. The lion is

315. (Right) *An illustration of the same clock from* Archaeologia, *Vol. XXXIV, 1852.* (Guildhall Library, City of London)

rather fine and reminiscent, on a small scale, of a good Augsburg animal; the shield is coarse, and it certainly appears to have been cut into at the top, left and right, in order to accommodate the supporting paws of the lion.

3. Beneath, the open-work cupola has a large missing section at the back; in any event, it is out of character with the rest of the clock, while the four busts in relief, one of which forms the central element of each of the curving triangular segments, has suffered badly. *See* 4, below.

4. Level with the base of the cupola and forming a parapet on the top of the rectangular—and largest—section of the case is a fretted gallery, using pierced fleurs de lys as the motif, interspersed at the centre of each side as well as at the corners with turned baluster finials on moulded rectangular plinths. Where these intermediate finials coincide with the relief busts referred to in 3, above, the latter have suffered badly by being, quite literally, squashed to accommodate the curved backs of the finials. It is an inconceivable and incomprehensible manifestation of artistic vandalism.

5. Next, beneath a moulded cornice, comes a cast frieze of which the central motif on each surface is a bust in relief, set in a round, concave recess. Apart from a small area missing, this does not seem to have suffered unduly.

6. At the next level come the large rectangular surfaces accommodating the dial, side doors and rear panel. One very strange feature is at once discernible. In the upper spandrel areas above the dial and doors, circular turned bosses have been superimposed on whatever engraved decoration filled these spaces. In at least one case, inspection from inside the case reveals that a triangular area corresponding to a spandrel has been cut round—and one imagines, temporarily removed, for some purpose or other. In any event, these bosses with their central protruding hubs, reminiscent of the iron plates that used to be employed to brace the bulging walls of old buildings, are wholly out of place and look it; as for any purpose they may have served, it is difficult even to form a conjecture. Turning to the side doors, their
310 gilding is of a different colour from the rest of the structure; and, for some strange reason, they are engraved both inside and out, the royal arms being always discernible when they are closed and a floral arabesque coming into view on opening.

7. Finally comes a cast plinth on a moulded skirting, the decorative elements of conventional design and not specially distinguished.

8. The case separates between the lower edge of the frieze and the upper edge of the dial plate and comparable levels on sides and back; thus, the cupola and frieze can be disengaged from the basic rectangular

316. *Coloured frontispiece depicting the clock from* L'Histoire de l'horlogerie *by Pierre Dubois, 1849.* (Clockmakers' Company, London)

317. *The clock and 'true lovers' knots' as depicted in Mr. George Robins's catalogue for the auction sale of the contents of Strawberry Hill, in 1842.* (British Library)

structure into which the clock mechanism fits, and this can be inserted, in fact, from either end of the rectangle, being held in place by pins. In practice, it is easier done by placing the case over the movement and sliding it down into place. When the upper part of the case is removed, it will be seen to fit on to brass angled uprights at each corner of the lower portion; it will also be clear that these have had extensions added to them at some time or another, and these extensions incorporate holes, some plugged, and the purpose of which is a complete mystery. The presence of these extensions must, however, of itself point to some corresponding alteration in the overall height of the case.

Currently, there are as many views regarding the authenticity or otherwise of this clock case as there are informed horologists to view it. There will, however, certainly be common ground in accepting that it has been very substantially altered in a variety of ways; and that, of itself, must tend slightly to diminish the likelihood that it is wholly bogus or nothing more than a nineteenth-century romantic evocation. Although, at the time of writing, no comparable clock case with genuine sixteenth-century antecedents has been located, certain features of this one do seem to strike familiar notes; this could simply mean that elements of an early case have been 'cobbled together', and what appear nowadays to be alterations and anomalies represent nothing more than the modifications that became necessary in order to give practical effect to such a construction.

The movement

1. The presence of brass wheels in this clock used to be regarded as prime evidence that it could not possibly be of sixteenth-century origin; nowadays, that is by no means so certain. Difficulties in preparing brass were certainly largely overcome by the second half of the period in question, when it became a much commoner
311 material in horological use. Whether one could extend
312 that usage backwards by the relatively short time span
needed to bring it within the present context—say, 1533—is a moot point.

2. The simple posted frame of the mechanism, with its plain steel corner pillars, could very well be accommodated within present knowledge of the practice *c.*1600 in such matters. The overall concept might well be Flemish. Again, however, it is a matter for speculation as to whether such usage could be entertained more than seventy years previous to that date; it must be said that it could certainly post-date it also.

The weights

1. These are of lead sheathed in gilt copper, which has been engraved. Not only are they not of the same size, even their shape differs: the longer has a rounded bulbous end to it, the other terminates abruptly.

2. There are most noticeable differences in the engraving, both in quality and content, as between one weight and the other. This ranges from such things as
different spelling of a word—'DIU' in one case, for 313
example, as against the usual 'DIEU' in the other—to the inclusion of a depth of detail in one by comparison with which the work on the other looks positively rudimentary. The representation of the true lovers' knots is entirely different on the two weights, as are also the representations of the initials 'H' and 'A'. Real similarity exists between them mainly in the deployment of the various decorative elements, and their respective proportions. Otherwise, careful examination can point only to the conclusion that one is a clumsy copy of the other.

So what is to be made of this clock? It has sometimes been said that the finer of the two weights is the only wholly original component, and the rest has been built to match! If so, it has involved a lot of imagination, not to mention artistic and technical licence, and it is no wonder that the clock has for long been the subject of investigation and speculatory interest. Artistic licence certainly comes into some of the earlier representations of the clock, as witness the squat, sinister-looking version shown in the Strawberry Hill Catalogue, and the elongated representation included by Pierre Dubois in his book. Endless time can be spent identifying the differences between these and the clock itself—even if you admit that the same object is concerned in all cases—yet it must be suspected that such activity will be largely unproductive. Most authorities seem to have agreed that the likelihood of any real connection between the clock—or, indeed, any part of it—and Henry VIII or his unfortunate spouse is so remote as to be discounted. In fairness, however, it must be said that one museum expert whose speciality has been early European domestic clockwork, John Leopold, of the Groniger Museum, in Holland, maintains that the machinery of this clock is wholly consistent with mid-sixteenth century Flemish practice. It seems that the clockmakers of Flanders were the first to use brass for wheelwork. This view is also shared by Beresford Hutchinson, of the National Maritime Museum in this country. Even so, sadly, it must seem doubtful whether it will ever prove possible to be categorical about the provenance of this fascinating object.

Emerging from the pseudo-sixteenth century—if that is the way to describe it—the first source that must inevitably be consulted in attempting to track down royal clocks and watches, surviving or not, and whether genuine, spurious or indeterminate, must continue to be Wood's fascinating review of 1866, *Curiosities of Clocks and Watches*. He quotes an extract from a treatise called *Humane Industry*, by Powell, 1661—probably Vavasor Powell (1617–70), who was an itinerant evangelist and prolific writer—in which reference is made to the Holy Roman Emperor Charles V, who had a watch which necessarily must have been very small since it was 'made in the collet or jewel of a ring; and King James had the like'. If true, then, considering the degree of technical development of the watch by the beginning of the seventeenth century, it can have been little more than an amusing toy if indeed it could be made to work on the hand at all. Another watch credited to James I is said by Wood to have been formerly in the collection of Sir Ashton Lever (1729–88), one of the great collectors of his time. He removed his museum to London in 1774 and disposed of it by lottery—a much favoured process for selling off unwanted treasures in the eighteenth century which, presumably, would be illegal under present-day laws—in 1788. This particular watch was seemingly bought in 1806, being exhibited and described to a meeting of the Archaeological Institute, on 9th May 1855, by Mr H. Syer Cumming. Of oval shape and French manufacture, it was said to measure 'without its case'—in other words, movement only since there is no mention of any protective outer or pair case—in length $1\frac{7}{8}$ inches, width $1\frac{3}{8}$ inches and thickness $\frac{5}{8}$ inch. Nearly all of brass—but presumably gilt—there is a silver chapter ring only $\frac{1}{8}$ inch wide, on which the hours are engraved in Roman numerals, each with its touch pin; in other words, this was a *montre à tact* for the benefit of the blind or to enable the time to be told at night without any need for artificial illumination. The single steel hand is 'in the form of a dart', while above the dial is engraved a scene of Leda and the swan, and below it a cherub's head on each side of which is a fox. The space between them, but still outside the dial ring, is filled with rich scrolling foliage. In the dial centre is a view of a river with swans, a bridge, horses, trees, fields, hills and a stag-hunt. The name on the movement is 'R. Dieu à Paris', and Wood continues to describe a typical watch of *c.*1630, with a catgut line instead of a chain between spring barrel and fusee, no screws whatever in its construction, no balance spring, and so on.

Tardy lists no less than three watchmakers by the name of Robert Dieu working in Paris during and just after the first quarter of the seventeenth century, so that chronologically, it might just be possible for this to have been the King's watch; yet he died in 1625, which most authorities might feel to be a handful of years too early for what seems to be a fairly conventional oval watch, of a well-established style. The operative word,

318. *David Ramsay table clock: general view.* (Victoria and Albert Museum, London)

319. *The underneath of the table clock, showing the 'royal' cartoon.* (Victoria and Albert Museum, London)

too, might well be 'conventional'; for a king does not normally wear just such a watch as might be owned by one of his subjects, with no special marks upon it to denote the rank of its possessor. Coats-of-arms on this kind of watch are not at all uncommon, and it would be reasonable to expect some such identifying feature.

King James I is said to have had a very ponderous sense of humour, so that a small square table clock in the Victoria and Albert Museum, which was formerly in the collection of Prince Soltykoff, would probably have amused him—if indeed he ever saw it. For years
318 this clock was wrongly attributed to a French maker
called David; a small plate obscured the remainder of the signature, and when this was removed, it became clear that the clock was the work of none other than David Ramsay, of whom much has already been written in an earlier chapter.

This small gilt-brass clock is surmounted by a pierced and engraved dome of the same material which conceals the bell yet allows its sound to be heard. In turn, the dome is capped by a small silver dial decorated with brightly coloured flowers in translucent enamel. On the sides of the clock case are four oval silver plaques engraved with figures representing the Evangelists.

However, the dominant feature of the clock—and the one which might well indicate a royal
319 association—is the cartoon, for want of any better
term, which is engraved upon the bottom, In this, James I accompanied by Henry, Prince of Wales, Prince Charles, Henry IV of France and one other person, who is thought possibly to be the Earl of Salisbury, is seen holding the Pope's nose to the grindstone, which is being turned by two English bishops. On the right of this scene, a cardinal and three friars watch in sorrow.

This clock is of the highest quality, as might be expected from Ramsay. Attempts to date it have been based upon considerations that it is unlikely to have been made after 1612, when the Prince of Wales died, and almost certainly also before the murder of Henry IV, two years earlier. If, as has also been hazarded, the concept of the cartoon relates to the failure of the Gunpowder Plot, this gives an opening date of 1605. It has been held, too, that the leading part given to James I in the cartoon indicates that the clock was made for him; this argument would be unlikely to hold water when subjected to the severely clinical analysis that is nowadays employed when assessing the provenance of works of art.

Inevitably, the name of David Ramsay associates itself with royal timepieces; so that it is not wholly surprising to find a watch of his in the erstwhile Evan Roberts collection, which purported to have belonged to James I. Although the collection has long since been dispersed, there do exist illustrated highlights from it,
especially in a book published in Chicago in 1897 320
which is mentioned elsewhere. The pictures show the 321
watch to be in an early seventeenth-century gilt-metal case, the back pierced and engraved in conventional style. The description states that the dial is gold, but doubtless this should read gilt. There is a silver hour ring, it obviously has an alarm disc, and it is also said to be a clock watch. The reproduction of the front view is by no means as clear as it might be, but the dial centre and border seem to be decoratively engraved. No clue whatever is given as to the evidence of a royal association involving this watch, which is a pity because, like all Ramsay's work, it is both fine and interesting.

A watch reputedly belonging to James I was included in the well-known sale of the horological and other works of art belonging to George III's sixth son, Augustus Frederick, Duke of Sussex, in 1843. Tracking this particular item provides an interesting example of
the processes used in establishing the 'pedigree' of a 322
notable timepiece. The watch formed Lot 35 in the 323
aforementioned sale—*see* Appendix Two—and there is sufficient descriptive matter, including the unique feature of a movement plate dated 1599, to be able to identify it with reasonable certainty as the watch forming item 421 in the Exhibition of the Royal House of Stuart—*see also* Appendix Two. This watch finally surfaces at the Usher Art Gallery in Lincoln, as part of the collection formed by James Ward Usher, a watchmaker and jeweller of that city; the gallery was built from his bequest and opened by the then Prince of Wales in 1927. As to the watch, it is in a gilt-metal case of cushion shape—a style which immediately superseded the type usually called 'tambour', where the flat recessed band has now become curved and projecting, but the cover over the dial remains elaborately pierced to enable the hands to be read without opening, for glasses over watch dials had not yet arrived. The date of such a watch would certainly be *c.*1600. This watch, which is apparently anonymous—as they often were at this period—is almost undoubtedly German. The complicated dial shows days of the month and phases of the moon, while the movement is both clock-watch and alarm, all on an internal bell. A rotating disc at the dial centre contains a round aperture through which the lunar information is conveyed, but this disc is also itself engraved with, so it is said, astrological information representing James I's horoscope, together with the legend 'J.Ist.Rex'. Whether this is, of itself, evidence of royal ownership must be a matter of opinion.

Several watches are accredited to Charles I. As has happened many times already, however, albeit in connection with other royal personages, a close investigation of the maker whose name appears on the

320. (Below) *A supposed royal watch by David Ramsay: this illustration is taken from* The Evan Roberts Collection of Antique Watches *published in Chicago in 1897.* (Private collection)

321. (Above) *An interesting comparison: the previous watch, as seen by* Horological Journal, *July 1888, page 163.* (Private collection)

322. (Left) *Early German watch, unsigned, and in 'cushion' case of gilt metal, the dial inscribed 'J. 1st Rex'.* (Usher Gallery, Lincoln)

323. (Below left) *The movement of the previous watch.* (Usher Gallery, Lincoln)

324. (Below) *Swiss form watch by Henry Beraud, resembling a fritillary; this view shows the dial.* (Christie's, London)

325. (Below right) *The bud-like case of the previous watch.* (Christie's, London)

object sometimes reveals a notable discrepancy between the established dates of his working life and the conjectured date of the royal association. The first watch to be described does not suffer this inbuilt
324 disadvantage. Traditionally said to have been given by
325 the King to his chaplain, this is a silver form watch, of *c*.1630, in the guise of a fritillary—a type of lily—with its petals of a naturalistic chequered design. The dial, visible in the middle of a petal, has a conventional centre engraved with an urban landscape surrounded by summer flowers upon a hatched ground; the shutter covering the winding-square is in the shape of an acorn, and the movement, with pinned-on pierced and engraved cock, is signed 'Henry Beraud fecit'. This maker was an early member of the Clockmakers' Company, his date of admission being uncertain but thought to have been during 1633.

The romantic enthusiasm for what booksellers nowadays call 'association items' is given much greater latitude if accompanied by lack of exact knowledge; and with a discreet admixture of wishful thinking, all the elements are present from which legend is created. Wood mentions another Carolean watch, however, which still exists and for which there does seem to be a much more likely royal provenance.

This is the watch that Charles I is said to have given to Mr (later Sir) Edward Worsley—who had risked his life for him in various escape attempts—when being removed from Carisbrooke Castle on 30th November 1647, with the words 'This is all my gratitude has to give.' The watch was carefully preserved in the Worsley family right up to modern times, when it was presented by Mr C. F. Worsley to the British Museum in 1948. Wood notes that it was exhibited by one Miss Worsley to a meeting of the British Archaeological Association at her home in Shorwell, in 1855; but this subsequent description of the watch, when compared with the reality, is unreliable in fine detail, to put it at its best.
The signature on the watch is 'Johannes Bayes, Londini 326
fecit', a beautiful and typical expression of the maker's 327 328
name; and the watch, in silver pair-cases, is quite large as these things go, the extreme diameter of the inner case being $2\frac{3}{32}$ inches and of the outer $2\frac{1}{4}$ inches. The movement is of that kind known as a clock-watch—that is to say, it strikes the hours on an internal bell automatically, like a clock—and the back plate of the movement is characteristically decorative, with the striking count-wheel of silver engraved with a central rose and with the hour notches numbered. The endless screw mainspring set-up is mounted in a blued-steel openwork frame and has a silver regulator dial numbered 1 to 8, a small pinned-on cock, and the plates separated by mixed pillars—available space determined the use of one, of turned baluster form, while the remainder are in the early elongated Egyptian pattern. The silver dial has large champlevé chapters, diamond half-hour marks and a very long and slender blued-steel hand which is so decorative that perhaps it may not be original. The outermost ring of the dial is divided into five-minute segments, an unexpected feature but not unknown at this period. The inner case, pierced to allow the sound of the bell to be heard, is enriched with the most beautiful engraving stemming from a central boss in the form of a rose, the remainder being an arrangement of large flowers in which can be discerned a sunflower, daffodils, tulips and so forth. The outer case is of that flattened contour which was fashionable at this time, giving the appearance of a thinner watch. Plain, it has holes in the band and bezel—Wood says there are nineteen, but it was not felt necessary to check this—which serve the same purpose as those on the inner case.

As for John Bayes, the Clockmakers' Company admitted him as a Brother in 1647, and he served two of the offices of Warden during a total period of four years, 1658–9 and 1661–2. He never seems to have become Master, however; and he was obviously in the clock and watch trade for some time before he joined the Worshipful Company of Clockmakers, for Britten cites a lantern clock by him, signed in the style used on the royal watch, which is dated on one of the frets

326. *The Worsley watch, by Johannes Bayes: general view.* (British Museum)

327. *Back of the inner case of the Worsley watch.* (British Museum)

1643. Baillie says that John Bayes had died before 1675; the evidence for this may be that he had a brother, Benjamin, who was apprenticed to him on 3rd November 1661 but was not admitted to the Freedom until 2nd August 1675, possibly as an essential element in carrying on a family business after the senior member of it had passed on. It is perhaps worth remarking, too, that another watch by John Bayes is said to have belonged to John Pym (1584–1643), whom Britten describes as having been Cromwell's secretary although he is more usually known as a statesman and leader of the Short Parliament of 1640. Unfortunately, however, the outer tortoiseshell case of the watch is reported as being inscribed 'Johne Pyme hes watch A.D. 1628', a date which does not accord with what is at present known about Bayes's working life; indeed, it is nearly twenty years prior to his admission to the Clockmakers' Company, and this might seem, despite the circumstances detailed above, rather too long an interval. It is clear, also, that Pym had died before Bayes's active life had really got under way.

Charles I's official watchmaker was, of course, the eminent Edward East. He was working under his own
329 330 name from 1627, two years after the King had
331 ascended the throne, and he lived to the remarkable age
of ninety-five. Wood cites a large silver 'alarum clock watch' made by East, which is said to have been

328. *The movement of the Worsley watch.* (British Museum)

constantly at Charles I's bedside and which the King is supposed to have presented to Sir Thomas Herbert, who was Groom of the Chambers, on his way to the scaffold on 30th January 1649. The watch is then said to have passed into the hands of a family called Mitford by intermarriage with the Herberts in the mid-eighteenth century and, in the mid-nineteenth, was still in the possession of a Mr William Townley Mitford. The story is then taken up by Britten, who reproduces two illustrations of the watch taken from the *Archaeological Journal*, volume VII. This shows a watch of typical early seventeenth-century format, the case most elaborately pierced and engraved with foliage and flowers and with a loose ring through the pendant boss as was usual at that time. The dial, with single hand but seemingly having a minute circle around the outermost edge, has its centre embellished with the usual little riverside vignette, a seated figure in the foreground playing a flageolet, birds on the water, trees, buildings and a church in the background. Britten comments, a little sniffily, that 'the Society of Antiquaries seems to be quite satisfied with their examination', but then goes on to point out that there is no sign, in the illustration, of any alarm disc or indicator, and that, presumably, there must once have been another hand which, at that time, while not an impossible adjunct, would certainly be unusual.

This particular watch does, in fact, seem to have come to the surface again of recent years. In 1951, the *Horological Journal*, at page 173 of its March issue, reported under the heading 'Watch that belonged to Charles I', a ceremony at York involving a Mr G. E. Herbert. He was a descendant of Sir Thomas Herbert, and the presentation of the watch is described in some
332 detail, including the bequest by Thomas Herbert to his grandson, George, in the words 'I give unto the said George Herbert the greate silver clocke, my gracious Master King Charles I gave me in testimony of his royall favour, a little before his death, hopeing that as a

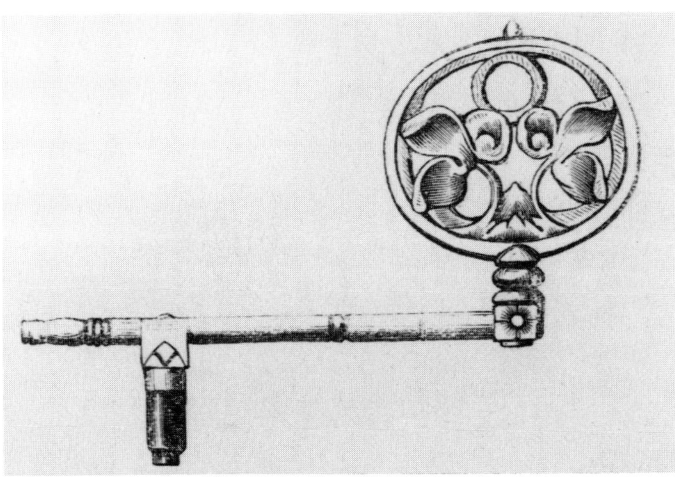

329. (Top) *The Thomas Herbert watch by Edward East: front view, as illustrated in* Sussex Archaeological Collections, *vol. III, page 103, 1850.* (Guildhall Library, City of London)

330. (Above) *The back of the case of the Herbert watch, from the same source.* (Guildhall Library, City of London)

331. (Left) *The original crank key for this watch, also as seen in 1850.* (Guildhall Library, City of London)

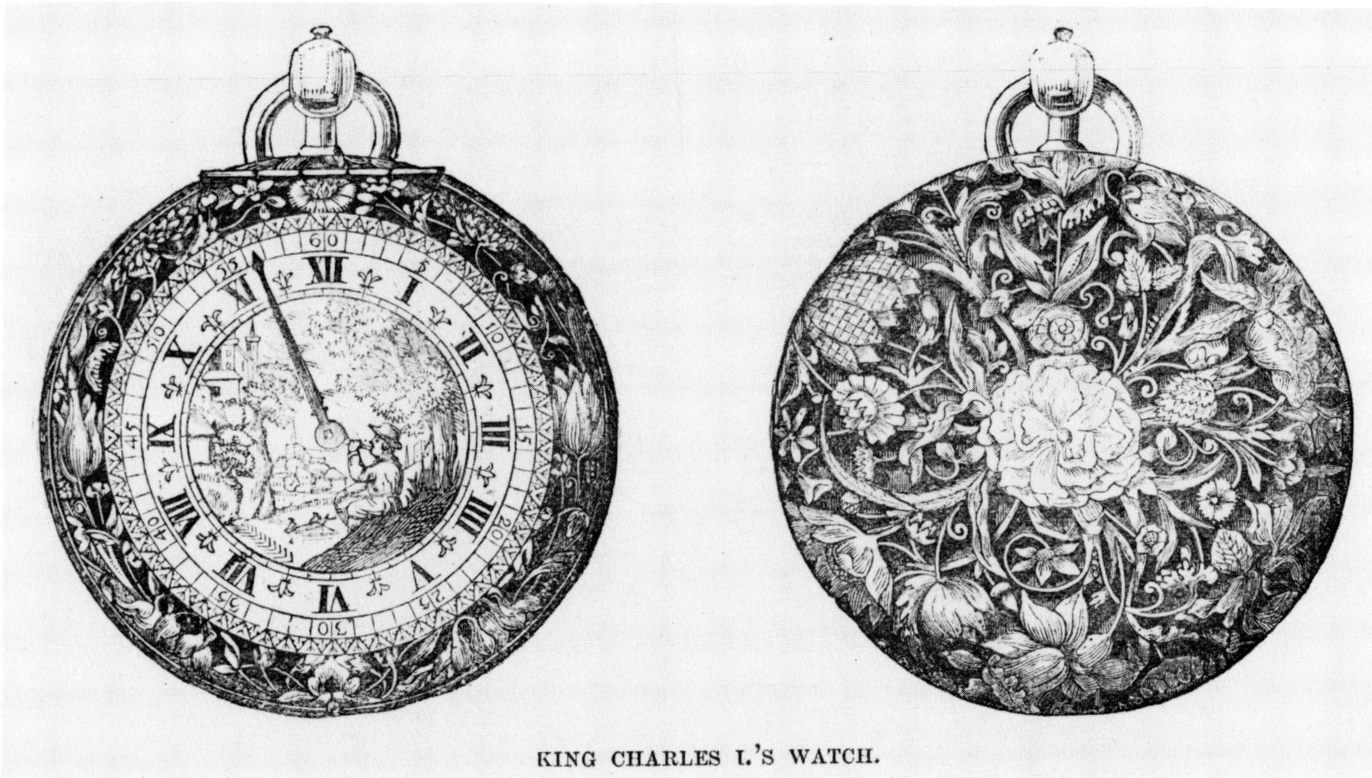

332. *An interesting comparison: an obviously different engraving—at least in fine detail—of the Herbert watch, from Robert Chambers's* Book of Days, *1862.* (Guildhall Library, City of London)

valuable jewell he will keepe the same.' Seemingly, the watch eventually passed, as has been stated elsewhere, into the hands of the Mitfords, of Pits Hill, their home near Petworth, in Sussex, by intermarriage with the Herberts. It must have been present when this report was filed—an accurate measurement of the diameter is quoted as $3\frac{5}{8}$ inches—yet the accompanying illustration, good though it is so that it could easily pass for a photograph, will be seen, on the closest inspection, simply to be a reproduction of the engraving used by Britten. The paragraph concludes by stating that 'this treasure . . . is now at the British Museum', but a recent check has revealed that it is no longer there.

Scaffold presentations, in connection with Charles I, have certainly proliferated over the years; Wood cites the example of a watch, kept on permanent loan in Ashburnham church, in Sussex, which was said to have been given by His Majesty to John Ashburnham, 'at the place of execution'; it seems, however, that John Ashburnham was nowhere near the King on the morning of his execution and certainly not upon the scaffold with him. 'The correctness of the legend,' opines Wood, 'may be doubted.'

Even so, this watch does turn out to be quite well documented. In a book entitled *The Ashburnham Archives*, a catalogue edited by Francis W. Steer, FSA, 333
and published by East Sussex County Council in 1958, 334
there is quoted an extract from John Ashburnham's Will, dated 7th February 1670—he died in 1671, and the Will was proved the following year—which leaves to his grandson John 'my Clocke Watch which was my Mother's And also my watch with an inamel'd case of Imagery which was given by my late deare Master King Charles the first of ever blessed memory and a case of gold which I made to preserve the same'.

Various accounts exist of the Carolean relics, including this watch, which passed down the Ashburnham line, being housed at Ashburnham Place, near Battle in East Sussex. It is said that they were kept, at one time, in Ashburnham church, where on special occasions they were brought out to be touched by the superstitious, to ward off 'the King's Evil'. A letter in *The Times*, for 11th January 1889, and signed 'Medicus', relates: 'There was, I believe, a watch with the clothes given by the King to Mr. Ashburnham on the day of his execution. This had a gold external case. However, some thieves broke into the church at Ashburnham and having stolen the gold case and done other damage, the then Earl had the relics removed into his house, where they have been carefully preserved since.' Parts of Ashburnham Place still exist, but much of it was considered uneconomic to maintain and pulled

333. *The Ashburnham Watch, showing the magnificent dial, the movement by Henry Jones, and the leather outer case enriched with gold piqué work.* (Private Collection)

334. *Both sides of the crank key associated with the previous watch: the ribbon also appears original.* (Private Collection)

down in the 1950s, after the death of Lady Catherine Ashburnham, the last of the direct line to live there.

There must be initial disappointment on examining this watch, in view of its apparently well-documented background; but this should be tempered with appreciation, for this was once a beautiful watch, even though now somewhat jaded, and still full of interest in the present context.

In round pair-cases, the inner is gold and plain, while the outer is leather-covered and enriched with a conventional design in gold piqué work. The movement is of that elegant kind in which the cock, with oval open-work foot and table, is pinned to a post projecting from the plate. This is, of course, pre-balance spring; the endless-screw mainspring set-up is located on the back plate in the usual pierced blued-steel framing, and there is a small indicator dial, so often missing in this situation. The plate is signed, in a style reminiscent of East, with a flowing 'Henricus Jones Londini'. The fusee still has gut fitted to it, and this is, in all respects, a quality watch of its period.

Yet, the watch can have no possible connection with Charles I, for Jones—who has been mentioned at some length in Chapter Two—was only bound apprentice in 1654: the King had been executed in 1649. The watch movement and cases, in fact, could well be ascribed to 1670 or thereabouts. The dial, however, is quite a different matter. Beautifully enamelled with a floral design that smacks of those sometimes seen in simple engraved versions, this could, in the author's view, have come from a somewhat earlier watch. There is some indication, too, of a 'marriage' between dial and movement in that, whereas under normal circumstances, three or even four single dial feet can be observed projecting through the plate, each one fixed by pinning, in this case the feet come in pairs, immediately abutting against each other and each pinned separately, save for a single foot in one instance only. There is also some indication that the dial surround, gilt-engraved and conventional, is separate from the enamelled dial itself and may never have been part of it. It would be rather unusual at this period to find an otherwise plain watch with such a very handsome polychrome dial—such components usually were allied to cases that were equally decorative and often, although not necessarily, enamelled *en suite*.

All this, at the moment, is pure speculation since it has not yet been feasible to remove the dial in order to inspect the situation behind it. It is hoped to accomplish this in due course, when it may be possible to make a more educated judgement. If this dial could have originated in the time of Charles I, is it possibly all that remains of the watch originally presented by the King to John Ashburnham? Had that watch, as the Will suggests, been a fully enamelled object—that is, case as well as dial, the former probably decorated inside as well as out—and had it ever been damaged, for enamel-work of this kind is very fragile, is it possible that the dial had escaped relatively unharmed and been allied to a fine Henry Jones watch to preserve at least some remnant of the original relic? It is a tantalizing thought—but it must be said that the Ashburnham family also served King Charles II, for whom Henry Jones did a little recorded work, and the watch could have come into their hands from that direction.

Another such pre-execution presentation relates to a watch said to have been presented to Bishop William Juxon (1582–1663), who was Bishop of London during the period 1633–49 and eventually Archbishop of Canterbury, 1660–63. The Bishop attended King Charles I during his trial and received his last words on the scaffold; he might well be considered a suitable recipient for such a gift. Wood, in his *Curiosities of Clocks and Watches* of 1866, mentioned in this work on many occasions, has this to say on page 275:

> In Brayley and Britton's 'Description of Cheshire' in the *Beauties of England and Wales*, we read that at Vale Royal Abbey, which was in 1801 the residence of Thomas Cholmondley, and since of Lord Delaware, was a watch said to have belonged to Charles I and to have been given by him to Bishop Juxon upon the scaffold. This watch came into the Cholmondley family by an intermarriage with the Cowpers of Overleigh, near Chester, who were related to the Juxon family.'

At item 387 of the catalogue of the Loan Exhibition of Royal Treasures, 1937—(*see* Appendix Two)—is listed a watch, said to have been handed to Bishop Juxon when on the scaffold, 'adding the word "Remember"'. The watch was left to the owner's great-grandfather, Admiral Rodney, by an aunt. The catalogue further shows that the watch was loaned by a Mrs. Ozzard, who was also presumably the owner; and Admiral Rodney (1719–92) is a well-documented figure.

Whether the Vale Royal Abbey watch, and that of Mrs Ozzard, were one and the same, is not clear; but as recently as June 1981, there has appeared on the market a superb Edward East watch, housed in a gold and enamel case with a protective outer case of silver, of 335
which the provenance is given as 'By descent through a family of title, in Ireland. According to family tradition, given by Charles I on the scaffold at his execution, to Bishop Juxon.' This watch was exhibited in 1911, at the Scottish Exhibition of National History, Art and Industry held in Glasgow, and before that, mentioned by Alan Fea, in *Memoirs of the Martyr King*, 1905, p. 55. While this beautiful watch could certainly be described as of 'royal' quality, there is sadly no proof whatever of such antecedents.

Even though there appears to be no contemporary documentary back-up for the gift of a watch to Bishop Juxon, one explanation for this particular legend seems possible. In a marvellous antiquarian miscellany compiled by Robert Chambers (1802–71) during the years 1862–4 and published under the title *Book of Days*, an account is given, under heading date 'JANUARY 30', of the execution of Charles I. This is accompanied by an illustration, of which Chambers has 336
this to say: 'A view of the dismal scene was taken at the time and published in Holland, and of this a transcript is here presented.' This drawing, insubstantial though it is, makes clear that, apart from soldiers, the only person actually attending the King on the scaffold itself is dressed as a prelate and must be Bishop Juxon. The King is shown in the act of handing over to him what certainly seems to be a watch, dangling on a chain: with magnification, it is easy to visualize hands on the front of what might be the dial. However, the only objects the King is recorded as handing over at this moment to the Bishop were his Bible and the jewel of the George, the Order of the Garter, to be kept for his son. It is at least conceivable that it is the latter which the print was intended to depict; but since it looked so much like a watch, it is more than likely that the spirit of romanticism that affected Britain in the nineteenth century may have inspired somebody to supply a suitable specimen!

335. (Left) *An enamelled watch by Edward East, said to be the one given by Charles I to Bishop Juxon.* (Christie's, London)

336. (Below) *A print of the execution of Charles I: the scene on the scaffold, as reproduced in Robert Chambers's* Book of Days, *1862.* (Guildhall Library, City of London)

There is a good documentary background to a watch that has been in the custody of an Oxford college continuously since 1685. A certain Thomas Bedford acted as executor for Sir Leoline Jenkins (1623–85) who was a multi-purpose man—academic, diplomat,
337 politician, judge and a Privy Councillor. The detailed
338 339 records of Bedford's executorship which still exist, show
that 'by verbal order an oval gold or guilt watch which King Charles the First used to carry in his pocket (which was given to his Honr. by Madame upon the buriall of the Queen Mother)' was to be deposited by Bedford at the college; and this was in fact done on 10th September 1685. The watch is of considerable intrinsic interest, whatever may be its royal antecedents. In a small oval 'Puritan' case, of a type which first appeared in the decade 1630–40, the movement is signed 'Jan Janse Bockelts A Haerlem'. It is recorded that this maker left Haarlem in 1626 for The Hague, subsequently changing his signature to 'Jan Bockelts Hagh'—there is an example of his later watches so signed in the Ilbert Collection in the British Museum—so that this crossing of co-ordinates gives a good clue to a date *c.*1630. The movement, however, constitutes the focal point of interest: of quite exceptional quality and original, its mechanism provides not only for hours and minutes but also seconds, to be displayed concentrically. Remarkable though it must seem, this innovation must have been a century ahead of its time; seconds were not generally indicated at all before the introduction of the balance spring, around 1675, and centre-seconds, as this arrangement is called, was a device first used extensively by George Graham in his famous cylinder escapement watches about 1725.

Finally, there remain all sorts of fragmentary references to watches supposed to have emanated from the ill-fated King; mostly these have been lost to sight, but it is always to be hoped that they may surface again, when perhaps a more thorough investigation of their claims might be made. Among these can be listed the following:

(a) Britten, on page 708 of his sixth edition, notes: 'A Richard Bowen was the maker of a large silver watch with two cases, the outer one chased and engraved with a border of flowers and the figure of the king praying, and the words "And what I sai to you I sai unto all, WATCH". It was said to have been given by Charles I, while at Carisbrooke, to Colonel Hammond, 1647.'

337. (Below) *Sir Leoline Jenkins's oval watch, said to have belonged to Charles I. The centre-seconds arrangement is unique at this period; the hand itself, however, was supplied by the British Museum as a more appropriate replacement for the later one hitherto in use.* (The Principal and Fellows, Jesus College, Oxford)

338. (Below centre) *Back of the movement of the previous watch: the signature betrays its Dutch origin. There is an associated plain outer case.* (The Principal and Fellows, Jesus College, Oxford)

339. (Below right) *Side view of the movement: the condition of the watch is impeccable.* (The Principal and Fellows, Jesus College, Oxford)

Wood also describes this watch; yet the only recorded London maker of this name was not bound apprentice until 1650—to Nicholas Payne, being subsequently turned over to Robert Smith—and he was only admitted to the Freedom of the Clockmakers' Company on 1st October 1657. Colonel Robert Hammond (1621–54) was Governor of the Isle of Wight and custodian of Charles I during 1647–8, while the King was, of course, executed in 1649.

(b) Among the list of articles disposed of by the King—his 'death-gifts', as one authority has called them—was a gold watch to the Duchess of Richmond. Just to make identification even more difficult, it is noted that 'he was accustomed to wear two of these articles'.

(c) Another large silver watch formerly the property of Charles I was supposed to have been given to Mr Spencer of Redleaf by Elizabeth, daughter of James I, when he entertained her at his house near Penshurst. This was loaned by a Mrs Boyse to the Exhibition of the Royal House of Stuart in 1888, and is catalogued as item 462—*see* Appendix Two.

The Stuart Exhibition did produce a fine crop of real or imaginary royal timepieces from that important period—important not only historically but also horologically—and it may be interesting to conclude considerations of Charles I's watches with an extract from the second notice about the show to appear in *The Times*, on 5th January 1889. This reads:

> Extremely fine is the gold watch given by Charles [I] to Sir William Dugdale, the celebrated antiquary, and lent to the exhibition by Mrs. Stratfield Dugdale, in the possession of whose family it has remained ever since Sir William's day. [Sir William Dugdale (1605–86) was eventually to become Garter King of Arms.] It is in design and execution a real work of art; the gold openwork of the case and the silver rim are wrought with great delicacy and an astonishing sense of effect. It should be compared with the two large silver watches (375 & 462) one of which is the identical watch or hanging timepiece which the King gave to Sir Thomas Herbert on the day of his execution and which has descended from him to Mr. Mitford. The other was given by Elizabeth of Bohemia to Mr. Spencer, of Redleaf, when he entertained her at his house near Penshurst. A fourth watch (396) is somewhat earlier; it has a portrait of James I and his Queen; it was made by David Ramsay, the watchmaker who appears in *The Fortunes of Nigel* and it seems to have been given by King James to his favourite Robert Carr, Earl of Somerset. It can be exactly dated, for it bears Carr's arms with an earl's coronet, and as he was made an Earl in 1613 and disgraced in 1615, the watch must have been made between those years. [Somerset was accused of poisoning Sir Thomas Overbury but pardoned in 1616.]

Oliver Cromwell has had the ownership of as many watches attributed to him as any English monarch of his century. Wood, as ever well to the fore in such matters, describes a clock-watch in a leather outer case studded with silver, by Jacques Cartier, a maker who is placed by Tardy, in 1650, at Montauban, this being a noted Protestant stronghold some 30 miles from
Toulouse. This watch was illustrated by Britten, sixth 340
edition, figure 229; but he had simply lifted the engraving from *The Illustrated London News*, issue of 9th February 1850 at page 96, which in turn had reproduced it from *Antiquarian Gleanings in the north of England* by Sir James Sibbald David Scott, FSA (1814–85), who was a well-known antiquary and writer. In fact, Scott described the watch as a repeater, but, said the metropolitan periodical, 'We apprehend it is a clock-watch, which strikes the hours, as repeaters, strictly so called, are of rather more recent date than this one.' The illustrations also suggest that the watch had an alarm facility. In 1850 the watch was said to be in the possession of J. H. Fawkes Esq. of Farnley Hall, an assertion which Britten was studiously repeating eighty-two years later.

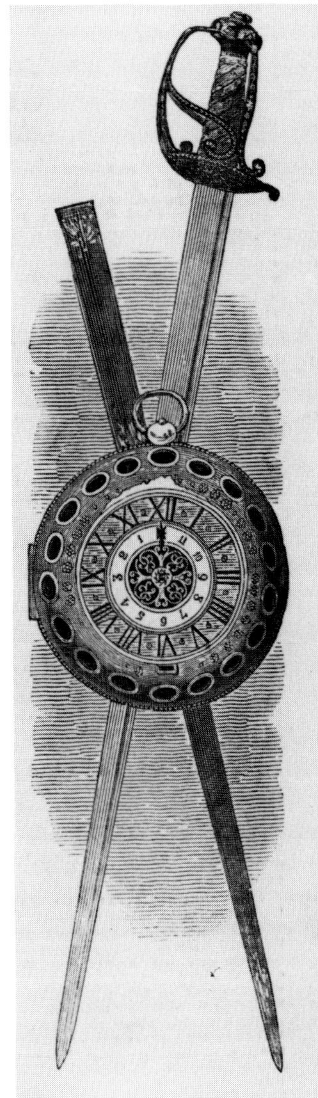

340. *Watch said to have belonged to Oliver Cromwell, by Jacques Cartier, as seen by the* Illustrated London News, *in 1850.* (Guildhall Library, City of London)

Another watch with a pedigree said to stem from Oliver Cromwell is preserved in the Founders' Room, Department of Western Art, Ashmolean Museum, at
341 Oxford. There might appear to be some links missing at
342 the beginning of the chain, but nevertheless the University received the watch in 1824 at the end of a line which can be traced to a Dr Ralph Schomberg (1714–92), a Reading physician and antiquary, who was elected FSA in 1752. He gave the watch to his son Captain Isaac Schomberg, RN, author of *Naval Chronology* (died 1813), who gave it in turn to a Mr William Bragge, of New College, Oxford (MA 1797), and it was he who eventually presented it to the University, *vide* Ashmolean Museum, 1836 catalogue page 140, number 377. The watch is in a cast silver-gilt melon-shaped case; the silver dial plate has deeply engraved

341. *Another watch with a similar association, this one by Timothé Hubert, Rouen: general front view.* (Ashmolean Museum, Oxford)

342. *Movement of the previous watch, which is in a fine silver-gilt case cast in the shape of a melon.* (Ashmolean Museum, Oxford)

343. (Right) *Watch by M. Bockel, London, dated 1648, and said to have belonged to Oliver Cromwell. Reproduced from the* Evan Roberts Collection *catalogue of 1897.* (Private collection)

344. (Below right) *A watch, conceivably the same as the previous one, and also dated 1648: this time the signature is said to be Bockels, Aachen.* (Reproduced from a dealer's advertisement, 1956)

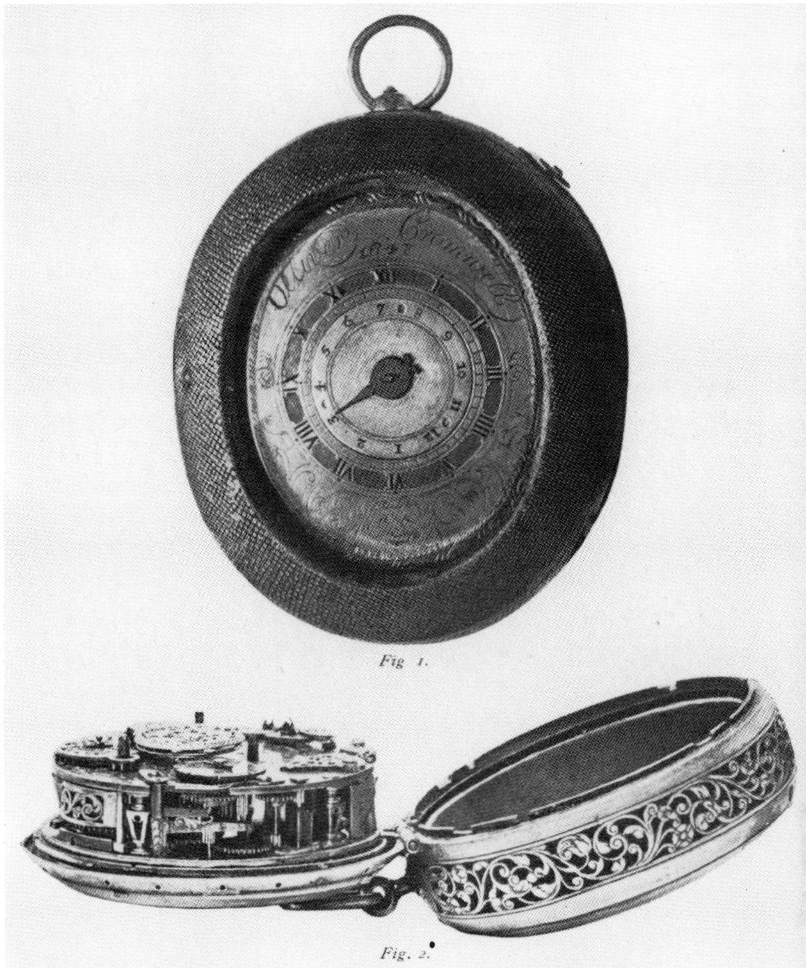

border decoration, a gilt chapter ring, and the dial centre engraved with a landscape scene. There is a single steel hand. The movement is signed 'Timothé Hubert à Rouen', a maker who became *maître* in 1646 according to Baillie.

Printed references to Cromwell's watches are legion—so many that it is inconceivable that they are all genuine. Earlier in this present century, a famous English collector called Evan Roberts had an alarm watch of large size, in an oval pierced and engraved
343 silver case with an outer protective case made of wood
344 covered with fish skin; this watch is depicted in an illustrated catalogue of some of the highlights of his massive collection of about fifteen hundred watches, which was published in Chicago in 1897. Its maker was described as 'M. Bockel of London', an unlikely-seeming combination—but a Mathys Bockel was at work in Haarlem from 1610 to *c.*1630, Baillie tells us. This watch has inscribed around the top of the dial 'Olliver [*sic*] Cromwell 1648', a date with which it is clearly difficult to identify the maker. The watch had also, at some time, graced the Roskell Collection and, in 1956, to judge from an advertisement illustration, passed through the hands of James Oakes, the London dealer, when the maker was said to be Bockels, Aachem. One can, perhaps, pass over another watch attributed to the Lord Protector and said to be the work of Jacob Collomby of London—no description of this watch seems to have survived, and the maker cannot be placed prior to *c.*1660; Britten, however, associates this watch with a certain Mr Ambrose Phelps, who must be assumed to be a collector.

One of the finest—albeit still elusive—watches with supposed associations with Cromwell, is by Henry Harper, a London watchmaker who was apprenticed only on 23rd July 1657, to Humphrey Pierce, being subsequently admitted to the Freedom on 4th August 1664. In this context, it must be remembered that Cromwell died on 3rd September 1658. Britten tells us in his sixth edition at page 180 and figure 230, and also page 763, that this silver watch had a plain inner case, upon which were engraved the arms of the Protector incorporated with the royal arms, a difficult combination to visualize! The silver dial of this watch has a day-of-the-month ring outside the chapter circle and, according to Britten, a pierced dial centre although his illustration suggests only a beautifully engraved floral design, typical of the time. The single slender hand has a long 'tail', and there is a quarter-hour ring bordering the centre. The outer case is fish-skin piqué with silver pins. Apparently, this watch eventually descended to Cromwell's eldest daughter, Bridget—he had a large family, some four sons and four daughters—and it is said eventually to have gravitated to the Schloss Museum in Berlin. As for Henry Harper, he had rather a chequered career, being elected to the Clockmakers' Company Court of Assistants in 1682, only to be hauled before the Lord Mayor's Court six years later, when some watch chains of his making were deemed to be of insufficient quality and ordered to be broken.

The *Gentleman's Magazine*, that bottomless well of information for the antiquary, supplies yet another example of a Cromwell watch—or so it says! In the issue for December 1808, at page 1074, a letter is reproduced in the following terms:

Nov. 4

Mr. Urban
I send you three views (fig. 8, 9 and 10), of a Watch formerly belonging to Oliver Cromwell, which he took out of his fob at the siege of Clonmell, and presented to the ancestor of the present Colonel Bagwell, whose it now is. The name of the maker, William Clay, is engraved on the work within-side. The outer, or golden circle, indicating the day of the month, revolves one division every 24 hours; whereby the number of the day is opposed to the index hand above.

P.Q.

The three illustrations show front, side and back views of a 'Puritan' oval watch, distinguishing features
345 including the pointer, in the form of a human hand, poised above the calendar ring at the XII o'clock position, and a disc-type rotating keyhole cover on the back.

On investigation, Colonel Bagwell does turn out to have existed—although trace of him was only found in the very last biographical source used by the author, and then only as a last resort! *The Record of Old Westminsters*—which is a biographical list of all those who are known to have been educated at Westminster School, in London—reveals, in volume I (1928), page 41, an entry as follows:

BAGWELL, William, elder son of John Bagwell, M.P., of Marlfield, co. Tipperary, by Mary, daughter of Richard Hare, of Ennismore, co. Kerry, and sister of William, 1st Earl of Listowel; b. [unknown]; admitted [to the school] Sept. 11, 1787; Lieut.-Col. of the Tipperary Militia Nov. 17 1794, Col. 1805; M.P. Rathcormac in the last Irish Parliament 1798–1800; Clonmel Feb. 1801–March 1819; Muster Master General for Ireland; P.C. (I); d. unm. Nov.4, 1826.

It is now time to consider three watches, all in the British Museum, and all of which purport to have Cromwellian associations, though none of them can be substantiated. The one to be taken first is, in general appearance, so like that illustrated in the *Gentleman's Magazine* and described above, that, were it not for the quite irreconcilable matter of dates, they could easily be mistaken for one and the same watch.

The museum records that, on 8th September 1786, there was bequeathed by Sir Robert Rich 'A small plain oval gold Watch in a double case going upon catgut, and I desire that the following inscription may be annexed to it, viz: "This watch usually worn by Oliver Cromwell was bequeathed to the Trustees of the British Museum for the use of the Public by Lieutenant General Sir Robert Rich Baronet". . . .' Sir Robert bequeathed to the museum at the same time 'a Picture of Oliver Cromwell presented by him to my Great Grandfather, Nathaniel Rich . . . then serving under him as Colonel of a Regiment of Horse in the Parliament Army'.

All these quotations are extracted from the British Museum's volume of *Original Letters and Papers* (volume II, 1785–1809); and it is reasonable to suppose that the donor was a relative of that same Robert Rich who had married the Lord Protector's youngest daughter, Frances. It is also a reasonable conjecture that, in 1786, the family tradition was unquestioned and both portrait and watch were regarded as having the closest possible associations with Cromwell. But, as Hugh Tait, of the Museum, remarks, there is no external evidence to confirm it; and, inevitably, Wood has noted the bequest in his Appendix.

345. *Three drawings of the watch by William Clay, said to have belonged to Oliver Cromwell: these appeared in the* Gentleman's Magazine, *December 1808, page 1074.* (Guildhall Library, City of London)

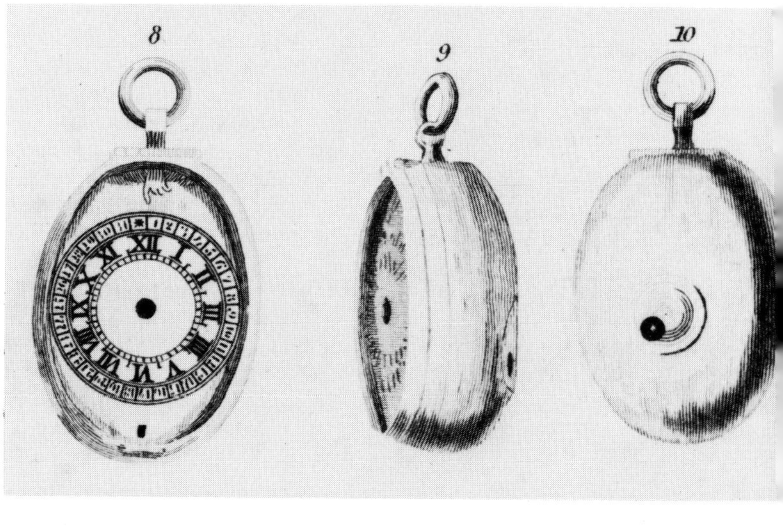

346. (Above) *Thin gold oval watch by Robert Grinkin: front view.* (British Museum)

347. (Above right) *Movement of the Robert Grinkin watch, said to have belonged to Oliver Cromwell.* (British Museum)

The watch is quite delightful. In oval gold pair-cases of the most 'Puritan' kind, it is very small, as these things go. The outer case is latched, as they very often were; the inner has an oval crystal glass set into the
346 front cover, through which can be observed the gold
347 dial plate, plain but for the silver rotating calendar ring,
and the 'hand' pointer, both outside the applied engraved gold chapter ring. On the back of this inner case is the revolving disc keyhole cover, just as in the magazine illustration. The verge movement has solid tapering pillars with feathered engraving and is signed 'Robert Grinkin, Londini'. This fine early maker had been a master in the Blacksmiths' Company in 1609, transferred to the Clockmakers' Company, soon after its formation, in 1632, served the office of Master in 1648 and died in 1660. It is abundantly clear that, however much this beautiful watch—well up to the standard to be expected of a royal watch, let alone one for Cromwell's use—may resemble the one described in the *Gentleman's Magazine*, it cannot have been in Colonel Bagwell's possession in 1808 if it had been given to the British Museum in 1786; this despite the fact that Wood, referring to the watch mentioned in the *Gentleman's Magazine*, states categorically that it is 'in a private room at the British Museum'. There is no record of any such watch ever having been deposited there. So, the precise details concerning the watch by William Clay—who, by the way, seems to have been active from *c*.1652 to 1680—remain, to the present, an unsolved mystery.

Of the two remaining watches to be described, one can be dismissed almost out of hand. This is an oval watch in a plain silver-gilt case. The signature on the movement has, for some reason or another, been erased leaving only the irrelevant—in the circumstances—'Londini'. The plain dial plate has a simple I–XII chapter circle engraved upon it. The cover has a circular opening within which the dial can be viewed; above this opening appear the initials 'O' and 'C' with a crown between them, while opposite this and below the opening appears a sword. On the back is the legend 'God and the Commonwealth', and, on the dial plate itself,
above the chapter circle, is inscribed 'T. Hooke 1661'. 348
All this extraneous engraving—which, since it matches in style and technique throughout, was certainly done at the same time—is of the poorest

348. *The very coarse watch with 'pounced' adjuncts, and erased signature.* (British Museum)

imaginable quality. When the watch was displayed at the Special Loans Exhibition at South Kensington in 1862, as item 7,482—*see* Appendix Two—the method was described as 'pounced', which indicates decorating with small punched indentations, or even holes. The effect is coarse and amateurish, and really there is little to be said in favour of this object; it is inconceivable that it ever belonged to Cromwell.

The foregoing watch, as well as the one about to be described—which is perhaps the most interesting of all—both came to the British Museum in 1874 from Dame Harriet Fellows, who had herself inherited them from the collection formed by her husband, Sir Charles Fellows (1799–1860), of West Cowes, Isle of Wight. Sir Charles was a noted traveller and archaeologist and the
349 350 author of a number of works dealing with his explorations and excavations. He was knighted in 1845. The watch in question is another of plain 'Puritan' oval shape, this time the case being silver. The plain silver dial has engraved chapter numerals, which have been heightened by filling with red *fil-en-col*, or engraver's wax. The typical verge movement is signed 'John Midnall in Fleet Street fecit'. Midnall was, in fact, an early member of the Clockmakers' Company, becoming a Warden in 1635; and Baillie gives an 'opening date' for him as *c.*1620. In all, a thoroughly nice watch of its period.

The excitement, however, centres on the short fob chain to which the watch is attached—arguably the earliest known example of this accessory. It consists of three short strands connecting the bow of the watch pendant to a shaped silver plate; from the opposite edge of this plate there extend beyond four shorter strands terminating in four hooks, presumably intended for the usual seals, watch keys etc, but now empty. On one side of the plate is engraved a shield with Cromwell's arms upon it, while on the other is his crest with the initial letters 'O.C.'. The crest consists of a demi-lion holding the handle of a tilting spear, a modification made by the Lord Protector presumably on account of the tameness of the authentic version, in which the lion's paw simply holds a ring. Taken together, the quality of the chain and its engraved elements, as well as the good, if not outstanding, watch suggest quite well their suitability to Cromwell's ascetic tastes and sensibilities, and no feature of them rules out the possibility of their authenticity.

Indeed, there is one other jot of evidence that, even if only in the 'hearsay' category, should not be discounted. James Benson, in his useful little book *Time and Time-Tellers*, which was published in 1875, only a year after the Midnall watch reached the British Museum, writing about it on page 51, mentions that

> The silver seals which were at one time attached to this chain are now absent, but they were a few years back in the possession of some descendants of the Cromwellian family, who allowed Sir Charles Fellows to take impressions of them. The watch, as it is here engraved, remained for upwards of a century in Holland, was there purchased by an English nobleman who presented it to his godson, and by him given to Sir C. Fellows, who believed that it was probably worn by Cromwell from 1625 until his death in 1658.

The present whereabouts of the seal impressions have not so far been discovered. There is also one small unexplained feature of this fob chain, in that the pierced terminal plate used to gather together the three strands of the chain and connect them to a hook for attaching to the watch has a tiny rectangular plaque forming part of it, on which appear the letters 'C.F.' If this was applied by Sir Charles Fellows, for purposes of identification, it was not a customary practice.

349. (Left) *Silver oval 'Puritan' watch by John Midnall: front view, also showing one side of fob chain and plate.* (British Museum)

350. (Below) *The movement of the Midnall watch and the reverse side of the fob plate.* (British Museum)

351. (Right) *Silver pair-cased clock-watch by Robert Seignior.* (Christie's London)

352. (Below right) *View of the movement of the previous watch, and of the back of the case.* (Christie's, London)

In case Oliver Cromwell's presence in a work devoted to royal timekeepers might seem out of place, he must be considered *in loco regis* during the period of eleven years when constitutional monarchy lapsed. It was clearly in such a capacity, for instance, that the application of the pendulum to clockwork—to quote the *Commonwealth Mercury* of 25th November 1658—was 'examined and proved before his Highness the Lord Protector'.

Passing now to the reign of Charles II, the first timepiece to be discussed remains a reality, rather than a mere dry-as-dust book reference. This particular object passed through Christie's sale rooms on 28th March 1973, making the considerable sum, for that time, of 9,200 guineas. Described by the auctioneers as
351 an important English silver pair-cased verge clock-
352 watch, and said to date *c*.1680, it was the work of Robert Seignior, an outline of whose life and times has already been given in Chapter Two. This again was a big watch—4½ inches in diameter—in silver pair-cases that closely followed the style of several other pieces from this period that have been noted, the leather-covered square-hinged outer having pierced roundels in bezel and band, and the back centred with a piqué rosette, while the inner was magnificently pierced and engraved with a design of flowers among which could be identified sunflowers, daffodils, carnations, daisies, tulips, roses and lilies. As for the movement, the auctioneers mention the pierced scroll brass and steel baluster pillars, four-wheel train with fusee and chain, three-arm steel balance with spring and slide regulator, the sector-shaped scale divided 1 to 6, working with worm-and-wheel mainspring set-up in blued-steel brackets and with silver indicator. In the notes it is pointed out that, whereas worm-drive on the back plate and hair-spring regulator is uncommon, it is by no means unknown, and an alarm watch by Thomas Tompion of *c*.1676 employs that arrangement. The movement detail concludes with reference to the balance cock, gilt, with round table and irregular border to the foot, screwed to the plate, and decorated with floral designs, and the striking-train with blued-steel gates and numbered silver count-wheel, striking upon an internal bell. As for the silver dial, this is centred with an engraved rosette, while the champlevé chapter circle has quarter-hour divisions.

The particular significance of this watch—apart from its intrinsic beauty—is that it has been traditionally held to have been a gift from Charles II to Nell Gwyn; and its descent to the present day has been attributed to the first Duke of St Albans (1670–1726), who was born Charles Beauclerk, the son of the King and this royal mistress, thence to his son Lord William Beauclerk, whose daughter Charlotte married the son of the founder of Drummond's Bank. Eleanor (Nell) Gwyn was born in 1650 and lived only to the age of thirty-seven; starting as an orange-seller at the Theatre Royal, she rose to become a famous actress, whose outstanding beauty was commented upon several times by the diarist Samuel Pepys. Her relationship with Charles II started when she was about seventeen, and she remained in favour until he died in 1685.

It would be nice to believe in this fairy tale; one has only to view an object like this to realize that this is the stuff of romance. Unfortunately, however, objective appraisal, while not by any means disproving the story, does not seem to substantiate it with concrete evidence.

References exist in plenty to other watches said to have belonged to Charles II or to have been given away by him—like that supposed to have been presented to Captain Nicholas Tatterell, or Tattershall, of the brig *The Surprise* in which the King fled to France after his defeat at Worcester in 1651—but as unusual a royal attribution as any normally to be met with concerns a watch key. Wood tells the story, repeating an account from the *Mirror* for 1833, of a curious heart-shaped key, given by His Majesty to the Pendrell family—Wood's spelling of the name has long since been superseded by the more usual Penderel—as a mark of gratitude for their having been 'very instrumental in his preservation'. Made of oak, $\frac{3}{8}$ inch thick and faced either side in silver, it was surmounted by an acorn in the same metal, and with a pipe of brass. On one side was engraved the head of the King, together with a branching oak; on the other, 'Quercus Car. 2d. Conservatrix 1651'. The Pendrell brothers helped to disguise His Majesty for his flight, after the Worcester episode.

While staying with the same auctioneers as were involved with the Robert Seignior clock-watch, atten-
353 tion can now be directed to a clock proper. A rare and superb night clock by Edward East, in ebony case surmounted by a griffin séjant, was sold in Christie's sale rooms on 8th November 1972 for 9,500 guineas. This was the clock traditionally made for Catherine of Braganza, wife of Charles II, which is said to be the subject of Samuel Pepys's diary entry for 27th June 1664: 'After dinner to Whitehall, and there met with Mr. Pierce and he showed me the Queen's bedchamber, and her closet, where she had nothing but some pretty

353. *Night clock by Edward East, said to have been made for Catherine of Braganza.* (Christie's, London)

pious pictures and some books of devotion, and her holy water at her head as she sleeps, with her clock by her bedside, wherein a lamp burns that tells her the time of the night at any hour.'

Seventeenth-century night clocks are not at all common, and one by East must inevitably be of the highest quality.* The case of this clock has a pie-crust moulding to the base, sides and door, and a broken pediment top, with the griffin supported upon a shaped central pedestal. The $10\frac{1}{2}$-inch dial, painted with a classical landscape, has a semi-circular aperture of which the edge is notched to indicate minutes, and outside this quarter-hour divisions numbered I to III only, with half-quarter dots between. Behind the aperture revolves a painted disc, once in two hours. This is pierced with two windows diametrically opposite one another, through which the appropriate hour numeral can be seen. The fusee movement of this clock has no fewer than twelve pillars separating the sloping-topped plates, which are latched in the manner favoured by Tompion. A tic-tac escapement with short bob pendulum completes the going-train, and there is also locking-plate striking, using a count wheel with numbered notches on the outside of the back plate. This is plain apart from the superb scrolling signature 'Edwardus East Londini'. Once, seemingly, the base of this clock was made to enclose a later musical movement, but this was thoughtfully removed before the clock came to be sold.

This clock had been formerly in the collection of James Oakes, a very well-known dealer in fine clocks in his day; his widow continued the business after his death. It must follow, too, that had there been any material evidence further to support the traditional royal attribution accorded this clock, the auctioneers would most certainly have specified it. An equally vague provenance seems to have surrounded an object sold by that other great London firm of auctioneers, Sotheby & Co, on 16th June 1975. Lot 289 of that sale, a watch that appeared superficially to have had associations with James II, fetched £2,600.

This particular watch had featured, as exhibit number 385, in the Loan Exhibition of Royal Treasures
354 held in 1937, and the related entry in the Catalogue of that event will be found in Appendix Two. Then it had been described as the King's property, but the auctioneers clearly had reservations. As for the watch itself, it apparently consisted of two parts—a move-

*One of the horological highlights of 1980 was the appearance on the auction market of a unique and superb long-case night clock by Edward East; the export of this clock was halted by the Review Committee, and, happily, it has now been acquired by the British Museum.

354. *Watch said to have associations with James II, by Richard Baker.* (Sotheby's, London)

ment which pre-dated 1700, and a case and dial which post-dated that milestone. The maker was Richard Baker, who was admitted to the Freedom of the Clockmakers' Company in June 1685 after a somewhat chequered apprenticeship, being bound first to John Chatfeild [*sic*], who was a Blacksmith rather than a Clockmaker, and being turned over as late in the day as June 1683 to Richard Browne. Baker had premises in Lombard Street, and Baille gives his death as occurring in 1710. His son, also Richard, followed in his footsteps, entering the Company in 1727, presumably by patrimony since he is not recorded in the Register of Apprentices.

Later seventeenth-century watches with real or supposed royal associations are nearly always either of the 'sun and moon' variety or of that other, rarer, kind known as 'wandering hour' watches. This watch was of the first kind and housed in a fine gold case repoussé with a scene of Penelope and one of her suitors, set within a rococo frame, and the bezel similarly enriched with scrolling swags supporting oak leaves. The dial, in its upper half, displayed a semicircular chapter of champlevé Roman numerals, running from VI on the left to VI on the right, with XII sited as in a conventional dial. Beneath this hour band was a shaped aperture behind which rotated a polychrome disc with sun and moon immediately opposite each other, for indicating the hours. The lower half of the dial was taken up with a miniature portrait of James II in a gilt oval frame, this being supported by a scrolling floral design in relief, in silver and set with rose diamonds. Surmounting this arrangement was a crown, free-standing and embrac-

ing the centre post. The auctioneers noted that both dial and case were in equally fresh condition, and it seemed possible that they had been substituted at a later date for whatever had gone before, perhaps by Baker's son. They put a tentative date for the case as *c.*1740.

The movement of this watch, however, was certainly *c.*1690. With tulip pillars and a four-wheel train with fusee but without a centre wheel, the winged balance cock was finely pierced and engraved with a formal design incorporating birds, the cock foot having a floral motif and an irregular edge, the slide plate similarly decorated. All in all, a most desirable object, but it does seem likely that any real connection with the monarch would be impossible to prove.

Another watch with supposed connections with James II has to be viewed *in absentio* since, sad to say, all but its outer case was stolen from the British Museum in

Note: Informed judgement upon the Strigner watch has hitherto been impeded by the failure of any photographs of it, apart from fig. 355, to survive the theft of 1971. Now, however, a recently-rediscovered magazine article of 1965 shows it to have an unmistakably eighteenth-century white enamel dial with gilt centre, thus making any association with James II so untenable as to be discounted.

355. (Left) *The only surviving photograph of the Strigner watch, showing royal arms on the inner case.* (British Museum)

356. (Below left) *The superb outer case of the Strigner watch, with its panels of carnelian set in gold, with, in the centre, a cameo head of a Roman Emperor.* (British Museum)

357. (Below) *Silver dust cap with suspect royal associations, from the Ilbert Collection.* (British Museum)

1971. Superficially magnificent though it appears at first sight—and a photograph survives—it has so many curious characteristics that it cannot fail to be suspect, despite an authentic-sounding history, or so one is led to believe. The watch seems first to have been given a public showing by a Mr A. W. Franks, who was not only Keeper of a Department at the British Museum but a Vice-President of the Society of Antiquaries. It was at a Meeting of that body on 14th December 1882—the account is taken from the official *Proceedings of the Society of Antiquaries of London*, second series, volume IX, p. 213 *et seq.*—that he produced the watch which 'the Earl of Mulgrave is good enough to allow me to exhibit'. After describing the watch, Mr Franks stated its provenance in the following terms:

> The watch is stated to have been given by James II to his natural daughter, Lady Catherine Darnley, whose mother was Catherine, daughter of Sir Charles Sedley. She married James, 3rd Earl of Anglesey, and by him had an only daughter, Lady Catherine Annesley, who married in 1718, William Phipps, Esq., the direct ancestor of the Earls of Mulgrave, now Marquesses of Normanby. After the Earl of Anglesey's death the Countess married, 2ndly, John Sheffield, Duke of Buckingham, by whom she had an only son, who died without issue, bequeathing his Yorkshire estates to his mother. With this history, the appearance of the watch seems perfectly to correspond.

But does it really? The appearance of the watch, when complete, must certainly have been striking—the outer case, on its own, is quite splendid, consisting of shaped and curving panels of orange-red carnelian
356 set in gold, among which are interspersed reserves of
gold, pierced and engraved in formal foliate fashion. In the centre is an eight-sided boss of carnelian carved as a cameo, showing the head of a Roman emperor. So far as one can tell from a picture, the gold inner case was pierced and engraved around the deep band with conventional motifs which included a mask at the six o'clock position and a shell diametrically opposite; in between ran an arrangement featuring birds and monkeys among foliage. The entire back of the case was occupied by a representation of the royal arms and supporters within a shaped border of interwoven strapwork. Few details of the movement survive save that it was a quarter-repeating verge, protected by a silver dust-cap. Franks describes this as follows: 'The works are protected by an inner case of silver with the royal arms under a crown, the heads of the supporters forming the termination of a scroll inscribed LONDON. On removing this the works are seen, and the name of the maker, Strigner, London.'

There are three dissonant characteristics that immediately cause the provenance of this watch, as stated, to be considered suspect. First, the maker, Strigner, is completely unrecorded—and careful
search has revealed no trace of any craftsman of this 355
name. Next, the dust-cap—and the dial, so Franks appears to suggest, although no proper description or photograph of it have survived—bore only the legend 'London' and no maker's name, an irregular practice for any reputable maker. Finally—and perhaps this has only been recognized since the British Museum mounted its admirable special exhibition, 'British Heraldry', in 1978—the arms shown on the back of the inner watch-case are not in any way similar to those associated with James II (reigned 1685–8) but are very similar to those appropriate to Queen Anne.

There is one strange phenomenon on the fringe of this issue, but it should be mentioned for the sake of completeness even at the risk that it is irrelevant. There came to the British Museum with the Ilbert Collection—and that famous collector's notebooks
show that he bought it from Captain Jauncey in 357
1934—a disembodied silver dust-cap that exactly matches such description as remains of that on the Strigner watch. There can be no possibility that they are one and the same, of course, but they must have been uncannily alike. The Ilbert specimen, it must be admitted, is of the coarsest imaginable quality, and Courtenay Ilbert himself noted that he considered it a Continental forgery. If the Strigner cap was from the same workshop, could that be what we are dealing with? In any event, it would be unheard of for any monarch to favour a watch by a totally unknown maker, while a repeating watch in the time of King James II by anyone other than Quare, who only received his Patent in 1687, would be inconceivable. Finally, the engraving of the inner case as revealed by photographs was not of the best quality and, even accepting that watch-case engraving was generally 'farmed out' to lesser artists in this field, such would not have been the case with any genuine royal watch.

It will be useful, here, just to mention briefly two other watches with stated royal connections, although the evidence for this is even less substantial than in the case of the watch just described. The first forms part of
the Usher Collection, in Lincoln. A French enamelled 358
watch signed 'Jaques Soret'—Tardy does not list this 359 360
maker at all, and Baillie, obviously working from the basis of this particular watch, simply says 'late XVIIth century'—it is enriched with miniature portraits of Louis XIV and Madame de Maintenon. There is an outer case of shark-skin studded with gold pins; and there even remains in place a piece of faded orange ribbon, said to have been on the watch when '*le roi soleil*' presented it to William III, who in turn is said to have given it to one of his favourites at whose house he slept on his march to the Boyne in 1690. The watch,

from its pictures, does indeed appear to be a very fine example of its period with a superb enamelled dial centred with a pink rose on a blue ground and a gold border, around which runs the fine early enamel chapter ring. For the rest, perhaps it would be wise to reserve judgement.

The other watch, which is to be found in Sir John Soane's Museum, in London's Lincoln's Inn Fields, is by Langley Bradley, a great name in horology in his day. This watch was said by the distinguished horologist R. W. Symonds, in his authoritative *Thomas Tompion, His Life and Work*, to have belonged to Queen Anne, who presented it to Sir Christopher Wren. Clutton and Daniels, in their well-known work *Watches* (figures 226–8, first edition), say that William and Mary made the presentation, the basis for this being the royal monogram 'W & M', which has been worked into the pillars separating the plates of the movement. Sir John Summerson, curator of the museum, writing to the author about this watch, says: 'The association with Wren is doubtful and we do not know where or at what date Soane acquired the watch . . . there is no authority for an association with Queen Anne.' Nevertheless, as one might well expect of Bradley, this watch is very fine. In plain silver pair-cases, the silver dial has a concentric calendar ring which includes divisions for months and signs of the zodiac, and might be expected to date *c.*1700. Langley Bradley himself spanned the turn of the century, being apprenticed in 1687 under Clockmakers' Company auspices and finishing up as Master of that body in 1726. He seems to be last recorded in 1738.

A clockmaker with a highly individual style who has

358. (Above) *Watch by Jacques Soret, dial view, with outer case at the side.* (Usher Gallery, Lincoln)

359. (Above right) *Back view of the enamelled inner case of the watch by Jacques Soret.* (Usher Gallery, Lincoln)

360. (Below) *Movement of the Jacques Soret watch: this watch is said to have belonged to William III.* (Usher Gallery, Lincoln)

not previously appeared in these pages is Edward Cockey, of Warminster, a town in Wiltshire. His speciality—indeed, almost all his known work, for very few conventional examples of his skill have survived—was monumental astronomical clocks in elaborate long cases, of which certainly five are recorded at the present time. The Cockey family started out as bell-founders, early in the seventeenth century, but the Edward Cockey who made the clock about to be described must have been born in 1701: his present-day descendants possess a mourning-ring which is inscribed 'Edward Cockey Ob. 26 March 1786 Aet. 85'. In 1968 the late J. K. Bellchambers, in a monograph entitled *Somerset Clockmakers*—geographically, the family operated in Frome (Somerset) and Warminster (Wiltshire), which are within 10 miles of one another—wrote: 'Edward Cockey was without doubt one of England's finest provincial clockmakers and one would have to search very far afield to find any maker who has produced five astronomical clocks. He had no doubt a very rich clientele and was in constant communication with the London makers from whom no doubt he obtained his castings and found his engravers.' Indeed, evidence as to the last assertion is to be found in the spandrels on one of his large clocks, which are identical to those on one of the equation clocks made *c.*1720 by Joseph Williamson, *q.v.*

This clock, then, came on the market in Sotheby's sale rooms on 8th October 1965, when it was
361 purchased anonymously for £1,500, and eventually
362 was acquired by the National Maritime Museum. Having an overall height of 11 feet 5 inches, the hood width being 2 feet 7 inches, the 20-inch dial has gilt spandrels exhibiting a seated figure of Queen Anne framed by cornucopias. Within these, the twenty-four-hour dial—two sets of I–XII numerals—has ten-minute numerals as well as fleur-de-lys half-hour marks. The dished dial centre houses all the complex calendar work, and the pierced hands conform to this module. The indications in this area include day of the month, month of the year, rising and setting of the sun, age and phases of the moon and sidereal time, with the sun revolving round an outer painted section and rising above blued-steel 'horizons' which adjust to the time of year. The case of this masterpiece is black japanned and parcel-gilt, the hood having a domed top surmounted by an ormolu figure standing upon crossed scrolls, beneath it gilt tracery of pierced foliage and husks and with flambeau finials at the corners, while the glazed door is flanked by pilasters at the angles and decorated with a Grecian frieze and entwined flowers. The trunk of the case has a giltwood fluted pilaster and a composite giltwood capital continuing round the sides and with unusual pendants beneath the overhanging,

361. (Left) *Astronomical clock by Edward Cockey, seen full length. This clock is said to have been made for Queen Anne.* (National Maritime Museum, Greenwich)

362. (Above) *Dial and hood of the previous clock.* (National Maritime Museum, Greenwich)

363. (Above right) *The royal astronomical clock by Edward Cockey, as revealed by the Pictorial Inventory. A number of differences of detail can be seen, by comparison with the clock shown in the preceding illustrations.* (Royal Collection)

concave cornice. The structure rests upon a rectangular plinth; and overall there is gilt decoration taking the form of classical scenes and groups of flowers on a black ground.

The curious arrangement of a hollow column built on to the trunk of the case, is to permit the massive weight of the three-month-duration movement a properly controlled drop. In such cases, it used also to be customary to place one or two sandbags in the base, to lessen the damaging effect of any sudden drop caused by the line breaking, a not infrequent occurrence before the advent of steel or nylon lines. The clock is, of course, timepiece only—any such additions as striking or chiming would have been considered superfluous in the astronomical context.

The royal provenance, so far as this remarkable clock is concerned, derives from an unsigned manuscript in the British Library (King's Library MS 277), headed 'A Description of a very curious Piece of Clockwork, made by Mr. Cockey of Warminster In Her Majesty's Drawing Room at St. James' [Palace]'. This document, however, describes the movement in great detail but makes no mention of the case—a curious omission, since it is obviously original and unorthodox—while the last paragraph is extremely puzzling. This reads: 'This Piece of Work, as I have been informed, was presented to Her Majesty Queen Ann, in the Year 1705; & was always looked upon as a very curious piece of Clockwork. . . .' From such biographical details as have come to light about Edward Cockey, however, this date would seem impossible; and that must throw doubt upon the whole attribution.

There is just one other piece of evidence on this
matter. Under reference B 12 in the Pictorial Inventory 363
is a drawing of a typical astronomical clock by this maker—indeed, even were it not obvious, a note of the

drawing states 'Made by Cockey'. It is also said to have been removed from St. James's Palace at the time of the fire there, which occurred in 1809. It must seem unlikely that more than one of these monumental clocks—of which so few seem anyway to have been made—would have gravitated to the Royal Collection, so that this drawing might be expected to represent the clock which was sold in 1965. Yet, when drawing and clock are placed side by side, very noticeable differences immediately manifest themselves. Was the artist indulging in undue licence in his representation, has the clock itself been altered—this seems unlikely, in view of the nature of the apparent structural differences—or are we looking at two different clocks? Up to the present, the answer is not clear. What is clear, however, is that this mystery is nothing new. B. L. Vulliamy, in an inventory dated 1st January 1835, where the clock is described as having a large japanned wood case, states: 'Lord Carrington has an exactly similar clock made by the same maker, & these are the only two clocks of Cockey making I every saw. The name of Lord C's clock is Edward Cockey Warminster.' In a further annotation dated 1st November 1850 he adds: 'I never could discover what became of this clock.'

By way of a small digression, it is interesting to note that the use of a watch as a vehicle for commemorating some great, even tragic, event is by no means a modern convention. A few years ago, there came on the market a fine silver pair-cased verge watch by no less a maker than David Lestourgeon, rated by Baillie as a fine craftsman and seemingly of French extraction: even were it not for the name, Britten notes that he features on the Register of the French Church at Spitalfields in 1689. He was admitted a Brother in the Clockmakers' Company in 1698, and Baillie specifies 1731 as closing the span of his working life, although not necessarily the year of his death. Watches of his make are in many well-known collections, and his own special style included transferring certain features from the back of the movement to the front, so that they could be incorporated in the dial. Such a one is that about to be described.

With a plain inner case, this watch has an outer with early square hinge, and engraved with inhabited foliage motifs. The silver champlevé dial has its chapter ring set off-centre towards the pendant, leaving space beneath it for a curved scroll containing the maker's name, and above this, a shaped aperture through which can be seen a mock pendulum. To the right of this, between and to the side of the hour numerals IIII and V, is another aperture for the blued-steel regulator disc to control adjustment of the balance spring. Moving the balance to the front of the movement thus leaves the back free for other purposes; in this case, a

364. (Left) *The clock known as the 'Barnard' Tompion. The original travelling-case still survives.* (Sotheby's, London)

365. (Right) *Back and side views of the previous clock.* (Sotheby's, London)

silver plaque chased with a portrait bust of William III flanked, on the one side, with the inscription 'Ob. March 8 1702' and, on the other, with a skull-and-crossbones above the monogram 'WR'. It will be recollected that William III broke his neck in a fall from his horse in Windsor Park: it is said that he tripped on a molehill. This does not seem to be the only watch of the kind that Lestourgeon made, for Britten mentions a pendulum watch, with medallion portrait of William III and the date 1702 on the movement, which he states is in the Pierpoint Morgan Collection; this is now, presumably, in the Metropolitan Museum of Art, in New York. Before leaving the subject of pendulum watches it is just worth mentioning that G. H. Baillie, in *Watchmakers and Clockmakers of the World*, states against his listing of Henry Wynne, 'Made a pendulum watch with shag-reen case, for the King.' Wynne himself was a reputable but relatively unknown maker, who was apprenticed in 1654 to Ralph Greatorex, becoming a Freeman of the Clockmakers' Company in 1662 and advancing to Master in 1690. Baillie gives his terminal date as 1708; the monarch concerned is indeterminate, and the author has been unable to find any other reference to such a watch.

In view of his proven royal commissions, it is almost inevitable that Thomas Tompion's name should be connected with at least some clocks traditionally held to have been made for the sovereign, but where the
supporting evidence is rather less capable of authenti- 364 365
cation. One such clock is known as 'the Barnard clock'—named after one of its earlier owners. Bearing Tompion's number 460, this is a small-size two-train repeating clock, signed by Tompion and Banger. Its height is $9\frac{1}{4}$ inches, and, like many other of Tompion's best-quality clocks, the ebony-veneered case has silver mounts. These even extend to silver open-work side panels, having as a central theme a mask against a radiating background with a basket of fruit above and all set amidst a design of entwining foliage, fruit and flowers. The panel in the back door is a fret of ebony backed by silk. The dial has a mock pendulum aperture below XII and small subsidiaries in the upper corners flanking the dial signature cartouche, that on the right for strike/silent, while on the left is the rise-and-fall dial. Another outstanding feature of this fine clock is the survival to the present of its original travelling-case, in wainscot oak and complete with wrought hinges and lock.

It is said that this clock was made for Queen Anne, although, as has been mentioned elsewhere, she was not particularly well-disposed towards Tompion when he tried to recoup the arrears still owed by William III at the time of that sovereign's untimely decease; and it has also been argued that her continuing ill health would hardly have predisposed her towards dabbling in such extravagances as one of Tompion's expensive clocks. Indeed, even he might have fought shy of the commission, in view of his earlier experiences with the Queen. However that may be, the story continues with the gift of the clock by George II to a certain Andrew Stone, who was tutor to his grandson George III. Stone, born in 1703 and educated at Oxford where he obtained his MA degree in 1728, became Under-Secretary of State and Member of Parliament for Hastings 1741–61. He enjoyed the confidence of the Court, becoming treasurer to Queen Charlotte in 1761: in other words, he became a man wielding considerable influence in high places by the time of his death in 1773. Stone left the clock to his sister Anne, the wife of William Barnard, Bishop of Londonderry (1698–1768), after whom it has come to be named and to whose descendants it has been passed down.

The other clock by Tompion to be reviewed in this context is said to have been given by Charles II to his
366 mistress, the Countess of Castlemaine, from whom it has passed to her descendant, the Duke of Grafton. A brief summary of this remarkable lady's life is germane to the story of the clock, since, for any proper consideration of its provenance, certain dates are of paramount importance.

Barbara Villiers, daughter of William Villiers, second Viscount Grandison, was born in 1641. An acknowledged beauty, she became the King's mistress in 1660, and Countess of Castlemaine by virtue of her husband's elevation to the Irish peerage in 1661. A year later she had been imposed upon Queen Catherine, as Lady of the Bedchamber. She subsequently became the centre of Court intrigue, and a political activist who could make or break those in power; she was also said to have trafficked in the sale of Court offices and privileges. Her amours became notorious and, by 1669, she had been pensioned off, being created Duchess of Cleveland in 1670. She was supplanted in the King's graces by Louise Renée de Kéroualle in 1671 and eventually went to live for some years in Paris (1677–84). Returning, she married Robert Feilding in 1705 and lived in Chiswick. The marriage was annulled in 1707, and she died in 1709. The King acknowledged paternity of five of her seven children.

In a sense, the clock itself reflects all the intrigue that surrounded its supposed original owner; this can be said to have culminated with an incident about 1845, when the clock was sent to B. L. Vulliamy for repair. He promptly changed the movement for one of his own and even added his name to the dial, although he was later ordered to erase this impertinence. As for the original movement, he left it to the Institution of Civil Engineers, where it remains to this day, in perfect working order, despite Vulliamy having written of it, in 1849, that 'within the last two years it was put into incompetent hands to repair and spoilt. I made a new Clock into the Case'. R. W. Symonds, in his definitive work on Tompion, regards Vulliamy as having chosen the course which would show him the greatest profit, irrespective of the morality of his actions; and it is hard to conceive of any other explanation for his depredations, consistent in their constant repetition.

For present purposes the clock and case will be described as if still one entity. The visual impact is greatly heightened by the use of a fire-gilt brass case with silver mounts; the finials, bud-like but with outer leaves, are most unusual, while perhaps the strangest feature of all is the absence of any back door. Instead there is a panel of open-work entwined foliage and fruit, held in place by screws. Similarly, the side panels are mainly of open-work metal, but incorporating a small round glazed lenticle. The main carcase of the case has both engraved and applied decoration; and, in the absence of a door, the only way to gain access to the movement is by bodily lifting the case off, first having removed the four screws which hold it to a base plate, upon which the movement is mounted. The back plate of the latter, since it was clearly not intended to be seen, is entirely devoid of engraved decoration.

If the case of this clock is considered remarkable, then the movement must be regarded as even more so. It is unnumbered, which places it as prior to 1680, when Tompion started to number his movements. Symonds has no doubt that it was an experimental piece, and it was certainly a highly complicated one. The sheer craftsmanship is superb and, in view of its necessarily early date, cannot but give rise to astonishment at its sophisticated design and construction.

First, the clock has *grande sonnerie* striking: that means to say that, after every quarter, the last hour is also struck. Usually, of course, the quarters are struck by themselves, the advantage of the former arrangement being that you do not have to be physically within sight of the clock dial to avoid any possibility of error in determining which hour is concerned. Even so—and this feature is unique by comparison with later clocks of the same type made by Tompion—only one train is employed for both quarter- and hour-striking, instead of one for each function. There is no auxiliary spring for the repeating-train which also derives its power from the striking one; pulling the repeat cord simply unlocks that train. In view of the multi-purpose power reserve required for these various indications, it is no wonder that the striking-mainspring is unusually large and powerful. There is also an alarm function, but this does have its own spring, which is wound, like the other two, from the dial.

This dial is remarkable, at first sight, for embracing, in addition to the aperture for mock pendulum, no less than four subsidiaries, one in each corner. The purpose of the mock pendulum—essential to a clock like this one, where access to the movement was by no means easy—was to determine visually that the clock was in fact going; and this clock is thought to be the first in which Tompion employed this feature. Another 'first' was the use of rise-and-fall regulation of the pendulum,

366. (Left) *The movement of the so-called 'Castlemaine' Tompion, after B. L. Vulliamy had re-dialled it.* (Alan Lloyd Collection)

367. (Below left) *The magnificent Tompion clock said to have been formerly in the Duke of Sussex's collection, and dispersed in 1843.* (Deposited on anonymous loan at the British Museum)

368. (Below) *Back view of the case of the preceding clock, showing decorative panel set into the rear door.* (Deposited on anonymous loan at the British Museum)

controlled by one of the upper subsidiaries, the other being for strike/silent, an arrangement which eventually became commonplace. The hands in the lower subsidiaries on the dial controlled the locking-mechanism which had to be brought into use to restrain the pendulum when the clock was moved.

There are entries in Hooke's diary in February and June 1677 which suggest that the scientist was helping Tompion with a royal clock which may have been this one. It is simply described as 'the King's striking clock'. Certainly the Castlemaine clock could not have been made before 1676, by which time that Countess had been supplanted by Louise de Kéroualle; and in 1677 she went to live in Paris, not returning until 1684. It must seem unlikely, therefore, that the King had the clock made specially for her. If, as has also been suggested, the clock was given to her after the King's death, then it may have been 'the King's striking clock' mentioned by Hooke. No obvious way of solving this impasse is immediately apparent although Symonds comments, a shade ruefully, that it would be interesting to know if the clock figured in the Royal Will. The testamentary dispositions of the sovereign are never revealed, however.

Comparable with the clocks just described, but perhaps not so well known, is the splendid bracket clock by Tompion said to have been owned by the Duke of
367 Sussex, the sixth son of George III. This is at present on
368 anonymous loan to the British Museum. Among the special features of this clock, possibly listed as item 75 in the Catalogue of the sale of the Duke's effects in 1843 (vide Appendix Two), is *grande sonnerie* striking. Other refinements include the complete absence of any back door to the case; this was to protect the spring-suspended pendulum, which could be locked rigid for travelling by manual operation of the two switches in the lower corners of the dial, and re-started by use of the 'mock pendulum' visible through an aperture therein. It should be stated that the principal evidence connecting this clock with the Duke of Sussex is the existence, on the back of the dial plate, of an apparently wholly authentic repairer's inscription, which reads 'Cleaned Gorham April 1834 Kensington'. James Gorham, as his watch paper reveals, had his premises conveniently 'opposite the Palace gate' in Kensington High Street so he may well have been appointed to the Duke some years before he received a Royal Warrant from the sovereign. This occurred in 1837—(*see* Appendix Three).

In contrast to the magnificence and mechanical ingenuity built into the clocks just described, there now follows a sequence of watches, each with its own royal pretensions. First comes a coach watch of large dimensions, the extreme outer diameter being in excess

369. *Coach watch by John Harris, said to be connected with Princess Augusta of Saxe-Gotha.* (Sotheby's, London)

of 5 inches, which is housed in fine silver-gilt pair-cases. 369
The royal association is to be found on the outer case, which is repoussé with formal scrollwork surrounding a central crowned monogram: this has been identified as belonging to Princess Augusta of Saxe-Gotha, wife of Frederick, Prince of Wales and eldest son of George II. Their eldest son—since Frederick died in 1751—succeeded to the throne as George III in 1760. The inner case of the pair is elaborately pierced and engraved with inhabited foliage, and a vignette of a landscape on the band around the base of the pendant and a grotesque mask opposing it. The verge movement has additional trains for quarter-striking and alarm,

there being in consequence three winding-squares at the back. In decorative terms, it has turned baluster pillars to separate the plates, and a large winged masked cock with broad foot which is finely pierced and engraved. The white enamel dial with Roman hour numerals and, outside them, Arabic five-minute figures, has a central rotatable alarm disc, indicated by the pointed 'tail' of the hour hand. This, of blued-steel, together with its companion for minutes, comprise the style known as 'beetle and poker'.

This watch is signed 'John Harris, London no. 2005'; and Baillie lists some half-a-dozen makers bearing this not uncommon combination of names who were working in London during the second half of the eighteenth century. It is not possible to distinguish between one and another of them, so far as the manufacture of this object is concerned. It was sold, incidentally, by Sotheby's on 21st July 1975.

A somewhat more speculative watch was sold by the same auctioneers on 16th June in that same year. Like at least one other object mentioned, it had been displayed in the Loan Exhibition of Royal Treasures in 1937 where it was said to have been given by the Prince of Wales to a certain Colonel Newton in 1794. The credibility of that attribution may be judged by the price made under the hammer—some £540.

As to the watch itself, it consisted of a quarter-repeating cylinder movement housed in gold plain pair-cases, into the back of the outer one of which had been inset—apparently at some later date—a gilt engraved medallion bearing the Prince of Wales's insignia and,
370 beneath, a presentation inscription dated 1794. This reads 'G.P.W. Col.Com X.L.D. Gulielmo Newton Hoc Pignus Amicitiae Nov^{rs} die XXII MDCCLXXXXIV D.D.'. Nevertheless, the watch itself was of late eighteenth-century style, the maker being James Wild, of Soho, number 4383. Britten places this maker in Frith Street, Soho, in 1790, and Baillie adds a closing date of 1808.

The ring-watch made by John Arnold for George III, known only from contemporary references, seems even so to have sparked off a fashion for such things; another such specimen, also attributed to that monarch, has already been seen to be of Continental origin. The British Museum has yet another, but in this case the
371 object itself is of fine quality and although anonymous
372 may well be English. With a full-plate fusee cylinder movement, the cock is formed almost like the letter 'A', from which springs a short extension into which the balance is pivoted. It has an unorthodox appearance

370. *Back of a watch by James Wild, of Soho, with inscription indicating a royal association.* (Sotheby's, London)

371. (Centre right) *Ring watch, unsigned, possibly English.* (British Museum)

372. (Right) *Movement of the preceding watch, said to have belonged to George III.* (British Museum)

such as might well be tried out by a good London craftsman. For the rest, the gold ring has shoulders and bezel set with brilliants, with a crystal over the dial and another inset at the back through which the movement can be seen. The white enamel dial with its five-minute figures and gold 'beetle and poker' hands adds to the wholly English appearance; and it must be regarded as a fine and interesting watch, but any royal connection must be seen as tenuous in the extreme.

For a complete change, but while still with the British Museum collections, one can turn to a garden sundial. Of octagonal shape, brass and apparently of early nineteenth-century date, the maker's signature is 'D.
373 Bolton, London'. The interesting part of this large dial is the circular cartouche, 80 millimetres in diameter, near the foot of the gnomon—which, incidentally, is so different both in character and colour from the rest as to suggest a replacement—containing a monogram 'C.R.' surmounted by a crown. This has been ascribed to Queen Caroline, consort of George IV, an attribution which is now generally considered quite plausible. The dial came to the museum from the Croft Lyons Bequest in 1926.

Occasionally, in describing objects with tenuous royal associations, one is encountered that encapsulates several mysteries within itself. Such an item was sold at Sotheby's on 9th December 1968, when it made £740, a not inconsiderable sum in those days for a watch of its quality. The ruby cylinder movement, with going-barrel, and enclosed by a dust-cap finely engraved with scrolling foliage, was signed 'Charman & Co., London, no. 9041'; it had a white enamel dial with subsidiary seconds and gold hands. The beauty of this watch was undoubtedly in the double-backed case, however. This had split-pearl-decorated bezels, pendant and bow while the back was enamelled in translucent

373. *Detail of large sundial signed 'D. Bolton London', showing evidence of royal association.* (British Museum)

blue over a *guilloche* ground, within a white serpentine border, and in the centre a Royal Cypher 'GR' surmounted by a crown set in diamonds. This fine case, surprisingly, bears a London hallmark for 1817, agreeing with Britten's entry for the maker: Peter Charman is located at 64 Piccadilly for ten years from 1816 onwards. However, what can be the inscrutable meaning behind the inscription to be found on the inner dome of the case, which reads 'Yuen-ming-yuen 1861'?

Perhaps the most difficult objects to authenticate are royal presentation timepieces. In the majority of cases
374 there is likely to be no back-up proof in the form of supporting documentation, and decorative elements that might seem to give credence to such claims are often open to suspicion when subjected to critical analysis. On 29th July 1969, Sotheby's sold a very fine clock which might seem to fall into the 'presentation' category, and it made £1,350, a pointer to its credibility. A bracket clock, the 8-inch dial with cherub spandrels was studded with coloured semi-precious stones while the arch contained a small painted porcelain plaque and mother-o'-pearl chime and strike/silent dials. The three-train movement, with verge escapement, utilized an eight-bell chime with associated pin-barrel. As to the fine mahogany case, the bell top was surmounted by a silvered figure of Cupid and elaborately mounted with ormolu on all sides, while the front and back of the dome were set with silver portrait medallions of Louis XVI and Marie Antoinette above fleur-de-lys and child supporters, the apron having a crown and the rest of the case mounted with a profusion of interlaced branches and leaves, terms, pineapples and cabochons. In other words, this was a really elaborate clock such as might be most acceptably received in French Court circles, and indeed it was said to have been presented by Queen Charlotte, the wife of George III, to Louis XVI on the occasion of his marriage, on 16th May 1770, to Marie Antoinette.

374. *Royal presentation bracket clock, unsigned.* (Sotheby's, London)

The strange feature of this clock was that it was unsigned; the auctioneers hazarded a guess that it might be Dutch, presumably because it had an arcaded minute band which is always associated with that country's horological practice, and certainly the enrichment of the case did not accord with normal English tenets in such things. The same spectacular element can be detected—albeit there is no question but that this is an English clock—in a fine long-case clock which was advertised for sale in June 1972, and which, according to an inscription inside the trunk door, was formerly at Carlton House in the time of George IV, being sold at the dispersal auction to a servant of Lady Sydney Inverurie. This clock has a fine month-duration movement with rack striking and plain knopped pillars. The break-arch dial, with strike/silent at the top, is made the more elegant by the maker's signature, which is deployed in an overlaid silvered semicircle straddling the lower half of the matted dial centre, within the chapter ring. The oak case, decorated with raised gilt chinoiserie on a brick-red japanned ground, and surmounted with three ball-and-spire finials, is well-proportioned and finely preserved. The maker signs himself 'John Taylor, London'—not a name to conjure with, and difficult to assign to any one individual since there were several such working in London during the eighteenth century.

An even more insubstantial wraith of a clock—because now the principal reference to it lies in the pages of Britten, and the only illustration his figure

534—must be mentioned here, if only because it came from the workshop of Christopher Pinchbeck, presumably the son. The style of the clock is definitely not English, and Britten compares it with German early eighteenth-century practice and its case with Louis XV taste. The materials are an unfamiliar mixture of 'pinchbeck', that alloy invented by Pinchbeck senior, and gilt metal. The shaped dial plate has a circular white enamel dial with central alarm disc set into a cast foliate surround rising to an arch with cast cherubs and foliage flanking a white enamel plaque containing the signature 'C. Pinchbeck'. This clock seemingly struck the hours and also had a pull quarter-repeating train as well as the alarm function, the latter being wound with a square sited just below XII. With the whole structure supported upon four elaborate scrolling feet, Britten illustrates yet a further element, which seems to be a cast plinth, of somewhat indeterminate form, although whether this was original or not remains unclear since it is not mentioned in the text.

This clock is said to have belonged to George IV when
Prince of Wales, and to have been kept at his house on 375
Hammersmith Mall. Afterwards it passed into the possession of the *maître de cuisine* at Carlton House, one Louis Welfe, who lived subsequently at the Hammersmith establishment; and when Britten knew the clock, it then belonged to a Mr Hansard Watt. Strangely, an almost identical clock appeared at Christie's on 21st June 1978—the case appeared to be a perfect twin—but the movement, with going-barrels and tapered pillars, and originally a verge escapement but now converted to anchor, lacked the repeating facility, while the alarm must have been differently

375. (Below) *Clock by Christopher Pinchbeck, sold by auction in 1978.* (Christie's, London)

(Below right) *Very similar clock illustrated by Britten in 1932, and said to have been once in Windsor Castle. There are noticeable differences in the quality of the gilt mounts, the alarm winding-squares are differently planted, and Britten's version seems to have acquired an addition in the form of an ornate base.*

376. *Clock by William Parr, with painting by William Hopkins Craft.* (Christie's, London)

planted since the winding-square in this example was located below XI. The hammer price was £750.

Yet another clock said to have associations with this same monarch appeared in Christie's in May 1979. Of a somewhat florid character, it consisted of a gilt-metal structure described by the auctioneers as of domed plinth-shaped outline surmounted by a twin-handled urn with detachable cover. Its upper corners were hollowed to accommodate 'finials' taking the form of smaller urns with detachable covers, these concealing compartments containing cut-glass scent bottles. The angles were formed of a columnar arrangement having, above, foliage and swagged drapery enclosing 376
an enamel plaque depicting a vase of flowers in an interior. In each column below the plaque there was a small drawer, cast on the outer surface to resemble

balustrading, and beneath these, splayed fluted obliquely placed square bases each on four ribbed stepped feet. The reverse of this unusual creation was set with a mirror: this, taken with the scent bottles and the small drawer compartments, immediately gives the clock a boudoir flavour. The gilt-metal shaped front plate, cast with scrolling foliage in an overlapping laurel-leaf border, served to frame an oval enamel dial plate, signed 'W.H. Craft, Invt et fecit 1785'. This is decorated with a figure of Peace, in a classical architectural setting against a landscape background, and garlanding the tiny central clock dial, which is seemingly supported by an enamelled truncated column at the base of which two putti, beside a discarded torch and quiver, attend two doves, at the same time displaying a scroll upon which is detailed the proportion of the National Debt incurred in connection with the American colonies. The two-train rack-striking fusee movement, with anchor escapement, has a back plate engraved with scrolls, garlands and Prince of Wales's plumes, the maker's signature—'Parr, Watch and Clock Maker, No. 20, Strand'—appearing on the bob of the pendulum, which is complete with securing-clamp for use when travelling.

The complicated design of this clock will be apparent from the foregoing; but it is, nevertheless, an interesting object which repays further study. William Hopkins Craft, the enamel painter, lived *c.*1730–1811. Working mainly on allegorical subjects, he exhibited regularly at the Royal Academy and lived for a time in Paris; later, in partnership with David Rhodes, he worked for Wedgwood in London. He seems to have declined in old age, for he was admitted to the Charter House in 1810, and the following year, aged eighty, he was 'suddenly taken ill on Clarkenwell [*sic*] Green, and, being conveyed home in a coach, expired on entering his apartment'. There was a series of three of these clocks, with allegorical subjects painted by Craft, variously dated, and all contained in similarly decorated gilt-metal cases with mirror backs. The first is dated 1779, the symbolism showing England as a colonizing power; this one represents the rebellious colonists granted independence; the third, which is signed 'Invented 1773, finished 1796', shows an allegory of the liberated New World being encouraged in the pursuit of freedom by the Old. The auctioneers, in their catalogue entry, speculated that the strong stand on the question of the colonists' outstanding financial liabilities, reflected in the decoration of this clock, might also represent the known antipathy then existing between the Prince of Wales and his father, George III.

Little enough seems to be known about the clockmaker William Parr. Britten notes watches made by him which span the years 1790–1808, and, in 1804, he published *A treatise on pocket watches; pointing out the defects so generally complained of in their construction . . .*, which is a rare forty-four-page booklet, of which there is a copy in the Clockmakers' Company Library.

As to the provenance of the clock, it was given by George IV to Frederick Thomas Malleson, the royal gardener at Claremont Park, Surrey: his dates are given as 1785–1866. Thereafter, it passed down through four generations of the same family, two of them also in royal service, to the present day.

Much has already been written in this book about the Vulliamys, that remarkable horological dynasty of which the first member was Justin. There exists in private hands the movement only of a remarkably sophisticated 'timer'—for want of any better 377
description—signed by him, which has a number of novel features and a tentative provenance which at least has some element of probability built into it. This machine has an arched silvered dial plate, measuring $9\frac{1}{2}$ inches by $7\frac{3}{8}$ inches, upon which are inscribed no less than nine 'subsidiary' dials, each with its single

377. *The nine-dial timer by Justin Vulliamy, possibly from George III's private observatory at Kew.* (Private collection)

blued-steel hand, and each dial marked to show the division of time being registered upon it, viz. minutes, seconds, $\frac{1}{8}$ seconds, 2nd, 3rd and 4th seconds and 2nd, 3rd and 4th minutes. The supposition is that this clock was intended for observational timing in astronomy and that it was originally used in George III's private observatory at Kew, for which it was specially designed by his royal clockmaker. It has a very short duration of going, making it quite unsuitable for normal time-keeping, even if the dials, or any one of them, were designed for it—which none of them is. Additionally, three of the subsidiary dials can be activated or halted at will, by the use of three spring clutches operated by knobs something after the fashion of organ stops. The other extraordinary feature is that, although weight-driven, the escapement, with its quarter-second pendulum, is an enormous version of the cylinder—much more usually a watch escapement. This would, in any event, appear to be the only weight-driven cylinder escapement ever recorded. As to the tentative attribution, it has to be said that no inventories exist in the royal archives which show the exact instrumentation of Kew Observatory; and two manuscript volumes which did list that Observatory's technical contents, and which were in the Library of King's College, in London, in 1926, cannot now be traced. There is one speculative entry in a list of certain items transferred from Kew to Armagh Observatory, and contained in a Minute Book of 1853 which is preserved there. This reads: 'Case of Vulliamy's curious clock'. However, whether this was the case of the nine-dial timer or not is never likely to be known, for it had already disappeared by 1951. To add insult to injury, it has sometimes been argued that a device of this kind could be very useful for lap timing in horse racing and other such sports.

Whatever may be the merits of the Justin Vulliamy timer, there has recently appeared on the market an interesting chronometer by Robert Pennington, which,
378 it is also suggested, might have graced the Observatory
379 in Richmond Gardens. This small 55-hour machine, bearing the maker's serial number $\frac{1}{430}$, can be dated accurately by reference to the twin mainsprings—mounted in two tiers, each spring in its own barrel unit, and similar to the arrangement favoured by Mudge senior in his No. 1 timekeeper—for they are signed 'K. Clark 1801'. Other curious features of this important instrument, with its Arnold pattern escapement, include separately planted steel detent and gold passing spring, each with depth adjustment facility; gold escape wheel of 16 teeth; and a compensation balance of Pennington's own 'Y-C-C' design, and 3-armed solid brass rim having two bimetallic affixes. The silvered dial is arranged on the regulator pattern, with subsidiary 24-hours and seconds dials, and peripheral minutes; it also incorporates a crown above the royal cypher 'G. R.' Movement and dial are contained in a brass drum, glazed at both ends, which in turn fits into an hexagonal two-tier box of Cuban mahogany, with hinged brass observation cover bearing the inscription 'Pennington London'. Winding is through the side of the case, in the manner originated by Margetts.

378. (Top) *Dial of chronometer no.* $\frac{1}{430}$ *by Robert Pennington.* (Christie's, London)

379. (Above) *Movement of the preceding chronometer.* (Christie's, London)

Altogether less assuming was a small—only $6\frac{1}{2}$
inches overall—brass timepiece lantern clock with
380 alarm by William Webster, of Exchange Alley, which
passed through Christie's auction rooms on 3rd
October 1979. With short bob pendulum and verge
escapement, this type of timepiece was for travellers, usually having a stirrup at the back from which it could be hung on any convenient hook, and a pair of spurs projecting from the base to hold it away from the wall. Behind the broken-arched gilt dial, with its matted centre and alarm setting disc, formal spandrels and maker's name on a silvered medallion in the arch, there was a posted movement with turned pillars, feet and finials. The Webster family of clockmakers were, of course, names to be conjured with throughout the eighteenth century, which was to all intents and purposes spanned by just two, father and son, and, just to make it more difficult, both named William. Exchange Alley is that tiny thoroughfare—it still exists—which housed over the years many famous horologists, such as Daniel Quare and Robert Seignior; running between Cornhill and Lombard Street, it was doubtless very well placed for business of all kinds. The other name on this particular clock, however, is not so familiar. Inscribed around the edge of the dial arch is 'Prince Rupert, Windsor Castle'. George I had an uncle so-named, who was Constable of the Castle in 1668, somewhat too early for this clock. The object itself was not of any special merit, whatever the standing of its maker, so that the authenticity of the implied association must be open to some doubt.

380. *Travelling alarm lantern clock by William Webster inscribed at the top of the arch 'Prince Rupert, Windsor Castle'.* (Christie's, London)

Also a somewhat speculative, if much more attractive, item was the watch that appeared twice—at an interval of six months—in Christie's, first on 4th October 1977 and then again on 19th April in the year following. This had that rare feature, a double dial: that is, a dial on each side. In a gilt-metal case that was pierced as well as engraved with scrolls and acanthus designs, for this was a verge clock-watch, and on which the bezels were further decorated with split pearls, the dial on one side showed the time in hours and minutes, with day-of-the-month calendar and with two winding-squares for the going- and striking-trains. On the reverse was a sweep centre-seconds hand, with subsidiaries for the time, at top, and strike/silent, regulation and the lunar day beneath. The provenance of this watch, according to the catalogue entry, started with William IV. About 1791 that monarch formed an association with an actress called Dorothea Jordan, when he was the Duke of Clarence, and one result of this relationship, which continued until 1811, was a natural son, George Augustus Frederick Fitzclarence, first Earl of Munster, who was born in 1794. The watch was given by the King to his son, who in turn gave it to Lord Northland, from whom it descended to the present day. The date of the watch was given as *c.*1790, which accords with such an origin. However, the maker's name, for the signature is quoted as 'Staplin, London, S.11', does not help very much. No such individual is listed in any of the standard reference works.

381. *Watch by Sam Houston with inscription concerning Princess Charlotte.* (Clockmakers' Company, London)

382. *Woven silk portrait of Princess Charlotte, intended to be carried in the back of a watch case.* (Clockmakers' Company, London)

Another unrecorded maker bears the credit for the next watch, which came into the Clockmakers' Company Collection via the Hurle-Bradley Bequest. A verge watch in a silver consular case, the signature on the movement is Saml. Houston, London. No. 794. Salient features of the latter also include a five-armed solid steel balance, and an early example of the wedge-
381 shaped cock. Winding is through the dial at IIII, the numerals being upright Roman, the hands gold, and of the spade and pointer design. The case carries the London hall-mark for 1807, and the case-maker is 'CC', possibly Charles Clarke. The royal association springs from the inscription on the back of the case, beneath a
382 crown, which reads: 'Worn by HRH/The Princess Charlotte/untill she was twelve Yrs/old & then presented/by HRH to/Heny. Kuper'. If one can assume that the royal Princess was Charlotte Augusta, only child of George IV and Caroline of Brunswick, then she can only have worn the watch for a year or so before giving it away; born in 1796, she died in childbirth in 1817. Nothing is known about Henry Kuper.

Concerned with a more recent historical event, if one can believe the inscription, but sharing with the last object described the phenomenon of having appeared twice in the big London sale rooms of recent years, is the next timepiece, a gold hunting-cased quarter-repeating lever watch. This first turned up in Sotheby's on 21st May 1973. The inside of the hunter cover is engraved with the following legend: 'To my faithful & devoted personal attendant John Brown Esqre in grateful remembrance of the presence of mind and courage he displayed at Buckingham Palace Feb. 29 1872 from Victoria R.'. The event in question occurred when the Queen, returning from an afternoon's drive in an open landau, was accosted, at the Garden Entrance to Buckingham Palace, by a student brandishing a pistol in one hand and a document in the other. The man was restrained by John Brown until the police arrived and arrested him.

Complete with gold chain, the watch appears to have been Swiss-made: it is signed 'Exam[d] by Lund & Blockley, 42 Pall Mall, London', a device often used by London makers when dealing with a bought-in product. The gilt and jewelled movement, of Lépine calibre, repeated with two hammers on steel gongs. An interesting instance of the enormous increases that have occurred, of late, in the market value of historic watches is to be seen to some extent in this particular example, for when this watch was sold in 1973, it made £580. When it next turned up, on 22nd June 1977 at Christie's, it fetched £1,050. As to the makers, Lund & Blockley, they enjoyed royal favour officially for one year only, in 1887, after which they disappeared from the list of Warrant Holders. It was not that John Brown's watch gave too much trouble, but simply that the firm went bankrupt (*vide* Appendix Three).

Watches seem to have been favourite gifts of monarchs through the ages, even at 'first remove'. A curious example of this seen at Christie's in 1971, was a plain gold half-hunter watch, the movement unsigned despite having an English lever escapement and therefore, presumably, English antecedents. On the back of the case was engraved the Royal Cypher of King Edward VII, and the cuvette was engraved: 'To S. J. Gale, from The King'. A note to the catalogue entry explains that Samuel J. Gale was a personal companion of Sir Ernest Cassel who was, in turn, a close friend of the monarch. Nevertheless, a somewhat involved kind of presentation, it might be thought.

Commemorative clocks and watches have occurred through the ages, and examples have already been noted. A somewhat out-of-the-ordinary one passed through Sotheby's rooms in 1976, in the form of a skeleton clock reputedly made to celebrate the marriage, in 1863, of Prince Albert Edward—later King Edward VII—and Princess Alexandra of Denmark. The chapter ring of this clock, which consisted of interlocking discs, displayed the hour numerals in red; a timepiece only, the fusee movement had an anchor escapement. The boldly scrolled and pierced frame, of substantial construction, was surmounted by Prince of Wales's feathers, as was also the chapter ring, in this last case incorporating the emblems of the three kingdoms and Wales and with the monogram 'AA' below the hour VI. This object was in a relatively restrained style, but the same could hardly be said of a silver watch which appeared in Christie's in 1971. Inscribed 'Chronometer Prima', but otherwise without manufacturer's identification, this lever watch had a silver dial bearing the royal coat-of-arms and was housed in a silver hunting-case. The cuvette was stamped, in high relief, with Britannia together with the inscription 'The British Empire Mourns Edward the Peacemaker'. The cover was similarly decorated with a portrait of Edward VII and an inscription—unfortunately, there is no record of this last feature—while the reverse displayed a portrait of George V and an inscription upon a band, which read, 'God Save the King'. The three portraits were apparently signed 'Adr. Huijbers'.

The foregoing examples of supposedly royal clocks and watches have been selected more or less at random, and any systematic search of likely documentary sources such as catalogues, not only of museums and exhibitions but also those of varying degrees of accuracy of description which derive from Britain's hundreds of auctioneers, would be bound to produce an untold abundance more. Watches, particularly, seem very prolific, yet one of the potentially most interesting episodes, so far as these are concerned, seems lost to posterity for ever, at least in regard to any surviving detailed record. There are several pointers to the belief that King Edward VIII, during his brief term as monarch, disposed of a number of fine watches that were either in the Royal Collection or deployed amongst members of his family, using as his selling-agents the then partnership as horologists and dealers of Philip Clowes and Captain J. H. ('Jack') Jauncey, RN, who were based at an address in London's Beauchamp Place in 1937. The latter partner disappeared back into the Navy at the beginning of World War II and does not seem to have played any further role in horological matters: both are now long since dead. Had any inventory of the watches involved in this transaction—if indeed it ever did take place—survived to the present time, it might have served to authenticate for the future a number of attributions which have probably still to be claimed, thereby avoiding the kind of suspicious approach to such things which is nowadays the normal practice, and which this chapter has set out to demonstrate.

It is, of course, difficult to measure accurately the overall attitudes towards royal relics, genuine or not, shown in the past, because they are not often reflected in contemporary literature. Therefore, it was a veritable delight to find the following authoritative view expressed in *The Times* and forming part of the first notice it published concerning the Stuart Exhibition of 1888.

This appeared in the issue for 31st December of that year:

With regard to the authentication which is, of course, the most important question in the case of an exhibition of this kind, it may be said that, generally speaking, it is good and trustworthy, more perhaps in the case of the personal relics than in that of the pictures. . . . They have for the most part been so highly prized by the families to whom they originally belonged, their value to those families has been so much greater than their market value, that they have, in five cases out of six, remained in the possession of one line from the beginning. The visitor may, therefore, accept with very great confidence the historical pretensions of the needlework, the trinkets, the prayer books, the arms that are to be found here. . . .

Unfortunately, after this revealing philosophy, the writer went straight on to extol the virtues of 'one of the choicest pieces of workmanship . . . Sir T. Dick-Lauder's "Memento Mori" timepiece'—which was the massive skull watch attributed to Mary, Queen of Scots, with which this present chapter commenced!

Nevertheless there does remain—both inside and outside the Royal Collection—a large number of the finest quality timepieces, of a wide variety of types and originating from many of the greatest craftsmen, that can without any doubt at all be connected with individual kings and queens of Britain, or members of their families. If the Royal Collection can properly be viewed as a highly important element in Britain's cultural heritage, rather than purely a private source of pleasure and enlightenment for the Royal Family—and since Her Majesty The Queen is graciously pleased to exhibit objects from it continuously in her gallery in Buckingham Palace, as well as making frequent loans to other public exhibitions, it is perhaps not such an unrealistic view—it must be a source of regret that any art objects should ever, over the centuries, have been allowed to escape from it. Perhaps, after all, a certain Henry Siddons, of Bath, who died in 1937, had the right idea. In his Will, he wrote: 'I trust that His Royal Highness the Duke of Kent may be graciously pleased to accept the gold repeater watch given by His Majesty King George IV to my grandfather George Siddons, of the Bengal Civil Service. From Royalty it came, to Royalty it should return.'

Relevant Royal Foundations—the Company and the Observatory

In Britain, the earliest public expression of royal interest in and concern for the crafts dates from the twelfth century, when the Weavers of the City of London received a Royal Charter of Incorporation. The mediaeval craft guilds were brought gradually into existence to control the City's trade during the Middle Ages; and indeed the guild system became an integral element in the economic, social and political climate of the time, throughout Western Europe. The guild concerned with clockmaking was only formed in the second quarter of the seventeenth century, for reasons which will be made apparent; but perhaps since this was one of the early technological guilds, formation of a suitable trade and craft body was not to be the only point at which contact was to be made with the monarch of the day. It was necessary for science to be encouraged, both to support the future development and prosperity of the nation and for purely practical purposes, like navigation. So, the Royal Prerogative was to be exercised on two different levels, commercial and scientific.

The Worshipful Company of Clockmakers

Workers in metal were scarce in Britain before the middle of the sixteenth century, and the Blacksmiths' Company did not receive its Royal Charter until 1571. As workers in iron—not, be it noted, shoers of horses since that was the job of the Farriers—the Blacksmiths tended to aggregate to themselves any craftsmen working in the same medium. In the end, most of these different crafts were to separate out from the parent body, but it was a matter of waiting until the time when demand for their specialist services had reached such proportions that it became desirable to set them up as entities in their own right.

The first mechanical clock arrived in Britain about the end of the thirteenth century, it would appear. Yet, three centuries later, any clockmaking was still confined to the large public clocks in churches and the like, and to substantial domestic miniatures of the same, known as chamber clocks, all of them being made of iron and all still made by blacksmiths.

However, from about 1600, watchmaking—which had certainly appeared in other parts of Europe almost a century earlier—started to make itself known in England, and English artists were soon competing with Continental practitioners and creating an English 'school', in both the mechanical and artistic dimensions of their craft.

By 1622, there were some sixteen clock- and watchmakers at work in London who were Freemen, mainly of the Blacksmiths' Company; but there were also a number of others plying the same craft, many of them from abroad

1. *The arms of the Worshipful Company of Clockmakers: a version used in the early nineteenth century.* (Clockmakers' Company, London)

including Huguenot refugees, who were not Freemen, a state of affairs that was frowned upon in the increasingly tight-knit craft community in the City. In 1627, clockmakers in the Blacksmiths' Company had induced that body to oppose on their behalf the intrusion of French clockmakers into the City of London, and the following year they tried to obtain recognition for themselves by means of a new joint blacksmiths' and clockmakers' Charter. A new Charter was indeed obtained, but it failed to give the clockmakers any special status.

Next, the clockmakers petitioned the Crown for their own Charter, a move that was naturally opposed by the Blacksmiths' Company, who were reluctant to lose any part of their special sphere of influence. This action and reaction was typical of the fragmentation and increasing specialization that occurred in the seventeenth century, and the opposite of the tendency to merge that had occurred in earlier periods.

In the course of time, the clockmakers realized their aspirations. Their Charter was granted in the reign of Charles I, on 22nd August 1631. It gave them authority to control their trade throughout the City of London and for 10 miles round about, under the official title of 'the Master, Wardens and Fellowship of the Art or Mystery of Clockmaking'. In this context, the word 'Mystery' (or 'Mistery') is thought to be from the Latin *ministerium*, or *misterium* in mediaeval Latin, meaning craft or vocation.

The Charter appointed the first Master, three Wardens, and ten Assistants who were to comprise the governing body of the newly formed Fellowship, by name. To constitute the Court of Assistants, these craftsmen were:

Master:	*Assistants*:
David Ramsay	James Vautrollier
Wardens:	John Smith
Henry Archer	Francis Forman
John Wellowe (Willow)	John Harris
Sampson Shelton	Richard Morgan
	Samuel Lynaker
	John Charlton
	John Midnall
	Simon Bartram
	Edward East

Both on the evidence of surviving artefacts and on contemporary indications, this was as mixed a bag of differing talents as one could wish for. The outstanding personality must have been East—yet here he is in a comparatively minor role. Both he and Ramsay held royal appointments, but the latter must have been the senior since his originated with James I. Ramsay was, in fact, to play a very small part in the early conduct of the Clockmakers' Company, and Henry Archer, appointed Deputy Master, presided in his place at most meetings of the Court of Assistants. As for the rest, some fine work survives from the *ateliers* of Archer, Shelton and Vautrollier, and Simon Bartram is a familiar name at this period; but only Willow, Shelton, Smith, Charlton, Harris, Bartram and East were subsequently to serve the office of Master.

The cost of obtaining the Charter was met by subscription of the then-existing members; and it was not an inconsiderable sum that had to be raised. In the next two or three years there are instances of members defaulting on their promises, but they were made to pay up in the end. In November 1634 the company paid £4 to one John Chappell, for 'flourishing and finishing'—that is to say, ornamenting and illuminating—this historic deed.

With the Charter safely achieved, the next stage—required of all new guilds by an Act of Henry VII in 1503—was to have Bye-Laws for the good government of the craft submitted and authenticated; this was done on 11th August 1632. On the following day, the Court of Assistants had its first formal meeting, when the Company's officers attended before the Lord Mayor to take the Oath of Office. Subsequently, and at a second meeting later in the same month, essential administrative parameters were agreed upon—prayers to be said before meetings, the hours of which were prescribed as from nine in the morning until noon, penalties to ensure the preservation of secrets as also for profane and blasphemous behaviour, penalties for members who neglected their duties, and so forth.

Despite this legitimization of the craft, its troubles were by no means over. It was still not obligatory for those working at making clocks and watches in the City of London to become Freemen of the Clockmakers' Company, and indeed many of them had already attained the same end by joining other Companies, and consequently owed allegiance to them. From the beginning, also, there was constant bickering with the Blacksmiths, who felt their influence waning as a result of break-away groups like the Clockmakers, not to mention the resulting loss of income.

In the case of Freemen of other Companies who were making clocks and watches, the Clockmakers were able to supervise the quality of their work; but of course they obtained no revenue from them. In an effort to alleviate the situation, the Company petitioned the Lord Mayor and Aldermen in 1697 for an Act to compel all apprentices working in the 'art' to take the Freedom of the Clockmakers' Company when their time expired. The Blacksmiths, for reasons already stated, actively opposed this application; and unfortunately, the decision went in their favour. In the event, it took another sixty-eight years—in 1765, in fact—before the Clockmakers' Company was successful in this particular issue.

The powers granted to craft guilds in the City of London, even as late as the seventeenth century, were extraordinarily extensive and, so far as the Clockmakers were concerned, for a long time rigidly enforced. Rather than reproduce the archaic language of the Charter and Bye-Laws, the following extract from the Company's official history* puts these powers in a nutshell:

> The Master, Wardens, and Assistants, or any two of them, the Master or one of the Wardens being one, had power to search and view all productions of the Art made within the Realm or imported for sale, and to seize and break work unlawfully made or composed of bad or defective materials, or in any way faulty; and to carry the

**Some Account of the Worshipful Company of Clockmakers* by S. E. Atkins and W. H. Overall. Privately printed, 1881.

same to the Company's Hall or meeting place, to be adjudged, and, if condemned, to be broken; to break open any place, if refused admission, to search it, and to seize work and tools therein concealed; to prevent aliens or strangers from working except with an allowed and professed Clockmaker, and also all persons who had not served a seven years' apprenticeship to the trade.

The authority thus exercised had the effect of bringing them into frequent conflict with members of the trade, but they seem to have carried out what was sometimes a difficult duty with moderation and firmness, thus protecting the public from being imposed upon, and the manufacturer from unfair and ruinous competition.

In practice, Searches were organized by dividing the City into 'walks'—e.g the City Walk, South-west Walk, Eastward Walk, etc—the necessary attendant costs being met by a quarterly payment of 4 pence from every Member of the Fellowship. Even with this small fee, the annual revenue deriving therefrom had, by 1708, reached the surprising sum of over £28. The Court Minutes of the Company contain innumerable examples of the results of such Searches,

18th January 1635 — The same day Thomas Hill a dyall maker at the Tower had 4 pocket dyalls cutt and did affront Mr Allen with opproprious words.

3rd November 1652 — Whereas at a general search by the Master and Wardens the 24 of October there was a Chamber Clock seized by Mr Thomas Holland, Warden, according to the orders of our Charter, being the work of Samuel Davis dwelling in Lothbury, London, the work being found very unserviceable and deceitful by the Court aforesaid. It was therefore adjudged to be defaced and broken that it might not be put to sale to deceive the people, which was done accordingly, Samuel Davis being present gave his consent thereto and was fined forty shillings according to the orders and he submitted thereunto.

29th September 1683 — Mr Robert Halsted's movements seized about six months since being viewed were judged to be absolutely insufficient, and uncapable of amendment and were therefore in their severall parts either broken or defaced soe as that they could never be usefull and in that condition were delivered to the Beadle that he should deliver them to Mr Halsted.

Exercise of powers such as the foregoing probably continued until near the end of the eighteenth century; but these by no means constituted the only active measures to protect the trade with which the Company concerned itself. In the latter half of the eighteenth century, for instance, there was a spate of fraudulent offences, in which the names of reputable craftsmen were deliberately attached to goods of inferior manufacture in order to enhance their saleability, and without any thought as to the effect on the reputations of the craftsmen concerned. In a sense, this was a permutation of an offence that had been detected very much earlier, in which certain Dutch artisans in Amsterdam had started using the names of well-known London makers, including Tompion, Windmills, Quare, Cabrier and others and selling the resulting articles as English. In July 1777, however, the situation is summarized in a Court Minute as follows:

1777. 7 July — Mr Charles Cabrier attended and acquainted the Court that he had entered prosecutions against sundry persons for putting his name to Watches which they had made up without his knowledge or consent, praying their assistance and advice, which was unanimously promised whenever he applied again, if he would indemnify the Company from every expense that may arise from the prosecution of this business.

The case went for trial in the King's Bench, when a defendant called Anderson was found guilty and fined £100, being £20 on each of five counts of fraudulently signing Cabrier's name on a watch. Meantime the Clockmakers' Court became so concerned at the apparent prevalence of this practice that a special meeting was called to determine what action should be taken, and it was decided, by way of caution to offenders as well as to protect the purchaser, to publish in the leading journals and newspapers of the day, a statement of the law applying to such offences, together with a declaration that the Court of Assistants was determined to prosecute in every such case that was brought to its notice. This probably had some effect, but even as late as 1818 the same kind of transgression was still occurring, and there is preserved among the Clockmakers' Company manuscripts in Guildhall Library (MS 3940, item 132) a printed broadsheet which was distributed throughout the London trade by Paul Philip Barraud, a famous watchmaker working in Cornhill, in which two men make a sworn statement admitting their guilt, in contriving to put Barraud's name on a watch that was not of his manufacture. By making such public confession they avoided prosecution, and simultaneously other potential offenders were warned off.

Over the years the Company fought many another cause on behalf of the members, a particularly protracted and injurious one, so far as the London craft trade was concerned, being the importation of foreign watches. At first, in the eighteenth century, the quarrel was with the Commissioners of Customs, who seemingly were permitting quantities of these to enter the country without paying duty. They could thus be sold cheaply on the market, undercutting the domestic product. By the following century, the blatant smuggling of large quantities of foreign watches, often complete with forged names and hallmarks on them, was rife, and the Company was again up in arms, demanding that such operations constitute a felony punishable by law.

While such time-consuming activities as these, often involving litigation and the briefing of counsel, were occupying much of the time—not to mention the finances—of the Court of Assistants, it nevertheless had many purely domestic issues to resolve. There was always the thorny question of apprentices—how many each Freeman could have bound to him at any one time, how many for the Assistants and senior officers of the Company, and so on.

Many occasions arose when efforts were made to circumvent the regulations, and appropriate penalties were inflicted in those that came to light. There was also an impediment in the constitution of the Company at its foundation, by which, for some strange reason which it is difficult to fathom at this distance in time, it had never been authorized to elect a Livery. This term originally related, of course, to the particular dress or uniform which each craft adopted, and by which it could be recognized, hence the term 'Livery Companies' which is often used to describe such craft guilds. It also had, and still has, a special meaning as denoting a particular grade of membership, an indication of seniority usually. An apprentice, having completed his training successfully, is admitted a Freeman of the Company; if he satisfies the Court of Assistants as to his rectitude and capabilities, he may, after a period of time, be elected to the Livery and take a very much greater part in the affairs of the Company and indeed of the City of London, for some ten thousand Liverymen of the City Companies are entitled to vote at elections in Guildhall. It is from the Livery, too, that the Court of Assistants recruits its members, always by the most democratic methods, and once a member of the Court, the road is fairly clear ahead to the office, first of each degree of wardenship—Junior Warden, Renter Warden (who is the Company's treasurer) and Senior Warden—and finally to the office of Master, for such appointments go almost entirely upon seniority and, although elections are held, these are usually a formality. There is really no answer to the argument that, if you are not fit to hold the office of Master, you will never even be elected to the Court of Assistants.

In any event, the Company felt the lack of a Livery and eventually, in 1748, petitioned the Lord Mayor and Court of Aldermen, within whose province it was to grant such an amenity. The matter dragged on, and in the end authority was refused; and indeed it was not until 1766 that it became possible for a Livery to be constituted, and even then it was limited in size to sixty members.

By the end of the eighteenth century most of the original functions of the Livery Companies had ceased to have relevance, although they have never been legally rescinded. Today, some crafts have simply disappeared without trace, while others have some present-day equivalent even if, in a few cases, it requires a stretch of the imagination to envisage it. The Clockmakers are fortunate in that the commodity with which they are concerned is just as important as it has ever been, perhaps, in this age of space-exploration, even more so. Nevertheless, with the advent in the last century of mass-production of mechanical timekeepers, and the sudden appearance, in the present one, of the quartz crystal and the electronic developments flowing from that discovery, the 'trade' is an entirely differently-composed entity from that which pertained throughout the earlier centuries of the Company's existence, so that most of the purposes for which it was founded have become extinct.

English institutions have a remarkable capacity for change and for acclimatization, however. During the nineteenth century the City Companies, rather than accept decline in a rapidly developing world that had little time, often enough, for the high standards of fine craftsmanship which they represented, found new life for themselves in charitable endeavours, in general and technical education and in promoting interest in their respective crafts even when such may have been features of a bygone age. The City and Guilds of London Institute is but one facet of the practical encouragement given to technological progress, in this new-found role.

The Clockmakers' Company, as such things are judged, has never been a rich institution. It never owned its own Hall—so that Court meetings, in the past, had to be held in taverns and inns within the City precincts, while its records and valuables were kept safe in a Strong Chest. This massive piece of furniture, with its four locks and keys, all of them different, and incapable of being opened unless the key-holders—the Master and the Wardens—were all present together, was frequently conveyed from one end of the City to the other, as might be required, yet it kept its contents safe and in good condition until a more permanent home could be found for them. There seem to have been several Chests over the centuries—doubtless they wore out and had to be replaced—the last one having been commissioned in 1766. This was eventually put in good order and handed over to Guildhall Library in 1873, where it seems to have been lost sight of for very many years. Rediscovered in a basement under the old Library in Basinghall Street in 1976, it has been renovated and is now on display to the public in the Company's Clock Room, which is accommodated in the new Guildhall Library in Aldermanbury.

The Company is singularly fortunate in possessing, in a fine state of preservation, a complete archive of its Court Minutes from its inception, as well as a number of other record series from its past, several in a complete or nearly complete state. It also retains not only its original Charter, but its Grant of Arms—obtained in 1671—as well as some 1
valuable plate, which is still used on certain ceremonial occasions. Probably its greatest asset, however, and the one on which much of its educational activity is based, is its Library and Collection. There is evidence that the Company first started seriously to collect the classic technical and historical works on horology, as well as examples from the finest periods of clock- and watchmaking, about 1815; the purpose then was to instruct apprentices in the best practices of their craft, and neither books nor objects were made available to the general public. However, when Guildhall Library was rehoused in 1872, the generosity of the Corporation of London in providing accommodation, and of the Company in displaying its Collection and depositing its by 2
now large collection of horological books, as well as its own manuscript records and other valuable horological documents, for reference use by readers in Guildhall Library, has helped to make this one of the world's great centres for research in this field. It can certainly claim to be one of the oldest specialist collections in horology in the world and is probably the oldest; and the arrangement entered into in 1872 has recently been reinforced when the new Guildhall Library was completed in 1974. Not only is the Company's Library beautifully housed in the main Reading Room, but a custom-built exhibition gallery, leading off the main entrance hall, has been provided which is substantially larger

2. The Clock Room in Guildhall Library, in the City of London, where the Clockmakers' Company Collection is housed; and, for comparison, the original Clock Room in the Basinghall Street building, which was in use from 1873 to 1975. (Author)

than the one in the earlier building, allowing the Company to show considerably more of its fine collection of clocks, watches, chronometers and associated objects.

The exercise of royal grace which gave life to the Company cannot be overlooked or forgotten. The magnificently illuminated initial letter of the Company's Charter embraces as its theme the monarch, King Charles I, seated upon the throne, crowned, robed and holding orb and sceptre. The Company has always been exceedingly proud of the circumstances of its foundation, referring back to them frequently in official documents of various kinds, and is even now looking forward to, as well as actively preparing for, the 350th anniversary of that occasion. The next institution to be examined, in which horology is now involved as a scientific aid to astronomy and navigation, was established in the reign of Charles I's son and, coincidentally, only four years after the Clockmakers' Company had obtained its Grant of Arms.

The Royal Observatory, Greenwich

Greenwich Observatory is known the world over as a centre for the pursuit of astronomical knowledge, where accuracy in all things is all-important, where observational and theoretical astronomy each has its properly recognized place
3 in the scheme of things—and, of course, as the site where Longitude 0°, or the Greenwich Meridian as it is more usually called, was first projected. In Britain, it is also famous as the home of the Greenwich Time Signal, and the provision of an accurate time standard has always been a fundamental part of its functions.

It is necessary to go back over three hundred years to trace its origins. The Royal Warrant of King Charles II authorizing its foundation is dated 22nd June 1675, the declared purpose being 'in order to the finding out of the longitude of places, and for perfecting navigation and astronomy'.

Time-measurement is an essential element in navigation, and particularly in finding the longitude of a ship at sea, and this may be a good point at which to deal with this subject. Historically, navigation must have been a nightmare for any master mariner, and if evidence of this be needed, it is contained in the endless stream of unnecessary shipwrecks and in the sorry plight of seamen dying of diseases of dietary deficiency like scurvy, with which the records of past centuries are filled. The fact is that, once out of sight of land, it used to be well-nigh impossible to plot any ship's position with predictable accuracy since the techniques available were just not good enough.

In simple terms, the method of plotting a position at sea is identical to that on land, in that it is located at the point where two carefully measured co-ordinates cross. These co-ordinates are known at 'latitude'—that is, distance north or south of the imaginary meridian we call the Equator—and 'longitude', being the distance east or west of the Greenwich Meridian, which runs through the Poles, as well as through Greenwich. Latitude can be measured by observation without too much difficulty, but longitude requires the existence on board ship of a timekeeper that will perform accurately in the special conditions of being afloat—that is to say, it will

3. *The original buildings of Greenwich Observatory on the skyline, with the Time Ball on its mast above the Octagon Room.* (Author)

not be adversely affected by the ship's motion, which immediately rules out, for instance, any use of pendulum clocks. This timekeeper carries Greenwich Mean Time which, when compared with local time as calculated by observation, gives a measure of the distance east or west that has been travelled; in other words, the longitude.

Charles II was an enlightened monarch with an enquiring and scientifically-inclined mind, and there is no doubt that he deplored the terrible waste of men and materials that took place not only in his mercantile marine but also in the Royal Navy. He had already, in 1673, founded the Mathematical School at Christ's Hospital, which instructed boys in navigation as well as mathematics; this was a provision for the future—the King also took an interest in the boys' later apprenticeships—but, for the present, the Observatory had to be functional as soon as possible. Strangely, things seem to have happened rather more rapidly in those days than might be the case today, for the Royal Warrant was signed in the June, and the first Astronomer Royal—although he was not called that yet—laid the foundation stone on 10th August 1675. The following year he started work.

'Our astronomical observator'—the King's own words—was a certain John Flamsteed, and once he had formally launched the building, which was to be designed by Sir Christopher Wren 'for the observator's habitation and a little for pompe' as he himself put it, he lost no time in planning and preparing for his task. Flamsteed himself had been born on 19th August 1646 at 7.16 p.m.—his accuracy, even in such a minor detail as this, spoke well for his future vocation—at a house called Crowtrees, in the village of Denby, during the family's temporary absence from their proper home, in Derby, because of an outbreak of plague.

Flamsteed's father was a prosperous maltster, and, at the age of nine, his son was sent to Derby School, then under the headmastership of the Reverend Richard Brandreth. While there, the lad was unfortunate enough to contract a serious illness—it is likely that this was rheumatic fever—and he had to withdraw altogether from school at fifteen, becoming an invalid for the next five years. To a certain extent his health suffered, probably on account of this bad start, for the rest of his life.

It was while Flamsteed's father was attempting to restore his son's health—he sent him first to Uttoxeter and subsequently to Ireland with this objective—that John seems to have become interested in science. He built himself a quadrant to measure the sun's altitude and—encouraged by a well-known mathematician called Immanuel Halton, whose sons also went to Derby School—studied mathematics, made himself some measuring-instruments and started to calculate the positions of the planets. At the age of twenty-three, he submitted the results of his calculations to the Royal Society and received a notably kindly reception, which even served to impress his father, who had, up to that time, been decidedly lukewarm concerning his son's scientific interests. Furthermore, he met many of the leading scientists of the day as a direct result of this manoeuvre, including Sir Jonas Moore, HM Surveyor of Ordnance, who took a liking to him and even gave him some scientific instruments.

By this time, Flamsteed's health was starting to improve, so that he was able to resume formal education, entering Jesus College, Cambridge, in 1672 and taking his MA degree two years after. Various options seemed open to him after that, his own inclination being to become ordained, take a small living near Derby and continue with his scientific work, a course followed by many another cleric in those days. Alternatively, Sir Jonas Moore wanted him to become tutor to his sons, and he even went to stay at the Tower of London while considering this.

In the end, on Moore's advice, Flamsteed submitted a number of his scientific innovations to the King and the Duke of York, including a set of tide tables and some rules for weather-forecasting, together with a barometer and thermometer. Next, he went with Moore to a meeting of the Royal Commission which was even then considering an improved method, or so it appeared, of finding longitude at sea. Flamsteed, invited to join the Commission and give his opinion of the scheme, replied that it was based on erroneous data as the positions of the fixed stars had been wrongly determined.

These eventualities had, if nothing else, brought Flamsteed to the forefront just at that precise moment when the King, having appreciated the significance of star positions in the general context of scientific advance, and especially in relation to navigation, decided to build an observatory at Greenwich and appointed John Flamsteed, already well immersed in the relevant problems to be solved, as its first 'observator'.

Flamsteed's salary was set at £100 *per annum* which, in the event, was a ridiculously small sum considering that he had not only to provide all his own instruments and pay any assistants but also coach two of the Christ's Hospital boys for nothing. Happily, people rallied around him. Moore gave him a sextant, two clocks, a telescope and some books, and the Royal Society loaned him some more instruments. They were as it happened, shortly to elect him a Fellow; this did not, however, cause him to become sufficiently enamoured of that august body that he failed to complain vigorously when they asked him for the return of their instruments in 1679, to help furnish their own observatory at Gresham's College.

Charles II had set aside £500 for the building of the Observatory within his royal park at Greenwich, the money being obtained from the sale of spoilt gunpowder. In fact, the modest little two-storey building—modest by Wren's standards, that is—cost £520.

Flamsteed, despite all the friendly help he received, was never free of money worries and indeed had to undertake additional coaching in order to make ends meet. Furthermore, he was not the easiest of mortals with whom to rub shoulders, being secretive in scientific matters, touchy and suspicious of his fellow workers. He quarrelled with two very eminent contemporaries, Isaac Newton and Edmund Halley, over the publication of his Star Catalogue, they being impatient for the data contained therein and he, the ever-cautious perfectionist as it might appear, refusing until he was absolutely satisfied with the accuracy of his results. Against Flamsteed's better judgement the Catalogue was eventually published in 1712, but he continued to maintain that his calculations were inaccurate and, two years after publication, bought back all the copies remaining unsold and burnt them. In the end, it was six years after his death and only after completion by his two assistants Crosthwait and Sharp that his massive catalogue of 2,935 stars appeared in three volumes under the title *Historia Coelestis Britannica*. That was in 1725.

Whatever he may have been to fellow scientists, Flamsteed seems to have been happy in his home life, and his marriage, though childless, was quite successful. It is said that his friends and servants adored him and that, in their company, he had a certain sense of humour. Towards the end of his life, and although he reckoned to have given £2,000 of his own money to the service of the Observatory—and he was there forty-three years—his affairs did show some improvement. In 1684 he had been given the living of Burstow, in Surrey, which he held until his death although he could hardly have given much time to his parishioners!

Flamsteed died on 31st December 1719—at 9.38 p.m., it is recorded—and lies buried under the chancel of Burstow church. His friend John Evelyn, the diarist, commented: 'An honest, sincere man', but a modern historian probably has a better perspective of him. Of his work he says 'it was not marked by any discoveries. It was distinguished by continuous industry and meticulous care, and by an accuracy far surpassing that of any of his predecessors or contemporaries. He realised, perhaps better than anyone else of his time, what was then needed for the promotion of astronomy'.

4. *Interior view of part of the Octagon Room, Old Royal Observatory, showing the twin Tompion regulator clocks set into the wainscot below a portrait of Charles II.* (Author)

Although the Observatory building was designed by Wren, it had been constructed under the supervision of Moore. Its two storeys above ground—there were kitchens and cellars in a basement—contained only four rooms for the Flamsteeds' living-accommodation. All on the ground floor, these were a dining-room, bedroom, study and hall. Above, and occupying the whole of the first floor, was the famous Great Room or *Camera Stellata*, nowadays called 'the Octagon Room'. This had to serve as Flamsteed's office as well as one
4 of his observation points. To this day this fine room—34 feet across and 18 feet high—remains in a nearly original state, and it can be compared with a print of seventeenth-century origin which was intended to form part of Flamsteed's book but, in the long-drawn-out interval before it was published, seems to have become separated from it. The print shows, for example, two full-length portraits over the door, one being clearly that of Charles II and the other probably either James, Duke of York, or Prince Rupert. Only one of these—that of the King—has been so far rediscovered, although there are slight differences in the pose which suggest that perhaps yet another version may exist. There is another mystery, too, in the two clocks which are set into the panelling to the left of the entrance door. These are the famous two-seconds-beating regulators, their pendulums suspended above the movements, which Moore commissioned from Thomas Tompion for Flamsteed's use. The print, however, shows yet a third clock, sited in the companion panel to the right of the door although, in reality, the panelling shows no sign of disturbance and looks as if it might always have been unoccupied. Incidentally, Tompion's contribution to the Observatory was by no means confined to the two regulators; he also made the famous Angle-Clock, which shows time in degrees, minutes and seconds of arc instead of on the conventional system, an arrangement specially useful in astronomy. This clock, which Tompion constructed to Flamsteed's design in 1691, still exists in working order.

When Flamsteed died, he can reasonably be said to have carried out to the letter, in so far as the techniques and instruments then available would permit him to do, his earliest instruction 'forthwith to apply himself with the most exact care and diligence to the rectifying the tables of the motions of the heavens, and the places of the fixed stars, so as to find out the so much desired longitude of places for the perfecting the art of navigation'—and therefore to have served his royal master well. In the event, his work turned out to be less significant than anticipated in the realm of navigation, by comparison with John Harrison's pioneering work in designing and perfecting marine chronometers in the following century, but of great importance to Isaac Newton in constructing his theory of universal gravitation; even so, the *Nautical Almanac*, first published in 1767 by the fifth Astronomer Royal, Maskelyne, remains an annual publication to this day, so observational astronomy can be said to have always played a part in finding ships' positions at sea.

Flamsteed was the first of a long line of distinguished

scientists to hold the appointment of Astronomer Royal; and these men, like Flamsteed, lived on the premises until comparatively modern times. Sir George Airy increased the accommodation, thereby screening one of the original elevations of the building, as seen today. The seventh to hold the royal office, Airy is chiefly remembered for his Transit Circle, advanced for its time, which came into use in 1851 and continued to define the Greenwich Meridian for more than a century. Even so, this standard was not adopted internationally until 1884. John Pond, who had preceded Airy, initiated the Time Ball signal, still to be seen on the roof of the Octagon Room. At precisely one o'clock each day the ball fell the full length of the 15-foot mast to which it is attached, communicating the time to seamen in the Thames and to those chronometer-makers who could take advantage of the service. This was the first time-signal, of course; but the better known version, the 'six pips' radio signal, was introduced by yet another Astronomer Royal, Frank Dyson, in 1924. However, these are almost superficial manifestations of the work of the Observatory which was always wholly science-based and in the nineteenth century, for example, was mainly directed towards satisfactorily representing the planetary motions by Newtonian theory.

Gradually the role of Greenwich Observatory had to change; the rise of astrophysics in the early years of the present century, with its need for the best observing-sites, and for ever larger telescopes, robbed it of its traditional pre-eminence in positional astronomy, while the increasing atmospheric pollution over and around the metropolis, coupled with more intense street lighting, finally led to the total transfer of the observatory, between the years 1948 and 1958, to a new site in the Sussex countryside, at Herstmonceux Castle. This move also brought with it a change in nomenclature. The newly located observatory is now called Royal Greenwich Observatory, while the original buildings at Greenwich, which have been preserved in their pre-transfer condition with all the historic instrumentation intact or replaced so far as this has proved possible—and the process is still continuing—has now become an integral part of the National Maritime Museum, the other main buildings of which directly adjoin it, and is generally referred to as the Old Royal Observatory.

Royal timekeepers in important catalogues

To illustrate the very large number of timepieces that have attained royal associations, genuine or spurious, over the years, the following verbatim extracts have been assembled from a small group of catalogues covering some of the more important auction sales and exhibitions held during the nineteenth century. For comparison, there has been included one example dating as recently as 1937. The paucity of the descriptive material, in some cases, demonstrates all too clearly how difficult it can often be to trace the history of specific objects when trying to establish provenance.

Catalogue extracts		*Commentary*
Auction Sale	*STRAWBERRY HILL, the renowned seat of HORACE WALPOLE* Mr George Robins is honoured by having been selected by The Earl of Waldegrave, to sell by public competition, THE VALUABLE CONTENTS of STRAWBERRY HILL, and it may fearlessly be proclaimed as THE MOST DISTINGUISHED GEM THAT HAS EVER ADORNED THE ANNALS OF AUCTIONS. It is definitely fixed for MONDAY, the 25th Day of APRIL, 1842 and twenty-three following days (Sundays excepted). And within will be found a repast for the Lovers of Literature and the Fine Arts, of which bygone days furnish no previous example, and it would be in vain to contemplate it in times to come. On the Seventeenth Day's Sale, May 13, 1842	
No. in Catalogue 48 Page 174/17	A singularly interesting and very rare specimen of mechanism of the early times in a fine state of preservation, the celebrated clock of silver gilt *presented by* HENRY VIII to his QUEEN, ANNE BOLEYN, on their marriage; it is richly chased, engraved and ornamented with fleur-de-lys, miniature heads, etc., on the top sits a lion bearing the arms of England, which are also on the sides, on the weights are the initial letters of *Henry* and *Anne* with true lovers' knots, one bears the inscription "The most Happye", the other the Royal motto. Also the curve-shaped and carved bracket for same studded with medallions in gold. *This bijou was a gift of Lady Elizabeth Germaine to Horace Walpole*	Purchased for Her Majesty Queen Victoria, who is actually listed as buyer although there is no evidence that she attended the sale in person, for the sum of £110 5s.

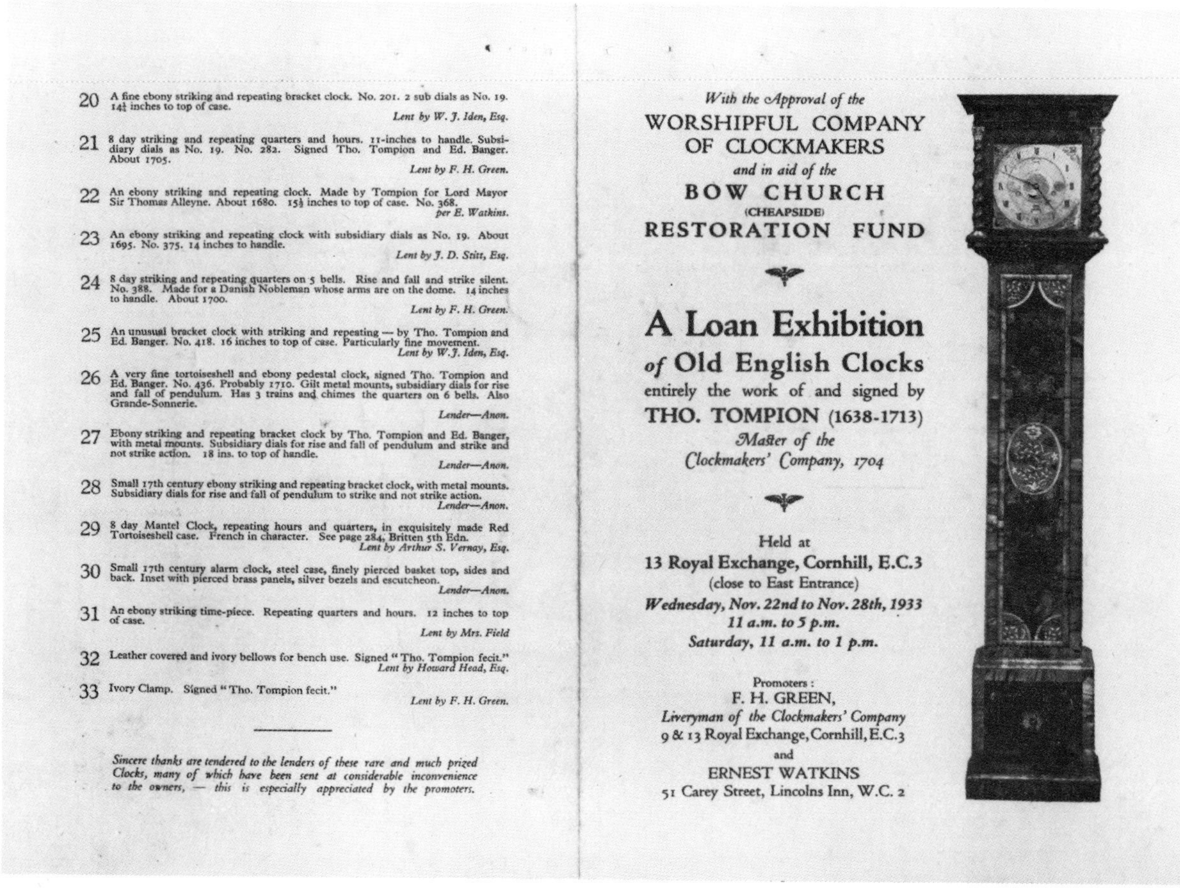

20 A fine ebony striking and repeating bracket clock. No. 201. 2 sub dials as No. 19. 14¾ inches to top of case.

Lent by W. J. Iden, Esq.

21 8 day striking and repeating quarters and hours. 11-inches to handle. Subsidiary dials as No. 19. No. 282. Signed Tho. Tompion and Ed. Banger. About 1705.

Lent by F. H. Green.

22 An ebony striking and repeating clock. Made by Tompion for Lord Mayor Sir Thomas Alleyne. About 1680. 15½ inches to top of case. No. 368.

per E. Watkins.

23 An ebony striking and repeating clock with subsidiary dials as No. 19. About 1695. No. 375. 14 inches to handle.

Lent by J. D. Stitt, Esq.

24 8 day striking and repeating quarters on 5 bells. Rise and fall and strike silent. No. 388. Made for a Danish Nobleman whose arms are on the dome. 14 inches to handle. About 1700.

Lent by F. H. Green.

25 An unusual bracket clock with striking and repeating — by Tho. Tompion and Ed. Banger. No. 418. 16 inches to top of case. Particularly fine movement.

Lent by W. J. Iden, Esq.

26 A very fine tortoiseshell and ebony pedestal clock, signed Tho. Tompion and Ed. Banger. No. 436. Probably 1710. Gilt metal mounts, subsidiary dials for rise and fall of pendulum. Has 3 trains and chimes the quarters on 6 bells. Also Grande-Sonnerie.

Lender—Anon.

27 Ebony striking and repeating bracket clock by Tho. Tompion and Ed. Banger, with metal mounts. Subsidiary dials for rise and fall of pendulum and strike and not strike action. 18 ins. to top of handle.

Lender—Anon.

28 Small 17th century ebony striking and repeating bracket clock, with metal mounts. Subsidiary dials for rise and fall of pendulum to strike and not strike action.

Lender—Anon.

29 8 day Mantel Clock, repeating hours and quarters, in exquisitely made Red Tortoiseshell case. French in character. See page 284, Britten 5th Edn.

Lent by Arthur S. Vernay, Esq.

30 Small 17th century alarm clock, steel case, finely pierced basket top, sides and back. Inset with pierced brass panels, silver bezels and escutcheon.

Lender—Anon.

31 An ebony striking time-piece. Repeating quarters and hours. 12 inches to top of case.

Lent by Mrs. Field

32 Leather covered and ivory bellows for bench use. Signed "Tho. Tompion fecit."

Lent by Howard Head, Esq.

33 Ivory Clamp. Signed "Tho. Tompion fecit."

Lent by F. H. Green.

Sincere thanks are tendered to the lenders of these rare and much prized Clocks, many of which have been sent at considerable inconvenience to the owners, — this is especially appreciated by the promoters.

With the Approval of the

WORSHIPFUL COMPANY OF CLOCKMAKERS

and in aid of the

BOW CHURCH (CHEAPSIDE) RESTORATION FUND

A Loan Exhibition of Old English Clocks

entirely the work of and signed by

THO. TOMPION (1638-1713)

Master of the Clockmakers' Company, 1704

Held at

13 Royal Exchange, Cornhill, E.C.3

(close to East Entrance)

Wednesday, Nov. 22nd to Nov. 28th, 1933

11 a.m. to 5 p.m.

Saturday, 11 a.m. to 1 p.m.

Promoters:

F. H. GREEN,

Liveryman of the Clockmakers' Company

9 & 13 Royal Exchange, Cornhill, E.C.3

and

ERNEST WATKINS

51 Carey Street, Lincolns Inn, W.C. 2

5. *The covers of the catalogue of the Loan Exhibition of Tompion clocks held in 1933.* (Alan Lloyd Collection)

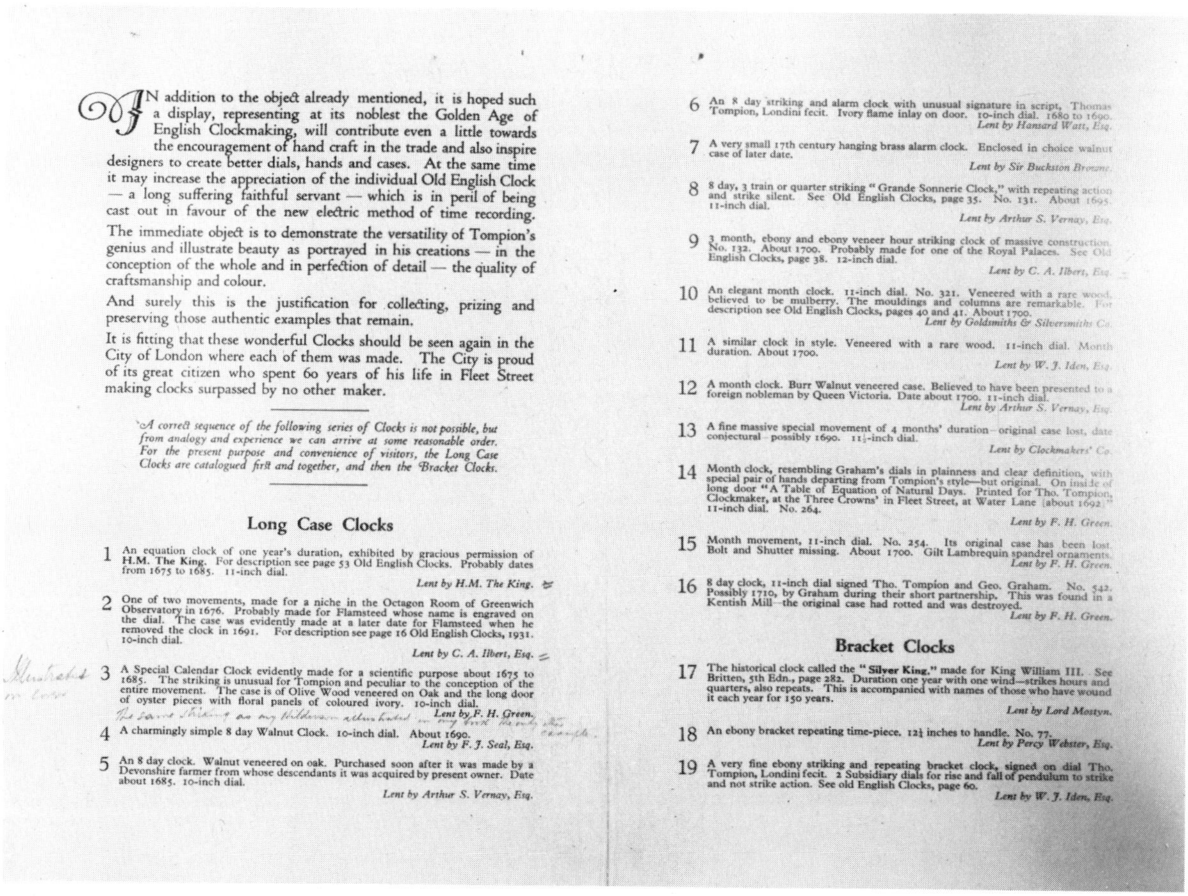

IN addition to the object already mentioned, it is hoped such a display, representing at its noblest the Golden Age of English Clockmaking, will contribute even a little towards the encouragement of hand craft in the trade and also inspire designers to create better dials, hands and cases. At the same time it may increase the appreciation of the individual Old English Clock — a long suffering faithful servant — which is in peril of being cast out in favour of the new electric method of time recording.

The immediate object is to demonstrate the versatility of Tompion's genius and illustrate beauty as portrayed in his creations — in the conception of the whole and in perfection of detail — the quality of craftsmanship and colour.

And surely this is the justification for collecting, prizing and preserving those authentic examples that remain.

It is fitting that these wonderful Clocks should be seen again in the City of London where each of them was made. The City is proud of its great citizen who spent 60 years of his life in Fleet Street making clocks surpassed by no other maker.

A correct sequence of the following series of Clocks is not possible, but from analogy and experience we can arrive at some reasonable order. For the present purpose and convenience of visitors, the Long Case Clocks are catalogued first and together, and then the Bracket Clocks.

Long Case Clocks

1 An equation clock of one year's duration, exhibited by gracious permission of **H.M. The King.** For description see page 53 Old English Clocks. Probably dates from 1675 to 1685. 11-inch dial.

Lent by H.M. The King.

2 One of two movements, made for a niche in the Octagon Room of Greenwich Observatory in 1676. Probably made for Flamsteed whose name is engraved on the dial. The case was evidently made at a later date for Flamsteed when he removed the clock in 1691. For description see page 16 Old English Clocks, 1931. 10-inch dial.

Lent by C. A. Ilbert, Esq.

3 A Special Calendar Clock evidently made for a scientific purpose about 1675 to 1685. The striking is unusual for Tompion and peculiar to the conception of the entire movement. The case is of Olive Wood veneered on Oak and the long door of oyster pieces with floral panels of coloured ivory. 10-inch dial.

Lent by F. H. Green.

4 A charmingly simple 8 day Walnut Clock. 10-inch dial. About 1690.

Lent by F. J. Seal, Esq.

5 An 8 day clock. Walnut veneered on oak. Purchased soon after it was made by a Devonshire farmer from whose descendants it was acquired by present owner. Date about 1685. 10-inch dial.

Lent by Arthur S. Vernay, Esq.

6 An 8 day striking and alarm clock with unusual signature in script, Thomas Tompion, Londini fecit. Ivory flame inlay on door. 10-inch dial. 1680 to 1690.

Lent by Hansard Watt, Esq.

7 A very small 17th century hanging brass alarm clock. Enclosed in choice walnut case of later date.

Lent by Sir Buckston Browne.

8 8 day, 3 train or quarter striking "Grande Sonnerie Clock," with repeating action and strike silent. See Old English Clocks, page 35. No. 131. About 1695. 11-inch dial.

Lent by Arthur S. Vernay, Esq.

9 3 month, ebony and ebony veneer hour striking clock of massive construction. No. 132. About 1700. Probably made for one of the Royal Palaces. See Old English Clocks, page 38. 12-inch dial.

Lent by C. A. Ilbert, Esq.

10 An elegant month clock. 11-inch dial. No. 321. Veneered with a rare wood, believed to be mulberry. The mouldings and columns are remarkable. For description see Old English Clocks, pages 40 and 41. About 1700.

Lent by Goldsmiths & Silversmiths Co.

11 A similar clock in style. Veneered with a rare wood. 11-inch dial. Month duration. About 1700.

Lent by W. J. Iden, Esq.

12 A month clock. Burr Walnut veneered case. Believed to have been presented to a foreign nobleman by Queen Victoria. Date about 1700. 11-inch dial.

Lent by Arthur S. Vernay, Esq.

13 A fine massive special movement of 4 months' duration—original case lost, date conjectural—possibly 1690. 11½-inch dial.

Lent by Clockmakers' Co.

14 Month clock, resembling Graham's dials in plainness and clear definition, with special pair of hands departing from Tompion's style—but original. On inside of long door "A Table of Equation of Natural Days. Printed for Tho. Tompion, Clockmaker, at the Three Crowns' in Fleet Street, at Water Lane (about 1692)." 11-inch dial. No. 264.

Lent by F. H. Green.

15 Month movement, 11-inch dial. No. 254. Its original case has been lost. Bolt and Shutter missing. About 1700. Gilt Lambrequin spandrel ornaments.

Lent by F. H. Green.

16 8 day clock, 11-inch dial signed Tho. Tompion and Geo. Graham. No. 542. Possibly 1710, by Graham during their short partnership. This was found in a Kentish Mill—the original case had rotted and was destroyed.

Lent by F. H. Green.

Bracket Clocks

17 The historical clock called the "**Silver King.**" made for King William III. See Britten, 5th Edn., page 282. Duration one year with one wind—strikes hours and quarters, also repeats. This is accompanied with names of those who have wound it each year for 150 years.

Lent by Lord Mostyn.

18 An ebony bracket repeating time-piece. 12¼ inches to handle. No. 77.

Lent by Percy Webster, Esq.

19 A very fine ebony striking and repeating bracket clock, signed on dial Tho. Tompion, Londini fecit. 2 Subsidiary dials for rise and fall of pendulum to strike and not strike action. See old English Clocks, page 60.

Lent by W. J. Iden, Esq.

6. *The inside of the Tompion Exhibition catalogue.* (Alan Lloyd Collection)

Catalogue extracts

Commentary

Auction Sale The Very Celebrated and Unique Collection of Regulators, Clocks, Chronometers & Watches . . . . the property of His Royal Highness The Duke of Sussex, K.G. Sold by Christie's at their Rooms, 8 King Street, St. James's Square, on Tuesday 4th July 1843.

The entire contents of this Catalogue were, in a real sense, royal since they had all belonged to the sixth son of King George III. The following extracts, however, only cover those objects where descriptive or identifying information might enable them to be recognized today.

No. in Catalogue

3 A large gold hunting watch, by Desmasrais, with dead seconds, double-bottomed, with His Royal Highness's cypher.
Bought by Isaacs for £14 15s. 0d.

14 A small gold double-bottomed hunting watch, with a modern Geneva movement, by Milleret, the bottom of the case contains a miniature of the eye of the Princess Charlotte, with a French motto. This watch was presented by the Princess to His Royal Highness.
Bought by Owen for £16

15 A very small gold horizontal watch, in a double-bottomed case, by Hamlet, from the Duke of York's Collection.
Bought by Jacobson for £24

19 A large gold musical repeater, by Girarde Hertz, formerly the Princess Augusta's.
Bought by W. Anson for 16 guineas

22 A gold horizontal watch, by Vulliamy, Sen., in a chased case, belonged to George III whose cypher is on the case
Bought by Vulliamy for £19 10s. 0d.

29 A gold seconds watch, by Vulliamy, Sen., with duplex escapement and compound balance, with the royal arms on the back.
Bought by Vulliamy for £13 2s. 6d.

33 A VERY BEAUTIFUL GOLD CASE, made by Milleret, containing writing implements, pencils and gold ruler, the case beautifully enamelled with the royal arms, and a very small watch in the cover, which opens by a spring.
Bought by Jacobson for £28

35 JAMES I's WATCH, a very curious ancient clock watch, dated 1599, showing the days of the month and the moon's age, with an alarum. The initials of James I are engraved on the face.
Bought by Anson for £26 5s. 0d.

This object appears to be now in the Usher Collection in Lincoln, q.v.

36 A gold eight-day watch by Westwood, No. 50., in engine-turned case, made expressly for His Royal Highness, with a Breguet chain and key.
Bought by Nathan for £38 10s. 0d.

42 A large travelling repeating and alarum watch, in a double gold case, richly chased, by Trequet, with a duplex escapement and compound balance; this clock was constantly carried by His Royal Highness when travelling; it cost £400.
Bought by Owen for £68 5s. 0d.

47 A large double-cased clock watch, with alarum, in chased silver-gilt cases, with ebony outer case. This watch belonged to Queen Ann, whose crown and cypher are on the back.
Bought by Speyer for £16

There then follows a section of chronometers, among which are listed:

49 Gold chronometer by Josiah Emery, 1089.
50 Gold chronometer by G. A. R. Cathro, 1788.
51 Gold chronometer by Breguet "with his celebrated Tourbillon escapement".
52 Gold chronometer by James Dallas, 133.
53 THE LARGE CELEBRATED GOLD CHRONOMETER BY ARNOLD, No. 36.
54 Gold chronometer by William Hardy, 597.
55 Gold chronometer by Barrand, 309. [Probably Barraud.]
56 Gold chronometer by Josiah Emery, 1289.
57 Gold chronometer by Molyneux, 963.

Finally, there is a section headed "Regulators and Clocks", among which are the following of interest in the present context:

70 A weight month timepiece, by Benjamin Gray, with the day of the month shown in an arch above the dial, in a walnut tree case; presented to His Royal Highness by B. L. Vulliamy. B. Gray was clock maker to George II.
Bought by Boane for £8 8s. 0d.

72 A weight clock by Joseph Knibb, from the Duke of York's collection. Knibb was clockmaker to Charles II; his works are very scarce. A large bell, striking once for the Roman number of five, and smaller bell striking for the units.
Bought by Phillips for £4 6s. 0d.

The second half of this description was erroneously lotted up as no. 73; the catalogue consulted by the author had been corrected in a contemporary hand.

74 A weight clock by Tompion, F.R.S., showing the moon's age and days of the month, in a very handsome inlaid case.
Bought by Simpson for £5 5s. 0d.

75 A small spring quarter clock by Tompion, F.R.S., in a black ebony case on a bracket. Tompion died in 1713, in the 75th year of his age, and was interred in Westminster Abbey. This and the preceding lot were presented to His Royal Highness by B. L. Vulliamy.
Bought by Simpson for £12 10s. 0d.

Catalogue extracts

Commentary

85 A CLOCK BY PINCHBECK in an ebony case and bracket; above the dial are figures of children, which move when the clock strikes, formerly George III's.
Bought by Vulliamy for £9 19s. 6d.

90 A CAPITAL REGULATOR, BY VULLIAMY, SEN., with a grid-iron pendulum, with Harrison's escapement, made for George III, expressly for the Observatory in Richmond Gardens, A.D. 1785. The whole of the train of wheels is supported upon friction rollers.
Bought by Vulliamy for £52 10s. 0d.

9 92 A VERY CURIOUS CLOCK, BY KNIBB, in an ebony case, with illumination apparatus, designed by Prince Rupert.
Bought by Richardson for £4 12s. 0d.

105 A VERY CURIOUS CLEPSYDRA, OR WATER CLOCK, BY ADAMS.
Presented to His Royal Highness by B. L. Vulliamy.
Bought by Bentley for £3 5s. 0d.

107 A BEAUTIFUL SMALL EIGHT-DAY STRIKING CLOCK, BY VULLIAMY, in tortoiseshell case, with festoons and mouldings richly chased in or-molu, with a Dresden face. This clock formerly belonged to George III.
Bought by Vulliamy for £28

114 THE CELEBRATED ORIGINAL CHRONOMETER, by MUDGE, with his Remontoir escapement, which obtained the premium from the Board of Longitude. This is a unique specimen, as the companion chronometer, by Mudge, was lost at sea . . . etc.
Bought by Foster for 11 guineas

119 THE CELEBRATED WOODEN CLOCK, BEING THE FIRST PRODUCTION OF JOHN HARRISON, OF BARROW, in a high modern oak case with plate glass front.
Bought by Weeks for £4 7s. 0d.

The movement of this clock is preserved in the Clockmakers' Company Collection.

There then follow some fine regulators, including an eight-month example by George Graham, one of William Hardy's with remontoir, and a Josiah Emery with grid-iron pendulum. The last clock of special interest is:

127 AN ORGAN CLOCK BY CLAY, the music is discharged every third hour by the clock, the angles of the dial and the sides are richly chased with arabesques of or-molu, in an ebony case, on a mahogany pedestal containing the weight, which is the maintaining power of the music. Clay lived in the latter part of the reign of George II and was a very celebrated maker of machine organs.
This was passed over, unsold.

Exhibition 'Ancient and Mediaeval Art', shown at the House of the Society of Arts, in London, 1850.

No. in Catalogue

440 Silver CLOCK WATCH, made by Edward East of London, Watchmaker to the King, about 1640; given to Mr. afterwards Sir Thomas Herbert, by King Charles the First, on the morning of his execution, January 30, 1649. It came by intermarriage with his female descendant a century ago into the possession of the family of the present possessor, William Townley Mitford, Esq., Pits Hill, Sussex.

The following extract from "Memoirs of the two last years of the reign of that unparalleled Prince of ever Blessed Memory, King Charles I", p. 132, has reference to this Watch. On being summoned to the Scaffold, "Some time his Majesty was private, and afterwards taking the good Bishop by the hand, looking upon him with a cheerful countenance, he said 'Come, let us go', and bidding Mr. Herbert take with him the silver clock that hung by the bedside, said 'Open the door, Hacker has given us a second warning'. Through the garden the King passed into the park, where, making a stand, he asked Mr. Herbert the hour of the day, and taking the clock into his hand, gave it him and bade him keep it in memory of him; which Mr. Herbert keeps accordingly."

[Lent by] W. T. Mitford Esq

Auction Sale The Hamilton Palace Collection, 1882. Extracts from an illustrated and priced Catalogue published by Remington & Co., New Bond Street, London.

Hamilton Palace, in Lanarkshire, seat of the Dukes of Hamilton, and built on the site of an earlier house, was pulled down after the First World War, following subsidence of the ground resulting from mining operations. The remarkable collection of treasures it contained was partly dispersed at this sale, and the remaining part just before the demolition.

884 A CHIME CLOCK in case of ormolu, of rare and beautiful design, with allegorical figures above, surmounted by a lion holding the arms of England, the feet formed as dolphins, and miniature of dancing bacchanals, by Degault, in the front, with enamelled dials and movement by James Cox.
Bought by H. Durlacher for £861

This clock quite clearly turns up again in the Loan Exhibition of Royal Treasures, 1937, item no. 212, *q.v.* where it receives a somewhat fuller provenance.

2,206 THE STUART WATCH in outer and inner case of gold, enamelled with portraits of the Stuart family.
Bought by the Earl of Moray for £514 10s. 0d.

Catalogue extracts

Exhibition Works of Art of the Mediaeval, Renaissance and more recent periods, on Loan at the South Kensington Museum, June 1862.

7,448 Silver-gilt clock on a hexagonal pedestal; the panels of gold scrolls on blue enamel having in the centre of each a medallion with a projecting head carved in ivory; enamel pilasters at the angles resting on six claws and agate balls, above this is a glass cylinder showing the works, and a silver dial with an index to show the minutes, a gilt border at top and bottom set with garnets and six scroll brackets supporting a pierced dome, set with garnets round the edge of which are triangular ornaments and dragons' heads, with small amorini between holding shields, and a large figure of Mars pointing with a spear to a white enamelled globe at the summit, on which are painted the numerals denoting the hour; Between the globe and the dome is an hexangular boss, set with carbuncles on blue enamel. French work, ca. 1520. Height 13½. in.

[Lent by] W. B. Stopford, Esq.

7,458 Large astrological clock, the framework covered with turtleshell and silver appliqué scrolls, engraved silver bands.

The pedestal is quadrangular with shaped sides; square clock with four twisted columns of Venetian glass in imitation of amethyst, and on each side a silver obelisk of repoussé masks and scrolls, with an eagle at the top. There are dials on all four sides, that on the front has a deep silver revolving plate with a calendar for every day in the year, and two smaller dials denoting the hour and signs of the zodiac; and a pendulum with a figure of Time. Astrological dials on the back. On the pediment are two silver seated figures. Above is a sort of temple with two twisted ruby glass columns, and two silver figures in niches, ruby vases at the corner, surmounted by a gilt figure of Atlas supporting a globe. By "Jacob Mayr Junger, Augsburg." 17th cent. Height 3 ft 10½ ins.

[Lent by] Her Majesty The Queen

There then follows a sequence of watches all loaned to the Exhibition by Lady Fellows, widow of Sir Charles Fellows (1799–1860), traveller and archaeologist, from whom she had herself inherited them. Two of these are:

7,482 Oval, silver-gilt watch, plain, with pounced letters O.C. and a sword in front, on the back—
"For God and the Commonwealth"
on the dial plate "A. Hooke 1661".

7,483 Small oval watch, silver-gilt, plain, with crystal face: silver dial. Maker Robert Grinkin, London. 17th century.

7,770 The silver bedside clock of King Charles I given by him to Mr Herbert on the way to execution, Jan.30, 1649. The outer case is of beautifully perforated work enclosing two silver bells, on which the hours and quarters are struck; part of the interior mechanism of the clock was unfortunately

Commentary

This catalogue was edited by J. C. Robinson, while Section 35, Clocks and Watches, was written by W. Chaffers, FSA. The museum in question is now known as the Victoria and Albert Museum.

This is, of course, the famous Royal Tudor Clock-Salt, see pages 16 *et seq.*

The movement of this clock is now in the British Museum, see page 171.

One of the watches attributed to Oliver Cromwell and now in the British Museum, see page 256. 'A. Hooke' should, of course, read 'T. Hooke'.

Lady Fellows is not known to have had another watch by Grinkin, so that this is, in all probability, another of the watches traditionally ascribed to the Lord Protector, see page 255.

modernised many years ago, and the original catgut spring replaced by a metal one. The name of the maker "Edward East, London" is engraved inside; his name is among those of the ten assistants of the Clockmakers' Company on its first incorporation in 1631; and he is mentioned in Sir Thomas Herbert's memoirs (page 103, London 1702) as the king's watchmaker, living in Fleet Street. Diameter $3\frac{1}{4}$ in.; depth $1\frac{3}{8}$ in.

This interesting relic came into the family of the present possessor by intermarriage with the Herberts. Thomas Herbert, a kinsman of the Earls of Pembroke, was in arms for the parliament during the civil war, until he was appointed a personal attendant upon the king, to whom he became sincerely attached, and remained with him to the last.

The following extracts from his "Memoirs",page 132, will best explain the history of the gift. On the morning of the 30th January. Colonel Hacker [subsequently hanged as a regicide, 1660] having knocked at the king's chamber door, and announced "that it was time to go to Whitehall, where he might have some further time to rest, the king bade him go forth, he would come presently. Some time his majesty was private, and afterwards taking the good bishop by the hand looking upon him with a cheerful countenance he said 'come let us go;' and bidding Mr Herbert take with him the silver clock that hung by the bedside, said 'open the door; Hacker has given us a second warning'. Through the garden the king passed into the Park, where, making a stand, he asked Mr Herbert the hour of the day, and taking the clock into his hand, gave it to him, and bade him keep it in memory of him, which Mr. Herbert keeps accordingly" Engraved in the Sussex Arch. Collection, vol. iii page 103.

[Lent by] W. Townley Mitford, Esq., M.P.

7,772 Oliver Cromwell's watch.
This watch was made about 1625, the maker, John Midnall, in Fleet Street, was on the Court of the Clockmakers' Company in 1631; warden in 1635; and died about 1638. The watch is a plain silver one in a double case, of an egg-shaped form, flattened on the sides, with a circular glazed aperture in the outer case to show the silver dial plate. It is attached by three short silver curb chains to a small plate, on which the arms are engraved. To this plate are attached four short chains of a similar make for seals. Length, $1\frac{7}{8}$ in; width, $1\frac{3}{4}$ in.

The crest of the Cromwell family was a demi lion holding a ring in the paw, but the Protector changed the ring for the handle of a tilting spear, as seen on the banner used at his funeral; this with the initials identifies it as the crest of Oliver Cromwell, and also the coat of arms.

There is every reason to suppose, from the appearance of the relic, that it was used by Cromwell, from 1625 until his death in 1658.

Commentary: This watch is also now in the British Museum, see page 257.

7. (Right) *This plate, no. XXIX, from* The Royal House of Stuart *(1890) shows three watches said to have belonged to Charles I:*
(Top) *The early German watch in gilt-metal case with perforated cover, said to have been given by the King to Sir William Dugdale;*
(Bottom left and below) *The Thomas Herbert watch by Edward East, with original key;*
(Bottom right) *Silver alarum clock-watch given to Mr. Spencer, of Redleaf, by Elizabeth, daughter of James I. This watch was also made by Edward East. These objects constitute items 442, 375 and 462 in the catalogue of the exhibition of 1888.* (Guildhall Library, City of London)

8. (Below right) *Another plate, no. XVIII, from the same work, illustrates a variety of objects, which include mourning and other rings and a bloodstone cameo; there are also three watches, identified in the text so that they, too, can be related to the Stuart Exhibition in London. They are:*
(Left) *A watch in elongated octagonal gold and rock crystal case,* $1\frac{5}{8}''$ *long and* $1\frac{1}{4}''$ *wide, said to have belonged to Mary, Queen of Scots. The movement is signed 'D. du Chemin, Rouen', a maker who can perhaps be identified with the subject of a listing by G. H. Baillie, under date 1570, and mentioning an apparently similar watch formerly in the Bernal Collection. The watch here illustrated is said to be the property of Lady Adeliza Manners and is presumably, therefore, item 331 in the 1888 Exhibition.*
(Centre top and below) *Two views of a gold watch, only* $1\frac{1}{8}''$ *in diameter or, with the outer case,* $1\frac{3}{8}''$ *in diameter. This is the watch said to have been given by Mary, Queen of Scots to one of her attendants, called Massie, the day prior to her execution. The maker of the movement is Estienne Hubert, Rouen; G. H. Baillie lists two makers of this name working in that city, the earlier shown as 1620. The shagreen outer case is studded with small gold flowers and 'on the back, formed of gold nails, are four lily flowers, arranged in saltire'. This watch is stated to have been exhibited at Peterborough in 1887, Glasgow in 1888, and London 1889, and to be the property of James S. Fraser-Tytler, Esq. It can, therefore, be identified with item 330 in the London exhibition.*
(Right, centre) *This gold watch is said closely to resemble the first of the watches described above, save that its maker is Estienne Hubert, who made the second one! In a similar octagonal gold and rock crystal case, it has a plain dial plate, as compared with the engraved landscape and scrollwork of the other example; it is also said to have belonged to Mary, Queen of Scots. It was exhibited in Edinburgh in 1888, London in 1889. It is also said to be the property of W. Murray Threipland, Esq.: of the two watches exhibited by him in London, items 327 and 328, it is probably the former, since there is no mention of an accompanying key.* (Guildhall Library, City of London)

Exhibition 'The Glasgow International Exhibition' 1888.

172 A WATCH by Etienne Hubert of Rouen, provided with catgut instead of a chain; the dial-plate enamelled with flowers and an inner case of gold filigree. It is stated that this watch was given by Queen Mary to Margaret Lyon, Marchioness of Hamilton, daughter of the eighth Lord Glamis, and that it passed through many hands until it came into the possession of the present owner, a lineal descendant of the Marchioness.

Lent by Captain Anstruther Thomson

This display is best summarized in the words of a book published in 1890 by James MacLehose and Sons, Publishers to Glasgow University, and entitled *Scottish National Memorials*, which introduces itself thus:

This volume is the outgrowth of the interest excited by the Historical and Archaeological Collection which was brought together in the 'Bishop's Castle'—a reproduction of the ancient Castle of Glasgow, designed by the late Mr. James Sellars for the Glasgow International Exhibition of 1888. That collection of Scottish National Memorials was the largest and most important that had ever been brought together. . . .

182 A TIMEPIECE in the shape of a skull in silver, attached to a chain of the same metal. Presented by Queen Mary to Mary Seton, one of her four Maries, Maids of Honour. On the forehead is the figure of Death, who stands between a palace and a cottage, and around him is the legend from Horace: 'Pallida Mors equo pulsat pede pauperum tabernas regumque turres'. On the back part of the skull is the figure of Time, with the legend from Ovid: 'Tempus edax rerum, tuque invidiosa vetustas'. The upper portion of the skull represents (1) Adam and Eve in the Garden of Eden, and (2) the Crucifixion, each with its own appropriate legend. The space between these designs is pierced with open work for the escape of the sound when the hammer strikes the silver bell which fills the hollow of the cranium, for the watch is a repeater. The workmanship is admirable throughout. A watch of similar design but of inferior workmanship of about the year 1600, and of Swiss origin, may be seen in the Department of Antiquities in the British Museum, to which it was presented by Lady Fellowes in 1874. The Seton timepiece has been figured in Wood's "*Curiosities of Clocks and Watches*".

Lent by Sir T. N. Dick Lauder, Bart.

For its part, the *Horological Journal* for November 1888, page 46, comments:

A few reminiscences of this remarkably successful Exhibition may be of interest to some of our readers. . . . Coming to those things most of interest to watchmakers, we would say that the exhibition in the Bishop's Palace calls for special notice on account of the antiquity of the objects exhibited and also on account of their authenticity. There are there several watches made for Queen Mary of Scots [*sic*] and given by her to some of her attendants. Remarkable for their exquisitely engraved and wrought cases, they are the production of a watchmaker of Rouen; the escapements are, of course, of the most primitive kind of verge and in place of the chains is a piece of catgut. . . .

Two illustrations, figures 57 and 58 on p. 58 of *Scottish National Memorials* show the Skull Watch now owned by the Clockmakers' Company, *q.v.*

205 WATCH, of octagonal form, the case of which is of rock crystal. The key bears the Crown and Sceptre over the initials M.R. It is said to have belonged to Queen Mary, and to have been given by Lord Seton to the family of Fingask, in whose possession it has long continued. It is in good preservation and in working order. It has only one hand, and bears no ornaments whatever.

Lent by W. Murray Threipland

184 GOLD WATCH and Key, by Etienne Hubert à Rouen (with catgut instead of chain movement) given by Queen Mary to Massie, one of her attendants at Fotheringay, the day before her execution. Of this watch Sir John Leslie, in a letter to Dr. M'Crie (M'Crie's *Life of Knox, Supplement*) says:- 'I have had the opportunity of inspecting an antique watch, through the politeness of Mr. J. Scott, late chemist in Edinburgh, the lineal descendant of a Frenchman of the name of Massie, who, having attended Queen Mary into Scotland, had received the relic from his mistress. It is a small round gold watch, scarcely exceeding an inch in diameter, and made by Hubert in Rouen.'

Lent by J. S. Fraser Tytler

There are illustrations of front and back of this watch, as also of its apparently quite conventional crank key.

No.	Catalogue extracts	Commentary
206	GOLD WATCH, which is said to have belonged to Mary Stewart. It is oval in shape, and no maker's name is visible. The works have nearly all gone. Lent by W. Murray Threipland	
207	JEWELLED WATCHCASE of filigree work, presented by the Chevalier St. George ('James VIII') to Lady Threipland when he visited Fingask, 7th January 1716. Lent by W. Murray Treipland	
535	AN OLD ENAMELLED WATCH, having on one side of the case a portrait of James Francis Edward Stewart (James VIII and III), in which he is represented in armour, and wearing a full wig and the ribbon of the Garter, and on the other a portrait of Prince Charles Edward, in which he is depicted as wearing a bob wig tied with black ribbon, while inside the lid there is a picture of a lady with a black page behind her. Lent by the Earl of Roseberry	
672	GOLD WATCH, set with brilliants, which belonged to Prince Charles Edward. On the back there is a portrait in enamel of the Duchess of Albany, the natural daughter of the Prince by his mistress Miss Walkinshaw. A few months before his death he executed a deed in which he legitimated her, and she became his sole heir. The portrait is surrounded by a circle of brilliants, and a similar circle surrounds the face of the watch, while the hands are also set with very small diamonds. On the Prince's death at Florence in 1788 the watch passed into the possession of his faithful follower Thomas Nairne, son of the attainted Lord Nairne, who brought it with him to Sancerre in France, a great resort of the adherents of the Stewart cause, from its being the residence of one of the Macnabs of Inishewen, who had married a French heiress. The watch was presented to the lender's father on his paying a visit to his kinsfolk the Macnabs at Sancerre about the year 1834. Lent by Col. John A. Macdonald of Glenaladale	The back of the watchcase is illustrated.
619	GOLD WATCH-CHAIN, which belonged to Prince Charles Edward, and was given by him to James Gordon of Cobairdy, on his taking leave of the Prince at Paris in 1747—'H.R.H. requesting Mr. Gordon's watch-chain in exchange'. This was a complimentary custom of the time. Lent by C. E. Dalrymple	

7 8 *Exhibition* 'The Royal House of Stuart', under the patronage of Her Majesty The Queen, at The New Gallery, Regent Street, London, 1888.

327 A WATCH, formerly Queen Mary's.
Lent by W. Murray Threipland, Esq

328 A WATCH of octagonal form, with a key, said to have been Queen Mary's. The case is of rock crystal, and the key has a crown and sceptre with the initials M.R. It is stated to have been given to the Fingask family by Lord Seton.
Lent by W. Murray Threipland, Esq

329 A GOLD WATCH formerly belonging to Queen Mary. Given by Queen Mary to Margaret Lyon, Marchioness of Hamilton, from whom it descended through members of the Hamilton, Crawford, Dundas, and Gray of Carntyne families, to the present owner. Lent by Capt. Anstruther Thomson

In the British Museum copy of this Catalogue, there are pencilled annotations, partially lost due to binding, relating to items 329 and 330, in both cases suggesting seventeenth-century dates for the objects in question.

330 GOLD WATCH, given by Queen Mary to Massie, one of her attendants, the day before her execution.
Lent by James S. Fraser-Tytler, Esq

331 WATCH, which belonged to Mary Queen of Scots.
Lent by Lady Adeliza Manners

360 "MEMENTO MORI" TIMEPIECE.
Given by Mary, Queen of Scots, to Mary Seton, inherited by the owner from the Seton family. The watch is in the form of a skull. On the forehead is a figure of death standing between a palace and a cottage; around is this legend from Horace 'Pallida Mors Equo Pulsat Pede Pauperum Tabernas Regum que Turres'. On the hind part of the skull is a figure of Time with another legend from Ovid 'Tempus Edax Rerum Tuque Invidiosa Vetustas'. The upper part of the skull bears representations of Adam and Eve in the Garden of Eden, and of the Crucifixion, each with Latin legends, and between these scenes is open work to let out the sound when the watch strikes the hour upon a silver bell, which fills the hollow of the skull and receives the works within it when the watch is shut.
Lent by Sir T. W. Dick-Lauder, Bart.

This watch is now in the Clockmakers' Company Collection.

371 WATCH formerly belonging to Charles I.
Lent by the Earl of Ashburnham

375 WATCH given by Charles I to Thomas Herbert. Charles appointed his death-gifts to some of his family and friends, including his large ring sun-dial of silver to the Duke of York; books to his other children; *Cassandra* to the Earl of Lindsey, Lord High Chamberlain; and his gold watch (he was accustomed to wear two of these articles) to the Duchess of Richmond; and his silver clock that hung by the bedside to Herbert himself:- "he asked Mr Herbert the Hour of the Day; and taking the Clock in his Hand, gave it him, and bade him keep it in memory of him; which Mr Herbert keeps accordingly". This watch, which descended to Mr. W. Townley-Mitford, is engraved in Chambers's "Book of Days", i.191.
Lent by W. Mitford Esq

Robert Chambers, 1802–71, founded with his brother the publishing firm W. & R. Chambers, of Edinburgh, wrote extensively on Scottish history, biography and literature, established *Chambers's Journal* in 1832 and compiled *Book of Days*, an antiquarian miscellany, 1862–4. (See page 246)

Catalogue extracts		Commentary
396	OVAL SILVER ENGRAVED WATCH with a portrait of James I and VI, and his Queen. Made by David Ramsay-Scotus. Lent by Sir Thos. Buchanan-Hepburn, Bart	
421	GOLD WATCH made for James I, with the date 1599. Lent by T. O. Barlow	It is tempting to identify this with the watch in the Usher Collection, also dated 1599, *q.v.* However, that is gilt-metal. Happily, the same hand which annotated earlier entries in this Catalogue has placed beside this entry the initials AE, conjoined, which is usually taken to indicate brass, bronze, copper or similar metal (Lat. *aes*=bronze); and, to put this attribution beyond all reasonable doubt, there is also inscribed the words "rosewindow lid", a description which could not possibly be bettered for the type of pierced decorative cover used on this type of early watch.
422	GOLD WATCH given by Charles I to Sir William Dugdale. Lent by Mrs Stratford Dugdale	It is worth recording that the annotator inscribed the symbol "AE" beside this item also, together with a date "*c.*1530".
433	A WATCH, given by Charles I to Bishop Jeremy Taylor, and inherited from him by the owner. Lent by Major Jeremy Taylor Marsh	
462	LARGE SILVER WATCH formerly the property of Charles I, given with other articles here enumerated, to Mr. Spencer of Redleaf, by Elizabeth, daughter of James I, when he entertained her at his house near Penshurst. Sir T. Herbert, referring to Charles's sojourn at Hurst Castle, wrote that, being "awaked" by some unusual noise, "rang his Silver Bell which, with both his Watches, were usually laid upon a stool near the Wax Lamp, that was set near them in a large Silver Bason". This referred to the arrival of Major Harrison, with orders for the King's removal to Windsor Castle. One of these watches was of gold, the other of silver, vide Herbert's *Memoirs*, above quoted. "One night, as the King was preparing to go to Bed, as his Custom was, he wound up both his Watches, one being Gold, the other Silver, he missed his Diamond Seal", a jewel of great value which was afterwards found by the King himself, when he saw it lying on the floor at Windsor, sparkling in the light of the fire. A third watch is mentioned by the same writer in respect to the King's desire that while at Windsor he should, one morning, be called an hour sooner than usual. Herbert on this occasion overslept himself "and awaken'd not untill Charles's Silver Bell hastn'd him in. Herbert, said the King, you have not obeyed the command I gave last Night. He acknowledged his fault. Well (said the King) I will order you for the future; you shall have a gold Alarum Watch which, as there may be cause, shall awake you; write to the Earl of Pembroke to send me such a one presently. The Earl immediately sent to Mr. East, his Watch-maker in Fleet Street, about it". Herbert related a curious anecdote, p. 172 of the same *Memoir*, which attests that this "Gold Alarum Watch" being entrusted by Pembroke to an officer for delivery to Charles, never reached his hands. For an alarum watch of this nature, see the watch of King James I, lent by Mr. T. O. Barlow, R.A. which, having the case perforated to emit the sound,	This item is annotated in the margin "fine E East style".

contains a large and audible bell. The King left his gold watch to the Duchess of Richmond; see *Memoirs* as above, p. 188. A silver clock "that hung by the Bed-side" of the King, Charles gave as a keepsake to Sir Thomas Herbert himself, p. 190 as above.

Lent by Mrs. Boyse

464 SMALL CLOCK enamelled, given to "Old Oscott" by Bishop Milner; formerly belonged to James II.

Lent by The President of Oscott College

483 WATCH given by Charles II to Mrs. Jane Lane, who aided him after the Battle of Worcester.

Lent by Alfred S. Merry, Esq

529 JEWELLED WATCH CASE, of filigree work, presented by Prince James to Lady Threipland, 1716.

Lent by W. Murray Threipland, Esq

A large work entitled *The Royal House of Stuart*, having an Introduction by John Skelton, C.B., Ll.D., (later Sir John Skelton, vide *Dictionary of National Biography*, lii, 332), no fewer than forty coloured plates by William Gibb, and descriptive notes by W.H.St. John Hope, M.A., includes many of the items from this exhibition. It was published in 1890. Among other important details, it confirms that item 442 is gilt, rather than gold; and it describes it as a German sixteenth century clock-watch, its dial "protected by an outer case of perforated work".

Exhibition "The Royal House of Tudor", at the New Gallery, Regent Street, London. 1890.

947 A GOLD WATCH, stated to have belonged to Queen Elizabeth.

Lent by Miss M. Lloyd

948 A MELON-SHAPED SILVER WATCH in shagreen case, said to have belonged to Queen Elizabeth.

Lent by Mrs. Charles Stuart

949 A SILVER WATCH, dated 1597, formerly belonging to Queen Elizabeth. Maker's name Johannes Bargis, Londini.

Lent by The Rev. Fanshawe Bingham

9. (Right). *The fine night clock by Joseph Knibb, once the property of the Duke of Sussex, which formed Lot 92 in the Sale of 1843.* (British Museum)

Auction Sale "The Valuable Collection of Objects of Art, Silver Plate, Watches and Clocks, Miniatures, Snuff-Boxes, Jewellery, Trinkets, and other articles of Vertu, of the Rev. W. Bentinck L. Hawkins, deceased, late of Bryanston Square", 1895.

141 Another [which, by inference, means 'A Repeating Watch, with gold dial, in engine-turned gold case' by Breguet] No. 1776 Engraved with the Royal Arms and Garter motto, surmounted by a Prince's coronet.

300 A Repeating Watch [by Breguet] with silver dial, in engine-turned gold case engraved with the Prince of Wales's feathers, Garter motto, and monogram G.P., in gold-lined shagreen outer case, No. 19.

494 A Repeating Watch [by Breguet] with gold dials showing day of the month, in engine-turned gold case, No. 83, with gold chain and key Engraved with the Prince of Wales's feathers and motto, and monogram.

1325 A Small Watch by Pierre Duhamel, with enamelled dial, in plain gold case and black shagreen outer case studded with gold, and with gold plate engraved with the monogram of Mary Queen of Scots.

1353 A Repeating Watch by Recordon, in engine-turned gold hunting case Engraved with a Prince's coronet and monogram G.P.

This remarkable accumulation was arguably one of the most important sales of its century, so far as horologists were concerned. Dispersed during February 1895 by Christie's, from their Rooms in King Street, St James's, it was spread over at least nine days during that month, although these were not consecutive. Apart from the watches by Breguet, of which there were no less than 145 examples, as well as three marine chronometers, the catalogue descriptions, averaging two lines or so, are nowhere near sufficiently detailed to render them reliable as evidence of antecedent history. In the case of Breguet, however, the auctioneers did at least quote the all-important serial numbers of the watches, a sad and tantalizing omission so far as all the rest are concerned. Nevertheless, several public and private collections—including among the latter that of the Clockmakers' Company—directly or indirectly acquired items from this source; the few watches whose descriptions follow might appear to have royal associations, but whether these could be identified with certainty today, except fortuitously, seems rather doubtful.

This watch would appear to be the one in the Usher Collection in Lincoln, *q.v.*

Loan Exhibition 'Royal Treasures', shown at 5 Great Stanhope Street, London 13th April–22nd May, 1937.

137 MUSICAL BRACKET CLOCK.
In satinwood case; it plays "God save the King".
From the Pavilion, Brighton.
Lent by Moss Harris and Sons

150 A LONG CASE CLOCK
It bears the cypher of William III, for whom it was made by Thomas Tompion, the famous horologist. The clock goes for three months without rewinding, and has a special perpetual calendar which makes an allowance for Leap Year. The veneered walnut case has gilt ormolu mounts.
According to tradition, the clock came from William III's bedroom at Hampton Court.
Lent by J. S. Sykes, Esq

200 CLOCK
Belonged to George I and was taken away by Queen Sophia when she returned to Hanover.
Lent by H. Artherton, Esq

This exhibition was deliberately designed to coincide with the Coronation of King George VI, and it was in aid of the Rebuilding Fund for Westminster Hospital. The premises were loaned for the purpose by Mr. J. A. Mactaggart, and the Exhibition was opened by Princess Helena Victoria. *The Times* reported that the appeal for exhibits had met an unexpectedly wide response, loans being made from some of the most famous private collections in the country; and it was also stated that all but four of the objects had never before been exhibited. Queen Mary paid at least one visit to the Exhibition.

This is the 'Record' Tompion, *q.v.*

212 CLOCK
In English ormolu case. Designed as two female figures standing on dolphins. Three dials. Below, a miniature painting in the manner of de Gault of two bacchanals dancing. A lion supports a shield which bears the old Stuart Arms of England with crescent for difference. The clock was made for Henry Benedict, Cardinal of York (1785–1827), who, on the death of his younger brother, the Young Pretender, styled himself Henry IX of England. Movement by James Cox of London. Circa 1780.
Lent by Francis Mallet, Esq

This clock constituted item no. 884 in the Sale of the Hamilton Palace Collection, 1882, *q.v.*

258D CLOCK
Chased ormolu in a leather case, with malachite ornaments on the top. Underneath is Queen Adelaide's monogram with initials F.G.H.C., 4th of December, 1840. The clock was given as a wedding present by Queen Adelaide to Miss Georgina FitzClarence, daughter of William IV and Mrs. Jordan, but she died before the wedding and the bridegroom kept the present and left it to his sister. It was sold later at Christie's. A mosaic figure of a parrot in coloured stone at the back.
Lent by Mrs. Villiers Hatton

258F SILVER WATCH
Given by Charles II to John Evelyn.
Lent by The Viscount Harcourt

258G GOLD REPEATER WATCH AND CHAIN
Belonged to Queen Charlotte.
Lent by Lt.-Col. H. E. D. Disbrowe-Wise

258H ENAMEL AND DIAMOND WATCH
Given by George III to George Simon Harcourt.
Lent by The Viscount Harcourt

258N REPEATER WATCH
Given by George IV when Prince of Wales to Colonel Newton.
Lent by Mrs. Knatchbull

258o WATCH
Silver-gilt, octagonal, with the Royal Arms.
Maker: David Ramsay, Dundee, 1605.
Supposed to have belonged to Patrick, 1st Earl of Panmure (ancestor of the present owner) who was imprisoned with Charles I at Carisbrooke Castle.
Lent by the Earl of Dalhousie

267 SILVER GILT CLOCK
Gilt clock traditionally said to have been presented by Henry VIII to Anne Boleyn. Subsequently presented by Lady Elizabeth Germaine to Horace Walpole, and bought by Queen Victoria at the Strawberry Hill Sale in 1842.
It is thus described by Horace Walpole:
Richly chased, engraved and ornamented with fleur-de-lys, little heads, etc. On the top sits a lion holding the Arms of England, which are also on the sides. On the weights are the initial letters of Henry and Anne within true lovers' knots; at the top "Dieu et mon Droit"; at the bottom "The most Happye".
Lent by His Majesty The King

275 SILVER CLOCK
Given to Queen Alexandra by King Edward VII on the occasion of their silver wedding, 1888.
Lent by Her Royal Highness The Princess Royal

381 WATCH
Silver, in case. Back and front covers engraved with subjects of "Actaeon and Diana" and "Narcissus admiring his image in the fountain". After designs of Etienne Delaune. On the dial plate is "Leda and the Swan" and within the hour ring a rustic scene. A silver band round the sides and the borders of the covers are chased with foliated scrolls with animals. The movement is signed David Ramsay, Scotus, native of Dundee, who was appointed clock maker to James I. He was the first Master of the Clockmakers' Company when the Charter was granted in 1631. The case was probably made in Blois, a town celebrated for its watches.

Inside the cover are engraved the old Stuart Arms with a label for difference and the letters P.H., indicating that at some time the watch belonged to Henry, Prince of Wales, elder brother of Charles I. There is an entry in the accounts of money expended by Sir David Murray, Keeper of the Privy Purse to the Prince: "Watches three bought of Mr. Ramsay, the Clockmaker (L61)".

Lent by Francis Mallet, Esq

385 WATCH
Containing a miniature of James II and a crown in diamonds. Belonged to James II.

Lent by Mrs. Knatchbull

387 WATCH
Belonged to Charles I. He handed it to Bishop Juxon when on the scaffold, adding the word "Remember". The watch was left to the owner's great-grandfather, Admiral Rodney, by an aunt.

Lent by Mrs. Ozzard

392 GOLD WATCH
Belonged to Prince Rupert and worn by him when Governor of Windsor Castle. It has two cases, the first case is of leather with a small round disc engraved "Prince Rupert". The second case is Silver-gilt, engraved "Prince Rupert, Windsor Castle".

Lent by Guy Kerrison Palmer, Esq

Commentary: Prince Rupert was Constable of the Castle in 1668.

501 WATCH
Silver-gilt, diamond-studded with Royal cypher in diamonds on blue enamel, the hands also diamond-studded.

It was one of several made for George III after he had become blind and deaf. As he could neither see the hands nor hear the chimes, the watch is so contrived that on pressing a lever it indicates the hour by jumping in his hand.

Lent by Kenneth Clark, Esq

Commentary: This type of watch is nowadays called a dumb repeater.

513B WATCH
In dark blue enamel with a white and pale blue enamel border, the outer rim is set with pearls, with diamond initials GR monogram under the Tudor rose. Made by McCabe in 1818.
Belonged to King George III.

Lent by E. W. Harden, Esq

518 JEWELLED WATCH
Belonged to Queen Anne.

Lent by the Countess of Ilchester

The progression of royal horologists: 1565–1900

So far as it has been possible to discover, within the limitations of the time available, it would seem clear that formal appointments to the position of watch- and/or clockmaker to the sovereign were slow to emerge. In the beginning, payments were made—often to foreign artisans brought in specially for the purpose—on the basis of work done and materials supplied. Gradually, incidental references to a craftsman as Clock Keeper (of one of the great palace clocks) occur: this title, and variations of it, is often coupled with entries showing payments of an appropriate stipend. Instances of this kind of record have been given in Chapter I. The next stage seems to be reward by privilege; grants or leases of property on preferential terms were made to such servants of the Crown, and one or two instances of this are quoted below. None of these, however, seems to have as its basis any properly-founded instrument of commission. Not until the beginning of the seventeenth century does a specific appointment as chief clockmaker first appear, and it takes the form of Letters Patent under the Great Seal. The first recipient of such a grant was David Ramsay, in 1618. Even after this, appointments were haphazard, as will be seen in the entry for Thomas Herbert, who is said to have served three monarchs. Not until Royal Warrants of Appointment issued by the Lord Chamberlain started to appear during the eighteenth century, does any consistent procedure seem to have been instituted; and even then the arrangement does not seem to have been foolproof.

The information set out below has been abstracted from two parallel but independent sources; so far as they match with one another, they provide a useful method of cross-checking and occasionally a little extra detail.

In the left-hand column will be found the results of a search in some of the principal contemporary printed works. Those used have been:

For the period 1669–1755: *Anglia Notitia; or the Present State of England together with Divers Reflections on the Antient State thereof*. . ., a most compendious work of reference upon all sorts of subjects compiled by Edward Chamberlayne (1616–1703) which appeared frequently if irregularly. The work was continued by the founder's son, John Chamberlayne, FRS (1666–1723); after the Act of Union of 1707, it was retitled *Magnae Britanniae Notitia; or, the Present State of Great Britain with Divers Remarks upon the Antient State thereof*. . . .

For the period 1744–67 and providing a little overlap with the foregoing: *The Court and City Register*.

For the period 1768 onwards: *The Royal Kalendar*.

The two last-mentioned are directory-type publications which listed each year, among a great deal of other information, all the currently-serving royal tradesmen and occasionally gave their annual salaries, which seem to have been more in the nature of a retainer.

In the right-hand column will be found entries extracted from the relevant record series held in the Public Record Office and still kept, for the time being at any rate, in the Chancery Lane branch in London. References to entries in the Patent Rolls are given below, where appropriate; to save space, however, appointments by Warrant issued by the Lord Chamberlain, which are preserved in Registers, will be found chronologically in accordance with the following PRO press marks:

Period 1660–1837 in ten volumes, refs. LC3/61–70.

Period 1837–1901 in four volumes, refs. LC5/243–246.

For interest, the signatories to the Warrants—usually, but not invariably, the Lord Chamberlain of the day—are noted. In the earlier Registers the entries are simple, almost in the form of minutes, but by the nineteenth century these had developed into elaborately printed deeds, headed by the royal arms, the official wording being interspersed with gaps where details of individual grantees could be inserted. Attached to many of these later copies of Warrants is a printed form of receipt signed by the grantee, to indicate that the original was safely in his possession. Sometimes, too, there are subsequent annotations to show when a Warrant expired, or was withdrawn, and, in the latter case, the reason why. One such inevitable ground for a Warrant being voided was the bankruptcy of the recipient, a fate that overcame Lund & Blockley in 1887.

Apart from a tiresome gap around the time of Cromwell, it is surprising how complete these records have turned out to be; but the odd discrepancy does occur, as witness the apparent absence of any grants either to John Ellicott or Benjamin Vulliamy. Appointments, however, frequently empowered the grantee to nominate his own deputy or assignee, which may explain the occasional enigma.

10. (Above) *A group of advertising watch papers featuring horologists holding the Royal Warrant. Printed paper discs such as these were customarily placed between the outer and inner cases of pair-cased watches, not only to prevent the cases rubbing together and to ensure a tight fit, but also to keep the owner of the watch mindful of its maker or repairer. The claim of John Barwise, an eminent maker, to the Royal Warrant would not appear to be substantiated by surviving records.* (Clockmakers' Company, London)

PRO manuscript sources

Nicholas Urseau

March 1572/3: "A Warrant unto the Exchequer to pay unto Nicholas Orseau, the Q. clockmaker, XXXVI li. for mending of the great clocks in Her Majesty's houses. And also to pay him from henceforth such money as the Keepers of her highness's houses where clocks are, and by those of her chamber, shall by their writing testify that the said Nicholas is to have for work to be done upon those clocks, during his life". (P.R.O.IND 6743)

This entry comes from the brief summary in a Privy Seal Docquet Book; the corresponding Warrant in the Exchequer records has not so far been traced. Even so, the wording suggests that it may mark Urseau's first appointment upon any regular basis.

It is interesting to note the difficulties experienced in the spelling of this craftsman's name, even in his own time. In a Patent Roll entry in 1573, he is described as "Nicholas Ursheaw alias Ursheus, the Queen's servant". The entry refers to the grant to him, and to his wife Joan, of the lease of a messuage in the Parish of St Martin-in-the-Fields, co. Middlesex, being a parcel of the manor of Westminster. This was to run for twenty-one years from 24th October 1573, the rent being 40 shillings *per annum*.

Bartholomew Newsam

So far, the only entries relating to this craftsman to come to light have concerned the grant of leases. These figure in the Patent Rolls, for which at this period, there are printed indexes. Thus, there is an entry dated 8th April 1565, having to do with the termination of a lease previously held by one Henry Baker "whose interest Newsam now holds". From Lady Day 1573, Newsam was granted a thirty-year lease of a tenement in Stronde Way [Strand] at a rental of 26s 8d *per annum*. Later still, under PRO ref. Patent Rolls C.66/1234, membrane 16, at date 6th September 1583, can be found details of the lease to Newsam for twenty-one years of a number of parcels of land, many occupied by tenants who are named; this includes no fewer than three tenements on "Strondwey".

Randolph Bull

Patent Rolls for the later years of Elizabeth I have been summarized in a typescript at the PRO, from which the following references are taken: Patent Rolls C.66/1375, membrane 10, is a Grant for life, dated 31st July 1591, to Randolph Bull, clockmaker, to be the Queen's ordinary servant as clockmaker, with Keeping of the privy clocks except the "Standinge clockes", at a wage of 12d per day, with livery money of £3 6s 8d yearly. The office was vacated by surrender dated 27th June 1603.

Period 1669–79:
"A List of His Majesties Servants in Ordinary above Stairs" includes: "Joiner, Copier of Pictures, Watch-maker, Cabinet-maker, Lock-smith, of each one."

The following day the post of Keeper of clocks at Westminster was granted to *Randolph and Emmanuel Bull.* (This entry occurs in C.66/1615.)

One or other of the Bulls clearly continued in royal service for some years thereafter; there is an entry, under date 13th March 1612, in the Earl of Salisbury's accounts kept in Hatfield House Library, which reads: "To Mr Bull, the k:Clockmaker, for a watch bought of him for your Ho: which was trimed with silver. viij. li."

David Ramsay
Appointed 'chief clockmaker' by Letters Patent under the Great Seal dated 16th July 1618 (PRO C.66/2169). Two annuities to Ramsay are similarly indexed, as follows:
£200 on 24th November 1613 (PRO C.66/1983 No. 9).
£50 on 18th April 1614 (PRO C.66/2041 No. 4)

Subsequently, there are a multitude of entries relating to Ramsay "his Majestie's clockmaker", in LC5/132, 133 and 134, covering the payment of lodging-allowances and reimbursement for work done. For more readily accessible detail the reader is referred to the July 1888 issue of *Horological Journal*, pp. 161–3.

William Partridge
Seems to have been appointed as clockmaker to Charles II when Prince of Wales, in 1645. In May 1660, he petitioned the King (see *Calendar of State Papers, Domestic Series*), "That he may be restored unto his said place of Clockmaker to yor Matie wth all such priviledges and Impunities as belong unto it according to his warrant". This was supported by his wife Sarah; and, at the foot of the Petition is the note "To succeede Da. Ramsay". Partridge seems to have had an adventurous life, serving for a year and a half in the King's "life Guards of foote; and afterwards did raise a Company at his owne charge; and hath been a great sufferer by Plundring,Imprisonm^{ts} and expulcõns". Sarah, in her note in support, mentions that William—who gives his rank as Captain—had spent much time in improving himself in his trade, in France and Flanders, after having been "bred under Mr. Este" [?East].

Even though nothing of Partridge's work seems to have survived, he did take up the Freedom of the Clockmakers' Company on 1st September 1640 and there is a later note, of 1652, indicating that he had presented a silver-gilt spoon to the Company. Baillie suggests his terminal date as 1660.

Edward East
Appointed chief clockmaker by Letters Patent under the Great Seal dated 15th November 1660. (PRO ref. C.66/2953 No. 29)

He enjoyed a tenure for life "in as large and ample manner as John Bull or Randolph Bull or David Ramsay, deceased, or any other heretofore had". East's pay is stipulated as 12 pence per day and £3 6s 8d annually for livery.

Contemporary printed sources	*PRO manuscript sources*
Year 1682 only: Watchmaker: Robert Seignior	*Robert Seignior* Appointed chief clockmaker by Letters Patent under the Great Seal dated 28th August 1674. (PRO ref. C.66/3157 No. 23.) His tenure was "without ffee, until the Death, Surrender or other Determinacion of Edward East"—who, in the event, outlived him.
Year 1684 only: "Mr Edward East and Mr Thomas Herbert, watchmakers to both their Majesties." *Year 1687 only*: "A List of some of his Majesties Officers and Servants casually omitted in their proper place, for want of right and timely information" includes: Mr Thomas Herbert, Watchmaker. *Period 1692–1710*: Thomas Herbert is shown as royal watchmaker throughout, save for the four years 1700–1704, when, among "Other tradesmen sworn servants to the King", no name is placed against the entry "Watchmaker". In 1707, Herbert's salary is stated to be £300 *per annum*, dropping the following year to £200.	*Thomas Herbert* There does not seem to be any trace of a grant under Letters Patent to this maker, which is surprising in the light of the long period during which he is thought to have served. In a supplementary record series dealing with household establishments and carrying PRO ref. LC3/30, at fol. 82, an otherwise wholly blank page bears the heading "Watchmaker & Clockmaker", with, beneath, the date 12th May 1686 and Thomas Herbert's name. This appears simply to record his swearing in. In another volume in the same series, LC3/3, which carries the description, on one of the early pages, "A List of all His Maj. Officers sworn by the Lord Chamberlain of His Maj. Household or by his Order", there is recorded a Treasury payment to Herbert, under date 14th March 1688, of £200, presumably a salary. This will be found on fol. 15.
Period 1716–23: Mr Joseph Antrim (later Antram) starts as royal watchmaker at £200 *per annum*; by 1723 has become watch and clockmaker at £300 *per annum*.	*Joseph Antram* Warrant dated 30th October 1714, as "Watchmaker and Clockmaker in Ordinary", signed "Shrewsbury".
Period 1725–7: Watchmaker and Clockmaker: Mr Will Vick (1725 salary: £300).	*Richard Vick* Warrant dated 8th December 1722, as "Watchmaker and Clockmaker in Ordinary, in the room of Joseph Antram", signed "Holles Newcastle".
Period 1728–41: Watchmaker: Mr Thomas Cartwright. Clockmaker: Mr Francis Robinson. (The salary of the former stated to be £150, that of the latter not stated.)	*Thomas Cartwright* Warrant dated 6th November 1727, as "Watchmaker in Ordinary", signed "Grafton". *Francis Robinson* Warrant dated 6th November 1727, as "Clockmaker in Ordinary", signed "Grafton".
Year 1743 only: Watchmaker: Mr Benjamin Gray. Clockmaker: Mr Francis Robinson. (The salary of the former £150, but that of the latter still not given.)	*Benjamin Gray* Warrant dated 30th March 1742, as "Watchmaker in Ordinary in the room of Mr. Thos. Cartwright dec'd . . .", signed "Grafton".
Period 1744–59: Watchmaker: Benjamin Gray, £150. Clockmaker: Francis Robinson, £150.	
Period 1760–61: Watchmaker: Benjamin Gray, £150. Clockmaker: [blank] £150.	*George Lindsay* Warrant dated 12th December 1760, as "Watchmaker in Ordinary", signed "Devonshire".

Contemporary printed sources	*PRO manuscript sources*
Period 1762–72: Watchmaker: George Lindsay, £150. Clockmaker: J. Ellicott, £150.	
Period 1773–7: Watchmaker: George Lindsay, £150. Clockmaker: Benj. Vulliamy, £150.	*Thomas Mudge* Warrant dated 10th December 1776, as "Watchmaker in Ordinary in the room of George Lindsay dec'd . . .", signed "Hertford".
[From 1778, lists of royal tradesmen are often prefaced by the note: "The following have no salary unless inserted after their names." It is also noticeable that they now rank as "Esq".]	
Period 1778–81: Watchmaker: Thos. Mudge, Esq., £150. Clockmaker: Benj. Vulliamy, Esq., £150.	
Period 1782–1812: Watchmaker: T. Mudge, Esq. Clockmaker: Benj. Vulliamy, Esq.	*Francis Perigal* Warrant dated 1st January 1784, as "One of the Watchmakers in Ordinary", signed "Salisbury". *John Duterrau* Warrant dated 20th February 1799, as "One of the Watchmakers in Ordinary", signed "Salisbury". *Manley Hart (or Smart)* of Plymouth Warrant dated 4th April 1803, as "Watchmaker in Ordinary", signed "Salisbury". [A listing of 'Samuel Hart' is given by J. K. Bellchambers in *Devonshire Clockmakers* (1962). He is shown as a watch- and clockmaker in Plymouth Dockyard from 1795.] *B. L. Vulliamy* Warrant dated 26th December 1811, as "Clockmaker in Ordinary in the room of Benjamin Vulliamy dec'd . . .", signed "John Thynne, Vice Chamberlain".
In 1813: Watchmaker: T. Mudge, Esq. Clockmaker: [blank]	
Period 1814–20: Watchmaker: T. Mudge, esq. Clockmaker: Vulliamy [*sic*]	[*B. L. Vulliamy* Received a second Warrant, this time as "Or' Molu Manufacturer in Ordinary to H.R.H. the Prince Regent", on 28th April 1819; this was signed "Ingram Hertford, Chamberlain".]
Period 1821–38: Clockmaker: Benj. Vulliamy. Watchmaker: Sigismund Rentzsch.	*Francis Perigal & John Duterrau* Warrant as "Clockmakers", dated 5th April 1820, signed "Ingram Hertford".

[During this period, no clockmaker was listed for the year 1828; and there is shown, under the trade "Or Molu Manufacturer and Gilder in Metal" the name "J. Th. Vulliamy". Justin Theodore is believed to have been brother to Benjamin Lewis, but even so, that particular Warrant seems to have been granted to the latter. Also, from this point onward, no further distinction is made between watch- and clockmakers.]

Sigismund Rentzsch
Warrant dated 22nd July 1820, as Watchmaker signed "Ingram Hertford". *Renewed* by Warrant dated 24th July 1830, in which designated Clock- and Watchmaker. *Renewed* (2) 11th August 1837.

George Warner
Of the City of Dublin to be Watchmaker in Ireland. Warrant dated 30th August 1821, signed "Graham, Vice Chamberlain".

[*Thomas Weaver*
Warrant dated 5th April 1823, as Keeper in Ordinary of the Kew Observatory, signed "Montrose".]

[*Rev. Stephen George Francis Triboudet Demainbray*
Warrant dated 12th December 1823, (but Appointment to date from 5th July 1823), as First Attendant in Ordinary to His Majesty at the Observatory in Richmond Gardens. Signed "Montrose".]

William Hanson
Warrant dated 17th February 1829, as "Clockmaker in Ordinary at Windsor". Signed "Montrose".

B. L. Vulliamy
Warrant dated 24th July 1830, signed "Jersey", has been ruled through and annotated "Not reappointed, to cease with the present possessor".

[*Thomas Weaver*
His Appointment at Kew was terminated at the same time and using the same form of words as the above although there was no indication of any connection between them; and Vulliamy, of course, continued in office until 1854.]

Stephen Henry
Warrant dated 14th August 1830, signed "Jersey". [A maker of this name is listed as active 1810–40, with addresses in Brook Street and Berkeley Square.]

Edward Buckwell
Clockmaker at Brighton. Warrant dated 16th August 1830. 10

Robert Bryson of Edinburgh
Warrant dated 31st May 1834, as "Chronometer, Watch and Clockmaker in Ordinary to His Majesty in Scotland". Signed "Devonshire". *Renewed* 24th November 1837.

William Hanson
Warrant dated 19th November 1835, as Clockmaker at Windsor, signed "Conyngham". [This may have been a son of the former grantee.]

Contemporary printed sources	PRO manuscript sources
	James Gorham of Kensington Warrant dated 7th August 1837, as Watch- and Clock-maker, signed "Conyngham".
	B. L. Vulliamy Warrant dated 7th August 1837 by which is re-appointed Clockmaker, signed "Conyngham".
	Edward Buckwell Warrant dated 16th August 1837, as Clockmaker at Brighton, signed "Conyngham".
	John Roger Arnold & Edward John Dent Warrant dated 13th November 1837 as Chronometer- and Clockmakers, signed "Conyngham".
	William Philip Warrant dated 4th January 1838, as Clock- and Watch-maker at Edinburgh, signed "Conyngham".
Period 1839–43: Ben. Vulliamy S. Rentzsch Arnold & Dent	*William Dobbie* Warrant dated 1st April 1839, as Clockmaker at Falkirk, signed "Conyngham".
	Edward John Dent Warrant dated 22nd April 1841, as Chronometer- and Clockmaker, signed "Uxbridge". [The copy of this Warrant is, however, annotated: "Void, not sent".]
	James Ogston Warrant dated 28th August 1841, as Clockmaker, signed "Uxbridge".
Period 1844–51: Ben. Vulliamy S. Rentzsch E. J. Dent	*James Muirhead* Warrant dated 22nd February 1844, as "Watchmaker at Glasgow", signed "De La Warr".
	John Bennett Warrant dated 20th February 1847, as Goldsmith and Watchmaker, signed "Spencer".
	David Gill Warrant dated 14th June 1848, as "Watch and Clockmaker at Aberdeen", signed "Spencer".
	John Scriber Warrant dated 29th January 1850, as "Watchmaker at Dublin", signed "Breadalbane". [This Warrant has been crossed through and endorsed "Cancelled 27 Oct 1859, see letter"; what the contents of this last may have been remains a mystery.]
	Henry Abraham Warrant dated 13th July 1850, as "Jeweller and Watch-maker at Southampton", signed "Breadalbane".

Contemporary printed sources

Period 1852–3:
Ben. Vulliamy
S. Rentzsch
E. J. Dent
J. Ogston

1854 only:
Benj. Vulliamy
S. Rentzsch
Fred Dent
Rich. E. Dent
J. Ogston

Period 1855–7:
S. Rentzsch
Fred Dent
Rich. E. Dent
J. Ogston
Chas. Frodsham

Period 1858–61:
Fred Dent
Marianna Dent
Chas. Frodsham & Co
John Bennett

Period 1862–3:
Fred Dent
Marianna Dent
Chas. Frodsham & Co
John Bennett
Aubert & Klaftenberger

Period 1864–75:
Fred Dent
Marianna Dent
Chas. Frodsham & Co
John Bennett
Aubert & Klaftenberger
Le Roy and Son

PRO manuscript sources

Richard Edward Dent
Warrant dated 28th April 1853, as Chronometer-, Clock-, and Watchmaker, signed "Breadalbane".

Frederick Dent
Warrant dated 9th May 1853, as Chronometer-, Clock-, and Watchmaker, signed "Breadalbane".

Charles Frodsham
Warrant dated 3rd April 1854, as "Superintendent and Keeper of H.M. Clocks at Buckingham Palace in Ordinary", signed "Breadalbane".

Mrs Marianna Fredericka Dent
Warrant dated 18th December 1856, as Chronometer-, Clock- and Watchmaker, signed "Breadalbane".

Thomas Russell and Thomas Robert Russell
"Chronometer Makers at Liverpool". Warrant dated 19th February 1858, signed "Breadalbane".

Messrs. Moise Aubert & Ignatz Klaftenberger
Warrant dated 1st March 1859, as Watchmakers, signed "De La Warr".

Monsieur Georges Desfontaines:
"trading under the Firm of Messieurs Le Roy et fils". Warrant dated 8th April 1863, as Watch- and Clockmakers, signed "Sydney". [A Warrant nominating simply Le Roy et fils is marked "Cancelled".]

Robert Bryson
Warrant dated 11th February 1867 in same terms as that of his father, (died 1852). Signed "Bradford".

[At the beginning of volume LC5/245 covering Appointments for the years 1868–83, there has been inserted a draft letter, dated 10th December 1883 but not addressed to anybody by name, declining to grant a Warrant since "Warrants of Appointment are now only issued to those tradesmen who habitually serve the Queen".]

Harrison Mill Frodsham & George Moore
trading as Charles Frodsham & Co. Warrant dated 21st September 1871, as "Superintendent and Keeper of H.M. Clocks at Buckingham Palace", signed "Sydney". [This copy Warrant is endorsed: "This Warrant is personal and does not extend to any future members of the firm".]

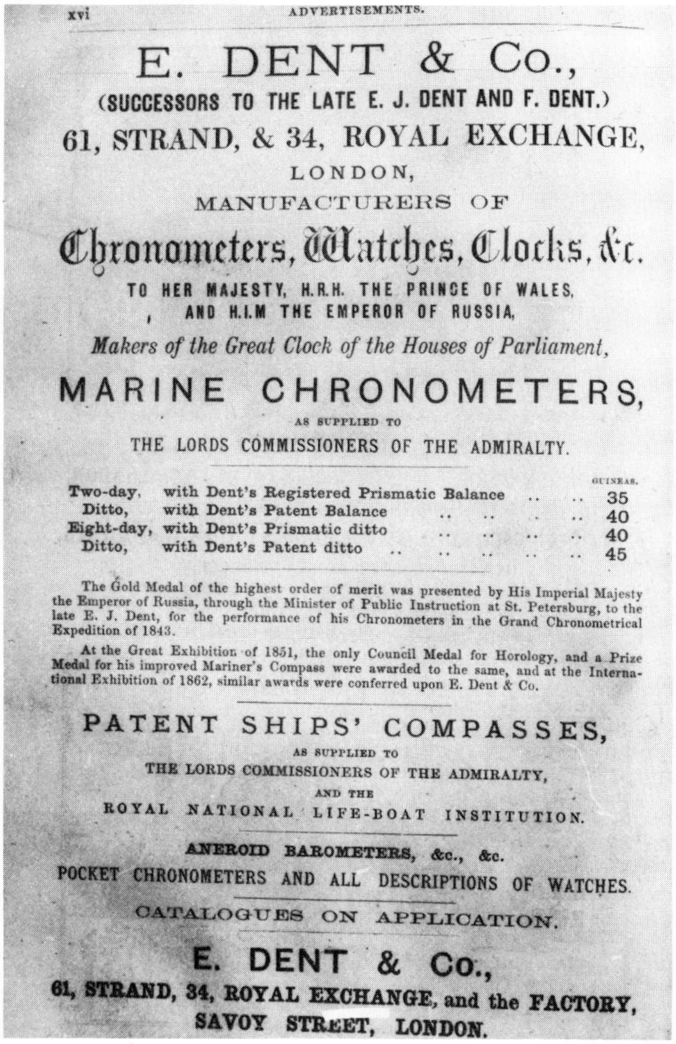

11. *A typical advertisement, by E. Dent & Co., which appeared in 1873.* (Author)

Contemporary printed sources

Period 1876–84:
Marianna Dent
Frodsham & Co
Sir John Bennett
Aubert & Klaftenberger
Le Roy and Son
[Bennett received his knighthood in 1872, but it took four years for *Royal Kalendar* to recognize it.]

PRO manuscript sources

William Wagland
Warrant dated 21st September 1877, as "Clockmaker to Her Majesty at Windsor" signed "Hertford". [The copy Warrant is endorsed "Strictly personal".]

[At the beginning of volume LC5/246 is a printed broadsheet headed: "PATENTS, DESIGNS AND TRADE MARKS ACT 1883 Section 106 (46 and 47 Victoria Cap. 57)". This gives due warning that anyone using the royal arms without authority is liable, on summary conviction, to a fine not exceeding £20.]

James William Benson
Warrant dated 14th July 1879, as Jeweller and Watchmaker, signed "Mount Edgcumbe". [The copy of this Warrant has been rubber-stamped "Cancelled January 1923".]

Harry Oscar Christensen
Warrant dated 16th June 1884, as "Clockmaker at Cowes, Isle of Wight", signed "Kenmare".

[From 1885 onwards it becomes customary to publish those holders of Warrants to serve the Sovereign in the Provinces and Scotland.]

Period 1885–6:
Sir John Bennett
Chas. Frodsham & Co
Le Roy et fils
A. A. Klaftenberger
M. F. Dent
E. Dent & Co

Provincial:
Thos. Robert Russell (Liverpool)
William Wagland (Windsor)
H. O. Christensen (Cowes, Isle of Wight)
Chas. Borelli (Aldershot: from 1886)

Scotland:
W. Dunningham (Aberdeen)
Jas. Muirhead & Sons (Glasgow)
Rob. Bryson & Sons (Edinburgh)

Edward John Dent, Maria Louisa Dent and Amelia Maria Dent
"trading as M. F. Dent". Warrant dated 16th June 1884, as Chronometer-, Clock- and Watchmakers, signed "Kenmare".

Thomas Buckney
"trading as E. Dent & Co". Warrant dated 16th June 1884 as 11
Chronometer-, Clock- and Watchmakers, signed "Kenmare".

Alexander Augustus Klaftenberger
Warrant as "Watchmaker to Her Majesty" dated 16th June 1884, signed "Kenmare".

Robert Kirkland Muirhead & John Myers
"trading as Messrs. James Muirhead & Sons, Watchmakers in Glasgow". Warrant dated 16th June 1884, signed "Kenmare".

William Dunningham & John Stevenson
"trading as W. Dunningham & Co. Watch and Clockmakers at Aberdeen". Warrant dated 26th June 1884, signed "Kenmare".

Charles Borelli
Warrant dated 10th November 1885, as "Clockmaker at Aldershot", signed "Lathom".

James Mackay Bryson
"trading as Robert Bryson & Sons". Warrant dated 8th April 1886, as "Chronometer, Clock and Watchmakers at Edinburgh", signed "Kenmare".

George Lund & Frederick Moralt Blockley
Warrant dated 4th May 1886 as Watch- and Clockmakers, signed "Kenmare". [The copy Warrant is endorsed, "This Warrant has lapsed owing to bankruptcy order." Fixed to it, in addition, are two cuttings from contemporary newspapers, giving details of the bankruptcy; the firm failed with liabilities of £15,319 having to be set against assets of only £8,732. *The Times* for 1st April 1887 recounts that Lund & Blockley had started trading in 1869, each principal introducing £1,000 capital to the enterprise. It is stated to have failed due to competition from co-operative stores and general depression in the trade.]

James Mackay Bryson
Attached to the front end-paper of volume LC5/246 is a typewritten copy of what must have been a rather special Warrant. The wording goes:

Our Sovereign Lady considering that the Place and Office of Her Majesty's Clockmaker and Keeper, and Dresser of Her Majesty's Clocks, Watches and Pendulums in Palaces and Houses in the ancient Kingdom of Scotland, is vacant in Her Majesty's hands by the decease of Robert Bryson . . . and being informed of the qualifications and fitness of James Mackay Bryson, Clockmaker of Edinburgh, to exercise the same . . . . Therefore . . . ordains a letter

Period 1887–92:
The firms serving under Royal Warrant were the same as during the period immediately preceding this one, save that, for one year only—1887—the list for London includes:
Lund & Blockley

For year 1893:
Sir John Bennett
Chas. Frodsham & Co
Le Roy et Fils
A. A. Klaftenberger
M. F. Dent
E. Dent & Co

Provincial
Thos. Robert Russell (Liverpool)
William Wagland (Windsor)
James Dimmick (Cowes, Isle of Wight)
Chas. Borelli (Aldershot)

Scotland:
W. Dunningham & Co. (Aberdeen)
Jas. Muirhead & Sons (Glasgow)
Rob. Bryson & Sons (Edinburgh)

passed under Her Majesty's Privy Seal giving, granting and disposing unto the said James Mackay Bryson during the days of his lifetime the said place and office . . . without however the ancient salary heretofore attached to the holder of that office, the said James Mackay Bryson being paid such remuneration for work actually performed by him as may by the Commissioners of our Treasury be deemed right and proper. Given at our Court at Windsor this seventh day of May 1886
(signed) Cyril Flower
G. Leveson Gower

James Dimmick
Warrant dated 10th November 1891, as Clockmaker at Cowes (Isle of Wight), signed "Lathom".

Robert Kirk Inches
"trading as Messrs. Hamilton & Inches Chronometer, Clock and Watchmakers at Edinburgh". Warrant dated 10th August 1893, signed "Carrington".

Daniel Buckney
"trading as Messrs E. Dent & Co". Warrant dated 30th June 1900, as Chronometer-, Clock- and Watchmakers, signed "Hopetoun".

Robert James & Joseph Potts
"trading as W. Potts & Sons, Clockmakers in Leeds". Warrant dated 1st August 1900, signed "Hopetoun".

Central to the theme—a select bibliography

The minutiae of research sources will usually be found in the main body of the text. However, there have been a number of works, some standard in their respective fields and others perhaps not quite so well known, which the author has consulted in respect of rather more than an odd detail; and a few of them have been at his elbow throughout. All such works have been gathered together below, in the hope that readers wishing to enquire into one or other of the various strata—clocks and watches, craftsmen, kings and queens, palaces and so forth—from which this book has been compounded, may at least find, among the titles that follow, a starting-point from which to approach the particular subject of their own choosing.

Background to the Royal Collection:

J. H. PLUMB and HUW WELDON: *Royal Heritage* (London, 1977)

BETTY WHITTINGTON: *A Short History of the Royal Warrant* (Privately printed, 1961)

Royal residences and their clocks:

W. B. ROBERTSON and FREDERICK WALKER: *The Royal Clocks in Windsor Castle, Buckingham Palace, &c. &c.* (London, 1904)

ALLEN BROWN: *King Edward's Clocks* (offprint from *The Antiquaries Journal*: volume xxxix, 1959)

CLIFFORD SMITH: *Buckingham Palace, its Furniture, Decoration and History* (London, 1930)

JOHN HARRIS, GEOFFREY DE BELLAIGUE and OLIVER MILLAR: *Buckingham Palace* (London, 1968)

W. H. PYNE: *The History of the Royal Residences of Windsor Castle, St. James's Palace &c. &c.* (London, 1819)

Horological anecdotage:

E. J. WOOD: *Curiosities of Clocks & Watches* (London, 1866)

F. J. BRITTEN: *Old Clocks & Watches and their Makers*, 6th edition (London 1932)
N.B. The seventh and subsequent editions of this work have been largely re-written and completely re-illustrated by other authors; in the process, most if not all the 'royal' content of the original book has been lost.

H. H. CUNYNGHAME: *Time and Clocks* (London, 1906)

ADAM THOMSON: *Time and Time-keepers* (London, 1842)

JAMES W. BENSON: *Time and Time-tellers* (London, 1875)

JAMES KENDAL: *A History of Watches and other Timekeepers* (London, 1892)

W. I. MILHAM: *Time and Timekeepers* (New York, 1947)

Biography, General

SIDNEY LEE (edited by): *Dictionary of National Biography: Index and Epitome* (London, 1903); second supplement (London, 1913)

Biography, Horological

G. H. BAILLIE: *Watchmakers & Clockmakers of the World* volume I (London, 1972)

BRIAN LOOMES: *ibid.*, volume II (London, 1976)

JOHN SMITH: *Old Scottish Clockmakers from 1453 to 1850* (London and Edinburgh, 1921)

TARDY: *Dictionnaire des Horlogers Français* (Paris, 1972)

VAUDREY MERCER: *John Arnold & Son, Chronometer Makers* (London, 1972)

VAUDREY MERCER: *Edward John Dent and his Successors* (London, 1977)

CEDRIC JAGGER: *Paul Philip Barraud* (London, 1968) and *Supplement* (London, 1979)

J. B. HAWKINS: *Thomas Cole & Victorian Clockmaking* (Sydney, 1975)

R. W. SYMONDS: *Thomas Tompion—His Life and Work* (London, 1951)

R. A. LEE: *The Knibb Family, Clockmakers* (Byfleet, 1964)

PETER FERRIDAY: *Lord Grimthorpe: 1816–1905* (London, 1957)

SIR DAVID SALOMONS: *Breguet (1747–1823)* (London, 1923)

GEORGE DANIELS: *The Art of Breguet* (London, 1975)

HUMPHREY QUILL: *John Harrison—The man who found Longitude* (London, 1966)

RITA SHENTON: *Christopher Pinchbeck & his Family* (Ashford, 1976)

PAUL CHAMBERLAIN: *It's about Time* (New York, 1941)

Comparative horology

HUGH TAIT: *Clocks in the British Museum* (London, 1968)

R. W. SYMONDS: *A Book of English Clocks* (London & New York 1947)

TARDY: *La Pendule Française* (Paris, 1974)

F. J. BRITTEN: *Old English Clocks—The Wetherfield Collection* (London, 1907)

HERBERT CESCINSKY and MALCOLM WEBSTER: *English Domestic Clocks* (London, 1913)

H. ALAN LLOYD: *Some Outstanding Clocks over 700 Years: 1250–1950* (London, 1958)

TERENCE CAMERER CUSS: *Antique Watches* (Woodbridge, 1976)

HENRY G. ABBOTT: *The* [Evan] *Roberts Collection of Antique Watches* (Chicago, 1897)

Horology, Historical and Philosophical

CARLO CIPOLLA: *Clocks and Culture: 1300–1700* (London, 1967)

R. T. GUNTHER: *Early Science in Oxford* (Oxford, 1923)

HERBERT CESCINSKY: *The Old English Master Clockmakers and their Clocks: 1670–1820* (London, 1938)

H. ALAN LLOYD: *The English Domestic Clock—its Evolution and History* (London, 1938)

Horological compendia:

H. ALAN LLOYD: *The Collector's Dictionary of Clocks* (London, 1964)

ALAN SMITH (edited by): *The International Dictionary of Clocks* (London, 1979)

G. H. BAILLIE: *Watches—their History, Decoration and Mechanism* (London, 1929)

CECIL CLUTTON and GEORGE DANIELS: *Watches* (London, 1979)

Technical horology:

THOMAS REID: *Treatise on Clock and Watch Making* (Edinburgh, 1826)

G. F. C. GORDON: (revised by A. V. May): *Clockmaking Past & Present* (Kingston Hill, 1949)

SIR EDMUND BECKETT, BART [Lord Grimthorpe]: *A Rudimentary Treatise on Clocks, Watches and Bells* 7th edition (London, 1883)

——: *Pioneers of Precision Timekeeping—A Symposium* (London n.d.)

Clocks and Barometers, by types:

ERNEST L. EDWARDES: *The Grandfather Clock* (Altrincham, 1952)

ERIC BRUTON: *The Longcase Clock* (London, 1976)

C. F. C. BEESON: *English Church Clocks: 1280–1850* (Ashford, 1977)

F. B. ROYER-COLLARD: *Skeleton Clocks* (London, 1969)

CHARLES ALLIX and PETER BONNERT: *Carriage Clocks* (Woodbridge, 1974)

RUPERT GOULD: *The Marine Chronometer—Its History & Development* (London, 1923)

NICHOLAS GOODISON: *English Barometers: 1680–1860* (London, 1968)

EDWIN BANFIELD: *Antique Barometers* (Bath, 1977)

Horological bibliography:

G. H. BAILLIE: *Clocks and Watches—an Historical Bibliography* (London, 1951)

TARDY: *Bibliographie Générale da la Mesure du Temps* (Paris, 1943)

The Worshipful Company of Clockmakers:

CECIL CLUTTON and GEORGE DANIELS: *Clocks & Watches in the Collection of the Worshipful Company of Clockmakers* (London, 1975)

JOHN BROMLEY: *The Clockmakers' Library* (London, 1977)

C. E. ATKINS: *The Company of Clockmakers Register of Apprentices: 1631–1931* (Privately printed, 1931)

S. E. ATKINS and W. H. OVERALL: *Some Account of the Worshipful Company of Clockmakers of the City of London* (Privately printed, 1881)

JOYCE BROWN: *Guild Organisation and the Instrument-Making Trade, 1550–1830; The Grocers' and Clockmakers' Companies* (*Annals of Science*, volume XXXVI, no. 1, 1979)

In addition to the above, the author has made extensive use of more ephemeral sources, such as catalogues of all kinds, and articles appearing in newspapers and periodicals. Space prevents any lengthy representation of these, but some of the more important are given below:

Catalogues, Exhibition, (in London):

a) The Queen's Gallery at Buckingham Palace:
   1) George IV and the Arts of France (1966)
   2) George III—Collector and Patron (1974)
   3) Sèvres porcelain from the Royal Collection (1979)

b) The Royal Academy of Arts, Burlington House:
   The Age of Charles II (1960)

c) Goldsmiths' Hall, Foster Lane:
   1) Pendulum to Atom (1958)
   2) Five Centuries of British Timekeeping (1955)

Catalogues, Auction (in London):

The author has had access to a run, covering almost the last thirty years, of catalogues of horological sales held by the leading London firms of auctioneers.

Periodicals and Art Journals, Articles in:

GEOFFREY DE BELLAIGUE: 'Martin-Eloy Lignereux and England' (*Gazette des Beaux Arts*, volume LXXI, May–June 1968)

SIR FRANCIS WATSON: 'A Clock decorated by Amigoni in the English Royal Collection' (*Studi di Storia dell'Arte*, 1971)

GEOFFREY DE BELLAIGUE: 'George IV and French Furniture' (*Connoisseur*, June 1977)

ALISON KELLY: 'A Clockmaker's Taste for Ceramics' (*Country Life*, 15th June 1967)

NICHOLAS GOODISON: 'Matthew Bolton and the King's Clock Case' (*Connoisseur*, June 1970)

E. CROFT MURRAY: 'The Ingenious Mr. Clay' (*Country Life*, 31st December 1948)

E. CROFT MURRAY: 'Musical Clocks by Charles Clay' (*Country Life*, 21st April 1950)

Finally, the author would wish to acknowledge his indebtedness to those many contributors, over the years, to the several well-known English journals devoted to horology, ranging from the long-since defunct *Practical Clock and Watchmaker—fl.* 1928 to 1935 but still remembered with nostalgia—to the now well-over-a-century-old *Horological Journal*, the twenty-eight-year-old *Antiquarian Horology* and the much more recent popular monthly magazine *Clocks*. In sources such as these is horological history continuously recorded, and no writer on the subject can afford to ignore them.

Acknowledgements

I would wish, first, to express my gratitude to Her Majesty The Queen who has graciously permitted the reproduction, in this work, of so many timepieces in the Royal Collection. I am particularly appreciative of the privilege of having been allowed to examine many of these same clocks, and especially the third royal clock by Breguet in Buckingham Palace which, since it has been in store for many years, has probably not been seen previously by present generations of antiquarian horologists.

Her Majesty Queen Elizabeth The Queen Mother, amidst all the bustle and celebration of her eightieth birthday year, has yet permitted me the freest access to her private collection of fine clocks, dispersed between Clarence House, Her Majesty's London home, and Royal Lodge, Windsor. Additionally, I have been greatly honoured by the Queen Mother's willingness to accept the dedication of this work. To Her Majesty, therefore, I offer my very warmest thanks.

Clearly little of the foregoing would have been possible in practice without much assistance from officials in the Households concerned. I would wish to mention, in this connection, John Titman, in the Lord Chamberlain's Office, who guided me skilfully and tactfully between the boundaries of what was, and was not, permissible; and Captain Alastair Aird, the Queen Mother's Comptroller, who went to enormous lengths to ensure that I enjoyed, completely undisturbed by anyone, the beauties of the many timekeepers to be found in Her Majesty's two principal residences.

My deepest gratitude in this context, however, must inevitably be reserved for Geoffrey de Bellaigue, Surveyor of the Queen's Works of Art. Over a period of at least twelve months I plagued him incessantly with long letters, each containing a series of detailed questions that required equally detailed answers. When we met, it was usually when I had accumulated further long lists of questions. He bore these constant interruptions to his normally busy life with unfailing courtesy and good humour, the latter even extending to the occasion when, inadvertently, I activated the burglar alarms in the King's Bedroom in Windsor Castle. It is no exaggeration to say that it would have been impossible even to contemplate this present work without being assured of his goodwill. I freely acknowledge my indebtedness to him and offer him my most sincere thanks. My warm thanks go also to his Assistant Surveyor, Mrs Julia Harland, who, once the photographic needs from the Royal Collection had been established, organised their fulfilment with great charm and efficiency. It was a very large order, involving photography at a number of locations, and hence the opportunities for mistakes were legion. They just did not occur.

Next, I offer my thanks to a group of people working in the environment which I have been exploring and who, in their different ways, have helped to smooth my path. They include Jane Langton, Registrar of the Royal Archives; Grace Holmes, the archivist of St. George's Chapel, Windsor; Peter Ashworth, the clockmaker at Windsor Castle, as also the Department of the Environment's District Works Officer there, Mr Knox; and finally Michael Potter, one of the clockmakers at Buckingham Palace.

In the museum world into which I first ventured some eight years ago now, many colleagues have willingly given me the benefit of their wisdom and experience when consulted upon specific issues. On a much broader front, however, I have come to lean so heavily upon the advice and judgement of Hugh Tait, Deputy Keeper in the Department of Mediaeval and Later Antiquities in the British Museum, that it is true to say that there are elements of this work which owe their inclusion to his advocacy of them. He has also been kind enough to share with me the results of the meticulous and detailed examinations he has made of certain relevant objects both inside his own Department and coming from without. For all these many services, as for his unfailing helpfulness and always wise appreciation, not only of objects but also of people and situations, I am pleased to record my gratitude. This I extend also, of course, to the Trustees of the British Museum for the formal permission granted me to reproduce objects from its Collections.

Colleagues of Hugh Tait's have also contributed substantially to the compilation of material for this book. Richard Good, Jeremy Evans and David Thompson, who operate in the Horological Students' Room, have favoured me with much relevant information as well as being ever-helpful and accommodating when I have unexpectedly arrived on their premises requiring their professional help. I am most grateful.

Turning now to other museums, I would like to thank my friend of very many years, Rodney Law, Deputy Keeper in the Department of Mechanical and Civil Engineering at the Science Museum, who was good enough to put at my disposal his personal copy of the Duke of Sussex Sale Catalogue of 1843, with its invaluable contemporary annotations. At the same museum Dr. Denys Vaughan, of the Department of Physics, not only facilitated photography there but was also particularly helpful regarding the clocks in George III's Observatory at Kew. At the National Maritime Museum, Beresford Hutchinson, Assistant Keeper in the Department of Navigation and Astronomy, has favoured me with his assessment of the Anne Boleyn clock; it is always useful to have another viewpoint when appraising such a controversial object as this one, about which I have endeavoured to reconcile the various opinions that have come my way. Chris Ellmers, Senior Assistant Keeper at the Museum of London, has been most helpful with information concerning certain of the art-objects accumulated by the late Queen Mary, which are now deposited there; and Sir John Summerson, Curator of Sir John Soane's Museum in Lincoln's Inn Fields, has advised me most kindly in connection with the Langley Bradley watch with its supposed royal associations. From outside Britain, John Leopold, of the Groniger Museum in Holland, also has strong views about the Anne Boleyn clock and I have done my best to reflect these accurately.

Several other museums have gone out of their way to be helpful, and I would like to record my thanks to the following:

The Victoria and Albert Museum: and Mr Claud Blair
The National Portrait Gallery
Rotunda Museum of Artillery, Woolwich: and Mr. S. C. Walter
Ashmolean Museum, Oxford: and Miss Noelle Brown
Fitzwilliam Museum, Cambridge
Usher Gallery, Lincoln: and Miss Judith Robinson
Herbert Art Gallery and Museum, Coventry: and Mr D. C. Janes

Before leaving our academic institutions, I would like also to record help received from Dr D. A. Rees, archivist of Jesus College, Oxford while I am especially grateful to an old friend, Dr Richard Edgcumbe, at that same university, for bringing his own photographic skills to bear upon a small problem which I had encountered there.

The long arm of coincidence has wrought some strange relevancies among those whose help I am now acknowledging. It so happens that Geoffrey de Bellaigue and Hugh Tait, as well as Beresford Hutchinson, have independently adopted, within the last few years, the Clockmakers as the Livery Company of their personal choice, so that that body of like-minded people might easily be thought to have some particular interest in this book, more especially since I must now pay tribute to one of its most eminent Past Masters. Colonel Humphrey Quill, my old friend and horological mentor, among so many kindnesses, has often searched his encyclopaedic memory for me, in order to isolate some tiny detail of essential information; he also pointed me towards a long-since-defunct periodical series, from fifty years back, which carried some articles on clocks in the Royal Collection. It was fascinating to note how far our knowledge of such things has progressed in the meantime; but it was wholly coincidental that Colonel Quill, in a long, varied and distinguished career, should have served for a time as an aide-de-camp to King George VI, making him personally conversant with many of the beautiful objects dealt with in the preceding pages.

Speaking of Livery Companies reminds me to record my appreciation to the Wardens of the Goldsmiths' Company, and also to their Librarian Susan Hare, for allowing me to reproduce their fabulous sixteenth-century royal clock-salt; while to my own Company, the Clockmakers', I offer my thanks for continuous and unencumbered access to an admirable Library and Collection, which have so often supplied the data base for works such as this.

Archives of all kinds, as well as printed books, have necessarily been consulted during the preparation of this work. At the Public Record Office in Chancery Lane, I am particularly indebted to Norman Evans, who has led me by the hand through various record series of which I had no previous experience, as well as so kindly checking himself certain rather intractable references upon which I had alighted. I must also acknowledge much invaluable help from my friends on the staff of Guildhall Library. Mrs Irene Pollock has suggested many useful sources over the months and has checked for me various obscure details which have emerged from time to time; Ralph Hyde, a modest man of great attainment, has drawn upon his enormous experience for the iconography of the earliest periods covered by this book; Tom Shaw and Michael Roberts have generously allowed me research facilities over and above the call of duty. To all of them I shall always be most grateful.

Having been an enthusiastic amateur photographer myself for many years, it has long been one of my real pleasures to be able to observe the professionals at work. In the present instance, I have especially to thank Gordon Robertson and his team, from A. C. Cooper, Ltd., whose fine large colour transparencies of clocks in the Royal Collection have provided such a sound base for illustrating this book. It was particularly nice, also, to renew acquaintance with John Webb, and I am grateful to him for braving two of our national institutions to take his customarily-excellent photographs for me. Finally Godfrey New, in the course of his normal service for Guildhall Library, found himself in the unenviable position of having to 'sweep up' for me, when other picture sources had proved either barren or inept; this he did with his customary skill and good humour, as well as undertaking for me the copying of various subjects in the Library's possession. I am most grateful.

Inevitably, a few photographs used have been drawn from the picture libraries so that, in this context, I can pay tribute to Sheila Corr, of the Hamlyn Group, an old friend who is one of the most skilled picture researchers it has ever been my good fortune to encounter; I am grateful to have been allowed to use a handful of Hamlyn's pictures, which are always excellent. I have also renewed acquaintance with Harriet Bridgeman and tender her my thanks for being allowed to draw upon the resources of the Cooper-Bridgeman Art Library. Finally, the Antiquarian Horological Society has permitted me access to its Alan Lloyd Collection of horological photographs, with permission to reproduce; this picture source has proved invaluable.

No book of this kind can hope to garner all the material it needs without the willing co-operation of those people whose business it is to deal in antiques, and especially old clocks and watches. I have been particularly blessed in this respect, and express my most cordial thanks to:

Charles Allix
J. F. Callaghan
Michael Cox
Terence Camerer Cuss
L. E. C. Dawson
Robert Foulkes
John Hoffman
Ronald A. Lee and Charles Lee
Jean-Claude Sabrier
Strike One Ltd.

and also, of course, to our leading auctioneers:
Christies: and Richard Garnier
Sotheby's: and Tina Millar, John Vaughan and Edward Jones

I now turn to a list of those whose help, even if modest when taken individually, adds up to a substantial body of useful knowledge when seen in the round. I would like them all to know how much I have appreciated their co-operation.

The Reverend John Bickersteth
Marcus Bishop
Eric Bruton
George Daniels
Percy Dawson
Brigadier Meyrick Neilson
Peter Roper
Jean-Claude Sabrier
John Steel

If, by some mischance, I have omitted somebody from the foregoing, let me seek forgiveness here and now: I am by no means infallible, I fear. Even at this late stage, for example, I almost omitted to mention Geoffrey Wadsley, the designer who has so patiently and painstakingly put this book together. His amiable competence has done much to bolster my flagging energy in the concluding stages of its production.

Finally, I wish to express my indebtedness and gratitude to my wife, and to my publishers. Chris has been my constant companion and helpmate throughout the entire operation: her skilful hands have typed the final copy, and she alone has prepared the index, at which task I regard nobody else as her equal. I offer her my most affectionate thanks. The publishing-house of Robert Hale holds, as an essential tenet of its practice, that authors need to recognize the end-product as their own work and not simply an emasculated version produced by a professional editor who has only commercial and print-production criteria in mind. I have been glad, therefore, to have been involved throughout the planning stages of the production rather than simply having been paid off on delivery of the manuscript; and I hope that John Hale and his colleagues may feel that this particular venture of theirs has been worthwhile.

C.S.J.
1982

Index

References to illustrations are shown in bold type, and those in the Appendices are prefixed by **App**. Reference to a footnote is indicated by **n** following the page number. The prefix 'biog.' denotes the main biographical entry for the person concerned. Reigning British monarchs are shown in capital letters.